Consumer Culture, Modernity and Identity

Edited by
Nita Mathur

www.sagepublications.com
Los Angeles • London • New Delhi • Singapore • Washington DC

First published in 2014 by

 SAGE Publications India Pvt Ltd
B1/I-1 Mohan Cooperative Industrial Area
Mathura Road, New Delhi 110 044, India
www.sagepub.in

SAGE Publications Inc
2455 Teller Road
Thousand Oaks, California 91320, USA

SAGE Publications Ltd
1 Oliver's Yard, 55 City Road
London EC1Y 1SP, United Kingdom

SAGE Publications Asia-Pacific Pte Ltd
3 Church Street
#10-04 Samsung Hub
Singapore 049483

Published by Vivek Mehra for SAGE Publications India Pvt Ltd, typeset in 10.5/12.5 Baskerville by RECTO Graphics, Delhi and printed at De Unique, New Delhi.

Library of Congress Cataloging-in-Publication Data

Consumer culture, modernity and identity / edited by Nita Mathur.
  pages cm
 Includes bibliographical references and index.
  1. Consumption (Economics)–Social aspects. 2. Consumers. 3. Group identity. 4. Social stratification. I. Mathur, Nita.
HC79.C6C6358   306.3–dc23   2013   2013036569

ISBN: 978-81-321-1127-6 (HB)

The SAGE Team: Sutapa Ghosh, Punita Kaur Mann, Rajib Chatterjee and Rajinder Kaur

Contents

PART III
Subaltern Concerns and Moral Subjectivities

Acknowledgements

A few discussions with academic fraternity around the conspicuous presence of consumer culture and concern with 'being modern' that, in fact, stare the traditional social order in the face pressed the idea that we should do something about it. Two options were available: first was to examine the rich and the poor, the young and the old people's tryst with consumer culture and aspiration to be modern in their everyday lives extensively drawing from a cross section of societies in different parts of the world; the second was to focus on a single society and develop insights into how people use consumption and a sense of modernity to promote normative ideas about individual and collective identities. Since both alternatives seemed irresistible, I chose to first invite contributions on societies from different parts of the world and task myself to engage with the intensive study of a single society sometime later.

This book offers analysis of people's articulation of consumer culture in five countries: the United States, India, Turkey, Czech Republic and Russia. Appreciating complexities and contradictions in the course of carving out the present volume has been an arduous yet enjoyable process and to which friends and colleagues have contributed generously. At the outset, I owe gratitude to Daniel Cook, Department of Childhood Studies, Rutgers University, New Jersey, who graciously consented to circulate my call for papers through the Consumer Studies Research Network (CSRN). I am grateful to all the contributors who responded to the call as also others who acceded to my personal request to write for this collection of essays. I much appreciate the encouragement and support of my colleagues and friends at the Indira Gandhi National Open University: Kaustuva Barik, Kiranmayi Bhushi, Neena Kanungo, Tribhuwan Kapur, Kapil Kumar, Rabindra Kumar, Saugato Sen, Jaideep Sharma, Debal K Singha Roy, Archana Singh, Jagpal Singh, Rashmi Sinha and R. Vashum. I am grateful to friends Himani and Umesh Pandey and Pralay Kanungo for sharing my concerns. Nilika Mehrotra from JNU was around and facilitated my work as always.

I acknowledge the Duke University Press for permission to reprint the following excerpted material from William Mazzarella's book: *Shoveling Smoke: Advertising and Globalization in Contemporary India*, copyright, 2003, Duke University Press:

'Citizens Have Sex, Consumers Make Love: Kama Sutra I', pp. 59–98. All rights reserved. Republished by permission of the copyright holder. www.dukeupress.edu

'The Aesthetic Politics of Aspiration: Kama Sutra II', All rights reserved. Republished by permission of the copyright holder. www.dukeupress.edu

R. Chandra, Alekha Chandra Jena, Archa Bhatnagar and their team at SAGE have pursued the manuscript painstakingly.

Vocabulary fails me to express gratitude to my family particularly Vidit for providing most happy moments of distraction to which I looked forward and my parents who kept pressing me for bringing out another book. I am waiting to see the glimmer of joy in their eyes when I present the first copy.

Introduction

The present age seems to be marked, among others, by consumer culture as an overarching and pervasive element of social life in both the mainland and the hinterland. Contemporary societies across the globe are largely marked by consumer culture that is made possible by the rise of disposable incomes in the hands of the middle classes and increasing availability of a large variety of commodities in the open market. Commercial brands and luxury commodities have come to serve as signifiers of identity in society and legitimized consumer culture that is made visible in terms of its referents: images, commodities and 'high-class' consumption as also their articulation in daily lives of people. By choice or by compulsion, people interpret and respond to it in different ways as they construct, deconstruct and reconstruct their social identities.

What makes for prolonged and rigorous interest of both lay-persons and academics in consumer culture, modernity and identity is their persuasive presence in their own lives, and reflection on the contemporary social situation and societal trends. Everyday lives of majority of people across the world have come to be gripped by commodities that serve as signs in the sense of acquiring meaning from the relative and hierarchical position in the social context. The use of commodities for social competition and impressing superiority can be traced to the last quarter of the sixteenth century when Elizabeth I was engaged in outrageous display of consumption at a massive scale that pushed the noble-man to follow at close quarters. This had deep implications as McCracken (1988: 12) writes

When noblemen began to establish new patterns of consumption as a result of Elizabeth's prompting and their own status anxieties, they began to change the fundamental nature of both the Elizabethan family and the Elizabethan locality. These changes had their own profound implications for the consumption of this and later periods in England's history.

Seventeenth and eighteenth centuries witnessed the spread of competitive consumption (Goodman and Cohen, 2004).

To use the term 'consumer culture', Featherstone (2007: 82) explains,

is to emphasize that the world of goods and their principles of structuration are created to the understanding of contemporary society. This involves a dual focus: firstly, on the cultural dimension of the economy, the symbolization and use of material goods as 'communicators' not just utilities; and secondly, on the economy of cultural goods, the market principles of supply, demand, capital accumulation, competition, and monopolization which operate within the sphere of lifestyles, cultural goods and commodities.

Consumer culture has deep roots in the Fordist mass production with emphasis on social class and later post-Fordist small-batch production with emphasis on choices of consumers. The transition from Fordism to post-Fordism, attributed to the late twentieth century, marked the subordination of production to consumption facilitated by an intelligent switch to flexible specialization geared to the consumers' taste, whims and fancies. According to Slater (1997: 10), Fordist mass consumption that is often regarded as the pioneer of consumer culture gave way to

a newer and truer consumer culture of target of niche marketing in which the forging of personal identity would be firmly and pleasurably disentangled from the worlds of both work and politics and would be carried out in world of plural, malleable, playful consumer identities, a process ruled over by the play of image, style, desire and signs.

The 'newer and truer' consumer culture is individual oriented in character and in contrast with its predecessor that was family oriented. Slater (1997) explains that consumer culture is, in essence, the culture of the modern West. It influences everyday lives of people since it is more generally bound up with central values, practices and institutions that underlie Western modernity in terms of choice, individualism and market relations.

The inextricable connectedness between consumer culture and modernity is historically tenable, as Slater (1997) presents, through four gateways. First is the sixteenth century in which consumer goods came to occupy place of significance in social lives of people. Fashion and style emerged as significant elements of consumption that led to the rise of consumer culture. The new kinds of markets led to the development of infrastructure organization and practices to deal with them. Fashion and style came to be treated as signifiers of social status. The second is the redefinition of consumption in relation to commerce largely in the eighteenth century. This was founded on the understanding that individuals had the freedom to make and exercise choices of commodities that they wished and could afford to buy. Third is the 1920s commonly identified as the first consumerist decade but which is the fallout of the development between 1880 and 1930. This was the era of mass production of consumer goods. Fourth is the period of neo-liberalism (the world-wide beginnings of which are ascribed to the 1980s) marked by economic progress, consumer sovereignty and wide ramification of materialism in people's lives as they get uprooted from core social identities. In fact, the 'ideological miracle carried out by 1980s consumer culture was to tie this image of unhinged superficiality to the most profound, deep structural values and promises of modernity: personal freedom, economic progress, civic dynamism and political democracy' (p. 11).

This book presents an understanding of the articulation of consumer culture and modernity in everyday lives of people in a transnational framework. It is envisaged to develop this understanding by juxtaposing specific, empirical studies on consumer culture, modernity and identity with critical traditions. The 13 theoretical chapters in the book trace manifestations and trajectories of consumer culture and modernity as they connect to develop a sense of renewed identity. The urgent questions addressed are: How do people imagine modernity and identity in consumer culture? What does modernity or 'being modern' mean to people in different societies? How does modernity contradict/coincide/develop an interface with tradition? The chapters are grouped into the following themes: lifestyle choices and the construction of modern identities; global markets, local needs: fashion and advertising; and subaltern concerns and moral subjectivities. Consumer culture is subject to specificities governed by social, cultural and economic factors. Given the wide variation in consumption patterns across the globe, it is nearly impossible to do justice to all the variants of consumer culture in a single volume. It is pertinent, however, to present select cases not overlooking the common features sweeping across societies. The chapters in this book deal with five distinct locales of consumer culture.

The first is the United States representing large-scale economies and high-end consumption societies. The roots of consumer culture in American society are deep. The period following end of World War II marked an increase in the rate of consumption in America that got checked to some extent in late 2007 when the economic recession set in. Ritzer (2010: 31) writes,

> On a per capita basis, Americans were apt to consume more of virtually everything than people in most, if not all, other nations of the world ... In the realm of services, Americans became the world leaders in the consumption of medical, psychiatric, legal, and accounting services. It is not just that they consumed more of everything, but more varieties of most things were available to, and used by, American consumers than those of most other nations.

Consumer culture seems to have trapped both the rich and the poor, the powerful and the powerless, and the well known and the lesser known.

The second is India providing fertile ground for study of consumer culture for the reason that consumption sets the benchmarks for middle classes' assessment of their position in society. Those with financial constraints feel pushed to engage with conspicuous consumption.

The economic reforms of the 1990s that opened the gates to the world market registered a fairly prolonged period of economic growth. The social consequence was the emergence of new lifestyles that fed urges of large section of people, particularly the middle classes, for exercising individual choice and engaging with leisure and pleasure of consumption generating a sense of confidence and feeling good (Brosius, 2010). Concomitantly, slogans such as 'India Shining' and 'Modern India' have come to represent it all both at the domestic level (providing confidence to the people at large) and international level (providing confidence to overseas investors).[1] What adds importance to the India case is the contradiction in the reception to economic reforms by the people. According to Ganguly-Scrase and Scrase (2011), economic liberalization is not an accepted dogma; its processes have evoked much dissatisfaction among the people belonging to different sections of society. For most, aspirations are not matched by the material gain. This may be appreciated in juxtaposition with their overall assessment that the consumer revolution in India is pushing a wide range of products (both locally produced, and imported) in the market space to feed the savings of 'consumer junkies'.

The third is Turkey, for the reason that it is negotiating for membership in the European Union and more importantly because it represents geopolitical connect between the west and the east. The resurgence of Turkey from the economic crisis of 2001 (in the course of which Turkish Lira depreciated and financial burden on the government increased due to sudden rise in the rate of government's debt instruments) has influenced modernity and consumer culture tremendously. With GDP per capita of US$10,000 (in 2012) implying proportionately large disposable income in the hands of the people it is an emerging free-market economy driven by its industry and service sectors. The World Bank classifies Turkey as an upper middle-income country. Predictably, it is an important destination for marketers. According to Yalcinkaya (2009), consumerism is most robust in the areas of retailing trends, use of credit or credit cards and consumption of imported goods. Unfortunately, the Gini coefficient of the country is 0.43 confirming wide inequality in income and wealth.

The fourth is Czech Republic because it has undergone several social twirls and twists in transition from centrally planned economy to market economy since the late 1980s; and remnants of communism that rested on moralistic distinction between 'necessities' and 'luxuries'[2] that continue to influence people's agency in consumer society. The Czech Republic is a special case in presenting the practice of consumer culture by the elderly. The present-day Czech elderly are cautious consumers. Contemporary consumer society holds out disorienting experience for many elderly people in the post-revolutionary Czech Republic. They have been witness to the transition from controlled economy to market economy and had had limited personal experience of life under communism but are now confronted with ubiquity of choice and the need to take full responsibility of their choices. This is extremely difficult for them given the fact that they were used to and appreciative of the availability of limited choice. Also, they suffer from a sense of loss as main providers in the family and seek to compensate it by buying commodities for the children which creates tension between the two generations.

The fifth is Russia and what makes it special for developing an understanding of consumer culture, modernity and identity is the transition from a conservative and centrally planned to consumer-driven economy. Soviet period witnessed production of goods with provision of repair. Notions of luxury and fashion, penchant for material things met with resistance as they are treated antithetical to spirituality. The end of communist regime in Russia and onset of massive inflation, coexistence of abject poverty with abundance and excessive wealth, and conspicuous replacement of Soviet ideology with sheer money-making enterprises and big man politics that came along with has brought about significant transformation in patterns of consumption, particularly in cities. The lifting of rationing and the incoming of foreign goods have encouraged the rich to express style in terms of acquiring greater number of a limited range of status goods rather than diversifying their choices to include a large variety of goods in their carts (Humphyery, 2002; Oushakine, 2000). Shevchenko (2002: 166) adds,

> The opposition between past and present strengthens consumers' attachment to the older objects of their household possessions but, at the same time, encourages them to acquire more. Representing the different life stages of their owners, these two classes of objects serve as the means through which both the socialist past and the (arguably) capitalist present are endowed with value and meaning.

Lifestyle Choices and the Construction of Modern Identities

Several studies have established that consumption of consumer goods and services addresses our identity directly in dual sense of estimating our own and others' position in society. Giddens (1991) succinctly suggests that the notion of lifestyle becomes exceedingly important in modern social life. As tradition weakens and the interplay between local and global becomes prominent, individuals are confronted with large-scale lifestyle choices that they are virtually forced to negotiate with. He adds that despite the standardizing influences such as commodification, the openness of social life, availability of diverse contexts of action and 'authorities' necessitates consideration of lifestyle choices as a significant constituent of self-identity. The emphasis on lifestyle choices influences even seemingly inconsequential decisions taken on an everyday basis such as what a person would wear, eat, do in leisure time, how s(he) would conduct herself/himself at workplace, etc. These are largely decisions regarding not simply how to act but who to be. The construction of identity and of a particular lifestyle is influenced by socio-economic conditions, group pressures and role models (Levy, 1959; McCracken, 1988). Self-identity is a reflexive enterprise, which is factored by an individual's selection of self-image or how/what s(he) chooses to project about herself/himself.

Shift in focus from production to consumption re-fashioned people's identities as they found themselves liberated from restrictive, sometimes oppressive constructs of identity and vested with the freedom to consume, make consumer choices and present their renewed identities. Commodities are connected with society not only in terms of their 'use-value' but also, and perhaps more importantly in the modern age, by their appropriation and usurpation in people's lifestyles. The consumption of commodities is, in effect, the consumption of signs for which reason commodities are defined not as much by their use value as by what they signify. Ritzer (1998: 7) clarifies, 'And what they signify is defined not by what they do, but by their relationship to the entire system of commodities and signs'.

More than maximizing satisfaction out of the utility intrinsic to a commodity itself that would in the long run set limit to nature and extent of consumption, consumers tend to consume a diverse variety of commodities and for several reasons. Another feature not emphasized often is the freedom to choose from a wide variety of commodities thereby out ruling the possibility of corner solutions. In fact, the insatiability of the present-day consumers is enhanced by the larger variety of commodities and by the paradoxical promise of consumer culture that either a commodity will satisfy the consumer or there is always another one waiting to be picked up. In a broad framework, consumers are sovereign, as Slater (1997) puts it, in at least two senses. The first is sovereignty of consumers in identifying and formulating their own desires, wants and identities constituting the domain of the private sphere which is free from the influence and interference of external agencies. The second is sovereignty in terms of enforcing the producers to respond to consumers' preferences and demands. According to Appadurai (1986: 32), demand of modern consumers for commodities is critically regulated by 'high-turnover criteria of "appropriateness" (fashion), in contrast with the less frequent shifts in more directly regulated sumptuary or customary systems. In both cases, however, demand is a socially generated and regulated impulse, not an artifact of individual whims or needs'. That demand is socially and not individually generated and regulated is what makes production and distribution of commodities a feasible enterprise. This does not, however, foreclose the need for product and price differentiation within a community and across communities.

Mike Featherstone (in this volume) focuses on the group of extremely rich people with enviable acumen of exploiting opportunities arising out of financial and social deregulation to their advantage that has emerged in different parts of the world. He critically analyzes their consumption spectacles and luxury lifestyles. The glamorized niche that the super-rich have created for themselves is highlighted by the media in a way that it captures public imagination more so because they are projected as highly successful people who live off their exemplary hard work and initiative. What makes a spectacle of the super-rich is not just their sprawling residences, fancy cars, private jets and yachts and overall luxurious lifestyle, but also their indifference to national interests such as contribution to taxation even in times of economic crises. Embroiled in the paper are the twin issues of power and national and social responsibility of such people.

In India, the meaning of modernity is produced through social, economic and cultural contexts and that it is generated out of different ways in which tradition and modernity get juxtaposed with each other. A person's ideas about what it is to be modern and what modernity *per se* is largely obtains from the process of socialization, personal experiences and interaction with the peer group. Modernity presents new ways of casting and interpreting tradition. Interestingly modernity creates globalized hybridities that are sensitive to both local value system(s) and nostalgia for traditional ways of being and people's craving for 'good and modern life' which it promises.

Sanjay Srivastava (in this volume) brings together two allegedly separate domains: the modern commercial market represented by the malls and construction of the self as he locates shopping in its social logics and dynamics. He demonstrates how people transpose practices, passions, aspirations and relationships from private settings to the mall bringing out their agency in expanding the scope of the mall from a commercial centre to a site for meaningful social interaction. Drawing on qualitative research in two malls located in Santiago and Chile, Stillerman and Salcedo (2012: 2) contend, 'Consumers have a reflexive relationship to malls: they are skilful, mindful, and self-critical shoppers, in contrast to the "seduced consumers" described by others.' Srivastava describes how shopping malls negotiate with the urban imagination to re-fashion the self. This provides a kind of strait between shopping malls, international chains of restaurants, print and electronic media, art and performances facilitated by spatial mobility and electronic communication on a global scale and impresses critical transformation in everyday, ordinary lives of people.

Shelly Pandey (in this volume) discusses the nature extent of urban women's engagement with consumer culture. She focuses on newly empowered young women working in the BPO sector. The situation is a complex one in that it is fraught with tension between two rival ideologies governed largely by tradition (within which they have grown up and remained committed to) and consumer culture (which attracts, pulls and lures them). At the outset, these women assert their sense of empowerment by adopting 'Western wear' (largely jeans/trousers and t-shirts and skirts), buying all that they ever had a fancy for, and having a say in matters (including those related to budgetary allocations) in their own marriage that was earlier ruled out completely. She concludes with the note that seeming social and financial empowerment has not, however, liberated women from the shackles of patriarchy.

The nostalgia of people for images and experience of tradition-bound ways of life (such as rural art dwelling space and cuisine) is commodified and presented in fabricated enclaves within the city that come for premium. Nita Mathur illustrates this (in the present volume) with examples (from India) of the Chowki Dhani village which is representative of the countryside in the state of Rajasthan, and Pind Balluchi which is a chain of restaurants known for serving 'authentic' cuisine from the state of Punjab in a village setting. Both, Chowki Dhani village and Pind Balluchi, draw on the fond memories and reminiscences of older people and familiarize the youth what 'goodies' the village had to offer. In the Indian situation, the subculture of modernity is not at crossroads with tradition, rather it branches out from tradition itself and in doing so retains certain aspects. Basi (2009) makes the same point in the case of Indian women working in call centre in mentioning that the local and global do not exist as binary opposites but are constitutive of one another. The markers of tradition-specific practices and motifs are picked up, hence disembedded, from their traditional contexts and remembered in contemporary context which makes them appear more relevant and amenable in the present age of modernity. The image of modernity implies not a total rejection of traditional ways of consuming and leading one's life, but identification of selective and often highly individualized strategy of making choice and maintaining status through one's consumption patterns. This, however, remains within limits for more people and is bordered by traditional values.

Elliott and Urry (2010: ix–x) write,

> ... changes in how people live their lives today are both affected by and reflect the border changes of global mobility processes. Or, more specifically, the increasing mobilization of the world—accelerating carbon-based movements of people, goods, services, ideas and information—affects the ways in which lives are lived, experienced and understood.

The present one is an age of 'network culture', in which Internet has largely influenced the construction, deconstruction and reconstruction of identities. Robert Rattle (in this volume) highlights the opportunities of and avenues that Internet and communication technologies afford for imagining as also expressing identity. Internet and communication technologies have revolutionized consumption insofar as they connect markets globally and offer opportunities of making choices and purchasing commodities through the World Wide Web. According to Ritzer (2001: 157),

> The consumer ceases to be an embodied figure in dealings with the dematerialized means of consumption. Rather, the consumer as subject is reduced to such abstractions as a credit card number and/or a password. The proprietors of cybermalls (themselves members, faceless and formless) deal with similarly disembodied consumers; ones they have no need of ever seeing or ever knowing

more about than a credit card number, an e-mail address, and maybe a snail mail address.

Rattle argues that Internet and communication technologies challenge social and economic hierarchies, wealth distribution and stifling competition that governed construction of identity in the past. They, in turn, provide enabling, distributive, cooperative and egalitarian social environment that has transformed understanding about consumer identity and consequently market structure.

Global Markets, Local Needs: Fashion and Advertising

The roots of 'globalization of markets' may be traced to the Bretton Woods Agreement of July 1944 that laid out a set of rules that would regulate commercial and financial relations among industrial nations. The period between 1947 and 1973 recorded high rate of growth in output and consumption, near-full employment and recognition of welfare rights in capitalist countries. The developing countries also recorded unprecedented rate of growth in the dawn of an era of free-trade across national boundaries. The enthusiasm for unrestrained free trade was somewhat reined in the meetings of General Agreement on Tariffs and Trade (GATT) wherein selective tariff reduction and provision of protection to states from unequal competition were worked out. In this economic climate, transnational companies that had hitherto (i.e. prior to the Second World War) invested in primary products came to venture into manufacturing. This had two major consequences, one that capital tended to accumulate in richer countries; two that position of the dollar as international currency got further entrenched.

The Bretton Woods Agreement collapsed between 1971 and 1973 due to several inherent inconsistencies. Thenceforth, there was weakening of the US productive output and consequent decline in international demand for dollar, general slackening of growth and high inflation. The aftermath of the post-war boom that prevailed till the close of 1970s paved the way for neo-liberalism in 1980s. Broadly, the policy of neo-liberalism comprised promotion of free market with minimal state intervention, high degree of privatization, and trade liberalization. Countries that had incurred high debts pitched foreign exchange earnings on higher priority than domestic consumption. In the context of the Third World, the period between 1979 and 1982 was characterized by focus of state policy on earning adequate foreign exchange. Two options were envisaged: increasing exports or decreasing imports. It was expected that pro-free market policies would open substantial trade and investment opportunities and that countries would exercise their comparative advantage in the world economy. In the advanced countries, policies favouring the 'free market' were launched (Kiely, 2005).

Neo-liberalism (especially in Thatcherism and Reaganomics) that entailed forceful advocacy of supply side policies was geared towards overcoming economic stagnation and urban deterioration. The objective was to usher-in conditions conducive to sustained economic growth which, it was realized, was being restrained by excessive regulation and state control. Regan favoured an advance towards a free market with reduced intervention of the government and freedom of international trade. He called for massive cut in government expenditure and unprecedented cut in taxation (Healey, 1991; Magazzino, 2012). Consumers gained a great deal from larger supply of goods and services at competitive prices as government lowered barriers for people (e.g. by reducing income tax and capital gains tax rates as also state regulation).

Intensification of worldwide market relations has resulted in availability of both local and branded commodities and/or services in distant markets, places and localities. This is a dialectical process in the sense that while commodities that had been restricted to better-known markets are made available in local markets and local labels are made available in better-known markets. The deterritorialization of markets has accompanied flow of finances and capital across nations. Cross-border flows of goods and capital have had at least two significant consequences. The first is global economic interdependence that makes revisiting state regulation policies imperative. The second is wide differentiation of goods and services to meet the needs and demands of different societies and development of diverse marketing strategies in terms of product concept and design, packaging, retailing and advertising, and promoting it. In anticipation of saturation of urban markets, some of the major companies are targeting the rural market well aware of people's low per capita spending and tough competition from local, indigenous products. The challenge to gain confidence of the rural masses is compounded by people's beliefs, longstanding familiarity and tradition of using the local, indigenous products and their price sensitivity.

In India, the Hindustan Lever, for example, found solution in making its products available in small sachets for price conscious consumers; and cola major Coke, decided to lower its price significantly in order to offer its products as a viable option to local soft drinks, beverages and other options (e.g. butter milk, lemon juice, etc.). Furthermore, Coke doubled its outlets in rural areas from 80,000 in 2001 to 160,000 in the following year and pursued more aggressive marketing. Consequently, rural markets came to account for 80 per cent of new Coke drinkers constituting 30 per cent of its total volume (IBEF, 2004). A fairly large number of companies dealing with durable goods have raised the number of their retail outlets and developed innovative means of distribution of their products in rural areas and remote regions. Multinational companies are known to carry out marketing research aimed at assessing both: the people's opinion about and the impact of their product(s)/service(s) on society. The ultimate objective is to develop appropriate marketing strategies (see Rajagopal, 1999 for details). The production of images of material prosperity is rooted in specific national and local cultural climate. Fernandes (2000: 616) explains how local national and global cultures are arbitrated in the following words:

> Multinational companies consistently attempt to associate their products with signifiers of the Indian nation, for instance through sponsorship of the Olympic team in the 1996 Olympics or through more subtle references to specifically Indian conditions such as the monsoon season. Businesses have also increasingly

attempted to consciously address social criticism of the negative cultural effects of multinational products.

This is a part of global cultural flows including in their ambit, what Appadurai (1990) referred to as ethnoscapes, mediascapes, technospaces, finanscapes and ideoscapes. The contention is, whether these flows, and as Castells (1991) mentions in the context of information technologies, space of places and space of flows, erode or impress cultural identities or generate a new identity. The issue is more complex than it seems in the first instance and has been contested in academic discourse for more than a decade.

Steve Derné, Meenu Sharma and Narendra Sethi (in this volume) critically examine the social and cultural implications of economic liberalization in India over a period of 30 years. Deregulation of the Indian economy, among others, opened the floodgate for transnational television. New programmes promoting largely different cultures many bringing with them role models, values and practices (often sharply contrasted with what the Indian audience were familiar with and/or used to viewing on the national channel all this while) captured the fancy of the middle classes. The exposure to 'foreign' culture and lifestyle set the terms of reference for renewed discourse of tradition and modernity in the country especially for the youth for whom modernity meant 'American lifestyle', 'Western education', 'use of international brands', 'dining at the international chain of restaurants', and 'living with a sense of individualism and self-identity'. As Butcher (2003) mentions, male students and low-income employees in Delhi described themselves as 'progressive' but not 'modern'. While they support the spread of education and demise of the caste system and superstition they are influenced by the socialist ideology and associate modernity with 'the West' and the 'rich people'. Elsewhere, Derné (2008) has brought out the tenacity of ideas about familial, kinship and marital relations. Notwithstanding the fact that globalization impacts social groups differently, he has demonstrated that the middle classes tend to selectively pick up those meanings, messages and images from the global media that they are able to relate with their own cultural stereotypes.

Fashion represents a social force with immense persuasive power to construct, deconstruct and reconstruct identities of people belonging to different classes. Friedman (1992) illustrates the travails of fashion-struck educated youth in politically and economically unstable African Congo between the 1970s and the 1980s. More specifically, fancy for European luxury goods especially *haute couture* originated from ready availability of access to Europeanized cuisine and clothes in Brazzaville—the French colonial outpost. Engagement with fashionable cuisine and attire was not merely for attracting peer-gaze but more for constructing a sense of distinctive identity that matched with their European masters. Veblen's (1957) chief argument was that fashion served to distinguish the upper classes and was, in fact, engineered by them for this very purpose. However, when the classes realized that their fashion and style practices were being imitated by or getting trickled down, they were impelled to reconstitute themselves. Simmel (1904) too notes that pursuit of fashion combines an individual's tendency towards imitation of a given example leading to social adaptation and social equalization with a resolve of differentiation and dissimilarity. The counter-tendencies juxtapose in a way that fashion of the upper classes remains distinct from that of the lower classes. In fact, the upper classes tend to give up fashion that characterized them no sooner than they realize that it has been appropriated by the latter. At this juncture brand names acquire significance.

According to Kellner (2012), fashion constitutes a significant site for consumer spectacle that informs the people of what is the 'in-thing' and what is outdated in the context of contemporary style. The best known performers in the entertainment industry serve as fashion icons and whatever they wear or do is treated as a statement of style. Interestingly, the spectacles of media culture script people's appearances and their behaviours. In this volume, Douglas Kellner argues that in consumer society, identity is produced and re-produced through fashion and advertising. Concomitantly, identity is fluid and expressive of predominant products, styles and images in the consumer market. Drawing from the example of Michael Jackson, Madonna and Lady Gaga who constantly change their identities, he discusses the complexity and contradictions inherent in fluidity of identity of individual, ethnic, and national levels. He employs critical approach to the visual culture of the image and spectacle to bring out the determinants and forces of identity in postmodern society offering new possibilities, styles and forms. Finkelstein (2012) writes,

> The invention of the fashion label or brand name has given the consumer a sense of social location which promises to neutralize the oceanic disorientation of a limitless horizon of commodities. This sense of location is made to seem part of the allure of fashionability and of the unexpected stabilizing of identity which accompanies signature goods such as McDonald's, BMW, Sony.

The brand name of commodity or a luxury brand acquires power and importance not essentially because of some intrinsic features of its own, rather 'partly through its endorsement and appropriation by people who are themselves icons of style, fashion and good life' (Nayar, 2009: 61).

In effect, brands serve as symbols, that refer among others, to shared values and meanings that are fashioned under the influence of the desire to be distinguished and identified with a specific group of people known for its upward social mobility and an enviable social position. It comprises those to whom the general public looks up for latest trends in fashion and style. In public discourse, particularly in Asian countries, it is usual to hear that the hub of fashion and modernity so to say is located in the 'West'. Jackson (2004), however, provides evidence of multiple modernities rather than grounded in simplistic east–west gradient. In fact, lifestyle choices of people suggest shared consumption patterns that could well be suggested by sets of cultural objects that are known to be vested with a distinctive social meaning that distinguish those who appropriate the whole set (Levy, 1959). Conversely, as Holt says,

> lifestyles may be viewed as product of relational differences between consumption patterns in which, differences in meanings embedded in consumption practices, serve as a basis for affiliating

with certain types of people and, likewise, as resource for distinguishing oneself from others, reinforcing social positions (and
because cultural and social structures are mutually constitutive,
the inverse holds as well). (1997: 336)

An individual tends to maintain a cultural consistency in her/
his use of complements of consumer goods. Better known as,
'diderot effect' (after Denis Diderot who first documented the
unity in complement of consumer goods) as also 'consumption
constellation' (Solomon and Assael, 1987), such a tendency fore-
grounds the practice of consuming distinct sets of objects by different collectivities that tell their identities. According to Holt
(1997: 328), 'This view assumes that categories of consumption
objects are imbued with distinct univocal meanings that appeal
to some collectivities more than others. Since, tastes in this view
are conceived as preferences for particular categories of objects,
they can be inferred directly from objects choices.' Product com-
plementarity occurs when symbolic meanings of different products relate with each other (Solomon, 1983). This understanding
has been exploited largely by marketers to present lifestyle concept through expressive symbolism to consumers. Group identities are known to consolidate around conglomeration of products
and activities that are used to define particular category (Englis
and Solomon, 1997; Solomon, 1983). The choice of products and
services incorporated by specific social groups into their lifestyles
provides opportunities for specific promotional and advertorial
enterprises. Mass production of commodities has necessitated
the mobilization of strategies of creating a matching demand for
them. Advertisers have struggled to encourage people to transcend the traditional consumer market and buying habits feeding
their own fundamentals needs.

The pursuit of creating a fancy for commodities and services
that call for additional financial burden has been arduous and
one involving close understanding of local cultures and ideologies of people. In addition, there is a need for webbing them
with the culture and ideology surrounding the commodities and
services produced for the global markets. William Mazzarella
(in this volume) describes how local culture(s), commitments,

anxieties, expectations and aspirations drive the advertising industry and themselves get influenced by global culture(s). In a significant addition to writings that suggest inclusion of elements of local culture in advertising, Mazzarella situates the discussion on the practices of advertising in the locale of public culture centring around productions of commodity images. He brings out the menaces, contradictions and concerns surroundings production of commodity images of 'KamaSutra' brand of condoms. The chapter integrates the practice of consumption with commercial, political and subversive practices as it focuses on representations and interface between local and global discourse. The challenge creates a market for commodities produced on a large scale which has got tougher as individualism to 'stand out' from the crowd has come to the forefront.

Nowadays, advertising is a complex negotiation between consumers' desire for exclusiveness and commodities actually available in the market (that may not be customized for each segment of consumers differentiated culturally and economically). By and large, advertisements emphasize the exclusiveness and contemporaneity of an object often justifying the price in terms of its elegance and authenticity. A conspicuous influence of marketing is the creation of universal consumer market segments in which similar meanings get associated with people, places and products) that together form a transnational consumer culture (Alden et al., 1999; Ueltzhoffer and Ascheberg, 1999, cited here from Hill, 2002a: 275). Rather than being adopted as a homogenising force, transnational consumer culture has met with resilience of local consumption cultures. In fact, one of the arguments that Mazzarella (2003) makes in *Shoveling Smoke* is that it is not just about resilience of already existing 'local' consumption cultures, but also about the way transnational marketing produces new conceptions of the local that then come to be experienced as 'authentically' local. Consumers indigenize the transnational consumer culture in a manner that it comes across as a fine blend between 'transnational' and 'local' culture even as modernity is interpreted, experienced and negotiated in terms of local subjectivity (Appadurai and Breckenridge, 1995). Focusing on the resilience of distinctive local consumption cultures, Jackson (2004) reviews Gerasimova's writing (2003) on artful tactics of ordinary consumers in Soviet private economy. Gerasimova presents the case of 'artful consumption' referring to personalization of things through mending and repairing them, handing them to successive generation or putting to new use things that have become unfit to serve the purpose for which they were bought in the first place.

Olga Gurova (in this volume) examines fashion retail as an indicator of the transformation of consumption in Russia in the last two decades. She charts out the trajectory of fashion retail in Russia and what it means to the people at the outset. The beginning of transformation in fashion retail has been traced to the 1990s. Small entrepreneurs came to develop their businesses surrounding fashion retail. Open-air markets, stalls, pavilions and other forms of retail sprang up. Over the years that followed, international and domestic retail chain stores, retail-entertainment centres, fashion centres and retail-parks mushroomed. As Olga Gurova mentions, all forms of retail receive equal patronage of the consumers. In fact, she divides the consumers into five categories: the advanced consumer, the squander, the socialist consumer, the alternative creative consumers and the convenience consumer based on their preference for and ideas about different forms of retail trade. In the process, she sheds light on people's aspirations and the market that sets the expectations from agenda for availability of products and selling environment.

Marketa Rulikova (in this volume) reinforces the major argument in Gurova's chapter that the socialist ideology continues to persist and manifest itself in people's lives including their values, identities, familial relations and economic and consumption behaviours even after its collapse in 1989–90. She describes senior citizens' participation in day-long promotional sales tours in buses that turn out to be arduous for the elderly in terms of inconvenience and humiliation meted out to them at the hands of the staff of the retail company that organizes promotional sales tour. Rulikova presents an insightful account of these tours and more importantly the contesting ideologies of the elderly who undertake such tours despite the physical and emotional hardships and the organizers of these tours who in effect, try extremely hard to promote and push their products even as they offer free gifts and other incentives to the prospective clients. Additionally, she locates the agency of the elderly in maintaining intergenerational solidarity in their attempts, of which one is engaging with sales tours in order to remain helpful to their children.

Subaltern Concerns and Moral Subjectivities

The history of consumer culture in general is one of exclusionary politics and at the same time an incessant run for mainstreaming lifestyles by the marginalized. Negotiation of identity and social status through consumer culture precludes a sense of fairness to the subaltern. An overwhelming number of people are forced to live with a sense of deprivation arising out of their inability to match up to the consumer lives and identities of their reference groups. Those who are not able to engage with mainstream consumer culture, or do so in a limited way, find themselves entrapped in a compelling situation. The struggle of poor consumers is understandably a hard one. As Lewis (1965: 40–41) explains,

> The culture of poverty is both an adaptation and a reaction of the poor to their marginal position in a class-stratified, highly individuated, capitalistic society. It represents an effort to cope with feelings of powerlessness and despair which develop from the realization of the improbability of achieving success in terms of the values and goals of the larger society. Indeed many of the traits of the culture of poverty can be viewed as attempts at local solutions for problems not met by existing institutions and agencies because, the people are not eligible for them, cannot afford them, or are ignorant or suspicious of them ...

The implication is that despite that poor consumers being well aware of middle class values are not able to incorporate these values in their lives. His contenders, however, maintain that whilst similar values prevail across socio-economic statuses, perceived differences arise out of restrictions on consumption (Jones and

Lou, 1999; Valentine, 2001, see Hill and Gaines, 2007 for an overview of critical discussion on the culture of poverty). It is unanimously accepted, however, that financial capital constraints drive them to struggle for survival and the pressure of consumer culture pushes them to engage with conspicuous consumption at the same time.

In the larger framework of consumer culture, two categories of the subaltern are visible. The first comprises those who are bereft of any means whatsoever to engage with consumer culture. We see them in rags, begging on the streets or toiling hard yet unable to meet both ends. They live below the poverty line, remain excluded from consumer culture and do not envisage a possibility of being a part of it ever. The second category comprises those who earn enough to manage two square meals a day and save a petty amount to meet the contingencies in life and engage with consumer culture. It is this petty amount at hand that makes them to aspire for, as they say, 'good clothing' and 'decent living' much like that of 'others', that is, the middle class in a general sense which serves as their reference group and the images of the luxurious life and living of the upper classes that they get to see in the programmes and advertisements on their television screens which create sense of discomfort, unease and inferiority. Reviewing critical writings on the behaviour of impoverished consumers (Calpovitz, 1967; Hill and Stephens, 1997; Holloway and Cardozo, 1969; Irelan and Benser, 1966; Lee et al., 1999; Richards, 1966; Sturdivant, 1969 among others), Hill (2002a) points out that early scholarship impressed the idea that the poor tend to compensate for their limiting resources and consumption opportunities by making irrational purchase decisions. This was, however, substituted by another one later, which established that rather than compensating, poor consumers pursue the very material goods that the affluent chase and look for their share of socialist wealth. Most of the studies find that the poor are surprisingly more resourceful than one would expect in terms of gaining control over their consumer lives.

The overbearing pressure to reach out to the ways and means of televised images of luxurious living makes them to cut-down on basic food and other necessities. Varman and Belk (2008) report the case of a low-caste washerman in India who purchased a colour television set out of the money he saved by reducing the consumption of milk by his children. They cite similar findings of Ger (1992) in Turkish society. This trend is representative of a common strategy adopted by the subaltern in order to secure a position of recognition in kinship group and neighbourhood. The other alternative is to incur debt. A number of banks and departmental stores across the world encourage purchase on credit and the convenience of buy-now-pay-later. Instead of planning and making provision ahead of large purchases, people are able to satiate their desires without prolonged delay (even if it calls for regret later). As Andreason (1975) mentions, in order to obtain material abundance, the impoverished obtain excessive debt obligations that are based on careful calculations of the consequences of their actions (cited here from Hill and Gaines, 2007). In the specific context of coping strategies of welfare mothers, Hill and Stephens (1997) propose that women enlarge the spectrum of available goods and services well beyond the limits of economic and social deficits by deploying resource strategies (e.g. social capital) within their communities (Hill and Gaines, 2007). Urban poor engage with consumerist activity and create a world of their own that assures them of showing a path that would lead them to a state of plentitude and abundance as in the case of *jhuggi jhopri* (shanty dwellers in New Delhi) dwellers (Srivastava, 2010). Hamilton (2008) demonstrates that the impoverished consumers are able to, in fact, employ coping strategies to create a positive self-identity and consumer empowerment. People could anticipate the difficult situations and employ coping strategies to deal with, avert them, or even be proactive in their efforts to manage them. In representing attempts to secure family's best interests, such coping strategies could be interpreted as acts of consumer agency.

Often, the poor who purchase commodities on credit are hit both by high rates of interest and lower quality products (see Calpovitz, 1967; Coe, 1971; Goodman, 1968; Hill, 2001, 2002a, 2002b; Williams, 1977 for discussion perspective on the plight of those with low income in consumer society). Many seek to enhance their earnings (whether by righteous or illegal means) in order to meet the demands of consumer culture, consumerist lifestyle. Using data from the Consumer Expenditure Survey, Krueger and Perri (2005) conclude that rise in income inequality in the United States is not proportionate to the rise in consumption inequality in the United States. They add,

> Moreover, income inequality has increased substantially both between and within groups of households with the same characteristics (such as education, sex and race), but even though between-group consumption inequality has tracked between-group income inequality quite closely, within-group *consumption* inequality has increased much less than within-group income inequality. (p. 1)

For the subaltern, consumer culture comes with several compulsive demands and restraints on free choice. Hamilton (2009) cites the case of an Irish woman who felt compelled to accept her friends' offers of handing old pair of jeans to her (which they would otherwise throw away) and a few other cases to impress the point that lack of resources results in discontentment with poor consumers' own life situation. The marginalization from consumer culture instills low self-esteem and perception of powerlessness. Melike Aktaş Yamanoğlu (in this volume) develops an understanding of how the poor youth in Turkey deal with the pressure to engage with conspicuous consumption on an everyday basis and establish their identity in a consumer society fraught with class-based hierarchy. She points out, the print and electronic media, Internet sources as also celebrity shows inform and impress the benchmarks of consumption in mainstream society. Overcoming the 'demonstration effect' and keeping up with the Joneses in such a situation is a challenging task for households with lesser income. Their narratives are those of exclusion from mainstream society and ones in which they see themselves as ridden with shame, humiliation, stigma and symbolic violence. Drawing from 65 interviews with poor and young people, Aktaş Yamanoğlu concludes that in an attempt to minimize social hierarchies by way of utilizing consumer goods and consumption practices, the poor youth tend to, in effect, reproduce them.

What is interesting to note is that fact that many a time consumer culture appropriates motifs and style of life from the social fabric of the middle and lower classes, refurbishes and subsequently presents them as coveted icons, fashions and style (e.g. cargo pants, jazz music and punk styles that were all associated with lower social status bearing groups). Street styles have a way of appearing in fashion shows, for they represent authenticity which is valued and treated as a precious commodity. In the words of Polhemus (1994: 8),

> But it is more than the price tag which distinguishes the genuine article from its chic reinterpretation. It is a question of context. And when fashion sticks its metaphorical gilt frame around a leather motorbike jacket ..., it transforms an emblem of subcultural identity into something which anyone with enough money can acquire and wear with pride.

The disjuncture between what was theirs for always and its newly acquired position in consumer culture that alienates the subaltern from it is hard to bear. They feel alienated, deprived and failed, for their's was the first right over all such appropriated elements.

Marxists developed a strong critique of consumer culture primarily on the ground that it is founded on the exploitation of workers. The protagonists of consumption tend to level off collective and individual anti-consumption sentiment. Consumer culture dismisses the puritanical ideas of austerity, self-restraint, community and nurturance and instead places undue importance on indulgence, individualism and self-interest, all of which are inimical to 'common good'. Marcuse (1973) mentions that the politics of corporate capitalism and the consumer economy creates strong ties between an individual and commodity form. In his words, 'The need for possessing, consuming, handling, and constantly renewing the gadgets, devices, instruments, engines, offered to and imposed upon the people, for using these wares even at danger of one's own destruction has become a "biological" need in the sense just defined' (p. 20).

Thompson (1971) draws attention to moral economy in the eighteenth century in which people would not seek to make profit out of necessities of others. In times of scarcity, the prices of commodities would remain at a customary level. The transition of moral economy to unregulated market economy was marked by assertion of rights by consumers. The latter brings with it extortionate mechanism that we tend to shrug off for their inconvenience and hardships. The demise of the moral economy is suggested, among others by people's acceptance of an economist interpretation of food riot, 'as a direct, spasmodic, irrational response to hunger—a picture which itself is a product of a political economy which diminished human reciprocities to the wage-nexus' (p. 136). Evidently, conflict of values lies at the core of consumer culture and modernity raising the issue of ethics and sustainability. Ethical consumption is acquiring currency across the world, at a great pace in the United States since the last decade or so. Nicki Lisa Cole (in this volume) examines the issue of ethical consumption cantering around ethically branded and certified goods that are popularly picked up for the contemporary values, desires and identities that they embody with an example of coffee. The paper has originated from her sustained study of promise and contradictions of ethical consumption with focus on the case of coffee. She mentions that ethically coded coffee acquires greater meaning for and success with consumers because of widespread awareness of the producers' struggle. The consumers are projected as saviours of the poor coffee cultivators. Lisa Cole presents a sociologically informed critique of the marketing strategy that appeals to the ethical and moral subjectivities of consumers of coffee. Despite growing awareness, ethical consumption remains confined as an ideology rather than serving as a viable alternative. Elsewhere she writes,

> By foregrounding the image and narrative of the laborer the industry has convinced consumers that they do not need to worry about the laborer. This is a more gripping form of Marx's commodity fetishism (1978), since the relations and real conditions of production remain obscured by ethical coffee. The narrative presented by it masquerades as a removal of the curtain, but in fact, it is the same curtain painted over with an enchanting scene. (Cole, 2011)

The concern surrounding labour and environmental exploitation gets dampened, mass consumption gathers momentum and global capitalist production and consumption get perpetuated. Sassatelli (2012) argues that political investment of the consumer bringing different facets of the politics of consumption is an important means of ensuring justice. The point that she makes is that while it is futile to expect that distinction and hierarchy of taste can be removed from the domain of critical consumption, this dimension of consumption could well be monitored 'through a more structural politics of justice at the systemic level'. Affirmation of consumer-driven social charge bears the possibility of sustainability, ethical uprightness and purposive lifestyles that would obviate the fallout(s) of mindless consumption. Consumer sovereignty in the domains of both the market and personal selves needs to rein sheer hedonism with various forms of discipline in a way that search for pleasure is guided and pleasure itself is moderated.

Roberta Sassatelli (in this volume) contests the notion of consumption as a 'private' act. One might say with her that rather than being confined as a private act, consumption is a site of politics and power relationships. She maintains that consumer is then a 'political subject' and concentrates on a viewpoint that treats individual consumers as agency for politics of justice. She discusses with precision and fineness the effectiveness of ethical consumption and limits of the market. While consumer society presents the freedom of choice to consumers, the political investment of the consumer needs to be grounded in political dilemmas of consumerism bringing together 'politics of difference' referring to choices of consumption as means of social inclusion as also exclusion; 'politics of normality' referring to normative view of the consumer ('normal consumption' as a social construct which is opposed to socially deviant forms of consumption such as addiction) and 'politics of effects' referring to systemic and implicit effects of consumer practices. Production is separated from consumption and politics from market clearing the haze around objects and services that are promoted as commodities available in the market in exchange of money by the advertising industry. This prepares ground for affecting consumer's awareness about and opinion on ethical and environmental issues related with their practice of consumption.

Acknowledgement

I am grateful to Professor William Mazzarella for his insightful comments. Usual disclaimer applies.

Notes

1. The 'India Shining' slogan was popularized by the Bharatiya Janta Party (BJP). The BJP launched its major electoral campaign under the same banner. It did not, however, enable the BJP to win elections in the year 2004. For details of the trajectory and fate of the slogan, see Brosius (2010).
2. The distinction between 'necessities' and 'luxuries' is not unique to communist ideology alone. In fact, a large number of puritan ideologies across the world have consolidated similar notions.

References

Alden, D.L., Steenkamp, J.E.M. & Batra, R. 1999. Brand positioning through advertising in Asia, North America and Europe: The role of global consumer culture. *Journal of Marketing, 63*(January), 75–87.

Andreason, A.R. 1975. *The Disadvantaged Consumer.* New York: The Free Press.

Appadurai, A. 1986. Introduction: Commodities and the politics of value. In A. Appadurai (ed.), *The Social Life of Things: Commodities in Cultural Perspective,* pp. 3–63. Cambridge: Cambridge University Press.

———. 1990. Disjuncture and difference in the global culture economy. *Theory, Culture, and Society, 7,* 295–310.

Appadurai, A. & Breckenridge, C.A. 1995. Public modernity in India. In C.A. Breckenridge (ed.), *Consuming Modernity: Public Culture in a South Asian World,* pp. 1–20. Minneapolis, MN: University of Minnesota Press.

Basi, J.K.T. 2009. *Women, Identity and India's Call Centre Industry.* Oxon: Routledge.

Bourdieu, Pierre. 1985. The Social Space and the genesis of groups. *Theory and Society, 14*(6), 723–744.

Brosius, C. 2010. *India's Middle Class: New Forms of Urban Leisure, Consumption and Prosperity.* New Delhi: Routledge.

Butcher, M. 2003. *Transnational Television, Cultural Identity and Change: When Star Came to India.* New Delhi: SAGE.

Calpovitz, D. 1967. *The Poor Pay More: Consumer Practices of Low-Income Families.* New York: The Free Press.

Castells, M. 1991. *The Information City: A New Framework for Social Change.* University of Toronto.

Coe, B.D. 1971. Private versus national preference among lower and middle income consumers. *Journal of Retailing,* 47(3), 61–72.

Cole, N.L. 2011. The Promise and Contradictions of Ethical Consumerism. *Consumers, Commodities and Consumption* (a newsletter of the Consumer Studies Research Network) 12, 2 (May). http://csrn.camden.rutgers. edu/newsletter/12-2/cole.htm, accessed on 30 May 2012.

Derné, S. 2008. *Globalization on the Ground.* New Delhi: SAGE.

Elliott, A. & Urry, J. 2010. *Mobile Lives.* London: Routledge.

Englis, B.G. & Solomon, M.R. 1997. Special session summary I am not therefore, I am: The role of avoidance products in shaping consumer behavior. In M. Brucks & D.J. MacInnis (eds), *Advances in Consumer Research* (Vol. 24). Provo, UT: Association for Consumer Research, pp. 61–63.

Featherstone, M. 2007. *Consumer Culture and Postmodernism* (2nd edition). London: SAGE.

Fernandes, L. 2000. Nationalizing 'the global': Media images, cultural policies and the middle class in India. *Media, Culture and Society,* 22(5), 611–628.

Finkelstein, J. 2012. Chic Theory. http://www.australianhumanitiesreview. org/archieve/issue.../finkelstein.html, accessed on 9 July 2012.

Friedman, J. 1992. Narcissim, roots and post-modernity: The Constitution of selfhood in the Global Crisis. In S. Lash & J. Friedman (eds), *Modernity and Identity,* pp. 331–336. Oxford: Blackwell.

Ganguly-Scrase, R. & Scrase, T.J. 2011. *Globalisation and the Middle Classes in India: The Social and Cultural Impact of Neoliberal Reforms.* London: Routledge.

Ger, G. 1992. The positive and negative effects of marketing on socio-economic development: The Turkish case. *Journal of Consumer Policy,* 15(3), 229–254.

Gerasimova, K. 2003. The life of goods in the Soviet private economy: Artful tactics of ordinary consumers, 1945–1991. Seminar presented to the Department of Russian and Slavonic Studies, University of Sheffield, 3 December.

Giddens, A. 1991. *Modernity and Self-identity. Self and Society in the Late Modren Age.* Cambridge: Polity Press in association with Blackwell Publishers.

Goodman, C.S. 1968. Do the poor pay more? *Journal of Marketing, 32* (January), 18–24.

Goodman, D.J. & Cohen, M. 2004. *Consumer Culture: A Reference Handbook.* Santa Barbara: ABC-CLIO Ltd.

Hamilton, K. 2008. I can do it! Consumer coping and poverty. *Advances in Consumer Research, 35,* 551–556.

———. 2009. Those left behind: Inequality in consumer culture. *Irish Marketing Review, 20*(2), 40–54.

Healey, N.M. 1991. The Thatcher supply side miracle: Myth or reality? *The American Economist, 36*(Spring), 7–12.

Hill, R.P. 2001. *Surviving in A Material World: The Lived Experince of Poverty.* Notre Dame: University of Notre Dame.

———. 2002a. Consumer culture and the culture of poverty: Implications for marketing theory and practice. *Marketing Theory, 2*(3), 273–293.

Hill, R.P. 2002b. Stalking the poverty consumer: A retrospective examination of modern ethical dilemmas. *Journal of Business Ethics, 37*(2), 209 –219.

Hill, R.P. & Stephens, D.L. 1997. Impoverished consumers and consumer behavior: The case of AFDC mothers. *Journal of Macro Marketing, 17*(Fall), 32–52.

Hill, R.P. & Gaines, J. 2007. The consumer culture of poverty: Behavioral research findings and their implications in an ethnographic context. *The Journal of American Culture, 30*(1), 81–95.

Holloway, R.J. & Cordozo, R.N. 1969. *Consumer Problems and Marketing Patterns in Low-income Neighborhoods: An Exploratory Study.* Minneapolis: Graduate School of Business Studies.

Holt, D.B. 1997. Poststructuralist lifestyle analysis: Conceptualizing the social patterning of consumption in postmodernity. *Journal of Micromarketing, 21*(2), 181–198.

Humphyery, C. 2002. *The Unmaking of Soviet Life: Everyday Economies after Socialism.* New York: Cornell University Press.

Indian Brand Equality Foundation (IBEF). 2004. *Fast Moving Consumer Goods.* Gurgaon: IBEF.

Irelan, L.M. & Besner, A. 1966. Low income outlook on life. In L.M. Irelan (ed.), *Low Income Lifestyles,* pp. 1–8. District of Columbia: US Department of Health, Education, and Welfare.

Jackson, P. 2004. Local consumption cult-type equation in a globalizing world. *Transactions of the Institute of British Geographers, 29,* 165–178. doi: 10:111/j.0020-2754.2004.00123x.

Jones, R.K. & Lou, Y. 1999. The culture of poverty and African-American culture: An empirical assessment. *Sociological Perspectives, 42,* 439–459.

Kellner, D. 2012. Media Culture and Triumph of the Spectacle. http://www.gesis.ulca.edu/faculty/kelner, accessed on 10 July 2012.

Kiely, R. 2005. *The Clash of Globalizations: Neo-Liberalism, the Third Way and Anti-Globalization.* Leiden: Koninklijke Brill NV.

Krueger, D. & Perri, F. 2005. Does Income Inequality Lead to Consumption Inequality? Evidence and Theory. http://economics.sas.upenn.edu/vdkrueger/research..., accessed on 18 July 2012.

Lee, R.G., Ozanne, J.L. & Hill, R.P. 1999. Improving service encounters through resource sensitivity: The case of health care delivery in an Appalachian community. *Journal of Public Policy and Marketing, 18*(2), 230–248.

Levy, S. 1959. Symbols for sale. *Harvard Business Review, 37*(4 July–August), 117–124.

Lewis, O. 1965. *La Vida: A Puerto Rican Family in the Culture of Poverty.* New Delhi: Random House.

Magazzino, C. 2012. The electronics policy of Ronald Regan: Between supply-side and Keynesianism. *European Journal of Social Sciences, 27*(3), 319–334.

Marcuse, H. 1973. *One-Dimensional Man: Studies in the Ideology of Advanced Industrial Society.* Boston: Beacon Press.

Mazzarella, William. 2003. *Shoveling Smoke: Advertising and Globalization in Contemporary India.* Durham, NC: Duke University Press.

McCracken, G. 1988. *Culture and Consumption: New Approaches to the Symbolic Character of Consumer Goods and Activities.* Bloomington: Indiana University Press.

Nayar, P.K. 2009. *Packaging Life: Culture of the Everyday.* New Delhi: SAGE.

Oushakine, S.A. 2000. The quantity of style: Imaginary consumption in the New Russia. *Theory, Culture and Society, 17*(5), 97–120.

Polhemus, T. 1994. *Streetstyle: From Sidewalk to Catwalk.* New York: Thames and Hudson.

Rajagopal, A. 1999. Thinking through emerging markets: Brands, logics and the cultural forms of political society in India. *Social Text, 60*(3), 131–149.

Richards, L. 1966. Consumer practices of the poor. In L.M. Irelan (ed.), *Low Income Lifestyle.* District of Columbia: U.S. Department of Health, Education, and Welfare.

Ritzer, G. 1998. Introduction. In J. Bandrillard (ed.), *The Consumer Society: Myths and Structures,* pp. 1–24. London: SAGE.

———. 2001. *Explorations in the Sociology of Consumption: Fast Food, Credit cards and Casinos.* London: SAGE.

———. 2010. *Enchanting a Disenchanted World: Continuity and Change in the Cathedrals of Consumption.* Los Angeles: SAGE.

Sassatelli, R. 2012. Self and body. In F. Trentman (ed.), *The Oxford Handbook of the History of Consumption,* pp. 633–652. Oxford: Oxford University Press.

Shevchenko, O. 2002. In case of fire emergency: Consumption, security and the meaning of durables in a transforming society. *Journal of Consumer Culture, 2*(2), 147–170.

Simmel, G. 1904. Fashion. *International Quarterly, 7*(22), 130–155.

Slater, D. 1997. *Consumer Culture and Modernity.* Cambridge: Polity Press in association with Blackwell Publishers.

Solomon, M.R. 1983. The role of products as social stimuli: A Symbolic interactionism perspective. *Journal of Consumer Research,* (December), 319–329.

Solomon, M.R. & Assael, H. 1987. The forest or the trees: A Gesalt approach to symbolic consumption. In J. Umiker-Sebeok (ed.), *Marketing and Semiotics: New Directions in the Study of Signs for Sale,* pp. 189–218. Bertin: Moutone de Gruyter.

Srivastava, Sanjay. 2010. Consumerism and object lessons for the urban poor. *Contributions to Indian Sociology, 44*(122), 103–128.

Stillerman, J. & Salcedo, R. 2012. Transposing the urban to the mall: Routes, relationships and resistance in two Santigao, Chile, shopping centers. *Journal of Contemporary Ethnography, 20*(10), 1 –28.

Sturdivant, F.D. 1969. *The Ghetto Marketplace.* New York: The Free Press.

Thompson, E.P. 1971. The moral economy of the English crowd in the eighteenth century. *The Past and Present Society, 50*(1), 76–136.

Ueltzhoffer, J. & Ascheberg, C. 1999. Transnational consumer cultures and social milieus. *Journal of the Market Research Society, 41*(January), 47–59.

Valentine, C.A. 2001. The culture of poverty: Its scientific significance and its implications for action. In E.B. Leacock (ed.), *The Culture of Poverty: A Critique.* New York: Simon and Schuster.

Varman, R. & Belk, R.W. 2008. Weaving a web: Subaltern consumers, rising consumer culture, and television. *Marketing Theory, 8*(3), 227–252.

Veblen, T. 1957 (1899). *The Theory of the Leisure Class: An Economic Study of Institutions.* London: George Allen and Unwin.

Williams, F. 1977. *Why The Poor Pay More.* London: The Macmilen Press Ltd. For the National Consumer Council.

Yalcinkaya, T. 2009. Is Turkish Capitalism Consistent with Capitalist Globalization? [online]. Local-Global Identity, Security, Community 6:78-92. http://search.informit.com.all/documentsSummary:dn= 107202151452579:res=IELHSS, accessed on 15 June 2012.

PART I

Lifestyle Choices and Construction of Modern Identities

1

The Rich and the Super-rich: Mobility, Consumption and Luxury Lifestyles*

Mike Featherstone

Introduction

In the wake of the global recession, the emergence of a new cohort of the wealthy, widely dubbed as 'the super-rich' has become more prominent. The expanding range of digital communications and transport technologies, coupled with 24-hour financial market trading and an array of offshore financial services provided in tax havens, has enabled a new type of mobile lifestyle for the growing strata of the rich and super-rich—increasingly referred to as 'high net worth individuals' and 'ultra-high net worth individuals'. Members of this group can be found in a number of locations around the world, moving between prestigious residential areas of global cities, financial centres and exclusive resorts. The leading representatives, along with the global billionaires who are found in the World Wealth List, feature prominently in the business and popular press, television

---

*Revised version of the lecture delivered at University of International Business and Economics, Beijing, May 2012.

and Internet. Their work and lifestyle are glamorized and put them in the public imagination in the same category as leading entertainers in music, film and television industries. Indeed, their public image is often associated with the media with the celebrity lifestyle (Turner, 2004). Some may seek to court publicity as a part of their brand strategy, while others attain notoriety for their style of business activities, leisure activities, adventures or scandals. The expectation is that they will engage in excessive luxury consumption, enjoy travel in the latest forms of transport (cars, yachts and private jets) and reside in homes full of art treasures, designer goods, fashion accessories and the latest gadgets. The media has highlighted the rate of growth of their fortunes, and questioned their contribution to national taxation along with the visibility of their luxurious lifestyles at a time of major economic downturn accompanied with increased national and private debt, unemployment and growing inequalities for many ordinary people. The super-rich justify their engagement with luxury lifestyle as a hard-earned reward for what they see as their extraordinary talent, hard work, risk and initiative.

With the extension of neo-liberalism since the 1980s and the deregulation of state support for welfare and privatization of many state services, the market is now presented as the most efficient social mechanism for expanding the national wealth, furthering social justice and rewarding individual enterprise. Those who are wealthy are presented, not as parasitic or exploitative, but as important contributors to the economy and social life. Nation states compete with each other to provide the most attractive taxation regimes not only to attract overseas investment from businesses, but also to pull in the super-rich, whose domicile, it is assumed, will necessarily help to stimulate and generate beneficial business and financial ventures. Since the economic crisis of 2008, as we enter deeper into global recession, particularly marked in Europe, North America and other parts of the West, there has been talk of a new age of austerity. Yet, unless the crisis leads to a collapse of the whole global economy, which is a possibility that should not be ruled out, given the financial imbalances and levels of indebtedness and endemic problems of the economic system, innovative solutions seem hard to find. For many economists and politicians it would seem that consumer culture is regarded as not just a part of the problem, but also part of the solution. The condition leading to the crisis—the encouragement of overconsumption and household speculative enterprise through the massive selling of unsustainable credit by financial agencies—is glossed over. The only viable way forward out of the recession, then, is seen as involving renewed consumption: To encourage consumers to buy more goods, for the very reason that from Beijing to New York, to London, to Johannesburg and São Paulo, the call is to find ways to renew consumer demand and increase the production of goods and services, as this will mean more jobs and the expansion of the economy. In the case of the United States' economy, around 70 per cent of US GDP now comes from consumer spending.

This chapter briefly considers a number of sites and facilities for the super-rich in various parts of the world. The luxurious lifestyles and expenditure of super-rich have become more visible, given their lack of contribution to national taxation at a time of a major economic downturn, with increased national and private debt, unemployment and inequalities for many ordinary people. Their high mobility and command of digital communications systems, meritocratic ethos and ready intermixing suggests they are the true cosmopolitans. Yet their capacity to opt out of national and social responsibilities raises many questions and has been designated as an unwelcomed and unsustainable 'revolt of the elites'. The intention of the chapter is to begin a preliminary investigation of the contemporary super-rich and their luxurious forms of consumption and glamorous lifestyles, which are increasingly held up as models for us all. Studies of the rich, of course, are few and far between in sociology and cultural studies. It is clear that researching the rich presents many methodological and practical challenges and it is no surprise that the vast majority of sociologists and cultural researchers have followed the long-term tendency of focusing on the middle and working classes.

Wealth and Luxury Dynamics: The Court Nobility and the Rise of the Middle Class

While markets and some level of monetization with the buying and selling of goods and the exchange of commodities have existed from early forms of human societies, the attitude towards wealth has varied a great deal. In religion-centred or theocratic societies, such as ones dominated by variants of puritanism (the English Republic and Interregnum of the seventeenth century, or the Communist Party in China with the Cultural Revolution, or the Iranian Revolution of 1979 with Khomeini and the ayatollahs), signs of wealth along with luxury and excessive consumption were deemed wasteful and frivolous and not to be manifested in public. In other societies, the display of wealth may have been tolerated, but highly circumscribed with strong prohibitions, or social sanctions, on its movement and transformation into more liquid forms such as money.

Nobility, Merchants and the Middle Class

In early modern times in particular, especially in Europe, the major dynamic would seem to have been the struggle between the nobility and the merchants, between the aristocracy and the middle class, between landed wealth and titles and trade and money. A strong tension developed between the purveyors of wealth and luxury goods, the merchants and financiers in the middle class and the king's court and aristocrats, with the latter attempting to restrict strongly the social power of the former group. A struggle was won by economic specialists in England and then other parts of Europe from the eighteenth century onwards, with the triumph of the middle classes entailing among other things: the birth of a consumer society, the expansion of luxury, and the development of economics into an independent science favouring *laissez-faire* and the reduction of sovereign restrictions.[1]

The tension between the nobility and the middle class was manifest in the use of different types of wealth. For the nobility, landed wealth was locationally fixed being consumption restricted and rule bound. For the middle class, wealth could be more readily traded through the purchase and sale of commodities. It is generally expected that rulers and powerful groups such as the monarchy and nobility will engage in more extensive and even excessive consumption, compared to those in the middle and lower orders. Consumption here needs to be seen as hedged in by social rules and rituals, and not merely directed to satisfy bodily appetites, pleasures and desires. In addition, consumption can be seen as a resource to reinforce prestige, with many types of consumptions taking place in setting designed to enhance the visibility and display and hence the status, of the ruling group. Indeed, the visibility of consumption events (eating and entertainment) and ceremonial activities (involving the observation of correct dress codes, adornment, demeanour and forms of self-presentation) as well as the decoration and design of the architectural spaces in which events take place, all work to reinforce the differences between those who possess the adequate resources and knowledge to be at ease in such settings and those who do not. The resultant sense of self-worth and appropriateness and legitimacy of access are important indicators of the ways in which consumption can be seen to create and reinforce social distinctions between those who are at ease with the legitimacy of consumption and display and those unable or forbidden to consume in the middle and lower orders.

Concomitantly, there is a marked contrast between the world of the courtier, noble and aristocrat where the emphasis is on display, reputation and status and that of the middle class. The middle class, however, are given more to fantasies and imaginative play in their consumption (Campbell, 1987). In effect, their consumption, not just of everyday staple goods such as food and drink, but often of emergent literary cultural forms such as novels, especially from the eighteenth century onwards, takes place in more isolated and private settings. This can be contrasted to the need for confidence, wit and panache in the social world of the aristocrat and courtier. The world in which performance and display skills were central, with imaginative play carefully circumscribed. The historical dynamic in the West has been one that has reduced the social power of courts, the aristocracy and landed wealth, while dramatically increasing that of the upper class (the bourgeoisie) and middle class, who derive their wealth from industry, business and finance. This has been particularly the case in Europe, although there are major differences between East and West Europe in terms of the persistence of the aristocracy, and even between countries as close as France and England in terms of the tensions between the aristocracy and new upper-middle-class money.[2] In various phases, the moneyed upper class gained major increases in their social power following on from their economic success. In some cases, as in England after the Republic of 1649 and the Revolution of 1688, greater interchange and intermarriage took place between the aristocracy and the expanding new rich members of the middle classes (Pincus, 2011).

In certain phases, elements in the middle class gained ground from the nobility and the aristocracy. But the middle class should not be seen as a unity and contains a number of fractions that have assumed great significance in certain countries at particular points in the history. At times the educated and cultural sectors of the middle classes have gained power; in other phases it is the business and financial parts which were prominent. It is also important to consider the emergence of professions and in the last century the growth of white-collar workers in the lower middle class. The educated middle class have, in some periods, sought to establish more their own cultural institutions and legitimate ways of life based more on education and self-formation in ways that implicitly criticized the obsession with wealth, display, status and material power; the importance of *Bildung* in the German context with the development of Romanticism and the veneration of the life dedicated to art is an interesting case, whose influence had ramifications in European and other parts of the world (Bleicher, 2006). There is clearly a tension between this group (referred to as the *Bildungsbürgertum* since eighteenth century Germany), the expanding culturally educated middle class and the industrial business and moneyed middle class (a tension we find existing down the centuries that is played out in Bourdieu's contrast between economic and cultural capital in France).

At the same time, there are other phases in which the generation of wealth by the new rich happened dramatically and brought a new cohort of arrivistes, and autodidacts into prominence, whose confidence in their own abilities grew with their numbers and power. In the United States Gilded Age, a number of new rich in the era of expanding monopolies, trusts and 'robber barons' were the iconic 'self-made men'. Figures such as Carnegie, Rockefeller and Ford were accompanied by an increase in the confidence of the new rich and visibility of their consumption and investment in leisure and cultural activities. The well-established rich or the 'gentleman' with his fine-graded sense of taste was, at times, seen as inappropriate, ill-informed and vulgar. This corresponds with the portrait of the American nouveau riche's conspicuous consumption of the 'leisure class' described by Veblen (1899). In some ways, today's global super-rich share some common characteristics with their forerunners in the upper and middle classes.

We can, therefore, understand the dynamic between the monarch, the court and nobility on the one side and the middle classes on the other, as a series of struggles, yet also interdependencies. Given that monarchs and courts from early times needed funding and taxation, the markets proved to be an indispensable resource. Courts, then, often encouraged markets as instruments to stimulate the use of coinage, money, credit and taxation that provided milieu for the financial expertise that could help finance their own state projects (Graeber, 2010). While there may have been strong antipathy between the aristocrats, courtiers on the one hand and the merchants, nascent bourgeoisie and middle classes on the other in terms of status, values and lifestyles, the merchants were effectively needed to raise revenue and furnish the goods for consumption in the courts. Royalty, as Foucault (1979) and others have argued, regularly sought to display their sovereign power through public visible ceremonial such as executions. But they also demanded splendour in formal court ceremonial events, which required sumptuous settings, opulence and luxury, to impress people with the monarch's magnificence. All this needed finance.

The interdependence played itself out in the way that merchants provided the resources for court wealth and display. A part of the magnificence demanded by monarchs, emperors and princes involved sumptuous display and lavish consumption. This did not just mean the excessive volume of rare food at banquets (the pies with thousands of lark's tongues at Roman banquets) served on exquisitely designed gold and precious metal tableware, but also fashion. Courts were early centres of fashion and information on the latest luxury goods for consumption; they were sought after and frequently discussed by courtiers and advisors for presentation to the king. Information about other countries, their courts, technology, weaponry, architecture, dress and fashions was much sought after. The trade routes between China and Europe are a case to point, with a long history going back several millennia and becoming important through the development of the Silk Road. The volume of trade was enhanced through the development of sea routes to Asia round the Horn of Africa in the wake of the Portuguese Explorers Ferdinand Magellan, Vasco da Gama and others to open up the spice trade, which sharpened the rivalries between European nations such as Portugal, Spain, The Netherlands, England and France and ushered in the early modern era of colonialism and empire in the fifteenth century.[3] They became increasingly embroiled in competition for trade to supply the expanding range of luxury goods to the European courts and aristocracy. The opening up of the Americas after 1492 not only intensified the competition, but also resulted in new fortunes making their way into the courts, aristocracy and middle classes resulting in more ostentatious architecture, fashions, artefacts and goods to display. The subsequent nascent global trade system was given a further boost increase through the involvement of China by the Spanish via their Philippines colony responding to the Chinese demand for silver after the opening up of the Potosi silver mines in Bolivia in the mid-sixteenth century. In the last two decades a good deal of research has helped to correct the dominant Eurocentric theories that have circulated globally, with their assumption that modernity first developed in the West as a result of Europe's monopoly of creativity, invention and scientific rationality (Frank, 1998;

Goody, 1996, 2006a, 2009). It is now clear that there were longer chains of interdependencies along with many parallel developments throughout Eurasia. There is evidence that merchant cities in Europe, China and Japan maintained similar levels of development until well into the eighteenth century (Pomeranz, 2000, 2009).[4]

Court Societies and Luxury

The demand for luxuries, then, initially came from court societies. Sombart (1967) makes the case for the significance of court societies as centres of luxury consumption that stimulated an appetite for new goods, fashion and exotica. In the premodern societies of Medieval Europe, princely and ecclesiastical courts acted as the centres of luxury. These have been regarded as key sites for civilizing processes (good manners, civility, refined taste and high culture) involving the taming of the warrior nobility who had to learn the restraint, wit and self-control of the courtier (Elias, 1994). In his depiction of the court society Elias (1983) argues that luxury was anything but superfluous, being part of the self-assertion of the ruling groups. Elias, following Sombart (1967), mentions the emergence of the Pope's court at Avignon as the first modern court that brought together churchmen, nobles and beautiful women. While princely courts in Italy soon followed, it was in France from the end of the sixteenth century onwards that we find the highest development of court life, especially with the court of Louis XIV.

Luxuries were meant to be enjoyed in highly coded and finely graded ways. The king, lords and courtiers all wore fine clothes and their significance was carefully marked and noted. There were numerous advisors on court rituals, who provided not just input on manners, but instilled careful and repetitive lessons in etiquette—how to bow, walk, greet people of differing stations in life; how to dance; sip one's wine. The public ceremonials in particular could be quite an ordeal. The slightest mistake, such as slipping in a dance, threatened to provoke ridicule and gossip. Masking one's feelings and controlling body language, along with the correct demeanour in wearing clothes and use of possessions, became essential. In 'good society' it was important to distinguish oneself from vulgar associations, provincialism and of course the despised middle class.

Consumption, the eating of gourmet food at elaborate banquets, the savouring of fine wines, the appreciation of paintings, of specially cultivated exotic flowers and fruits, was not just sensory pleasure, but involved highly qualified and discriminatory taste; the training of the sensibilities to appreciate is what we have come to know as high culture. The provision of such rituals, along with the elaborate-staged spectacles involving actors, animals, music, fireworks, in pageants and masques, was prohibitively expensive. But such was the power of Kings like Louis XIV that it was impossible to avoid the royal request and lords and courtiers were obliged to engage in the provision of competitive display and entertainments to the point of ruin.

Courts became centres of display for new fashions, including fine clothes, artefacts, cuisine, entertainment and the arts. This helped in the establishment of Paris as the centre of high culture, and its new fashions became imitated throughout Europe. Food became an important part of this concern with style, fashion, display and conspicuous consumption. Great banquets and fine food were ways of demonstrating the power of the ruler and his court. In Europe since the sixteenth and seventeenth centuries, first in Italy and then in France, we observed the development of culinary art along with the printing of cookery books with the status shift of cooks from craftsmen to artists (Mennell, 1996). There was also a greater formalization of table manners.

It can therefore be argued, following Elias and Sombart, that courts played an important role in stimulating consumption in the middle class and lower orders (also see McCracken, 1988, on Elizabethan England). They were the centres of luxurious consumption and display which was meant to be exclusive, to exclude those outside. But the world that courtiers thought of as 'the world' was one in which they were carefully observed by a range of others: the servants, tradesmen, fashion designers, cooks, architects, artists, artisans, lawyers and financiers, with whom they came into regular contact. Lower outsiders were required to pay attention to their masters or pay the cost, and observational skills led to appreciation and imitation. Some of these groups had cultural specialists, others were cultural intermediaries, who helped to circulate official and unofficial accounts of the cultural activities, to those outside this world, who were eager to know the gossip and scandal, as well as the latest fads and fashions. Yet despite all the attempts by courts to regulate consumption by the lower orders courts, sumptuary laws which were imposed in Europe, China and Japan ultimately failed and outsider groups gained purchasing power and the capacity to begin to satiate their taste for luxuries. There may have been a strong antagonism on the part of courtiers and aristocrats towards the middle class, but court societies like those of Louis XIV were ultimately unable to halt the flow of interchange of tastes, styles and fashions with other groups and the generation of alternative centres of influence. Although the aristocrats' recreational time in the city of Paris brought them into contact with the bourgeoisie and lower orders, this did not necessarily serve to reinforce their status and power. The despised bankers became more important as family fortunes fluctuated and debt increased. It was more than a clashing of codes, as some of the encounters took place in spaces where codes were made to become more indeterminate and status differences counted less.

Markets: Making Opulence and Luxuries Productive

The display of wealth then and enjoyment of luxuries provide a complex set of possibilities involving processes of formalization to establish greater distinctions between social groups; however, at the same time the need for interactions between the nobility and the middle classes, and the long-term accumulation of wealth on the part of the latter, created the need for milieu where they could meet more informally. Luxury consumption aroused considerable ambivalence, being regularly condemned by religious and cultural specialists as well as philosopher scholars such as Confucius and Mencius, who emphasized the virtues of poverty (Goody, 2006b). Luxuries were dangerous sinful things from the point of view of the Church, yet despite moral condemnation and sumptuary laws, the demand for luxuries flourished both within court society and outside. The luxury trade between Europe and Asia stimulated the exchange of goods and ideas that linked cities together. This encouraged occupational specialism: not only were merchants in demand, but also artisans and in some cases manufacturers, as well as lawyers, bankers, accountants, plus people to work in schools and hospitals. Cities became centres of innovation in luxury and learning, consumption and culture (Featherstone, 2007; Goody, 2006a).

In addition, merchant communities developed their own subcultures that displayed some notable similarities across Eurasia, encouraging the growth of literary forms such as the realistic novel, along with performance arts such as the theatre as well as secular painting and sculpture. Indeed, as Pomeranz (2000) argued in the period 1400–1800, there is a process of the transformation of luxuries into everyday goods for elite groups and some sectors of the middle classes, along with the development of new canons of taste, in various parts of Eurasia, including China and Japan. That was despite attempts by authorities to restrict consumption and re-impose sumptuary laws. Connoisseurship also developed in Ming China at around the same time as Western Europe (Clunas, 1991). While court societies proved to be a stimulus to luxury consumption, the middle classes who traded in luxuries also financed and organized the crafting of luxury goods, along with the building and design of luxurious settings in which they were displayed, experienced and consumed. From the eighteenth century onwards luxury began to be seen positively and as something to be endorsed by the middle classes as having general social benefits for all.

The pursuit of luxury ceased to be seen as sinful, morally corrupting or something restricted to the decadent aristocracy; now it was seen as leading to positive social benefits by encouraging innovation and new economic production and trade. For Smith (1776), the desire for luxuries was positively linked to the desire for material self-betterment and would be socially beneficial; yet there was still some unease amongst economists and others in the nineteenth century as well as the eighteenth century about the attack on thrift and the encouragement of the pursuit of status, display and emulation (Roberts, 1998). There is a dark side to the production of luxuries, which has been well documented (Pomeranz and Topik, 2012; Said, 1993; Todorov, 1992).

Amongst many critics, Veblen's (1899) writing at the end of the nineteenth century stands out for his attack on the 'conspicuous consumption' of the idle new rich 'leisure class' in the United States. Yet the amassing of fortunes and luxury consumption among the upper classes was strongly evident in Europe in the last decades of the nineteenth century and the rundown to the First World War. This was a phase of intensified globalization and international trade—a time in which the aristocracy and the new rich middle class came together in a phase of renewed formality with strong military themes in dress and demeanour evident in the upper-class society. Social divisions were sharp; the upper class displayed the rewards of prosperity in fine settings amidst servants and deference while many of the lower orders continued to live in slums under conditions of abject poverty. It was the *Belle Epoque* period in France, with the expansion of upper-class sociability and civility, a time for the flourishing of the arts, culture and connoisseurship, especially in the Paris captured by Proust in his *A La Recherche de Temps Perdu* novel series. This era came to an end with the onset of the First World War.

What were the similarities and differences between the rich and the super-rich in the epoch ending with the First World War, from those of the contemporary period (i.e. from the 1980s onwards)? Both are eras of intensified globalization, increased trade and financial integration. Yet in the former phase the rich lived in a world without a sophisticated infrastructure of globalized financial markets and the web of transnational companies and myriad of subsidiaries, which makes moving money around much easier. Some of the rich in the earlier phase, as mentioned earlier, were attracted to, or more confined to, entering 'society', a more formal upper-class world that connected directly with the aristocracy, a world of titles, greater formality and sense obligation. The world had its international dimension, yet mobility, both spatial and social, would seem to have been more restricted and circumscribed. It is frequently argued that today's rich and super-rich can opt to forego national identifications to pursue their own financial advantage. Being a part of an aristocratic set is just one of the games they can play, and by no means the most absorbing or exciting one. Mobility, increasing speed and digital connectivity within an intricate globalized financial system enable financial fortunes to be moved instantly and profitably. Coupled with similar transformations in the means of physical communication, the ability to travel easily and comfortably around the world is helping produce a new mobile group of rich and super-rich people. The super-rich have access to a different world of rapid unencumbered mobility and can travel easily across frontiers and are welcomed in most parts of the world. They, therefore, could be regarded as 'the true cosmopolitans', and it would be expected that some will develop new orientations, attitudes, values and lifestyles as they enter this new milieu. It would now be useful to consider some of the main parameters of the emergent rich and super-rich milieu.

The Rise of the Super-rich

There is a popular cultural fascination with wealth, as well demonstrated in television programmes such as Chris Tarrant's British hit show 'Who Wants to be a Millionaire?' The quiz show on the millionaire theme is taken up in Danny Boyle's film *Slumdog Millionaire* (2008) which won eight Academy Awards and a host of other honours. The film was adapted from the novel *Q & A* by Indian author Vikas Swarup (2005) which also won a range of awards and accolades, now being translated into over 40 languages. There are also a host of popular self-help and 'how to do it' texts with titles such as *How to Get Rich* (Dennis, 2006), *The Millionaire Next Door* (Stanley and Danko, 1996). This form of 'how to succeed in business' or 'become a millionaire' books has a long history, especially with autobiographies and biographies of the successful, the rich and the famous.[5] There is also a good deal of interest in the aftermath and downside of ordinary people's realized dreams of riches, with numerous autobiographies, novels and movies about the destructive consequences in the lives of lottery and football pools' winners. More recently, there have been attempts to question the social contribution of the super-rich, with the return to greater social inequalities and the destructive consequences of neoliberalism in terms of climate change and ecological problems. Today, while academic accounts of the super-rich and rich are still thin on the ground, there has been a flood of popular books, feature articles, research material and discussion in both the popular press and Internet.[6] Public attitudes towards the rich swings from admiration and identification to indignation and moral outrage; either way, the conduct and lives of the rich prove to be good copy.

The super-rich and rich have come into increasing prominence since the 1980s. In the immediate post–Second World War era, the upper class and rich retained a relatively low profile. At the time of post-war reconstruction in the United Kingdom, budget deficits and high taxes, welfare reforms such as state education and social services, were seen by many as collective rewards for the social participation of the middle and working classes in the war effort, in which the ideology was still one of pulling together. Taxation on the rich reached high levels in a number of countries.[7] After the 1973 Oil Crisis, with runaway inflation, balance of payment deficits and government spending shortfalls, a neoliberal programme to lower taxation and offer incentives for the rich to invest was developed first by Richard Nixon and Ronald Reagan in California and then implemented nationally with the Reagan presidency after 1981. In the United Kingdom, Margaret Thatcher followed similar policies in the 1980s. At the same time there had also been a long history of using offshore strategies for tax avoidance amongst businessmen in England and the United States. London, which has become the world's leading financial centre, with the help of British governments developed a strategy since the 1960s, first with petro-dollars and euro-dollars, to offer a range of offshore financial transactions to people around the world that ushered in an era of using trusts, tax havens and other shadowy strategies to facilitate the reduction of tax bills for companies and rich individuals.

Trusts have had a long history, being secret compacts administered by third parties under oath of non-disclosure, can be traced back to the European middle ages. What has changed has been the capacity to widen their use to move money in inventive financial ways that were tax economical, through offshore locations. These were often ex-British colonies (Cyprus, Malta, Singapore, Hong Kong, the Bahamas, Virgin Islands, etc.), as well as special status quasi-independent crown domains such as Jersey, Guernsey and the Isle of Man. With the globalization and the integration of the world economy over the last two decades, a phase of intensified financial deregulation has gathered pace. The new digital communication technologies have not only enabled the rapid development of the financial markets, especially after the 1986 'Big Bang' of 24-hour trading (Dezaley, 1990), but also permitted the movement of money around the world at the press of a button.

One consequence has been the rapid expansion of offshore financial services and tax havens that are widely used by transnational corporations for greater tax efficiency. It is estimated that well over 80 per cent of US and European companies use offshore subsidiaries, which enable profit to be extracted in the most tax favourable locations. It has been remarked that more than half of world trade passes on paper or electronically, through tax havens, as well as over half of the banking assets of transnational corporations are routed offshore (Caletrio, 2012; Shaxson, 2011). London and New York have become the global centres of offshore finance, with the banking and financial services sectors expanding rapidly since the 1980s. This has meant an increase in the number of highly paid financiers and financial intermediaries, who deal directly with moving money, market trading, hedge funds, derivatives and other financial instruments. Members of this group have become extremely well paid and several prominent banks have attracted attention through the payment of massive chief executive bonuses. The annual bonuses paid, not only to top managers but also to traders and other financial specialists, have created a wave of new money for investment, which has also distorted the London and New York property markets.

Not only the financial sector is able to generate massive salaries for the successful, but also existing businesses along with all forms of established and old money can take the option to invest their fortunes offshore, with the result that the richest people in the United Kingdom and other countries frequently pay minuscule amounts of tax. Hence, a group of extremely wealthy people have emerged, who have learned how to exploit the business and financial advantages of the new system. The World Wealth Report published annually by Merrill Lynch and Capegemini refers to two categories of rich people. The first high net worth individuals (HNWIs—people having investible assets of over $1 million) had their numbers increased by over eight per cent in 2010. The second category, ultra high net worth individuals (UHNWIs) are defined as people with over $30 million in investable assets and the global population of this group increased by over 10 per cent in 2010. The latter group of UHNWIs makes up approximately one per cent of the total number of HNWIs (Beaverstock, 2010). The global HNWI population remains highly concentrated in the United States, Japan and Germany, which together account for 53.0 per cent of the world's HNWIs. The United States is still home to the single largest HNWI segment in the world, with its 3.1 million HNWIs accounting for 28.6 per cent of the global HNWI population. A *Financial Times* survey in June 2011 of high net worth individuals found that 47 per cent had directorships, 81 per cent were male and 63 per cent were frequent international travellers. Their average income was £223,508 (US$360,000) and their net worth £1,080,684 ($1,600,000).[8]

At the same time, it is important to note as Beaverstock (2010) argues that there is clearly a major gap between this group, the HNWIs, with their limited millionaire status, who might be considered super-gentrifies rather than rich, and the Ultra–HNWIs, who are the mid-tier millionaires who could be seen as rich. Yet there is a further massive gap between the UHNWIs and the billionaires who are the genuine super-rich (Beaverstock et al., 2004). It is the latter two groups, the UHNWIs and the billionaires, who are highly cosmopolitan, transnational, mobile and who engage more fully in luxury consumption. These are the people who appear in the various rich lists compiled around the world, with *Bloomberg* of New York recently announcing a daily ranking of the world's 20 richest people that competes directly with the *Forbes'* well-known list.

A further recent trend to be noted is the increase in the numbers of billionaires outside the West and with the United States now joined by Russia and China who also now have more than 100 billionaires each (Forbes Insights and Société Générale study referred to in the *Financial Times*, 30 March 2012). The average ages of China's 115 billionaires and Russia's 101 are, respectively, 50 and 49. This makes them over a decade younger than the next youngest cohort, from India, and a quarter-century younger than the oldest cohort, from France. (The average age of US billionaires is 66.) Many of this new group of Chinese and Russian billionaires are self-made men.

Despite the global recession, HNWIs are now clearly a global phenomenon, with the expansion of the volume of their wealth in Asia Pacific overtaking that of Europe in 2009. A recent study of Chinese high net worth individuals by Merchant's Bank and the consultancy firm Bain & Compass remarks that the majority were entrepreneurs with at least 100 million Yuan (around US$15.3 million) to invest. At the end of 2010, nearly 500,000 high net worth individuals, including more than 20,000 ultra-high net worth individuals, held about 15 trillion Yuan available to invest. The survey also suggests that around 60 per cent of this group have emigrated or are seriously thinking of doing so. The propensity to seek to emigrate is highest among China's wealthiest; 27 per cent of those entrepreneurs with a net worth of $15 million or more have completed the formalities required to emigrate through investment schemes in countries like the United States or cities like Hong Kong. Many rich Chinese often prefer to immigrate to countries such as the United States, Canada and Australia. High taxes were cited as a reason for leaving China (Chen, 2011).

India's population of high net worth individuals (HNWI) grew by 20.8 per cent in 2010, according to the 15th annual World Wealth Report, making India's HNWI population the world's 12th largest. Increasingly, as they gain greater knowledge and confidence many Indian ultra-high net worth individuals are investing in vehicles that are generally considered to be at the riskier end of the financial spectrum, such as hedge funds, private equity, structured products and derivatives and private equity managers have been very active in India in recent years. The growth of the private equity sector and hedge funds has produced greater investment in start-ups and new companies, which has, in turn, helped to develop a new class of first-time entrepreneurs, who are now also joining the club of the super-rich.

Offshore finance is often seen as secretive, with non-disclosure rules operated by a set of trustees. They manage multiple companies and subsidiaries registered in various parts of the world in a way so as to facilitate low taxation, high investment return and low traceability on the part of outside parties. Their lifestyles offer evidence of their actual wealth. It is not that members of the super-rich necessarily seek conspicuous consumption, although some nouveau riche clearly are motivated to enjoy and display their wealth flamboyantly. A consumer culture set of luxury industries has grown up to cater for high-end tastes with highly crafted ultra-luxuries that are unavailable to the mere rich. There are also sets of professionals, cultural intermediaries, architects, designers, financial experts and others who feed off the super-rich and seek to attract their attention and money. This group needs to sell their wares and attract publicity, however discretely. The closeness of the super-rich to celebrities, and media interest in their activities, furthers the visibility.

Luxury Consumption Sites for the Super-rich

The nobility and aristocracy are generally seen as located, tied to their titled land or estate. It could well be more accurate to see them as moving regularly between the country house on the family estate and other locations, particularly the monarchical or princely court, the capital city and in some cases summer resorts. The aristocracy, then, were under obligation to participate in 'society' and to follow the 'annual season' or calendar of social events. As mentioned earlier, some members of the new rich succeeded in gaining membership of this exclusive circle by purchasing titles and other means of access. This world broke down in 1914 with the onset of the First World War. In the inter-war years, a new and very different model for the lifestyle of suc-cessful rich people gained prominence—that of Hollywood with its stars such as Douglas Fairbanks and Mary Pickford. The new Hollywood ideal endorsed the importance of appearance and 'the look', being an attractive personality, along with the pleasures of today and the enjoyment of leisure lifestyles (Featherstone, 1982; Hepworth and Featherstone, 1982). This helped popularize and establish new fashionable resort destinations around the world, in Europe notably the French Riviera and Monte Carlo, which had gained initial impetus in the Belle Époque in the late nine-teenth century. The image of the rich was changing. In some ways they were becoming more visible, as they rubbed shoulders with celebrities and stars and enjoyed lifestyles that were becom-ing glamorized in the consumer culture imagery and publicity in outlets such as the features press, magazines, newspapers and of course, movies. In the post-war era, the term 'Jet Set' came into prominence with the inauguration of jet passenger travel in the 1950s, which given the expense of tickets, maintained an image of upper-class exclusivity. Over the last 20 to 30 years of glo-balization and improvements in jet travel along with new infor-mation technologies has greatly increased the mobility potential for everyone. This is particularly noticeable for the rich, and has meant that the attachment to a particular nation state has become increasingly unnecessary as a base for their social relations and modus operandi.

There are a wide range of sites that are attractive to the super-rich. Global cities that are the major centres of offshore financial services (such as London and New York) are of prime importance closely followed by a range of other global cities and financial centres (such as Tokyo, Hong Kong, Singapore, Shanghai, São Paulo, Mumbai, Los Angeles, Sydney, Amsterdam, Paris, Zurich, Geneva, Luxembourg and Frankfurt). While many global cities provide tax-efficient conditions for foreign residents, others may prove to be attractive through their cultural capital heritage, or outstanding scenic beauty such as Rome, Istanbul, Barcelona,

Rio de Janiero. Still other smaller resort cities that are gathering places for the rich are significant (Beaverstock, 2010). Some of them have their own version of the 'season', with sporting or fashion events, cultural festivals or other reasons for annual gatherings. In a few of these locations the accent is on protection and seclusion, with gated communities becoming the norm for the super-rich.

Fortified gated communities for the rich can be seen as at one end of the continuum. There is a danger in urban settings such as global cities that the fortification and security could be off-putting, or the neighbourhood is open to easy access from lower class outsiders who destroy the ambience and sense of safety. One attractive option for the super-rich would be a place that allows freedom of movement and ease of contact with people, yet in a totally secure environment. Small resorts may achieve this with the security largely hidden, but it is rare to find in a global city.

As many cities experience a rise in house prices in their downtown centres, the working class and poor are increasingly driven out in favour of the 'dual city model' with the rich and upper-middle classes able to live in gentrified, 'museumified' or redeveloped central areas, with the poor moved out to mass housing developments on the periphery (e.g. Paris, New York, London, São Paulo and many other cities). Certain areas in London and New York have become subjected to what has been referred to as 'super-gentrification', the focus of intense investment and conspicuous consumption by a new generation of super-rich financiers working in the global finance and corporate services' sectors. Yet it is not just the financial service sectors' high earners, but also the influx of overseas money, which sees the property market in leading global cities as a good investment. Miami, for example, has been targeted by Latin American High Net Worth Individuals. New York's Manhattan currently has one-third of prime market sales going to foreign buyers, with Chinese investors since 2011 targeting the $1–3 million Manhattan market (Bailey, 2012).

Similar developments along with inflated property prices at the top end are occurring in many other parts of the world as the super-rich market continues to expand and there is a race to provide the latest in architectural design and lavish interiors, which are perceived as good investments.⁹ It is a noticeable new trend that skyscrapers and the new category of 'super-tall' buildings are now designed to house not just offices, but exclusive apartments.

One of the most ambitious building and real estate developments in the world has been taking place in Dubai and has entailed massive infrastructural investment to build a series of artificial islands, waterfronts and series of major shopping, entertainment and leisure facilities. Dubai contains Burj Khalifa, at 829 metres by far the tallest building in the world. The scale of the completed work and projects underway and planned in the Dubai is massive with over a dozen of skyscrapers that are more than 300 metres tall. Not far from the Burj Khalifa is the world's largest shopping mall. Dubai continues to develop a large number of megaprojects, including the artificial islands' complexes such as 'Island World', Palm Jumeirah, and the Dubailand 'thempark of themparks'. Dubai and the United Arab Emirates contain some of the highest density concentrations of ultra–high net worth households in the world and many of the projects are designed to create the perfect business, residential and leisure combination of facilities. It closely follows neoliberal free enterprise directives and has no income tax, trade unions, opposition parties or elections. In some ways it is a 'gated society' with high levels of security, containing many private developments with additional private security for the super-rich, UHNWI and HNWI groups. One of the most interesting mega projects in this respect is Palm Jumeirah that is an artificial island in the shape of a palm tree which provides 520 kilometres extra shoreline for Dubai and has villas, marinas, themed hotels, restaurants, etc.¹⁰

This type of development is by no means unique and developers around the world have sought to imitate the Dubai formula. Artificial islands have the advantage of having no original inhabitants to be displaced and demand compensation or access rights; they also are ideal for surveillance and policing, yet at the same time retain the seaside resort ambience with outside mooring or nearby marina access for yachts and pleasure craft.

A further possibility is for the rich to be permanently on the move and largely live in transit. To have a private jet fuelled and standing on the runway, or a private super yacht moored in an attractive resort location, is to open up life to many possibilities for business and leisure mobilities as well as for the exploration of the slightest whim. One alternative is to opt for a lifestyle that is constantly on the move, yet offers all the comforts of a secure apartment home. This is the promise of *The World*, a 165-apartment luxury liner on which it is possible to rent or purchase cabin apartments.[11] For the very wealthy super-rich, of course, there is no need to share the space of a cruise liner, but enjoy one's own. One noticeable trend over the past 20 years has been a rapid increase in the numbers of private yachts. More recently another variant has emerged, 'the super yacht' owned by wealthy multi-billionaires like Bill Gates or Roman Abramovich.[12]

These developments draw in the full range of critics; the combination of business, politics and resort facilities and conduciveness for networking, making deals, luxury consumption and high-end leisure has seen many of the new super-rich spaces dubbed 'Evil Paradises' by Davis and Monk (2007). The excessive carbon consumption lifestyles and transport oil consumption of the rich at a time of intensified climate change have also come in for criticism (Urry, 2010a).

Mobility and Assembling the Flexible Lifestyle

Mobility is clearly highly valued by the super-rich and in a hypermobile world of speedy digital communications and means of transportation; the capacity to purchase the latest technologies offers an important advantage for the new 'globals' (Elliott and Urry, 2010). What have been referred to as 'miniturized mobilities' (smartphones, digital devices) are seen as extending the 'globalization of mobility to the core of the self' (Elliott and Urry, 2010; see also Sheller and Urry, 2006, 2010b). The capacity to communicate instantly through the digital technologies and have the latest and most extensive market data as well as information about business possibilities, along with the technological gains of jet and helicopter travel to quickly arrange face-to-face meetings around the world, offers new major forms of logistic empowerment. Rather than relying on brokering forms, a better option for the super-rich is to directly employ a set of financial specialists to handle their investments, given that the most lucrative ones are often the most risky and need an attentive group of experts who can pull out or move into stocks and financial instruments at the optimum point. In some cases this entails the formation of a 'family office', a full-time team of financial experts, accountants and lawyers who have the sole aim of protecting and enhancing the family wealth. The long-term planning evident here and the focus on the family as the key unit are interesting. Rather than risk the family wealth eaten away by divorces or gambling, family trusts represent an attractive option as they curtail potential individual irresponsibility and enable families to plan two or three generations into the future to conserve the wealth for the long-term benefit of the dynasty. This suggests that for the very rich the prime attachment is to their own family—this has been referred to as the move to being a 'citizen of their own family' rather than a citizen of any one country (Meek, 2006).[13]

For the super-rich then there need not be a strict separation between work and leisure, given their capacity to communicate through personal assistants on any aspect of their business, financial and other activities, when the inclination takes them. The new mobile technologies such as mobile phones and the Internet along with the constant availability of datasets and metrics on the latest financial developments and investment opportunities enable the super-rich to micromanage at a distance, to the extent they choose. In this sense while they may have the family bound together financially through family trusts and other instruments administered by the family office, they also have the potential to disengage, take time out, explore new business, financial and personal adventures, as they see fit. This may lead to a more fragmented life, but it also offers the possibilities of greater control.

It is this range of sensibilities through handling, planning and protecting vast wealth, along with the fluidity of forms of sociation made on the move, or in the face of pressing deadlines, that it is suggested to bring to the fore new character types such as 'flexians' (Caletrio, 2012; Wedel, 2009). Flexians operate in flexible networks between financial, business, political and official elites and can act as specialist policy advisers, in effect a shadow elite, whose work takes them through a constant range of new projects. They possess a new transnational mobile habitus and thriving on turbulence and disorder and further a 'networked individualism'. The 'flexians' and super-rich are the groups above all able to develop this new type of self, suited to greater informational connectivity and the elaborate architecture of informational networks. It is in this flexible work life, with the potential to blur the lines between work, play and family and shift contexts at will, but calculate the costs and benefits of all, amidst the shifting matrix of network alliances and possibilities that luxury exists. The idea of luxury, of what luxury is meant to bring with it in the form of enjoyment and satisfaction, becomes elusive yet all the more tantalizing. Indulging in new pleasures is often linked to new purchases: yet the satisfaction that new goods provide can tend to be short lived as they soon migrate down the line from luxuries to necessities or fail to deliver what the advertising imagery and their artificial memories promise.

Luxury Consumption

There are a number of dimensions to luxuries. Luxury goods can be those that offer immediate sensual satisfaction that are in short supply—at various points in history, sugar, tea, spices, white bread, meat, wine, have all been ruled out of the diet of the majority of ordinary people. Yet, despite shortages and low wages in many parts of the world, for the vast majority of people today, almost all of these goods are available in supermarkets and other outlets throughout the world and are regarded as necessities. As this happens, it can be argued, members of the upper classes and rich will find or have provided for them new food and drink alternatives and concoctions, whose market price will be high and availability more restricted. The same can be said for categories of luxury goods, those worn and kept close to the body—clothes, jewellery and forms of adornment, make-up and perfumery. Silks and fine fabrics were once restricted high-value luxury items, but increasingly have become mass luxuries. Similar arguments can be made for furniture, housing, household equipment, internal décor, means of transport from the carriage to the motor car and private jet. Not all of these have passed down the line from extremely restricted or short supply luxuries to widely available mass luxuries—but many have. The expansion of a mass consumer culture from the mid-nineteenth to early twentieth centuries onwards has broadened the availability of cheap versions of luxury goods, as well as raising the visibility of existing luxuries.

In this sense there have been some diffusion and even tendencies towards the 'democratization of luxury', which has built on two processes within the development of consumer culture (Ewen, 1976; Featherstone, 2007). First, new sites, such as the department store 'dream worlds', provided opulent and luxurious settings for their goods in show windows and carefully designed displays, which emphasized glamour, extravagance and exotica (Tamari, 2006; Williams, 1982). As long as members of the middle classes and working classes were well dressed, good mannered and orderly, they could walk amongst and observe luxuries at close quarter. The visibility of luxurious goods and lifestyles was furthered by a second process: the expansion of the capacity to circulate convincing images of luxuries. This was not just through the expansion of photography, colour photography and paintings in advertisements, important though they were in providing close-up sumptuous images of luxuries. More significant was the framing of the people captured using luxuries and the accompanying textual elaborations. An important innovation here was the ways in which luxury goods and lifestyles were prominently featured in movies, particularly the Hollywood films that became a global force in the 1920s. Both the ready availability of images and the new sites of consumption stimulated dreams of the consumer culture good life lived amidst luxurious abundance and style, rare and beautiful things and people. It was not just a question of the ready availability of luxury goods, or the emergence of new ranges of mass prestige luxury brands as manufacturers sought to expand their markets through globalization. Images of luxury operate strongly in today's ubiquitous digital media and are used to sell all manner of consumer culture goods, sites and people. Consumer culture publicity presents glamour as within the reach of all, especially women, with endless advice on how women can transform their appearance and revamp their 'look'. This is notable in the recent fascination with celebrity and the spate of reality television programmes concerned with 'makeover', transformations of ordinary men and women into celebrities (Featherstone, 2010; Gundle, 2008; Turner, 2004). Glamour is about image and transformation: it offers a seductive aura that can be attached to objects and places as well as people. Both glamour and luxury, then, are readily mobilized in consumer culture advertising and publicity. Both have been diffused to wider audiences and subjected to democratization dynamics.

For the rich and super-rich the democratization of luxury and the pressure from below hold out the potential for a range of responses. For the aristocracy, it may well be that new luxuries are to be ignored, with the preference for established ones that fit into the regular routines and calendar. The classic, or traditional look, the old country house, the vintage Rolls Royce and tweed suit are there and used because they have always been used and signify a certain timeless status. In some ways these are not luxuries, but have become incorporated into regular routines and rituals and are now the necessities; the material props which help to provide the texture of an exclusive world in which it is the detectable style of presentation and manner of speech that convey everything, not the expense of lavish display, or the newness of possessions. Some members of the super-rich may seek to temporarily play at being a member of this world, or temporarily seek to join it and become enthralled with acting the part of lady of the manor and joining the country set, as was the case with the entertainer Madonna and her Wiltshire English country house. This need not of course lessen their mobility and capacity to jet around the world, rather such sites can operate as one of a range of temporary respites from intense bouts of work, or indeed, even be fitted out with recording studios, rehearsal stages, etc., and become a central place of work as well as leisure. Celebrities and stars prove fascinating to ordinary people in the media, given the vast majority started out as ordinary people. Watching them helps learning how to handle immense riches and negotiate the various learning curves of a new lifestyle in which they can purchase everything, which was previously confined to daydream, has proved popular media copy. In the accounts of the expansion of HNWIs and ultra HNWIs and billionaires, the numbers of self-made men are often emphasized, and there is the fascination with how the nouveau riche cope with the learning curve of their new lifestyle and potential luxury consumption.

For many members of the super-rich group, however, luxury consumption does offer the satisfaction of reinforcing status distinction between them and other groups along with the satisfaction of enjoying, possessing and commanding the latest luxuries. As the numbers of the super-rich and HNWI people grow, and the pressure from the middle class and aspirants to sample and experience the expanding range of new luxuries available and endlessly reviewed and talked about in the media and Internet intensifies, one logical outcome is for a new category of super-luxuries to be created with higher price tags. Of course, the rich themselves may decide to opt out of branding altogether and go for customization—bespoke tailoring with fittings by craftspersons who display their wares and help replenish the wardrobe. The whiff of mass production is anathema to the major luxury brands and they make every effort to suggest their goods are crafted, by constantly highlighting the narrative and images of their craft origins as well as trying to retain craft hallmarks and iconography in their new ranges.

The super-rich, of course, can employ craftsmen directly and part of the skill set they may seek to acquire if they have aristocratic pretentions is to come to know some of the trade secrets and skills of the craftsmen, to be knowledgeable about the goods they order. It is here that indirect knowledge is also important, the capacity to have an office able to research and investigate the qualities and range types of goods to be purchased and marry them against their own taste. The super-rich in particular employ personal assistants who can readily summon up experts to provide advice, scenarios, simulations and samples of new goods. There are a growing number of consultant firms that offer luxury services with experts on all aspects of luxury consumption to take all the effort out of choosing and will let them know what to go for in a super yacht, where to get it and what features are needed; or how to equip a new home with all the latest high specification kitchen, entertainment and security electronic gadgetry; or what type of luxury private mobile mansion jet to buy and how to customize it. In short, the super-rich can easily buy the expertise and assistance to make themselves information rich, to help themselves to craft and customize their lifestyles for maximum returns and least hassle. Incidentally, there is no shortage of people seeking to acquire expertise in this area and develop a career in luxury marketing as the rise in masters' degree courses in luxury brand management in recent years testifies.[14]

At the same time contemporary consumer culture spaces, be it city centres with their shopping malls, or airport malls, or traditional department stores, have increased the profiles of luxury goods and in particular the global luxury brands. There would seem to be a dynamic between ordinary luxuries and super luxury goods in which traditional luxury brands seek to expand their market and draw in new consumers globally. There has been a massive growth in brand-motivated mergers and acquisitions. Brands are seen as major corporate assets, with more major brands in the hands of fewer corporations. In the field of luxury cosmetics, most major brands are in the hand of a small number of powerful groups (Oyama, 2009). There is also considerable optimism that the luxury industry is successfully riding out the recession. World-leading luxury group LVMH recorded a 17 per cent rise in first-quarter sales in 2011 and Swiss luxury goods group Richemont reported pre-tax profits 83 per cent up on the previous year.

Enormous care is taken in every aspect of the marketing of luxury cosmetic brands from advertising, Internet sites and blogs, to the design of the display units and cosmetic counters, to the expertise, style and look of the beauty advisers. Particular attention is given to constructing affective experiences between customers and the beauty advisers and customers are encouraged to develop strong emotional experiences and loyalty through all the various aspects of the affective and synesthetic 'brandscape' (Oyama, 2012). One interesting recent trend has been the way in which some luxury brands have sought to enhance their image by pulling out of department stores and seeking to establish their own outlets in exclusive shopping centres and malls, or stand-alone city centre street stores. Great care is taken with the architecture and interior design and décor of the stores. Notable here is the investment in prestigious exteriors, the so-called designer shrines (Senatus Online Magazine, 2010). Striking buildings that stand out in the cityscape have been built through the employment of high-profile architects.

Luxury Experiences and Memories

Luxury goods often seek to draw on glamour, exotica and sumptuous imagery. Yet the images provided by advertising and marketing have to relate to the product. What is it that the luxury provides for the rich and super-rich? In an article on how to market to high net worth individuals, Baouamina (2011) argues that the perfect combination is to present the owners with luxury status symbols that have high psychological value and additionally stir the emotions. The former aspect relates to the HNWI's need to feel exclusive, to be treated with the utmost respect and attention through their possession and consumption of rare brands. The assumption that brands must seek to 'stir the emotions' relates to the distinction between luxury goods and experiences discussed by Bob Deutsch (2010). He argues that extraordinary experiences yield incredible stories and memories and that 'having incredible stories is the enduring luxury'. In effect the rich, who one assumes have sampled many luxuries and pleasures, want to seek out surprising, new, unscripted memorable experiences. They want to be pulled out of the everyday routine into something eventful, an occasion that offers an intense experience, which can be remembered in its emotional and sensory vividness and potentially relived and retold. They want to experience a different sense of time, from that of everyday routine duration.

One of the powers of being rich is the potential to move in and out of situations that bring one into contact with vital experiences: be it the intensity of concluding deals working against the clock, the adventure in the manner of Richard Branson's transatlantic balloon flights, the romantic interlude and the sporting event. It is also one of the reasons why those who are rich often sponsor sporting events, or purchase football clubs, buy racehorses, etc. This enables them to get close to and associate with people who are not only in the arena of excitement and fate, but also who may risk their lives in seeking excellence, perfection and fame. There is also the power of making things happen, of developing a project, or team, through wise investment and prudent decision-making. The vitality, excitement and involvement not only generate strong social bonds and memories, but also are seen by many as a key ingredient of an eventful and fulfilling life.

This may in some cases lead to a variant of the heroic life (Featherstone, 1992). Normally we think of the consistently goal-directed sustained life as leading to extraordinary achievements and events and recall the lives of charismatic figures such as Jesus, Mohammed and Buddha, or military heroes such as Alexander the Great or Genghis Khan, or artists such as Beethoven, Wagner, Cezanne and Picasso. Some would wish to see a few industrialists and businessmen as leading a similarly motivated life, following a similar single-minded sense of mission, and as a result attaining a charismatic force and reputation. There are a range of possibilities between attempting to live one's life in a total eventful way in line with some prior narrative and a more episodic life comprised of eventful segments or adventures. On the latter case, it is possible that a life lived in the gaze of the media may be one in which scandal and negative events are a continual possibility. There is also the fascination with those amongst the rich and famous who squander fortunes, indulge themselves, break the rules or just seem to court trouble and disaster—the high rollers, villains and fools.

Suffice to say that the super-rich provide more than their share of people who are seen to live out eventful lives. The power of such events lived in the glare of media publicity is such that the tales need to be told and retold in the press, novels, biographies, movies, television programmes and a host of associated media. It may be that certain events or lives become retold, by not only cultural intermediaries, but because of interest to artists working in a range of media, because of the dramatic way they unfold and can be represented. There is a continuing interest in fame, and the way lives can seemingly be fateful and dramatized from within, as they are lived, the intertwining of life and art and the ways in which lives can seemingly become works of art. It is no accident that the super-rich are interested in art. This is, of course, partly for investment potential, but the patronage of the arts, the closeness to artists and performers, is also of interest for the reasons mentioned earlier. It is, therefore, not unexpected that the world's richest man, Mexican Carlos Slim, has a passion for fine art collection and has opened a museum in Mexico to house his collection. There are, then, connections between the pleasures of collecting art, connoisseurship and luxury. Art would seem to inhabit a world akin to the one promised by luxury and there are many interesting questions here to be opened up.[15]

This is not meant to be an argument justifying luxury and the super-rich. Rather, it is in part an attempt to understand the power of luxuries, which is also manifest in the old lady saving up to buy luxuries items for her grandchildren, as well as enjoying the sharing of little luxuries, special food, saved, purchased and lovingly prepared, for family and friends at Sunday afternoon tea, or more festive occasions. Such occasions by their very designation and special quality are deemed to be outside the mundane routine. The super-rich are no different in wanting to seek out and experience luxuries, and experiment with the memorable, to dwell on and share and re-experience memories that too often are evanescent; it is just their financial scope and potential to do so is that much larger than others. Of course, the rich do not just aspire to luxuries, they are drawn to the power to command things and enjoy mobility, to be able to purchase any commodity they fancy and visit any destination of their choice.

The Future of the Super-rich

Since 1980s, we have seen the growing supremacy of neoliberalism throughout the world. There are still of course nation
states that seek to operate strong state agendas and have some
adherence to alternative projects, but the conventions and rules
of global economic life have been increasingly written in neoliberal language. This does not mean there are no critics of the
heightened social inequalities in Western countries, which are
now moving us back to early twentieth century levels. Yet it is
difficult to see an end to the ruthless global search to minimize
wage costs, which has progressively undercut the conditions of
the working class in the West. There are also signs that similar
processes are underway with regard to the middle classes. In
China, where the middle classes have grown exponentially, the
super-rich in commercial centres like Shanghai have pulled away
strongly. Income inequalities between the richest, one per cent,
and the rest have also increased in India and Russia and many
other parts of the world. The middle and working classes are
caught in a series of far-reaching changes that have seen income
levels increase significantly not only between the upper class and
those at the bottom, but also the inequalities within class strata
are also expanding. It is clear that the billionaires and ultra-high
net worth individuals are seeing their income grow much faster
than those who are merely rich or high net worth individuals.
Those at the top of the scale are benefitting disproportionally
from the increase in productivity many companies are achieving
through globalization, and of course, as mentioned earlier, they
have the financial resources to buy in the expertise and invest in
hedge funds and other financial instruments to rapidly expand
their fortunes. Some professional groups in the middle classes
are also benefitting by the increasing global demand for specialist skills, including financial services. Yet many of the middle
income groups are seeing employment options narrow and
incomes stagnate as their work is pushed offshore; in the United
States, this has made headlines such as 'Capitalism Is Failing the
Middle Class' (Freeland, 2011b).

Clearly these shifts along with the move to low taxes for the rich and the reduction of state welfare benefits continue to threaten the quality of life of the majority of the population, especially in times of recession. Neoliberalism tends to operate with a neo-Darwinist philosophy of the survival of the fittest. Competition, league tables, performance measurement and metrics that reward the winners and punish the losers have become the order of the day (Smart, 2011; Terranova, 2009; Venn, forthcoming). Yet, there are still many who remain to be convinced that this is the only viable logic for contemporary societies. The recent 2011 and 2012 protests against bankers and financiers in London, New York (the 'Occupy Wall Street' demonstrators), Madrid and other cities, focus on the greed and seeming immunity of bankers and the financial sector, which contrasts with the austerity, difficulties and reduced quality of life experienced by many ordinary people in the current economic crisis. The recession, increased unemployment, wage freezes, inflation, reduced public services, negative equity on house purchases and unsustainable levels of debit generate widespread hardships. An increasingly alert media and Internet now remind us that the rich, the bankers, financiers and corporate CEOs continue to award themselves massive salaries and manage to pay very little tax.

One of the problems with the new super-rich is that many of them feel they are doing a good job and making a genuine contribution to society; in effect they regard themselves as deserving global winners (Freeland, 2011a). A high proportion of this new generation of super-rich see themselves as self-made men, not the aristocrats and old money of the past, but economic meritocrats, who believe they deserve all the rewards they have worked hard to achieve. But as has been suggested, this is a difficult group of people to track down and research, which contains many sub-groups with different agendas. Not all follow the headline-grabbing excessive lifestyles of the Russian oligarchs who buy super-yachts, associate with super-models and buy super-league football clubs. Some may choose to live modest lives and practices austerity. Others have sought to follow philanthropy and develop foundations and think tanks like Bill Gates, Warren Buffet and George Soros. Yet others may develop ideas forums, or explore new cosmopolitan projects, sponsor the arts or engage in philanthropy.

One of the problems with philanthropic foundations and charities is that they are designed to follow closely the aims and priorities of the wealthy. Worthy as they may be, they signal an opting out of the model of paying taxes and allowing the elected government to decide on spending priorities. The problem is that many of the super-rich distrust and side-step governments, or do not wish to see their contribution swallowed up in what they see as a black hole of public debt and nation state deficit financing. There are also arguments that the rich can at the same time pay more taxes and be better off. The resistance to providing finance for the government, through either taxes or mutually beneficial tax breaks, suggests that part of the problem for the super-rich is a distrust of the way taxes are used by politicians. This is coupled with a sense that they would run things differently. Over the time it is possible that some members of this group may become more global in orientation and evolve a programme that better integrates their piecemeal and seemingly capricious interest in financing a wide range of charitable projects around the world, couples with support for medical and scientific projects, such as finding a cure for malaria. In the longer term then, there is some potential for some of the super-rich to develop broader global identifications and responsibilities for others in various parts of the world, and make some bid to be involved in emergent forms of global governance. This remains premised on a general maximization of their own financial resources and continued avoidance of state taxation, unless some form of global taxation or financial transaction tax emerges, which puts them at odds with many of the people they aspire to help.

Information technologies and the digital communications systems that are central to the financial markets and contemporary business communications, along with continuing financial deregulation, and increasing speed and ease of global trade, means that information, money, people and ideas travel faster than ever.

The fruits of the efficiencies and savings do not seem to percolate down to those on the lower rungs, while those at the top have recovered a good deal of the ground lost since the 2008 recession and continue to see their wealth increase. If history is any guide, when massive inequalities build up and the social bond and responsibilities are reneged on, questions of social justice will resurface. At the moment it is relatively easy to suppress dissent and protest, as there would seem to be no global alternative to neoliberalism. The demands to tax the super-rich on a fairer basis through direct taxation, or indirectly through some form of transaction tax, will continue to grow.

Notes

1. See McKendrick et al. (1982) on consumption, Berg and Eger (2003), Sekora (1977) on the luxury debates, Foucault (2008) and Elias (1984) on the development of biopolitics, physiocracy, political economy and the science of economics.
2. In both countries, the monarchs from the sixteenth century onwards sold titles to raise money. There continued to be tensions in France between the *noblesse de robe* (special official posts granted by the king, which were eventually sold) and *noblesse d'epée* (established aristocracy). Both groups came to adopt similar dispositions and manners and looked down on those below in the middle class (Elias, 1983).
3. The relatively short phase of Ming imperial maritime expansion should also be mentioned. This occurred especially under Admiral Zheng He (1371–1433) whose voyages to South East Asia, the Middle East, the Horn of Africa and possibly Mexico, opened up the flow of new and exotic 'treasures' and goods to China in its phase of proto-modernization.
4. It was not only 'the spice trade' that merchants pursued, but also silks and the valuable blue dye, indigo, often more valuable than gold (Taussig, 2008). This highlights the importance of appearance, display and the emergence of fashion dynamics.
5. Here we think in recent years' (since the 1960s) books such as Getty's (1983) *How to be Rich* and Branson's *Losing My Virginity* (2009). Some, like the classic account of the nineteenth century self-made men, Andrew Carnegie's (2006) *Autobiography* and *The Gospel of Wealth*, first published in 1901 do not just address business success, but argue for philanthropy. For a discussion of self-help advice books and the general role of self-improvement and self-transformation in consumer culture, see Featherstone (2010) and Hepworth and Featherstone (1982).

6. Popular books include: Armstrong (2010) *The Super-Rich Shall Inherit the Earth*, Kempf (2010) *How the Super-Rich Are Destroying the Earth*, Frank (2007) *Richistan*, Haseler (2000) *The Super-Rich*, Irvin (2008) *Super-Rich*, Nowell (2004) *Generation Deluxe*, Rothkopf (2009) *Superclass*, Shaxson (2011) *Treasure Islands. Tax Havens and the Men Who Stole the World.*

7. In the USA, in the 1950s, wealthy Americans were paying a top rate of tax of 90 per cent; today, the top rate of tax is 35 per cent. In the United Kingdom, the top rate of income tax was in the range of 70–90 per cent until the 1980s when the Thatcher government reduced it to 60 per cent along with a 4 per cent drop in the standard rate; this was offset by increases in indirect taxation such as VAT (Atkinson, 2004).

8. Incidentally, Merrill Lynch Global Wealth Management who are behind the *World Wealth Report* describe themselves as 'a Private Banking and Investment Group that provides tailored solutions to solutions to ultra-high net worth clients, offering both "the intimacy of a boutique and the resources of a premier global financial services company". These clients are served by more than 160 Private Wealth Advisor teams, along with experts in areas such as investment management, concentrated stock management and intergenerational wealth transfer strategies'.

9. India, China, the Gulf States and many others have joined the race.

10. It has been referred to as 'One of the greatest Mega Projects in world history ... right up there with the Great Pyramids of Egypt ... a true wonder of the world' (Siegel, 2012, http://uaemegaprojects.blogspot. co.uk/).

11. *The World* is massive cruise ship of 43,500 tonnes with 12 decks and almost 200 metres long. It houses around 150–200 passengers with a crew of 250. It has a global itinerary of exotic seaports, along with the usual range of cruise-ship comforts with the addition of a library, golf driving range, business centre and medical centre. *The World* is registered in the Bahamas and unfettered by national regulations. Residents are required to have a net worth of at least $5 million, and need to pay an annual maintenance fee of $100,000. A dress code operates, with a schedule of different types of clothing permitted at different times (Atkinson and Blandy, 2009; see also the discussion of the similar *Freedom Ship* project, Miéville, 2007).

12. Bill Gates, the second richest man in the world, owns the super yacht, the 110 metre *Attessa IV*, said to be worth $250 million. It can accommodate 30 guests and 26 crew members. Roman Abramovich, 68th richest man in the world, possesses a fortune of £12.1 billion. His super yacht *Eclipse* is 175 metres long, and costs an estimated $1 billion. There are nine decks with a cinema, discotheque, as well as a missile defence system and its own miniature submarine. It has a crew of 70 with running costs at some $20,000 a day (Paterson, 2011).

13. To describe the shift to becoming a citizen of the family could seem too strong as the two forms, 'citizenship' and 'family', would at first seem to work on different dynamics. Yet there has been a process of the formalization of rights and obligations and more general codification and rationalization of the family within modern societies (e.g. emergence of women's rights, spelling out husband and father's obligations, then children's rights, etc.). But the formalization of citizenship within the contemporary upper-class would prove to be an interesting variant: this being a family that essentially establishes its own laws and obligations and seeks to avoid the normal nation state citizenship duties linked to representation and taxation, for more informal modes of operating across societies, in conditions of mobility and multiple affiliations. Likewise the upper-class family is bound together by money, not just blood: the legal rules governing money flows, as well as blood ties make an interesting mix of obligations and rights. The use of the medieval notion of trusts, now transformed into a financial instrument for secrecy and tax efficiency aimed at securing the long-term transmission of wealth, with safeguards against squandering the fortune by capricious family members, is also interesting. An economic relationship involving money quantification and calculation, and used in the midst of the mobility, speed and flows of the global financial system, can therefore sustain a dynastic form, which in many of the more advanced parts of the world is becoming obsolete—with family structures being sidestepped or breaking up through divorce and separation, in many of the leading countries of the world. Returning to the affective and economic ties of family as opposed to those of nation could be seen as a positive step by some; but it also contains the dangers of romanticizing the mafia type family as the prime defensive unit to face an allegedly hostile world. The emphasis on dynasties in the upper classes, in the face of opposite trends in the bulk of the population and its relation to finance, would have been a worthy topic for Simmel (2004) in his *Philosophy of Money*, with his wonderfully flexible capacity to see reverse tendencies and the way quantitative phenomena give rise to qualitative changes and vice versa.

14. One of the first was in Monaco; other recent ones are at the London School of Business and Finance.

15. Luxuries then are not art, yet they can be seen to inhabit the same space as art, the pre-experience from which art is drawn and in their finished state, stand in the annex or waiting room next to works of art. The relationship between art and memory is complex.

References

Atkinson, A.B. 2004. Income Tax and Top Incomes over the Twentieth Century. *Hacienda Pública Española/Revista de Economía Pública, 168*(1), 123–141.

Atkinson, R. & Blandy, S. 2009. A picture of the floating world: Grounding the secessionary affluence of the residential cruise liner. *Antipode, 41*(4), 92–110.

Bailey, L. 2012. Prime luxury properties. *The Wealth Report 2012*, Knightfrank.com. Retrieved from http://www.thewealthreport.net/prime-property/prime-numbers.aspx

Baouamina, C. 2011. Tips on marketing to high net worth individuals in 2011. *Ultra Marketing.Com*, 13 June.

Beaverstock, J. 2010. The privileged world city: Private banking, wealth management and the bespoke servicing of the global super-rich. *GAWC Research Bulletin*, 338.

Beaverstock, J., Hubbard, P. & Short, J.R. 2004. Getting away with it? Exposing the geographies of the super-rich. *Geoforum, 35*, 401–407.

Berg, Maxine & Eger, Elizabeth, eds. 2003. *Luxury in the Eighteenth Century: Debates, Desires and Delectable Goods.* Houndmills, Balsingstoke, Hampshire: Palgrave.

Bleicher, J. 2006. Bildung (in special issue on problematizing global knowledge). *Theory, Culture & Society, 23*, 2–3.

Caletrio, J. 2012. Global elites, privilege and mobilities in post-organised capitalism. *Theory, Culture & Society, 29*(2), 135–149.

Campbell, D. 1987. *The Romantic Ethic and the Spirit of Modern Consumerism.* Oxford: Blackwell.

Chen, G. 2011. High net worth individuals: China's new export. *Reuters* 20 April.

Clunas, C. 1991. *Superfluous Things: Material Culture and Social Status in Early Modern China.* Oxford: Polity Press.

Davis, M. & Monk, D.B. (eds). 2007. *Evil Paradises: Dreamworlds of Neoliberalism.* New York: New Press.

Dennis, F. 2006. *How to Get Rich.* London: Random House.

Deutsch, B. 2010. 'Luxury Products or Luxury Experiences?' *Luxury Society.* Retrieved from http://luxurysociety.com/blog/2010/08, accessed on 24 August 2010.

Dezaley, Y. 1990. The Big Bang and the law. In M. Featherstone (ed.), *Global Culture.* London: SAGE.

Elias, N. 1983. *The Court Society.* Oxford: Basil Blackwell.

———. 1994. *The Civilizing Process.* Oxford: Blackwell.

Elliott, A. & Urry, J. 2010. *Mobile Lives.* New York: Routledge.

Ewen, S. 1976. *Captains of Consciousness: Advertising and the Social Roots of the Consumer Culture*. New York: McGraw-Hill.

Featherstone, M. 1982. The body in consumer culture. *Theory, Culture & Society* 1(2); reprinted in M. Featherstone, M. Hepworth and B.S. Turner (eds), *The Body*. London: SAGE.

Featherstone, M. 1992. The heroic life and everyday life. *Theory, Culture and Society*, 9(1). Reprinted in M. Featherstone (1995) *Undoing Culture: Globalization, Postmodernism and Identity*. London: SAGE.

———. 1995. *Undoing Culture: Globalization, Postmodernism and Identity*. London: SAGE.

———. 2006. Genealogies of the Global, in special issue on Problematizing Global Knowledge. *Theory, Culture & Society*, 23, 2–3.

———. 2007. *Consumer Culture and Postmodernism*, 2nd Edition. London: SAGE.

———. 2010. Body, image and affect in consumer culture. *Body & Society*, 17(1), 193–221.

Foucault, M. 1979. *Discipline and Punish: The Birth of the Prison*. Harmondsworth: Penguin.

———. 2008. *The Birth of Biopolitics: Lectures at the College de France 1978–79*. Houndsmills: Palgrave Macmillan.

Frank, A.G. 1998. *Re-ORIENT: Global Economy in the Asian Age*. Berkeley: University of California Press.

Freeland, C. 2011a. The rise of the new global elite. *The Atlantic*, January/February 2011.

———. 2011b. Capitalism is failing the middle class. *Reuters*, 15 April 2011.

Goody, J. 1996. *The East in the West*. Cambridge: Cambridge University Press.

———. 2006a. *The Theft of History*. Cambridge: Cambridge University Press.

———. 2006b. From misery to luxury. *Social Science Information*, 45(3), 341–348.

———. 2009. *The Eurasian Miracle*. Cambridge: Cambridge University Press.

Graeber, D. 2010. *Debt: The First 5000 Years*. London: Melville House.

Gundle, S. 2008. *Glamour: A History*. Oxford: Oxford University Press.

Hepworth, M. & Featherstone, M. 1982. *Surviving Middle Age*. Oxford: Blackwell.

McKendrick, N., Brewer, J. and Plumb, J.H. 1982. *The Birth of a Consumer Society: The Commercialization of Eighteenth-Century Century England*. London: Hutchinson.

Meek, J. 2006. Super Rich. *The Guardian*, 17 April 2006.

Mennell, S. 1996. *All Manners of Food*. Urbana and Chicago: University of Illinois Press.

Miéville, C. 2007. Floating Utopias: Freedom and Unfreedom of the Seas, in Davis, M. and Monk, D.B. (eds), *Evil Paradises: Dreamworlds of Neoliberalism*. New York: New Press.

Oyama, S. 2009. The emergence of Pan-Asian brands: Regional strategies of Japanese cosmetics brands. *Media International Australia, 133*, 85–96.

————. 2012. *The East Asian Brandscape: The Globalization of Japanese Brands in the Age of Japanization*. Ph.D. Thesis, University of London.

Paterson, T. 2011. Yachts with Champagne Showers Tempt the World's Super-Rich to Germany. *The Independent,* 2 February 2011.

Pincus, S. 2011. *1688: The First Modern Revolution*. New Haven: Yale University Press.

Pomeranz, K. 2000. *The Great Divergence: China, Europe and the Making of the Modern World Economy*. Princeton, NJ: Princeton University Press.

————. 2009. Putting modernity in its place(s): Reflections on Jack Goody's the theft of history. *Theory, Culture & Society, 26*, 7–8.

Pomeranz, Kenneth & Steven Topik. 2012. *The World that Trade Created: Society, Politics and an Emerging World Economy*, 3rd Edition. Armonk, NY: M.E. Sharpe.

Roberts, M.J.D. 1998. The concept of luxury in British political economy: Adam Smith to Alfred Marshall. *History of the Human Sciences, 11*(1), 30–35.

Said, E.W. 1993. *Culture and Imperialism*. New York: Vintage.

Sekora, J. 1977. *Luxury: The Concept in Western Thought, Eden to Smollett*. Baltimore: Johns Hopkins University Press.

Senatus Online Magazine. 2010. http://senatus.net/article/designer-shrines/

Shaxson, N. 2011. *Treasure Islands: Tax Havens and the Men Who Stole the World*. London: Bodley Head.

Sheller, M. & Urry, J. 2006. The new mobilities paradigm. *Environment and Planning A, 38*, 207–226.

Siegel, Brett. 2012. Palm Jumeirah Projects Update, UAE Mega Projects. Thursday, 29 March 2012. http://uaemegaprojects.blogspot.co.uk/

Simmel, G. 2004. *The Philosophy of Money*, 3rd Edition, translated by D. Frisby. London: Routledge.

Smart, B. 2011. Another great transformation or common ruin: Prospects and possibilities. *Theory, Culture & Society, 28*(2), 113–151.

Smith, Adam. 1776. *An Inquiry into the Nature and Causes of the Wealth of Nations*. London: W. Strahan.

Sombart, W. 1967. *Luxury and Capitalism*. Ann Arbor: Michigan University Press.

Stanley, T.J. & Danko, W.D. 1996. *The Millionaire Next Door*. New York: Simon & Schuster.

Swarup, V. 2005. *Q & A*. London: Black Swan.

Tamari, T. 2006. The rise of the department store and the aestheticization of everyday life in early twentieth century Japan. *International Journal of Japanese Sociology, 15*, 99–108.

Taussig, M. 2008. Redeeming Indigo. *Theory, Culture & Society, 25*(3).

Terranova, T. 2009. Another life: Political economy in Foucault's genealogy of biopolitics. *Theory, Culture & Society, 26*(6), 234–262. (Special issue on Michel Foucault.)

Todorov, T. 1992. *The Conquest of America.* New York: Harper.

Turner, G. 2004. *Understanding Celebrity.* London: SAGE.

Urry, J. 2010a. Consuming the planet to excess. *Theory, Culture & Society, 27,* 2–3. (Special issue on Changing Climates.)

———. 2010b. Mobile sociology. *British Journal of Sociology, 61,* 347–366.

Veblen, T. 1994. *Theory of the Leisure Class.* New York: Dover. (Original 1899).

Venn, C. 2009. Biopolitics, political economy and power: A transcolonial genealogy of inequality. *Theory, Culture & Society, 26*(6), 206–233. (Special issue on Michel Foucault.)

———. Forthcoming. Bankrupt capitalism: Debt, the crash, and neoliberal accumulation, in *Protocols for a Postcapitalist World.*

Wedel, J.R. 2009. *Shadow Elites: How the World's New Power Brokers Undermine Democracy, Government, and the Free Market.* New York: Basic Books.

Williams, R.H. 1982. *Dream Worlds: Mass Consumption in Late Nineteenth Century France.* Berkeley: California University Press.

2

Shop Talk: Shopping Malls and Their Publics

Sanjay Srivastava

To say that the Indian consumers [sic] are evolving everyday
would be an overstatement, but that they need to be understood
as much, is not!

'Best Food Forward', Editor's Note, *Progressive Grocer*,
Vol. 4, No. 1, 2010

Introduction: Goodbuy to All That

This chapter presents an ethnography of new consumerism,
through locating it within the wide range of social and cultural changes that have begun to transform public and private
lives in India in the wake of the policies of economic 'liberalization' undertaken by the Indian state since the early 1990s (Dutta,
2004; Fernandes, 2006; Guha, 2009; Kamat, 2004; Sengupta,
2008). The chapter explores the meanings attached to the practices of consumption—and ideas regarding the 'global' and the
'local', urban life, as well as gender and family—through focusing upon a specific new space of consumption, namely shopping
malls. The discussion is particularly interested in exploring the

various ways in which ideas of a 'new' India find expression through quotidian acts of shopping. Although shopping malls are still a relatively new phenomenon in India (Brosius, 2010; Voyce, 2007), and the relationship with them (in terms of shopping preferences) continues to be an ambivalent one (Mathur, 2010), there is, nevertheless, sufficient evidence to indicate that they have begun to play a substantial role in the ways in which social and consuming lives become conjoined to produce new narratives of individual and collective transformations. The broader context of these recent ways of creating the self—which are new for segments of the Indian population that earlier did not possess resources to take part in mass consumption—is related to changes in the cultural and political economies of Indian society. The decline in the prestige of the Nehruvian model of national life—characterized by 'saving for the national good'—is a significant context in this regard.

As has recently begun to be argued, the last two decades in India have witnessed a sustained shift in public discourses about 'ideal' citizenship. To wit, what we are witnessing is the displacement of the 'Citizen worker' (Roy, 2007) and 'Five Year Plan Hero' (Srivastava, 2006) from the imagination of national life that gathers around texts of popular culture such as films, advertising (Mazzarella, 2003) and public pronouncements on dominant cultural tendencies. It is in this context that we might locate the following statement by prominent Delhi architect Anurag Chowfla. 'Philosophically', Chowfla noted during a discussion of new urban spaces, 'we've all kissed Nehruvian socialism goodbye' (Balakrishnan, 2008). The farewell to 'Nehruvian socialism'—the pronouncement is a precis of a zeitgeist, rather than a careful sociological reading of an age, to be sure—is accompanied by a substantial engagement with the market in a manner not seen earlier. It is certainly, as the scholarship cited here indicates, a post-1990s phenomenon. Chowfla's comments are of particular significance in this regard; they suggest that new spaces and architectures of consumption—malls, multiplexes, theme parks and gated communities—strikingly summarize the change in the national mood, notwithstanding the asymmetrical nature of the new practices of consumption (Chandrasekhar and Ghosh, 2007).

New spaces of consumption such as shopping malls are, in fact, part of a broader landscape of recent developments within commercial, residential and leisure activities that include gated communities (Brosius, 2010; Srivastava, 2012) and theme parks (Srivastava, 2009). They share the imagination of these new spaces through being located in overlapping narratives of consumerism and its putative characteristics of unsettling older ways of being. In 2009, there were 172 operational malls across India, a figure that was set to double by the first quarter of 2011 (Kapoor, 2009). While there has been a recent shift in mall construction towards Tier II and III cities, it is the major cities that are still home to the largest number of malls. Of the 79 operating malls in North India, 44 were in the Delhi National Capital Region (which includes the satellite towns of Noida and Gurgaon), whereas 56 were in western India and 37 in Mumbai. North India, and the Delhi region in particular, has been identified by industry observers as the site of the strongest consumerist activity. The India City Competitiveness Report for 2009 ranks Delhi as the highest in terms of 'demand conditions' (Kapoor, 2009: 28), ahead of Mumbai. Further, all five cities identified by the aforementioned study as characterized by high demand for 'luxury goods and big ticket durables' are located in North India.[1]

Meaghan Morris points out that 'Shopping centres show why you can't usefully treat a public at a cultural event as directly *expressive* of social groups and classes, or their supposed sensibility'. Further, she says, 'Publics are not stable, homogenous entities' (Morris, 1998: 76; emphasis in the original). In the discussion that follows, one that builds upon the emerging scholarship on consumerism, lifestyle changes, consolidation of new class identities and changing relationships between the state and its subjects, I explore the different kinds of publics that frequent shopping malls located in Delhi and Gurgaon. The discussion will move across a number of territories—both actual and discursive—in order to explore the localized *affective* relationships (Morris, 1998: 67) between Indian malls and their visitors. These differ from contexts that, scholars suggest, are relevant for those in Western countries. These include, Jonathan Goss suggests, their role in recovering 'narratives of lost authenticity'—the putative loss suffered in the onset of Western modernity—that take place in carefully designed 'spatial settings [of] Public Space, Marketplace and Festival ..., and in temporal settings [such as] ... Nature, Primitiveness, Childhood and Heritage' (Goss, 1999: 50). This chapter will suggest that visitors in Indian malls bring their own histories of class, gender and relationships with the market in their engagements with malls. Also, that this produces strikingly different narratives of attractions to malls.

When Everyone Is Shopping You Don't Want to Be Seen at the Wrong Mall

I once asked Anita Kapoor, a resident of the up-market Kingston Park condominium in the DLF City in Gurgaon, about the malls she frequents and ones she liked. Anita and her husband lived overseas for several years, where the latter worked for an American bank and oversaw its outsourcing activities, before settling down in the DLF City. They live in a ground floor flat in Kingston Park, a gated community on a road with highest concentration of malls in Gurgaon (11 at last count). In fact, Kingston Park is wedged between two large malls. Anita's sitting room has several wall-size oil-paintings. In one, there is a clown slumped on a chair, and another Orientalist Ravi Verma influenced piece features two women and a young girl. Anita said that she and her husband didn't know much about art, but that luckily, their 'investment has appreciated greatly over time'. The room is full of art and various decorative pieces.

Anita volunteered the information that apart from malls she is also an avid Internet shopping customer and often buys clothes for her children at 'sale' times in the United States, spending as much as $700–800 each time. Since her husband now heads the credit card department of a major American bank, she says she is not worried about credit card fraud. Anita has two small children, a boy and a girl, and she believes that Indian-made kid's clothes are not 'good enough'. She doesn't appear to be bragging about her 'international experience', and states this in a matter of fact manner. However, she *has* moved some distance from her early life experience: her parents ran a school in western Uttar Pradesh town of Meerut. But every holiday, she says, 'my parents sent me to Delhi'. Later, she studied at Delhi University's prestigious Lady Shri Ram College. Recently, her father passed away, and her mother spends a lot of time with her, and, when she is in Gurgaon, she too frequents the malls 'since it is walking distance ... she gets her hair done, something she didn't do very frequently earlier'.

Anita and her husband are renting in Kingston Park and have 'booked' their own flat in the nearby Unitech World Spa gated enclave which, at the time of our meeting (2008), was still under construction. At 5,000 square feet, their new home will be large. However, construction is behind schedule by some 18 months, so they continue to rent. When they decided to move to India, they first rented in the gated enclave of Laburnum, paying a rent of ₹100,000 per month. Perhaps it is her experience of living in the West that makes Anita remarkably open with me about her personal life. She told me about her miscarriages and thinks aloud that her first miscarriage might have been due to the frequent power failures in the South Delhi locality where she began her married life. And, how she could have had biological children (her children are adopted), but it would have required several operations.

In one of our earlier conversations about her 'favourite' malls, it was Anita who suggested that I visit Select City Walk, profusely praising it and describing it as the one she liked the most. Anita also likes the newly opened Ambience mall (area: 1.8 million square feet) that sits at the entrance of the Ambience-Island-gated community in Gurgaon; in effect, the gated community has its own mall. The mall has seven floors, each a kilometre long, and its promotional material describes it as 'seven kilometres of shopping'. The store she frequently visits is Debenhams. However, Anita is very disappointed that one of the 'anchor stores' at the mall is the Big Bazaar, an extremely popular discount chain that sells everything from plastic buckets to cooking oil.

At the nearby Sahara Mall, the Big Bazaar store is the scene of hectic and crowded shopping by shoppers who are particularly attracted to its 'buy-one-get one-free' strategy. 'At Sahara Mall', Anita says, the crowd is very different. It's really like Lajpat Nagar or Sarojini Nagar (popular shopping precincts known for 'bargains') … pushing and shoving'. Ambience mall, she continues, 'is confused … it will become like a bazaar'. She likes malls where she can have a 'pleasant experience', and that's why she prefers the Select City Walk. 'There are no stores there like Big Bazaar, so you get a very different crowd', she tells me, adding that 'we were invited to its launch party, and you could tell it was a different crowd … people who could spend'. She has another story to tell, by way of driving home her point: 'We went the other day to the movie hall in Sahara (Mall)—as there were no tickets available elsewhere for the film we wanted to see. It was a horrible experience, there were *paan* stains [from beetle nut juice]!'

'We are not targeting any one group', the Customer Relations Manager at Ambience Mall had told me, 'but everyone [sic]. Our mall is particularly popular', he had added, 'because of its mix: it has very high-end shops as well as shops for every day shopping such as Big Bazaar. It has the biggest Big Bazaar in Delhi National Capital Region (NCR)'. The front of the mall is occupied by the luxury Leela Kempinsky hotel, and there is also a BMW dealership on the premises. I had been told by several industry professionals that, given its size, the mall's key aim was to maximize tenancy and that it was not particularly choosy about the 'mix'. As Anita describes her discomfort with Ambience Mall and its seeming lack of attention to identity politics, I was reminded of a comment made to me by an architect who is involved in mall design that Select City Walk exemplified 'careful thinking' since 'you don't want to be seen at the wrong mall!'.

Forty-two-year-old Sangeeta Mehta, who lives in an independent house in the DLF City, is also someone who is careful in her choice of malls. Sangeeta worked for 17 years with a prominent American bank and her husband is the head of a large outsourcing firm located in Gurgaon. She quit her job a few years ago. 'Ideally', she says, 'I would like to shop at somewhere like

Galleria', speaking of an open air market built by the DLF real estate company, which is designed to look like a European city square, and includes a fountain at its centre. 'However', she adds, 'places like that get dirty very quickly, and maintenance is always a problem'. Further, she added, a mall worth visiting must have a place for having coffee, shops for children and clean toilets. Comparing mall to other kinds of shopping areas, she feels that they are a 'great improvement. You don't have to put up with the dirt'.

Sangeeta is originally from Bangalore, and her father worked as a manager in the state-owned Bhillai Steel Plant [see Roy (2007) on the significance of 'steel towns' in the making of state-sponsored post-coloniality]. She comes, as she puts it, from an 'older middle class'. It was a milieu where there was familiarity with the world of consumption, though certainly not in the intense manner that characterizes the present. Sangeeta's father's professional background, the relatively frequent interactions with visiting Western 'experts' and non-resident Indian (NRI) relatives during her growing-up years were all sources of information about, as well access to, goods that have only recently become part of a more wider spheres of consumption. Often times, I got the feeling that this—her own longer-term familiarity with consumerism—was a significant aspect to her attitude towards contemporary trends where many from vastly different backgrounds had, in a manner of speaking, become like her. Consumption, for her, was simultaneously the task of being a 'different' kind of consumer.

She moved in social circles, Sangeeta once told me, where 'brand consciousness is very high'. Many of her acquaintances liked brands with 'big logos', so that from a distance 'you can tell it's a Louis Vuitton'. As for her, this was not very important: she could spend a very large amount 'on a solitaire, but it can be a small one'. She was emphatic that while she may buy branded products, but 'never something that has a large logo … people actually have to peer to work out what the logo is'. By way of an example, she narrated how she had recently bought a Korean-made four-wheeler that cost around ₹700,000. She could, instead, have bought 'a Mercedes'. However, 'my husband and I had a long discussion about this, and I said "No let's downplay it, and not buy a Merc'".

A significant aspect of being a consumer with the capacity to 'downplay it' relates to having been part of a 'savings mentality', as Sangeeta characterized her own upbringing. Of course, she added, it is a good thing to have 'grown out of it'. However, to have had the experience of control over money is a significant differentiating factor from 'new' consumers whose relation to the world of goods is in the nature of control consumerism exercises over them. Further, the experience of locality in a time of globalism is significantly tempered through the habit of careful evaluation that comes from the sustained experience of the culture of savings. Echoing a remark that Anita had once made to me, Sangeeta noted that:

> We are all internationally travelled people so we know the prices at the same store in Gurgaon, as in London. Earlier Marks and Spencers used to be very expensive, and my husband [who] travels overseas every month … would buy exactly the same clothes at cheaper prices in London or New York. Price is important for me…. I like the international brands, because you get a sense that India is moving ahead. Being internationally travelled, we also know the significance of brands, we know which foreign brands are actually 'luxury', and others, run of the mill.

Shopping in the Time of Personality Development

Sahara Mall—with its popular Big Bazaar store that stocks the kind 'run of the mill' goods that Sangeeta refers to—is a great favourite with Ravi (25), Amit (23) and Rishi (21). All three young men live in villages surrounding DLF City, the ones that are slowly being absorbed into the urban limits as farmers find it more profitable to sell and move further inland. I met them through Ram Singh, who worked as a driver for a family in Victoria Park gated community. Rishi and Ravi live in the village of Ghata, whereas Amit lives with Ram Singh (his maternal uncle) in nearby Ulwasnagar. Both villages—dominated by the cattle owning Gujar caste—are within half an hour's motor cycle ride from the DLF City. The families of Ravi, Amit and Rishi have each sold some or all their land to developers such as the DLF corporation and Sun City (another active player in the local real estate market). Sometimes, Ravi, tells me, they strike a deal for 'collaboration', where the developer hands over 30 per cent of what has been built on their land to them, and sells the remaining part on the open market. From the money they have made through sale of their land, Amit and Rishi have, in turn, established their own real estate businesses. Ravi is an 'agent' for the Indian arm of the American Max Life insurance company and also has a real estate business. They are all married, with Rishi having been married at the age of nine. Child marriage, Ravi, tells me, is not an uncommon practice among Gujars, though one that is slowly changing. As we talk, I can see the skyscrapers of the DLF City in the distance, where the cafes are full of unattached young people, some on 'dates', and others just 'hanging around'. I express surprise that Ravi has clients for his insurance business in villages. 'The majority of my customers', he tells me, 'are from the surrounding villages … they are the ones who have sold their land and become crorepatis [millionaires] … whereas in the city, the service-class person is going to think twice about paying a premium of ₹25,000 per year.

Ravi, who is married, tells me that on 14 February he decided to have a night out with his 'girlfriend', and that they had to go to several venues before they could find somewhere to eat at one of the malls. 'We always do this on Valentine's Day', he says. I asked what would have happened if he was to run into someone from his village. He says that people from his village don't hang around the places he frequents with his girlfriend. All three men go to malls and prefer Sahara Mall. 'This mall is for the *aam admi* (common man), whereas we occasionally go to DT Mall and MGF Mall to watch films', he says. Amit chimes in to say that when he got married, he took his wife to a mall, 'but when the elders in my house found out, I was severely reprimanded. They said "abhi se mall ja raha hai to baad mein kya hoga" [if he starts taking her to the malls from now on, what will they get up to later?]'. Even now, he says, there is a lot of 'respect' for elders. There is really no such thing as 'love marriage': 'either you become an outcast, or they shoot you!' So, love happens at the malls.

But not just love. For these young men, there is another significant aspect to do with malls. Amit tells me that in his house 'everyone wears jeans ..., even the girls'. And,

> at least once a month I take the youngsters in my family out to Sahara (mall), it's a question of 'personality development'. The government school in my village is up to the 8th standard, but it only has 40 students. These are mainly the children of the *mazdoors* (labourers) who are working on construction sites. Most of the villagers send their children to private schools.

The spatial aura of malls, gated communities and glass-fronted offices (that house offices of key transnational corporations) is the palpable stuff of 'personality development', and the older populations of Gurgaon now take part in a barter of dispositions. It's an exchange made possible through the new economies of land and older arrangements of labouring. There are many like 'us', Ravi told me, who have sold their land. Many, he said, have bought in the interiors of Rajasthan (that borders Haryana) at about '20 per cent' of what they sold their land for. However, they no longer farm themselves and have given it over to sharecroppers. Some others, he added, have bought houses in DLF city, 'mainly for the sake of their children, because they want them to grow up in a different environment'. Going out with the girlfriend to a mall on Valentine's Day—while the wife stays at home—caters to the requirements of this 'different environment'; for Ravi and his friends, young men at the cusp where the city meets the village, the malls are both processes of this environment, as well as the sites of acting out the new times.

> Amit: When I was 10 and saw women smoking and driving, it was very *ajeeb* [peculiar] ... now in my village women from many of the better off families drive around in cars ... we have grown up in that environment, so it's not unusual any more.

'There are only two ways of improving yourself [in our villages]', Ravi once told me, '"graduation" or money. There is very little "graduation" here, so it's mostly money'. Malls allow for improvement, if you have the money.

We Prefer Going with the Family

'Improvement' is also a term that came frequently into use in a series of conversations with a group of four women who work in clerical positions in a government organization in Delhi. All four were aged between 45 and 55, had grown up children, and lived in west Delhi in self-owned flats within Cooperative Group Housing Scheme (CGHS) complexes. The CGHS has its origins in the state's Social Housing Scheme that came into existence in 1952 (Madan, 2007: 337). Housing societies formed under the Scheme were 'meant primarily for persons of small means' (Madan, 2007: 342), with the state providing both land and financial assistance at subsidized rates. The CGHS aimed to assist both 'low' and 'middle' income groups. Unlike Ravi and his friends, the women, when asked about the company in which they most often went to the malls, responded 'we prefer going with the family'. The group also expressed preference for shopping at Big Bazaar, and malls that hosted the store were frequently visited.

While there are a number of malls in West Delhi, there is one particular stretch of land in the locality of Rajouri Garden in—now bisected by the Delhi Metro light rail—that has the greatest concentration. There are five malls in close proximity to the metro station, as well as a few minutes walking distance apart. I was directed to this area by the women in this group who were frequent visitors to these malls. The City Square mall is the nearest to the Metro station. Like most Delhi malls, it is covered, and hence air-conditioned. It has four floors built around a central courtyard, which is the most common design in Delhi (an aspect mentioned by those in the group who had visited Select City Walk and who were able to point to this difference in design). The top floor—called Café Terrace—has cafés and various eating outlets and there is also a coffee shop on the ground floor. There are also sit-down restaurants that offer, among others, Thai, Chinese and North Indian cuisine (the last two include the up-market Yo! China and Punjabi By Nature, respectively). There are strict security checks, followed by physical frisking at the entry. Around the mall, there are flyovers, the metro line, and the incessant hum of traffic on the major roads that criss-cross the area.

Shoppers Stop is another nearby mall. Designed to be an up-market store, it has four floors of shopping, with different sections on each floor. On the first floor, there are plush leather chairs for shoppers and a newspaper stand. Nearby, there are two mock *mandaps* (small pavilions where marriage ritual are performed) with life size mannequins dressed in Bollywood style wedding finery. The first *mandap* has a sign 'Varnmala: Shadi Ka Bandhan' ('The Garland: Marriage Ties'), whereas the second is called 'Mehendi Ki Raat' ('The Henna-Ritual Night'). On the same floor, there is a section called 'Men's Ethnic Wear', and another for 'Women's Ethnic Wear'. Many young couples wander around, mostly unmindful of the goods on display. They appear lost in themselves, holding hands. One stops to admire the wedding tableaux. The relatively shabby Paragon mall and only slightly better TDI mall (both owned by the same company) are also in the vicinity. The former is scantily tenanted whereas the latter appears to be thinly visited. The fifth mall is Westside, which is reached after crossing a large area of vacant, rubble strewn land. Around the malls, there are half-made roads and the frequent danger of being hit by cars that come down the wrong side. Inside, however, it is another world.

Adventure

To begin with, for this group of women, malls are the world of new adventures: escapades and experiences that have specific gender dimensions and fold across the registers of time, commerce, kin networks and the restrictions of 'purpose'. Unlike Anita Kapoor and Sangeeta Mehta, however, the manner in which the group relates to malls is not through a system of ranking of spaces that are more or less desirable, depending on kinds of stores and their (imagined or real) clientele. Rather, they are open to visiting all kinds of malls, accumulating new experiences that distinguish the current phase of their lives from earlier ones, rather than seek to differentiate one mall from another as a way of positioning themselves as different kinds of shoppers; shopping itself is the act of distinction. At one of our meetings, I asked the group what they thought the differences were, if any, between various malls in Delhi. Their recounting of difference was exclusively in terms of the kinds of goods a mall might specialize in—'women things', for example—and that some may have a multiplex cinema and others not. No one outlined a hierarchy of malls, where some may be more 'common' than others.

A mall, by its very nature, is an uncommon place; it facilitates particular kinds of urban experience—market-sociality—that has been open to men, but has been out of bounds for most women. The places might be too far and the distance considered 'unsuitable' for a woman to traverse, or, the transport, erratic.

> Rekhaji (around 55 years): Sometimes there are shops (in a mall) that sells things that are only sold in places that you might never have been, or don't go. ... so sometimes we 'explore' these goods ... things that we have never seen before ... we can find those things (at a mall).

> Sanjay Srivastava (SS): Like what?

> Rekhaji: Like Kalpana (saree store) ... I will never [be able] go to the Kalpana shop in Connaught Place (central Delhi), but I will go them in the mall in Pritampura (west Delhi).

The mall is also the context of a significant change in the relationship between gender and 'purposeful activity' through the consolidation of a new imagination of 'loitering' (Phadke et al., 2011). This relates to the popular perception that there are specific conditions under which men and women may access public spaces. Hence, it is generally understood that men's access to public spaces need not be tied to a 'purpose' (i.e. carrying out specific tasks); however, the idea of women loitering in such spaces becomes both incomprehensible and condemnable. A recent study carried out in Mumbai that asked respondents to indicate how men and women use space summarizes its findings as follows:

> ... it is always men who are found occupying public space at rest.... Women, on the other hand are rarely found standing or waiting in public spaces—they move across space from one point to another in a purposeful movement.... Women occupy public space essentially as a transit between one private space and another. (Ranade, 2007: 1521)

The idea of the necessity of the purposeful activity by women is one that emanates from many sites of which the domestic is one of the most powerful. It is, perhaps, also the most stringent in its enforcement of the rule of 'purpose'. As another study points out, 'Restrictions over time are completely absent in case of upper-caste men. The only condition for men is that they should inform a family member in case of delay' (SWSJU, 2010: 30). In the context of this discussion, malls provide an alternative logic of loitering. So, frequently, the women narrated, what might be called, the fracturing of the reason of purpose and diversion from the immediate task at hand.

> SS: So, if you go to Noida, say to visit a relative, will you also visit mall there?

> Kusumji (around 45): Yes, definitely. But it's not that I have gone specifically to visit a mall, it's because I have gone there for some other reason ... if we are in that area for some other reason, then we go and see the mall, we don't go there just for the purpose of seeing the mall.

Consider, however, Kusumji's reflections on an earlier phase in her life and the imperative of purpose:

> When I first got married and wanted to go out we [she and her women friends] used to have to make the excuse that are going to the Gurudwara ... now we don't care, as long as they [referring to her son and daughter and in law] get along ['unki bani rahe']!

It is of course true that ageing confers certain freedoms upon women. However, that is not the only factor. For, as a recent gender 'safety audit' for Delhi points out, older women also feel unsafe in Delhi (Viswanath and Mehrotra, 2007). Malls have created an environment that combines the legitimacy and desirability of consumerism (Srivastava, 2007), with a discourse of public safety, where 'publicness' is of a very specific kind.

SS: Many women I have spoken to say that they feel very comfortable inside malls ...

Kusumji: Yes, there is a greater sense of security, there is no eve teasing ... my daughter's purse was stolen twice [in a bazaar] ... also it's about neatness and the 'gentry' ...

SS: What do you mean by that?

Kusumji: The kind of people who go there ... so there is far less probability of meeting the kinds of people who do 'chain snatching'.

Lataji (around 50): The Great India Place (mall) is worth seeing ... I had gone to Noida specially to visit it ... of course I won't now specially go to see it, however, whenever in future if I go to Noida, I'll make it a point to make some time to visit it.

The mall space is, apparently, the site of a new relationship between purpose and its antithesis, through the logic of commerce, and without any assistance from the traditional guardian of public safety, the state.

Lataji: I also like malls because you hang around as long as you like ... there are no shopkeepers to hassle you ... as to how much time you are spending there ... wasting his time. Also, at the open shopping areas, you always had to be careful, whereas at a mall you can be 'free' (carefree).

It is the logic of commerce that is the context for another kind of adventure, which relates to the minutiae of transactions themselves. It concerns the idea of 'credit', which is utilized to repudiate prevalent notions regarding the 'worthiness' of women, particularly those who have lived most of their adulthood within traditional family structures, under the restraining hand of fathers, brothers, husbands and in-laws. The changed nature of transactional activity is also an alternative narrative of freedom. One of our discussions concerned *how* this group made purchases. All the women possessed credit cards, either in their own right, or as a 'spouse'. Since credit cards are relatively easy to obtain, particularly for salaried men and women, this was not a surprising fact. Nirupmaji pointed out that apart from the 'convenience' factor, an additional incentive lay in the fact that her card 'is also a loyalty card, and (every time I buy) my points increase'.

> Nirupmaji (around 45): The bill comes a month later ... and when the bill comes I think 'surely this is not right!' Then we verify against the receipt (every one laughs) ... you think 'just buy it and worry about it later!'

Notwithstanding the concerns expressed by the groups regarding the possibility of 'overspending' when a credit card was involved, the dominant sentiment was one of pleasure, one that incorporated the complaints against the long history of 'purpose' as a rule of gender such that places to be visited and resources to be expended were strictly aligned with properness and propriety.

> Nirupmaji (around 50): Yes, but also we buy other thing, just waste our money! (laughs and is joined by the others) ... in my house we always have a surplus of things ... if I like this, I buy it, if I like something else, I buy that ... that's why our 'frequency' (of visiting malls) is far less, compared to teenagers ... for them it's a meeting place, if they want to eat something they go there.

It is a mark of the adventure that the mall—and its modus operandi—offers that middle-aged women, otherwise subject to the rules of female adulthood, articulate a new sensibility of space through comparisons with teenagers; 'It's a good change, all good', one of the women said when I asked the group whether they thought there was anything 'bad' about malls. 'Loyalty'—as that embedded in credit cards issued by specific stores—could now be split as a concept, no longer exclusively signifying devotion to the household, and the capacity to purchase *faltu cheezein* (goods not needed) also signifies a reformulation of the strictures of gendered expenditure and consumption patterns.

So, while it is true that women still bear the burden of the physical provisioning for the household and 'you get everything at the same place' in a mall, the latter also generates the sense of impulsiveness that has historically been the preserve of men.

SS: Do you go to malls after planning or just on the spur of the moment?

Lataji: Well, the other day, I was watching TV and a friend rang to ask what I was doing, and then she said, 'let's go to a mall'. So I said 'OK!' … when our children were small and we used to go to [the] India Gate [monument] to show them these things … we used to go for a picnic, packed our food and went to India gate. Nowadays the 'service class' [with which the women self-identified] mostly goes to the malls …

Kusumji: *aadat bhi pad jaati hai* … [it becomes like a habit].

New Relationships

The new 'habits' of the women of the 'service class'—practices that militate against habituation, feminine norms and those of 'service'—are also the site of new kinds of relationships formed in the crucible of the mall space. The first of these relates to the family and broader kin networks. Reflecting upon their lives as adults, the women divided their experience of sociality into three distinct phases. First, there was the time when as young married women with small children—say, 20–25 years ago—they experienced a great deal of organized familial interaction. This was the time when weeks of planning preceded all-day family picnics to one of the four or five regularly visited leisure sites: the shopping precinct of Connaught Place, the India Gate monument and Children's Park in Central Delhi, the Qutub Minar historical complex, and the sprawling Lodhi Gardens in central Delhi. The second phase relates to when the children were older but both the lack of suitable public transport and 'security' fears made it difficult for large family groups to meet for public leisure as often as they would have liked. Perceptions of harm in public spaces were linked both to the influx of labouring populations into Delhi—mainly from surrounding economically backward states of Bihar and Uttar Pradesh—and 'terrorist' threats that were also magnified through active 'awareness' campaigns by the state (such as those that asked passengers in buses to look under their seats to see if there was a bomb placed there). The third phase, this group of women reported, relates to a reinvigoration of family ties.

> Nirupmaji: Yes, that's true [that families spend more time together because of malls] ... I often call up my sister and ask her to come with me ... 'otherwise', I say, 'you'll just be stuck in the kitchen, we'll go out and eat something' ... so this is how we have our get-togethers ... sometimes my husband comes home early and we decide to go out ... the basic thing is that you can do everything at once, shopping and dinner, a movie.

Noting that the 'safety' offered by the mall—from a multitude of threats—has led to a 'great change' in the ways that families are able to meet and socialize. Nirupmaji suggested that this included 'a shift towards outside dining ... so now it's 'let's go and eat there today, let's go to a mall, etc.'. There was spontaneous laughter when I asked the group if they could remember when they last visited, say, the Qutub Minar:

> Kusumji: If someone comes from outside (Delhi), then we take them out [to show the tourist sites] ... I think about 'six years back' I went Qutub Minar.... In any case, we have seen these places earlier, how will Red Fort and Raj Ghat (Mahatma Gandhi memorial) change in the intervening years? We have been here (in Delhi) for the last 40 years....

Further, malls are also *preferred* sites of interaction with out-of-town kin, a renewing of relationships around new spaces:

> Kusumji: Earlier, when we had relatives visiting from Punjab, they had a 'set plan', they would want to go to such and such gurud-wara [Sikh temple] and to Lal Quila [Red Fort] and to Qutub

... but now when they come to Delhi, they don't want to go to these places, they say 'take us to a mall', or they want to go for a 'joyride' on the metro....

Whether accompanying relatives from out of town, or going with family members from within the city, the mall is a favoured site of new kin sociality. While the food court might be more expensive than similar independent outlets, 'at the food court, everyone can order according to their choice ... it offers great choice: there is Chinese, South Indian, North Indian, everything is available'; family ties are constituted through the instrument of 'choice'.

If malls are the site of a putative return to a period before fear and discomfort led to a decline of family interactions upon public spaces, then the new cultures of commerce also offer a different relational model of civility and equality with the market. Kusumji noted that she felt that in a mall 'they (the shopkeepers) "attend" to you better' and that 'there isn't the kind of rush you see (in bazaars)'. However, and perhaps, more significantly, customers negotiate the new sites of commerce through entirely different matrices of equality that, in turn, make the experience an empowering one.

Kususmji: Shoppers Stop has an excellent 'returns' policy: you can return goods purchased from them to any of their stores, anywhere in Delhi. You just have to go to their 'customer care' section and they will give you a 'voucher' and willingly exchange your goods ... at any shop. They just have to look at the 'invoice', and they will exchange it [this point was reiterated later in the conversation as well].

SS: But many say that the earlier forms of shopping when you went to a shop, you developed a relationship with the shopkeeper ... you got to know him.

Kusumji: Well, that's true ... however, if you keep going to the same branded shop, you can build the same 'rapport'. And, nowadays the sales people in the small [independent] shops also keep changing....

The minutest mechanisms of capital are translated into the language of social life. So, Lataji explained that some of the new practices—particularly prevalent at malls—had also been effective in improving the relationship between consumers and the salespersons who attended to them. 'Competition' is the grounds of a new environment of welfare and sociality. Lataji explained the process—*deus ex machina*—as follows:

> ... when you have bought [at a shop in a mall], there is a code on the bill [identifying] the person who has been attending to you.... I remember once a man was showing me something then he had to go somewhere, and another came. However the earlier salesperson came back and when I was purchasing he said 'put this in my name', so there is competition. It's quite clear to see that the benefit goes to the consumer, she gets the best rates ... if there is competition then they attend to you better.

Genuine Brands and Genuine Spaces

A significant reason for visiting malls is the growing clamour for brands by younger members of the family. This has also rubbed off on the parents in the ways in which they have begun to reformulate consumerist desire. 'Branded' products also serve to announce a transition in family circumstance, both economic as well as cultural.

> Rekhaji: ... our children are now earning in lakhs (hundreds of thousand) ... and they like to spend ... in my 'life time' we would go from one shop to another to see what is cheap, what is expensive ... now they want to buy 'brands' ... and within brands, particular styles ... *so within Levis they want particular styles.* (Emphasis added)

As brands become intimate part of household purchases, their presence—and necessity—comes to be expressed through the logic of antique custom:

> Kusumji: [The difference between branded and non-branded goods is] ... 'quality', definitely, there is no guarantee with the

other clothes ... so if you buy a brand like 'Monte Carlo' [an Indian clothing brand and a great favourite with this group] ... you also feel good that you are wearing 'branded' clothing ... there's the quality and the comfort, reliability ... there is that old saying *Mehnga roye ek baar, sasta roye baar-baar.* (If you buy something expensive you cry once, if you buy something cheap, you'll cry again and again.)

Brands are also, of course, on display in other shops that are not in malls. However, the 'open' market, unlike the mall, is full of 'defects'. Malls have an aura of certainty whereas the bazaar is a milieu of doubtful transactions:

> ... (at a mall) ... the brands are genuine ... so if they say it's 'Monte Carlo', then it will be a Monte Carlo brand ... so if you buy an Adidas in a mall or in Kamla Nagar (a shopping area in North Delhi) ... it will be better in a mall.... The branded material that you get in a mall will not have a defect ... it will be the best quality ... the company will send their best quality (to a shop in the mall) ... whereas at other places, it may have defects, they will sell it anyway ... *halka sa bhi defect ho to chal sakta hai* [they'll sell goods that have minor defects]....

Other experiences also carry the insignia of certitude, genuineness and transparency, particularly those that personal memory can juxtapose to a time before the appearance of malls. One of these concerns the significant activity of watching films at theatres.

> Kusumji: The other thing is that when you go to a mall to watch a movie, you are likely to get the tickets, whereas earlier, you went to a hall and there were no tickets available and you had to buy in 'black', or come home ... there must be 'independent' cinemas in my locality ... but [now] I think I will have to think hard to be able to name them.

> Earlier we would have to look around to see which film was running in which hall, now you can go (to a multiplex) and you can choose from a several films ... it's all about choice. The older halls had broken chairs, but we had to sit on them, whether they were comfortable or not.

At one of our meetings, I asked the women what they thought about the suggestion—frequently made in the media—that malls would lead to the eventual decline of the *kirana* store (the corner shop). Lataji appeared to speak for everyone when she stated that 'It's all positive … I think it [the "new" shopping environment] is an improvement … there has been an economic impact upon the small shopkeepers, but it's an improvement'.

Between Consuming and Saving

The advent of shopping malls and their reputation as 'safe' spaces for women, a youth cohort that has launched upon highly successful careers within the new economies of the post-liberalization period, and the rapidly growing reputation of consumerism as a respectable activity have combined to conjure certain freedoms that, otherwise, mainly derived through ageing (Lamb, 2000). However, the aura of the mall—its promises of sociality and adventure and assurances of authenticity—sits alongside memories and practices of another era. Situated at the juncture of traditional family structures and emerging market forms—say, between taking part in the rituals of *Karva Chauth* to pray for the well-being of their men-folk, and, visits to multiplex cinemas—the women, unlike their children, articulate a more complex sense of being than might at first be apparent. It is a sense that comes from imbrications with the savings economies of the past and the consuming imperatives of the present, forming a joint narrative of gendered 'responsibility' and the excitement of 'irresponsible' behaviour.

One day, Kusumji was talking about her last visit to watch a film in a multiplex located in a mall. 'Of course', she said, only one 'level' of person can afford to go to a multiplex.[2] 'In a (multiplex) picture hall', she noted, 'a cup of coffee costs ₹75'. She meant to say that she now considered herself part of the group that could, if only occasionally, watch a film at a multiplex screen. During her last visit, she ordered a cup of coffee. But then, she added,

I felt very scared. I thought that for that money I can buy a kilo of tea for the whole family ... but my kids say 'This is nothing [not very expensive]'. But of course the kids, if they don't like something, they will use it for a short while and throw it away. Whereas me, if I have paid Rs. 75, I will drink all of it ... if I can't finish, take it home!

Everyone laughed at this anecdote, as if recognizing themselves in the situation, as women situated within an uneasy transition from being the sacrificing mother and wife to a carefree consumer devoted to self-satisfaction.

I have noted earlier that malls provide an altered temporality, one where women might take part in activities at times—late evenings, night times—that are otherwise out of bounds. However, the sense of a new freedom is frequently tempered with discourses of responsibility and duty of care to the household. I asked the group how long, on the average, they spent at the malls:

Lataji: Hmmm ... 2 to 3 hours is normal. (But) 'Sales' are ... very attractive, even though I may not have thought of buying at a (particular) shop, if there is a sale on, I will say, 'let me go and have a look!' If in winter, you are getting cheap summer clothing then you say, 'let's buy it, it will come in use later'.

Kusumji: But I want to emphasize that we tend to go to malls much more often during sales, thinking that we will get goods at a cheaper rate ... we'll see an 'ad' in the paper about a sale in mall where branded goods are being sold. So, I'll certainly think that I need to make at least one round....

But, as if the responsible housewife is pursued by the seductions of the market, she added: 'And then (having bought at a sale) ... we sometimes come home and repent ... because it might not be latest variety'. Balancing is a hard act.

The malls that are most liked are those that allow for the articulation of the cultures of consuming and saving, where one can move between desire and constraint. To have 'everything' does not just relate to material goods:

Lataji: I like Shoppers Stop, it's very spacious and everything is there ... and there is a lot of space to move, and it has both local and global brands, so if you don't want to spend too much money, you can go for the local brands....

In fact, there is folklore—narrated with some amount of admiration—about those whose consumption activity is a reminder of another time. 'I know a family', Lataji told me, 'that buys the entire year's spices at the (India International) trade fair (at Pragati Maidan exhibition grounds, where bulk purchases can be made). And, she added, 'when we go to watch a film at a mall, we prefer a morning shows, where the tickets are much cheaper!'

Conclusion

Malls in India are, then, sites of multiple dramas of distinctions (Bourdieu, 1984), meeting points of the promises of urban culture and aspirations of its hinterlands, and reflective of social and cultural changes that relate to the emergence of the middle-class female consumer. Their appeal lies in being open to differing personal and social trajectories that make up the contemporary tumult that is a relay between changing ideas of class, gender, 'personality', trust, 'branding', consumption and saving. It was perhaps the recognition of their increasing cultural and social roles in her own life that led Kusumji to relate with increasingly incredulity an anecdote about a visiting friend. 'A friend of mine came from the United States', she told me, 'and I said to her "a new mall has opened, let's go and see it"'. But, the friend responded that 'she didn't want to go! She said she was fed up with malls!'

For the women and men discussed in this chapter, malls are significant places in the new urban imagination and spurning their attractions is to pass up on the opportunity of re-fashioning selves that consumerism is seen to offer.

Notes

1. These are Faridabad, Amritsar, Ludhiana, Chandigarh and Jalandhar.
2. Ticket prices vary from ₹150 to 250. At older, single cinemas, ₹50 is the average.

References

Balakrishnan, P. 2008. An office space odyssey, http://www.rediff.com/money/2003/jan/11spec.htm, accessed on 24 July 2008.

Bourdieu, P. 1984. *Distinction: A Social Critique of the Judgment of Taste.* Translated by Richard Nice. London and New York: Routledge.

Brosius, C. 2010. *India's Middle-class. New Forms of Urban Leisure, Consumption and Prosperity.* New Delhi: Routledge.

Chandrasekhar, C.P. & Ghosh, J. 2007. Women workers in urban India. www.macroscan.org, accessed on 12 December 2008.

Dutta, D. 2004. Effects of globalisation on employment and poverty in dualistic economies: The case of India. In C. Tisdell & R. Sen (eds), *Economic Globalisation: Social Conflicts, Labour and Environmental Issues,* pp. 167–185. Cheltenham, UK and Northampton, MA: Edward Elgar.

Fernandes, L. 2006. *India's New Middle Class. Democratic Politics in an Era of Economic Reform.* Minneapolis: University of Minnesota Press.

Goss, J. 1999. Once-upon-a-time in the commodity world: An unofficial guide to mall of America. *Annals of the Association of American Geographers, 89*(1), 45–75.

Guha, A. 2009. Labour market flexibility: An empirical inquiry into neoliberal proposition. *Economic and Political Weekly, 44*(19), 45–52.

Kamat, S. 2004. The privatization of public interest: Theorizing NGO discourse in a neoliberal era. *Review of International Political Economy, 11*(1), 155–176.

Kapoor, A. 2009. Retelling retail. In A. Taneja (ed.), *Operational Shopping Centres and Mallsnext,* pp. 24–28. New Delhi: IMAGES Group.

Lamb, S. 2000. *White Sarees and Sweet Mangoes: Aging, Gender and Body in North India.* Berkeley: University of California Press.

Madan, G.R. 2007. *Co-operative Movement in India.* Delhi: Mittal Publications.

Mathur, N. 2010. Shopping malls, credit cards and global brands: Consumer Culture and lifestyle of India's new middle class. *South Asia Research, 30*(3), 211–231.

Mazzarella, W. 2003. *Shoveling Smoke. Advertising and Globalization in Contemporary India.* Durham, NC: Duke University Press.

Morris, M. 1998. *Too Soon, Too Late: History in Popular Culture.* Bloomington: Indiana University Press.

Phadke, S., Sameera, K. & Shilpa, R. 2011. *Why Loiter? Women and Risk on Mumbai Streets.* New Delhi: Penguin.

Ranade, S. 2007. The way she moves: Mapping the everyday production of gender-space. *Economic and Political Weekly,* 42(17), 1519–1526.

Roy, S. 2007. *Beyond Belief. India and the Politics of Postcolonial Nationalism.* Durham and London: Duke University Press.

School of Women's Studies Jadhavpur University (SWSJU). 2010. *Re-Negotiating Gender Relations in Marriage: Family, Class and Community in Kolkata in an Era of Globalisation.* Kolkata: Jadhavpur University.

Sengupta, M. 2008. How the state changed its mind: Power, politics and the origins of India's market reforms. *Economic and Political Weekly,* 43(21), 35–42.

Srivastava, S. 2006. The voice of the nation and the five-year plan hero: Speculations on gender, space, and popular culture. In V. Lal & A. Nandy (eds), *Fingerprinting Popular Culture. The Mythic and the Iconic in Indian Cinema.* New Delhi: Oxford University Press.

———. 2007. *Passionate Modernity. Sexuality, Class, and Consumption in India.* New Delhi: Routledge.

———. 2009. Urban spaces, and moral middle classes in Delhi. *Economic and Political Weekly,* 44(26), 338–345.

Srivastava, Sanjay. 2012. National identity, kitchens and bedrooms: Gated communities and new narratives of space in India. In Mark Liechty, Carla Freeman & Rachel Heiman (eds), *The Global Middle Classes: Theorizing through Ethnography.* Santa Fe: School of Advanced Research Press.

Vishwanath, K. & Mehrotra, S.T. 2007. Shall we go out? Women's safety in public places in Delhi. *Economic and Political Weekly,* 42(17), 1542–1548.

Voyce, M. 2007. Shopping malls in India: New 'social dividing' practices. *Economic and Political Weekly,* 42(22), 2055–2062.

3

Consumer Agency of Urban Women in India

Shelly Pandey

Introduction

This chapter explores how globalization has contributed to the consumer agency of urban women in India. Globalization has been looked through the emergence of the business process outsourcing (BPO) sector in India, which got clustered in certain locations in and around the metropolitan cities. Globalization brought many sectors of employment in India, such as BPO sector, information technology sector (IT), etc., and many women got opportunity into the labour market, due to the increase in the demand for unskilled, semi-skilled and skilled labour. The growth of the IT sector worldwide and availability of large English-speaking and low-cost labour pool have resulted in India emerging as one of the desired destinations for BPO (Ramesh, 2004).

BPO is the delegation of one or more IT intensive business processes to an external provider that in turn owns, administers and manages the selected process based on defined and measurable performance criteria. There has been a phenomenal growth of the BPO sector in India accompanied with an increase in its employee base. The rise of the Indian BPO industry has been impressive from US$6.3 billion in 2005–2006 to US$9.5 billion in 2007–2008 and with growing employee base from 415,000 in 2006 to 700,000 in 2008 (NASSCOM, 2009). Participation of women is constantly increasing from 25 per cent of the total workforce in 2006, and is expected to touch 45 per cent in 2010 (NASSCOM, 2008). The advent of BPO sector has substantiated the employability potential of English-speaking women into the workforce.

There are different types of services being offered by the BPOs in India such as customer support services, technical support services, telemarketing services, employee IT help-desk services, insurance processing, data entry services, data conversion services and others on similar lines. Some of these services such as customer support services, technical support services and telemarketing services require having telephonic or online conversation with the customers sitting across the globe. In India, the clients or owners of the organizations under BPO are from developed countries such as United States and United Kingdom (Singh, 2007). In this scenario, the work culture of these organizations is driven by the Western corporate world. This sector opened up a big service sector in India along with many employment opportunities. Most of these jobs are contractual, informal and peripheral and are also feminized as many women with limited educational qualifications found employment in these sectors before getting married. However, the earlier studies show that women were relegated to lower level of employment in the era of globalization (Ng and Mitter, 2005) but the salaries offered in these sectors are good as per the Indian standard. For example a call centre employee with a degree of graduation is offered ₹15,000 to ₹30,000 per month at the age of 20 or early twenties.

The consumption patterns of the Indian middle class have been postulated by acquisition of material objects. However, there is undoubtedly indulgence in conspicuous consumption and display of wealth and privilege for the public gaze (Scrase and Scrase, 2009). In addition to the knowledge of middle class consumption, it is important to understand that in today's globalized India, when the unmarried women in the middle class have started earning and they do not have family responsibility due to their unmarried status, what kind of consumption patterns are becoming visible among them. The power structure within household, operating through specific gender hierarchies, lies not only in the highly visible form of domination and control but also in the more subtle and somewhat invisible equations. These equations, in the domestic sphere, relate to the expenditure of the income, its allocation and consumption. The study of consumption pattern shows how gender articulates with other socio-cultural structures and whether it reinforces or changes the existing gender inequalities.

Based on the sample of 50 young unmarried women working in the BPO sector at Delhi NCR region, this study locates the impact of globalization, on their consumer agency. Though the respondents self-identified themselves as belonging to the middle class, but the analysis of their family's income and expenditure shows that they belong to a particular economic bracket and cultural milieu. The average salary of their fathers was ₹20,000 and majority of the respondents have two or more siblings. These women are the beneficiaries of the English medium education. However, their consumption and household survival strategies revealed that they have limited household budgets. Given the complexity of defining middle class, which include non-manual wage earners, low-grade technicians and professional employees situated between proletariat and petty bourgeoisies (Wright, 1985), the self-ascription of respondent has been relied by putting them into the category of the middle class.

The Context

The historical writings on women as consumers have posited them as frugal housewives and responsible and caring mothers (Benson, 1986). In India, especially in the pre-globalization era, the home envisioned in the urban locations reiterated male breadwinner and dependent wife and children. The participation of women in the labour market was very limited due to lesser opportunities available. The trends of working women in that era showed that women used to cluster in a few occupations: teaching, nursing, and clerical and in the lowest rungs of the prestigious professions and received lower salaries than men (Ahmad, 1979). Until the early 1990s India seemed to be at the receiving end of modernity and positioned at the margins of the developed world. However, one of the major consequences of the changes operating in India has been the emancipation of women from their tradition-bound ethos. Earlier, the educated women had to choose between career and marriage but now the question of either marriage or profession has been abandoned and a combination of two roles—job and marriage—has become more common. Now, apart from economically hard pressed women, those who wish to live a socially useful life and add to the family finances are also getting engaged in paid jobs. They have come to realize that work gives them personal status and an independent social standing (Medora, 2007). The advent of the BPO sector has substantiated the employability potential of English-speaking women into the workforce.

The feminist studies on the industrialization insisted that for understanding the implication of industrialization for women, it is needed to examine the impact of women's earning on intra-household decision making. However, in the context of globalization when it reaches the patriarchal society like India, it is important to examine whether the opportunity of employment impacts their agency. This chapter looks into their agency through their consumption patterns, like how and where these women spend their income.

The changing consumption pattern among women is needed to be examined in the backdrop of the other changes as the outcomes of globalization. The economic liberalization polices, which intensified the globalization of the Indian economy, were initiated in early 1990s. During the same period another change happened, which gradually transformed the face of shopping in the urban location of India. This change was that an Indian departmental store chain called Shoppers Stop started taking off in 1991, with its first store in Mumbai. Now it has 47 stores across the country with a range of branded apparel and private labels under the following categories of apparel, footwear, fashion jewellery, leather products, accessories and home products. These are complemented by cafe, food, entertainment, personal care and various beauty-related services. The purpose to discuss the rise of Shoppers Stop store is to reflect upon the face and the growth of numerous shopping malls that have come up in many Indian cities especially in the first decade of twenty-first century, which run on the principles of more choice, glossy buildings as market place and hyper visibility of brands.

In this scenario, many scholars have located that there is a shift from dutiful nation-citizens to consumer-citizens in India as creating another form of identity (Fernandes, 2006). Even, the workers in the new sector of employment under globalization are viewed as not 'Nehruvian nationalists' but as professionals who are more committed to living their lives in India's aspirational middle class (Fuller and Narasimhan, 2007). The notion of 'belonging to world-class' is cropping up among the people in urban areas along with a strong desire to come to terms with the emerging middle class in India. The new middle class is highly heterogeneous, made up of professionals, administrative, managerial, clerical and other white-collared occupations (Beteille, 2001). However, the group that has caught the attention of this study is young women working in the BPO sector of Delhi NCR region.

BPO and Consumerism

The responses of the study indicate how the work culture is inducing a consumerist culture among young women and this kind of consumerism has become a way of self-expression among young working women. In this self-expression, their agency plays many roles in terms of quantity and the frequency of shopping.

The BPO sector in India represents the corporate sector having the ideologies of Western corporate world. As the client base of Indian BPO sector is essentially the Western countries, the work culture in the BPO organizations is driven with Western ideology. The nomenclature used for the employees such as 'executive' or 'analysts' and the interior of the workplace replicating the Western setup induce the modern outlook among the employees. Taking insights from the studies on gender and built environment (Desai, 2007), which indicate that the meaning of a space can be beyond its physical boundaries and there can be an emotional meaning of the space (i.e. space that is mentally inhabited), the analysis of the architecture of the BPO organization suggests that it creates an identity with the space inhibited. Apart from the modern outlook, the BPO sector also provides salaries to young women at the age of early twenties, which are sometimes more than the salaries of their fathers at the time of retirement. These factors construct new discursive orders that promote the idea of a self-propelled womanhood. In this way, a new identity of a modern corporate woman is created among the young women working in the BPO sector that goes parallel to the new, liberated, modern woman's image commodified as a selling strategy for conspicuous consumption (Chanda, 2004). To quote one migrant respondent from Uttar Pradesh:

> When I came to Delhi to work in BPO I did not used to wear much western clothes but after coming here I have started wearing and buying more western clothes because in my office most of the women dress-up in western style, so, I also started dressing-up like that. Secondly, I go to shopping malls in Gurgaon to spent time on weekends with my roommates. There I find such attractive clothes which complement my looks at my office so I buy them.

Many respondents talked about their changed looks (from traditional to Western) after started working in the BPO sector. According to them, the surrounding of young people as colleagues fosters a feeling of competition in looks and ultimately in consumption. Another respondent from Delhi said:

> There is always a feeling among women in my workplace that who is wearing what and who is looking good and smart, especially during office parties. We have team parties and office parties almost every month. Then every woman wants to dress-up

in a special way. On most of the weekends, I buy clothes to wear at my workplace.

Here it is important to understand the spatial location of the BPO sector that further fosters the consumerism. The majority of BPO organizations are located in Gurgaon (a satellite city of Delhi). All the migrant women in the sample of the study were staying in the paying guest houses in Gurgaon, which is also famous for its shopping malls amalgamation. On one hand, Gurgaon is a hub of BPO sectors and on the other hand, it has nearly 40 shopping malls. Hence, there are many locations in Gurgaon city that are represented as spaces having BPO organizations and shopping malls together. The architecture of both the BPO organizations and the shopping malls represents the Western settings in the mind of the viewer. The glass buildings, the modern and glossy interior produce the kind of atmosphere that replicates a Western city, induces a more Western identity among people working in that area, which impacts their lives by impacting their consumption patterns.

It is argued that shopping malls also create an image of the self-dependent modern woman. The analysis of some of exterior look of the shopping malls in Gurgaon explains that how the images used as marketing strategy in shopping malls also create an identity of a woman who is consuming for herself.

The images at the shopping malls indicate that new spaces of consumption are structured by the construction of femininity as modern, Western educated women who spend for her own pleasure.

The built environment of both the BPO organizations and the shopping malls indicates that how the corporate sector and advertisements focus on the construction of the ideology of individualism, consumption and free choice. This finding of the study goes parallel with Chaudhari's (2004) work, which talks about the image of women in the print media that sought to project an image of a liberated individual woman who makes her own autonomous choices, who is free to pursue her own work and leisure and is not tied to any impositions.

According to one respondent from Punjab,

now I buy all those things which I want to buy for myself. Last month I gifted myself a 'Rado' watch. Next I will buy a laptop for myself.

The analysis of the space, in which the work and leisure of women working in the BPO sector is located, makes it apparent that apart from the relation between selfhood and consumption, the 'created selfhood' is also playing a crucial role in this new consumerism of self-expression among women. The created self-hood can be understood through the term used by Appadurai (1996) that is the fetishism of consumer, which indicates that how through commodity flow, the real social agency of the consumer is masked for the real seat of agency, which is not the consumer but the producer. Here, the *created selfhood* indicates the identity created by the new work culture and new spaces of consumption, which are driven by Western ideologies and self-expression through consumption.

However, the study does not want to negate the role of electronic media for creating the new image and identity for young women but the focal point of the study is the space (Gurgaon city) where these women are located to either work or to recreate or to stay in rented accommodations. The architecture of BPO setups and shopping malls in Gurgaon flags off a marked differentiation from the urban spatial lay-outs of the tier II cities in India from where the women migrate to work in BPO sector in Gurgaon. On the similar lines, Bourdieu's (1977) work demonstrates that how space enters into the very constitution of social life and identities. His concept of habitus reveals how a spatial classification is fundamental to one's social and cognitive map, providing individuals with a set of parameters within which to deal with everyday lives and situations. In Bourdieu's conceptual scheme, the habitus plays a major role in shaping and orienting our practical acts. The study argues that the identity created by the habitus of women working in BPO sector in Gurgaon city provides impetus to consumption in the garb of created consumer agency.

However, the consumption for self is not the only consumption pattern that has come forward in the study. The study also found that women are also contributing in the family's consumption patterns, which will be discussed in the following section.

From Provider to Purchaser

'Earlier, I used to help my mother in household work but now I sleep in the free time at home due to my changing shift timing. Now I do not contribute in the household work' (respondent from Delhi).

The changing gender relations due to the newfound employment opportunities for women, with the rise of the BPO industry, have also impacted the gender division of labour in the household. Analyzing women's work in Indian context, Banerjee (1999a) explains that the intra-house division of labour proceeds the labour market and that it is the burden of housework imposed on women through the former that makes them weaker in the latter. However, the earlier studies on the BPO sector have shown that parents are getting supportive to their daughter's employment and the burden of household work is not faced by young women anymore (Tara and Illavarasan, 2009). Employment in the BPO sector has not only contributed to the financial autonomy of educated, urban middle-class women but also has had a positive impact on the cultural standing of daughters, whose career aspirations are supported by their parents, as inferred earlier by Clark and Sekher (2007). In the context of parents' reluctance and/or limitations to provide resources for higher education for their daughters, the BPO sector provides them with employment opportunities with handsome pay packages, without having demands for any higher educational qualifications. The idea of the absence of any higher eligibility criteria for BPO jobs need to be seen with two background features in mind. First, the criteria of a plus two or a graduate degree as an eligibility benchmark for a BPO employment must be seen in the context of the background of its employees. If the eligibility criterion is evaluated, in general, with the national literacy rates in mind, they might appear to be considerably high benchmarks for eligibility. However, when the eligibility criterion is evaluated with specific reference to the background of its employees, the criterion begins to appear fairly moderate. The employees, broadly, have middle-class origins. Herein, they belong to that sub-section of the Indian middle class that comes from English medium education, at the school level or at the college level or both, to their wards. As per the norms of this sub-section of the Indian society, the milestones of being a plus two pass out or a graduate are perceived as very basic educational qualifications. As a general practice in this sub-section of the Indian society, parents normally support their wards' life and education until graduation. The eligibility criterion of a plus two or graduation aligns well with the existent social norms of the employee's family of orientation. It is perceived as a fairly moderate eligibility criterion, as far as the educational qualifications are concerned. If the parents were to support their wards' education beyond the point of graduation, they are more likely to construe it as an above average commitment and investment towards the education of their wards, as per their social norms and patterns. The parents might not always feel encouraged to engage into it due to a, generally prevalent, bias against higher education of daughters, that it may become difficult to arrange a marriage for girls who have higher educational degrees. In addition to this, they may sometimes not be in a position to undertake such a step given the financial constraints that the expenses of higher education may turn out to be an additional debit entry over and above the expenses of the marriage of their daughters. Second, the BPO sector provides the rare combination of a handsome salary, company-sponsored dedicated transport facilities with home pick-up and drop, plush working environment and all this waiting to be taken by anyone who is just a graduate or in some cases even a plus two pass out. In the pre-1991 India, that is, before the Indian economy was opened up, such working conditions were almost unimaginable for a person with normal looks and average non-technical education being at the graduate level. Thus, the interface between the Indian middle class and the rise of the BPO sector in India throws up a unique opportunity that not only enables young unmarried women to be financially independent but also imparts them with the capacity to contribute and enhance to their family's income and consumption levels. This transition in the roles of the daughters from being providers of household support to being financially independent purchasers seems difficult in the absence of the rise of the BPO sector as far as the life chances of an average young unmarried woman with a non-technical graduate degree are concerned. Such young urban middle-class women would have otherwise stood lesser chances to be educated further and was more likely to be married off by the family, had she not have got a BPO sector employment and thus augmented the income levels both for herself as well as the family and the consequent escalation in their purchasing power parity.

The responses of some of these women show how these women have started contributing to the family's consumption. A migrant from Uttar Pradesh said, 'Now I feel the freedom to spend money after getting into the job. I gifted my mother a microwave on Diwali and earlier I gave her washing machine.' Another respondent from Delhi said, 'My job has allowed me to buy many home appliances which were unaffordable due to the limited income of my father. I have bought microwave, LCD TV for home and I have also taken loan for the car that we have recently bought.'

Feminists have used the concept of 'social reproduction' to refer to the gendered division of labour and to indicate the activities and responsibilities involved in the maintenance of life on a daily basis. The social reproduction includes how food, clothing and shelter are made available for immediate consumption (Barbara and Brenner, 1989). In India, the practices of socialization involve even the young women of the family into these activities, where they help their mothers into managing the demand of social reproduction. However, the rotating shift timings of the BPO sector allow women to escape from the household work but at the same time they are indulging into buying energy saving appliances for their homes. This indicates that how the gender roles are undergoing changes from traditional provider of household services to the modern purchaser or consumer of household gadgets and services.

The consumption of married women as purchaser of services has been posited into the demands of housemaids, cooks and caregivers at home (Lutz, 2002). However, the unmarried working women's income, which many a time is the additional income to the income of the father, posits her as the purchaser of home appliances. However, the findings also reveal the reason for the inclination towards the buying of home appliances is the changing division of labour in the household. Since women are getting into such sectors of employment that render them with little time for the household and even in the social reproduction, it is the mother of the unmarried women who are doing all the work for the daughters. The mothers are taking care of timely food, clothing and other logistic demands, which in turn is enabling the daughters to pursue their career in the unprecedentedly demanding work environment.

Since most of the household work is done by the mothers without much help from the daughter of the family, the daughters are spending on the energy saving device for the household work. Talking about the young women's contribution in the household work, Datta (2005) says that there is a trivialization of young women's contribution to the household in terms of their labour. However, this study found that this trivialization of the young women's contribution to the household in terms of their labour is accompanied by increasing contribution in the family's income. This additional income is generally routed in buying white goods and/or other energy saving devices that manifest in mitigation of the burden of household chores on their mothers. Thus, while prima facie it might appear that the hitherto contribution to the household work in terms of their labour has declined as a result of their employment in the BPO sector, the form and the direction of their purchases of the white goods suggest that they are intended, either manifestly or latently, to compensate for their absence from their family and household of orientation. This trend becomes more apparent when we consider the form and direction of consumption, in general, and white goods, purchases, in particular, in the lives of the migrant young unmarried

BPO sector employees. They save not to buy white goods for themselves as much as they save to buy the same for their families back home. This differentiation is further highlighted if we compare and contrast it with what would happen in the occident, in similar circumstances. In most likelihood, a young migrant unmarried woman working in a sector (comparable to the BPO sector in India) in west would have predominantly bought white goods for herself than for the household of her parents. However, it must be conceded that this difference of outcome in the west stands over and above an iceberg of a variety of reasons such as the difference in the structure and function of the family in the west, the social customs and norms and the general patterns of consumption and living. This comparison and contrasting clarifies that the form and direction of the purchases of white goods in the life of a young unmarried BPO sector employee is more than being just a standalone decision. It suggests that these young women, when they cease to be providers of household assistance, acquire a new rather compensatory role of being purchasers for the benefit and comfort of their family and household of origin.

Saving Dowry

The evolution of the practice of dowry has been seen in the context of rising consumerism in the earlier scholarships (Banerjee, 1999b; Clark-Deces, 2011; Davids and Driel, 2005). These studies postulate the shift from bride price to dowry into the effects of industrialization, urbanization and consumerism. The goods and wealth given under the system of dowry may include cattle, land, gold, silver, cloths, utensils, furniture, cash, vehicle, and so on. The form of these items changes with change in consumerism (Kramarae, 2000).

In the globalized India, dowry is embedded in the context of economic and monetary developments, the 'consumer revolution', represented by newly available luxury items in the market, provoke Indian consumer to use dowry as a means of obtaining these goods. On the other hand, the dowry has become a part of modern self-made man rather than the part of old world of ascribed status (Kapadia, 2002). By giving the example of IT professionals in Andhra Pradesh, India, who also migrate to United States to work, Biao (2005) suggests that education and migration have not made people more liberal in the Western cultural sense. Rather, IT professionals are particularly proud that they can maintain Indian culture and at the same time succeed in the global IT market.

According to Botticini and Siow (2003), growing consumerism and affluence have contributed to dowry inflation. The competition to get men with jobs in an organized sector suggests a new form of hypergamy, that is, women marrying with more economically successful spouse; this has influenced the larger part of the society. Hence, to fulfil the desire of this new form of hypergamy, parents are willing to pay dowry because the marriage of their daughters links their family to a high status family or higher salaried son-in-law.

However, the responses of the study indicate that the new sources of income for young unmarried women allowed them to bid up the size of their dowry. Their income is becoming an additional resource to their parental finances for their marriage. As these women start working immediately after their graduation, they typically work for five to six years before their marriage. On an average these women save more than half of their salary every month, which contributes a significant amount of savings before marriage.

> I spend on my clothes and shoes, I also buy some home appliances as and when needed and on weekends I go out for dinner either with my family or with my friends. Rest of my salary is saved every month. (A respondent from Delhi.)

> I go for shopping on weekends to buy something, which I like. I also pay rent of paying guest house accommodation and meal. When I go home I take some gifts for my family members and rest of the amount I save. (A migrant woman from tier II town.)

This economic empowerment, of young women, plays twin-fold functions. In short term it induces an instant jump in individual, collective and family consumption levels. In the long run, when juxtaposed against the enhanced commercialization and dowry in the marriage market, their considerably high saving rates affect additions to the funds of their marriage. The parents of these young women, in general, have some savings that exist as what they would call as funds for their daughter's marriage. The new addition to this fund plays more than just one function. In effect, it hedges the marriage funds against inflationary pressures. While marriages continue to get increasingly commercialized, these additions serve the function of giving the potential means of adding more colours to their marriage celebrations. On a parallel note, it imparts the capacity to pay higher dowry which may mean that the chances of getting a better groom in the marriage market get boosted.

The contribution to the marriage corpus fund of their parents also makes space for changes in the way these funds get operationalized. The fact that these women have contributed in their marriage corpus fund renders them with a higher agency, in the qualitative and quantitative expenditure decisions of this fund, at their disposal. For instance, they perceive that they would have more say in deciding the budgetary allocations for their lehngas (the popular marriage dress for the bride in the northern part of India) and/or the decision regarding budgetary allocations for a preferred beauty parlour for the purpose of bridal makeup. In general, they perceive a potential increase regarding their say in the overall shopping and other preparations of marriage.

Such qualitative and quantitative enhancements in the marriage ceremony hold significance in the minds of young women in India. More so, when they would have not been possible, had it not been for the economic empowerment that they got as a result of their employment in the BPO sector.

This trend marks a tangent from the traditional mode of thinking where the issue of arranging for marriage of the daughter of a family used to be an exclusively parental and paternal prerogative. The fact that these young women are now contributing to the funds of their marriages reflects that these contributions from daughters not only are accommodated but have also silently acquired acceptance from their respective parental and paternal quarters. It marks a significant change as daughters have silently been accepted as the new contributors to their own marriage funds and likewise boosts the qualitative and quantitative consumptions at and around the time of their marriages.

Conclusion

The consumption patterns of young women in contemporary urban India indicate that they are neither too traditional nor too modern in their consumption as the interplay between the traditional and modern institutions is acquiring a crucial role in the construction of their feminine self. Here the modern institutions are the modern world of work and traditional institute is the system of dowry or marriage money. Entering into the world of work has allowed them to attain confidence and autonomy, enabling them to assert their sense of self and personal agency. This gets reflected in their consumption for self and consumption for parental family as a result of financial independence. However, their savings for their marriage and dowry expenses, for the consumption of their marital family, reflect that how their consumer agency is still within the confines of patriarchal ideologies. The analysis of different portions of consumptions indicates that there is a nexus of self, family and marriage in the consumption pattern of young women in urban India.

Reference

Ahmad, K. 1979. Studies of educated working women in India trends. *Economic and Political Weekly, 14*(33), 1435–1440.
Appadurai, A. 1996. *Modernity at Large: Cultural Dimensions of Globalization.* Minneapolis: University of Minnesota Press.
Banerjee, N. 1999a. Can markets alter gender relations? *Gender Technology and Development, 3*(1), 103–122.

Banerjee, N. 1999b. Analysing women's work under patriarchy. In K. Sangari & U. Chakravarti (eds), *From Myths to Market: Essays on Gender.* Shimla: Indian Institute of Advance Studies.

Barbara, L. & Brenner, J. 1989. Gender and social reproduction: Historical perspectives. *Annual Review of Sociology, 15,* 381–404.

Benson, S.P. 1986. *Counter Cultures: Saleswomen, Managers and Customers in American Department Stores, 1890–1940.* Urbana: University of Illinois Press.

Beteille, A. 2001. The Indian middle classes. *The Times of India,* 5 February.

Biao, X. 2005. Gender, dowry and the migration system of Indian information technology professionals. *Indian Journal of Gender Studies, 12*(2–3), 357–380.

Botticini, M. & Siow, A. 2003. Why dowry. *American Economic Review, 93*(4), 1385–1390.

Bourdieu, P. 1977. *Outline of a Theory of Practice.* Cambridge: Cambridge University Press.

Chanda, I. 2004. Birthing terrible beauties: Feminisms and 'women's magazines. In M. Chaudhari (ed.), *Feminism in India,* pp. 228–245. New Delhi: Women Unlimited.

Chaudhari, M. 2004. *Feminism in India.* New Delhi: Women Unlimited.

Clark, A.W. & Sekher, T.V. 2007. Can career-minded young women reverse gender discrimination? A view from Bangalore's high-tech sector. *Gender Technology and Development, 11*(3), 285–319.

Clark-Deces, I. 2011. *A Companion to the Anthropology of India.* USA: John Wiley & Sons.

Datta, A. 2005. MacDonaldization of gender in urban India: A tentative exploration. *Gender, Technology and Development, 9*(1), 125–135.

Davids, T. & Driel, F.V. 2005. *The Gender Question in Globalization: Changing Perspectives and Practices.* UK: Ashgate.

Desai, M. 2007. Introduction. In M. Desai (ed.), *Gender and the Built Environment in India,* pp. 1–29. Delhi: Zubaan.

Fernandes, L. 2006. *India's New Middle Class: Democratic Political in an Era of Economic Reforms.* Minneapolis: University of Minnesota Press.

Fuller, C.J. & Narasimhan, H. 2007. Information technology professionals and the new rich middle class in Chennai (Madras). *Modern Asian Studies, 41*(1), 121–150.

Kapadia, K. 2002. *The Violence of Development: The Politics of Identity, Gender and Social Inequality in India.* London and New York: Zed Books.

Kramarae, C. 2000. *International Encyclopaedia of Women: Global Women's Issues and Knowledge.* New York: Routledge.

Lutz, H. 2002. At your service madam: The globalization of domestic service. *Feminist Review, 70*(1–2), 89–105.

Medora, N. 2007. Strengths and challenges in the Indian family. *Marriage & Family Review, 41*(1–2), 165–193.

NASSCOM. 2009. *The IT-BPO Sector in India: Strategic Review 2009.* New Delhi: National Association of Software and Service Companies.

NASSCOM Foundation. 2008. *Indian IT/ITES Industry 2007–2008: Impacting Economy and Society.* New Delhi: NASSCOM.

Ng, C. & Mitter, S. 2005. Valuing women's voices: Call centre workers in Malaysia and India. *Gender Technology and Development,* 9(2), 209–233.

Ramesh, B.P. 2004. Cyber coolies in BPO: Insecurities and vulnerabilities of non standard work. *Economic Political Weekly,* 39(5), 492–497.

Scrase, R.G. & Scrase, T.J. 2009. *Globalization and the Middle Class in India: The Social and Cultural Impact of Neoliberal Reforms.* New York: Routledge.

Singh, N. 2007. Call centres. In K. Basu (ed.), *The Oxford Companion to Economics in India.* New Delhi: Oxford University Press.

Tara, S. & Illavarasan, V.P. 2009. I would not have been working here: Parental support to unmarried daughters as call center agents in India. *Gender, Technology and Development,* 13(3), 385–406.

Wright, E. 1985. *Classes.* London: Verso.

4

Modernity, Consumer Culture and Construction of Urban Youth Identity in India: A Disembedding Perspective

Nita Mathur

Introduction

There is distinct shift in the consumption pattern of urban youth in India from necessity-based consumption to conspicuous consumption that is fuelled by their newly founded desire for coveted commodities and services and enhanced propensity to consume. The market forces tend to keep pace with latest trends and choices of the youth who have flair to establish and 'show off' their identity as 'modern people'. A large number of such people treat possession of consumer goods, engagement with leisure enclaves retailing global brands and services, spas and other personal service stations prioritizing the self over community hitherto characterizing 'high life' as a means of entrenching their own position and estimating others' position in society. A critical social consequence for society is the interception of face-to-face interactions and social relationships largely with Internet, long-distance telecommunication technologies and other forms of modern media. Understandably, the situation is more complex than plain transition from face-to-face relationships to non-face-to-face ones. Face-to-face relationships are now increasingly mediated and informed by non-face-to-face relationships. The process disembeds people from their former and familiar social and cultural settings and re-embeds them in newly carved out contexts. In order to view consumer culture and modernity from a fresh perspective, it is worthwhile to accord centrality to twin notions of embeddedness and disembeddedness.

Polanyi (2001) employed the concept of embeddedness in a broader framework of economy and market society. Given the fact that all economies are embedded, he did not use embeddedness as a distinguishing character of pre-modern and modern economies. Prior to the rise of modernity in a robust form, Polanyi argues, economy was embedded in social relations. Rise of modernity, however, was accompanied with rise of market society—one which was governed by by market order rather than organic human relationships. In Polanyi's words,

> The market pattern, on the other hand, being related to a peculiar motive of its own, the motive of truck or barter, is capable of creating a specific institution, namely, the market. Ultimately, that is why the control of the economic system by the market is of overwhelming consequence to the whole organization of society: it means no less than the running of society as an adjunct to the market. Instead of economy being embedded in social relations, social relations are embedded in the economic system. (2001: 60)

According to Beckert (2007), Polanyi's concept of embeddedness enfolds two connotations: first, institutional regulations connect all markets to the moral webwork of society and second, in being limited by institutional regulations, markets tend to stabilize a (democratic) organization of society. These two connotations imply that the reference point of embeddedness is 'the larger social system in which economies are located' and not economy as such [Barber, 1995: 406, cited here from Beckert (2007: 8)]. As individual gain comes to organize economic life in market society, economy tends to get disembedded from it. When this happens, a counter-movement geared to protect the society from the market gains momentum. The history of market economy demonstrates that the protective counter-movement impedes the rush for gain and in doing so restructures economic life and embeds the economy again. The play of 'double movement' shapes market society (Block, 2003). Polanyi maintains that the oscillation between embedding, disembedding and re-embedding accounts for the process of social change. Granovetter (1985) differs from Polanyi in arguing that economic action is embedded, so to say, in systems of social relations which imply that social networks have a bearing on economic outcomes. Later, Zukin and DiMaggio (1990) added three types of embeddedness to Granovetter's 'structural embeddedness': cultural embeddedness, cognitive embeddedness and political embeddedness. In the context of Algerian peasant society, Bourdieu (1963) demonstrates how social dislocation is caused as logic of the household is prevailed over by the logic of calculation in the process of modernization [cited here from Beckert (2007)]. Modernization does not generate disembeddedness by simply weakening networks and social institutions and making them irrelevant. Rather, structural changes push actors into new modes of social organization as specific forms of embeddedness get devalued. Reflecting on the concept of embeddedness in sociological writings, Beckert (2007: 10) states his own position,

> Following Polanyi, I take it as axiomatic that the embeddeness of economic exchange makes economic and social integration possible: The attempt to establish a system of self-regulating markets based on commodification of the "fictitious commodities" land, labour and money produced the dehumanizing social conditions that Polanyi held responsible for the social and political instabilities he witnessed in his lifetime.

This chapter develops what may be referred to as 'disembedding perspective' on modernity and consumer culture. It examines how urban youth in India (hereafter youth[1]) uses the consumption to shape the meanings of the category 'modern' and promote normative models of modernity that equate modernity with conspicuous consumption. The objective here is twofold: to determine youth's construction of modernity and modern lifestyle; and to explore the processes by which this group uses

consumption as a means to establish distinction in society, negotiate inter-personal relationships and affirm a 'modern' identity. More specifically, I examine the following questions: how
is modernity defined and negotiated reflexively; why and how
consumption lifts social relations from their local contexts and
re-locates them in new contexts of space and time; and how consumption serves to establish identity in terms of 'group identification' and 'social categorization' (see Jenkins, 1996). First, I briefly
explore the sociological literature on modernity and propose a
disembedding perspective that complements and improves on
available approaches to the understanding of patterns of consumption by youth. Thereafter, I present a profile of urban youth
in India and their proclivity to consume developed from youth's
own narratives followed by reflexive interpretation of modernity
through the practice of consumption. The data on which the
chapter is based draws from 275 survey respondents (113 women
and 162 men) between 15 and 34 years of age (with average
age of 23.4 and 24.7 years respectively) with average monthly
income of ₹15,500 (representing the urban new middle class)
and in-depth interviews with 25 informants (in mixed groups of
men and women) centring around three key areas of the survey:
brand value of commodities as signifier of status in society, social
and economic value of money for them and perceived influence
of consumer culture in their lives. The field-based study was conducted in New Delhi between March and September 2008.

Modernity and the Study of Consumption

The issue of modernity has gripped the interest of sociologists
since several decades. Fehér and Heller (1983) establish that the
central logic of modernity lay in simultaneous existence of capitalism, industrialization and democracy in a symbiotic relationship. The chief markers of modernity are: rationalism, rational
planning, technocentrism, standardization of knowledge and production and faith in linear progress, universal truths and values
associated with the development of capitalism. In the words of

Wood (1997: 544), 'These features are supposed to be associated with the development of capitalism, either because early capitalism, in the process of unfolding itself, created them, or because the advancement of these principles, such as rationalization, brought capitalism with it.' In fact, ephemerality contingency and fragmentation that mark modern life and associate it with capitalism necessitate the giving-in to the preoccupation with universality and absolute truth (Berman, 1983). It emerged as a cultural order and out of an economy of conveyor belts through fordism and the new way of life associated with it (Beilharz, 2009; Smith, 1993). Beilharz (2009: xii) puts it succinctly,

> Fordism represented a new way of producing but also of consuming: it promised a whole new way of life, and indeed a New Man (women still had to wait). This promised a new civilization, a mass society based on closed national circuits of mass production and mass consumption—not just Detroit but Hollywood, later suburbia and Levittown.

The modes of life that characterized modernity initiated major transformation of traditional social order. According to Marx, modernity would usher in a more genial and benign social environment. For him, the seeds of modernity lay in expansion of productive forces and the creation of world market attributed to capitalism and the rise of revolutionary bourgeoisie. He maintains that the value of a commodity derives from the social framework and in no case from an attribute inherent in it. Marx argues that the relation between labour (production) and consumption in capitalism is largely estranged. Rather than engaging in labour to produce objects to satisfy their own needs directly, they sell their labour for wages. Consumption gets disjointed from production when the act of production is not performed with the basic purpose of satisfying needs but for gathering profits. When both production and consumption get alienated, people develop relations with the commodities they possess and associate their identity with it.[2] Marcuse (1986: 92) explains in the following words, 'The people recognize themselves in their commodities; they find their souls in their automobile, hi-fi set, split-level home, kitchen equipment. The very mechanism which ties the individual to society has changed, and social control is anchored in the needs which it has produced.' Weber proposes that modernity is accompanied with a secular world-view as it advances institutional differentiation, disenchantment[3] and intellectualization of culture[4] over religion-based cultural order. As the grip of bureaucracy—the forerunner of material progress—tightens, order and security take over belief and knowledge systems. They get relocated in modern political ideologies but cease to be effective in developing a sense of personal identity. Individuals, however, assimilate values in the occupation goals that are pursued within the institutional context of everyday life (Seidman, 1983). Durkheim's analysis of modernity revolves around twin concerns of weakening of collective sentiments and consequent rise in the incidence of anomie and suicide, and spread of contractual relationships. In such a situation, morality and system of collective beliefs, traditions and aspirations get jeopardized (Shilling and Mellor, 1998).

Being 'modern' as Campbell (1987) notes, is, in effect, the search for novelty and a kind of hedonism. According to Campbell, a modern hedonist consumer

> is one who often withdraws from reality as fast as he encounters it, ever-casting his day-dreams forward in time, attaching them to objects of desire, and then subsequently "unhooking" them from these objects as and when they are attained and experienced. (pp. 86–87)

Consequently, modern hedonist consumers tend to search for and experiment with newer forms of gratification. They come to appreciate objects for their meanings and images rather than for utility. Campbell's hedonistic model of human action accounted for consumer revolution[5] in terms of pleasure (rather than satisfaction accruing from subsistence) as the goal of human conduct. He envisaged a distinction between traditional and modern hedonism in the following words:

> The former traditional hedonism was identified as a preoccupation with a sensory experience, with 'pleasure' regarded as

discrete and standardized events, and in the pursuit of which there is a natural tendency for the hedonist to seek despotic powers. Modern hedonism is marked in contrast, by a preoccupation with 'pleasure', envisaged as a potential quality of all experience. (1987: 203)

In prioritizing novelty, meanings and images associated with products, and longing for purchase and use of commodities, hedonism explains consumption as a voluntary, self-directed activity that implicates cultural ideals. The 'middle sections of society' displayed the new propensity to consume in their demand for luxury goods. Campbell provides an explanation of how the middle classes themselves committed to an ascetic, and puritanical 'Protestant ethic' and consequently to ordered, regular pattern of productive work characterizing capitalism, could give in to a form of consumerism based on hedonism. The middle classes, as his analysis goes, were characterized with 'moral interdirectedness' and mannered ethics opposed to the absence of emotionality and hedonism so characteristic of the upper class. Instead, what lay that at the core of its sensibility (but lacking in the Protestant tradition) was the concern with aesthetics. The middle classes incorporated the component of aesthetics into their ethic which hitherto had been dominated by twin ideas of morality and spiritually. Campbell argues that:

The middle classes, by contrast, true to their religious heritage, regarded "taste" as a sign of moral and spiritual worth, with an ability to take pleasure in the beautiful and to respond with tears to the pitiable equally indicative of a man (or woman) of virtue. It was an ethic that inevitably provided powerful legitimation for the pursuit of emotional pleasure. (1987: 205)

Modern life is marked by a longing to realize the pleasure created in imagination. This amounts to dissatisfaction with what is available in real life in the wake of striving for ceaseless consumption of novelty and new experiences.

Renewed connection of modernity with emergent social institutions and lifestyles makes revisiting previous sociological insights imperative. That the institutions of modern society can best be understood by employing the framework of but redefining classical theories and adapting them to the new context was emphasized by Giddens (1990, 1991). Thus, Marx's theory of capitalism, Durkheim's of industrialism and Weber's of rationalism need to be reconsidered in the study of modernity. Giddens (1991) equates modernity with the industrialized world[6] in which social relations are influenced by widespread use of material power and machinery in its production processes. He states that the interconnection between seemingly polar processes of globalizing influences and personal dispositions representing what he refers to as 'extensionality' and 'intentionality' is a distinguishing feature of modernity insofar as it transforms the existential reality of people's everyday lives and experience. A significant fallout of this interconnection is the understanding that, in his words, 'The self is not a passive entity, determined by external influences; in forging their self-identities, no matter how local their specific contexts of action, individuals contribute to and directly promote social influences that are global in their consequences and "implications"' (1991: 2).

Everyday lives of people get transformed even as time–space are reorganized and escaping out of the grip of specific locals, social relations recombine across widely separated time–space distances. The dynamics between global processes and local concerns mediates people's experience and their identity. The mediated self-identity and daily activity drive them to negotiate lifestyle choices from a wide variety of options. An individual grapples with day-to-day options in order to construct self-identity in the modern world. As Giddens writes,

> Modernity it might be said, breaks down the protective framework of a small country and of tradition, replacing these with much larger, impersonal organizations. The individual feels bereft and left alone in a world in which she or he lacks the psychological supports and the sense of security provided by more traditional settings. (1991: 33–34)

He points out that the most obvious criteria of the modern era are the extreme dynamism of modernity fuelled by three elements: separation of time–space,[7] disembedding mechanisms[8] and reflexivity.[9] A manifestation of modernity is the globalization of social activity even as most distant happenings influence local activities and events. This is facilitated by the print and electronic media as much as by world-wide connectivity through the Internet. The separation of time and space serves as the prime condition of the process of disembedding mechanisms. Two means through which disembedding mechanisms operate are: 'symbolic tokens' and 'expert systems' (together referred to as 'abstract systems'). Symbolic tokens are described as media of exchange that can be circulated or passed around, for example, money. Symbolic tokens are standardized because of which they transcend territoriality and time. In a practical sense, symbolic tokens are able to lift transactions from their local contexts and relocate them in new settings creating fresh patterns of interaction for which reason they are treated as a means of time–space distanciation.[10] Another means of generating space–time distanciation is putting modes of technical knowledge and expertise to use in a way that the practitioners and clients are de-linked, that is, they can operate independent of each other.[11] Expert systems largely depend on trust which '… is a form of "faith" in which the confidence vested in probable outcomes expresses a commitment to something rather than just a cognitive understanding' (1990: 27).

Urban Indian Youth as Consumers

Indian youth in general, and urban Indian youth in particular, is a heterogeneous category differentiated along several dimensions (gender, caste, class, religion and education, to mention only a few). National census figures (2001) indicate that youth population in urban areas is 37.29 per cent as against 32.45 per cent in rural areas; the percentage of youth in total population of the country being 33.80. The youth (particularly teenagers) in India can be classified into the following categories on the basis of their propensity to consume as Bijapurkar (2007) does: (i) the creamy layer (including 'rich brats') comprising 2 million but fast-growing group of people that the premium brand marketers target; (ii) the consuming class constituted of 'big city well-off kids' (p. 199) with high aspirations attracted to local and global fashion trends, hangout places, shop displays but not given to consumption that youth marketers could be happy about; and (iii) stretch-a-bit consumers incorporating between 5 and 12 million young people who are slow but sure to reach out to premium priced products. The remaining (i.e. about 44 million people) are aware of what is available in the market from movies, television programmes and the richer peers but extremely conscious of value for money. They buy cheaper varieties bearing the same look, style and functionary as the premium-priced commodities. Shukla (2010) mentions that by and large, the youth prefer to invest in consumer durable goods. What makes the Indian youth distinctive is their strong affiliation to the family. Comparing the Indian youth with their cohorts in BRIC countries, Bijapurkar (2007: 204) writes:

> Indian youth, in contrast, are very family centric; the cultural codes amongst Indian youth are about kinship of an extended family, about family obligation, and a home as a shared space.

It is commonly held that familial relationships in India have been extended and strengthened through use of, among others, technologies like cell phones, text messaging and cheaper air travel. Interestingly, two opposing tendencies operate concurrently: modern technology has seemingly increased connectedness of individuals with families; it has also distanced them from the family in a certain way. Young people who have had to leave old parents and relatives behind in villages or small towns in search of livelihood would, before cell phones were available, visit them on several occasions including festivals and major events in the family. Now a large number of them make do with a telephone conversation or just a quick visit. A 30-year-old call centre employee from Bihar has not gone back to his family for 3 years. He does, however, engage in long conversations with his parents and brother and feels it is good enough to do that.

He is also the one who defines 'good life' as one which is free of tensions and spent happily with one's parents. Relationships, expectations and aspirations seem to be re-contextualized in a way that they are lifted out from tradition and re-placed in a different context and life situation.

The Konard–Adenauer–Stiftung study on 'Youth Attitudes' in India endorsed the family as critical to their happiness. In fact, 87 per cent youth across caste groups, marital status, educational levels and gender said that they needed a family in order to be happy. Only 10 per cent youth in metropolitan areas stated that their happiness had nothing to do with the fact of having or not having a family at all (DeSouza et al., 2009). Male and female informants who were interviewed unanimously said that family is an important institution. This was not, however, unconditional, for many of them expressed that it was so only to the extent that members of the family did not interfere with what they did with their lives. According to Mazzarella (personal communication), it is an inherently contradictory fantasy. They wanted the freedom, but they also wanted the security and support that family represents, particularly in a country where there are few impersonal safety nets. Most of them did not want their parents and/or siblings to raise questions or challenge their decisions particularly those concerning where they went, whom they socialized with and how and on what they spent their money. When this was violated, they stopped sharing everyday concerns and adjusted their commitment to ensure the happiness and well-being of the parents by taking them to the malls and/or restaurants on weekends. This is a win–win situation for both parties. The youth feel good that they take care of the parents, and share with them a slice of their happy experience of shopping or just 'hanging around' in the malls. The parents, at the other end, feel that notwithstanding the week long indifference (which they prefer to believe is because of the pressure of professional work), the children come back to them *albeit* for a brief while.

The common perspective on the ideology and behaviour about the urban youth in India is that they are highly individualistic, the 'no-cares-in-the-world' kind, irrational, erratic and gullible when it comes to adopting fashion codes and latest styles. The study, on which this chapter is based, provides an alternative perspective. Interestingly, while making the case for consumerism, youth seem to be ambivalent about it as their following statements reveal: 'To some extent being materialistic is good and valuable, but I think materialism should not be man's priority';[12] 'Extreme of everything is bad but a bit of consumerism is important for better quality of life. Money is meant to fulfil needs and it is necessary to move in society with an identity of your own but it is not everything in life'; 'A demand for high class commodities and trend towards materialistic values brings in a more stylish lifestyle but at the end of the day, it's a waste of money'. In fact, they are largely value conscious and look for purpose even behind a luxury purchase. Also, they tend to reject those high-end foreign products with which they cannot relate or which they cannot afford.

Sinha (2008) seems to have touched the pulse in mentioning,

> For historical reasons, the designers were associated with some codes which alienated regular consumers of luxury goods, The couture stuff, the heavy sequin worked, ramp walk models made pretty pictures and inpus for gossip columns. But somewhere, in that code was also hidden the fact that 'it is not for me'.

The indulgent and confident youth enjoy spending on personal grooming, food and entertainment. Insiya (2009) reports the case of an advertising professional Cherry Batra as a representative of the earning urban youth in India who spends, on an average, 35 per cent of her salary on credit card and bills, 30 per cent on everyday expenses (i.e. conveyance, food, etc.) and 15–20 per cent on socializing. Batra explains that most of her credit card and spending is on socializing, the rest is on shopping. Cherry Batra and others like her who enthusiastically spend on retail fashion, eating out, modern electronic gadgets and other forms of enjoyment (that seem to be 'wasteful' to the older generation) actually represent a generation colloquially called 'youngistan'. Those whom I interviewed stated candidly that while it was perfectly fine to buy all that one desired and could afford without a sense of guilt, the endeavour should not 'alienate' one from the family. Interestingly, all the informants identified connectedness with the family as a chief marker of 'good life'.

Being Modern: The Practice of Consumer Culture

Goodman and Cohen (2004) state that consumption does not reflect cultural values, rather it has itself become a cultural value. This implies, among others, that people engage with consumption for the sake of it. Youth assign a critical value to consumption; many of them said that they felt impelled to consume. Rather than unwillingly and unquestioningly following the values and lifestyle laid down by age-old tradition emphasizing austerity and voluntary poverty, more and more of them now tend to customize their lifestyle. The possession of consumer goods, engagement with leisure enclaves and personal choices, preferences and tastes, hitherto characterizing high life are used as a means for establishing one's own position vis-à-vis others in society.[13] Increasing propensity to consume among urban youth in India is attributable to the pressure of the peer group that measures their success and 'coolness'[14] by the ease with which they are able to engage with commercial brand names and commodities that hold status-enhancing appeal (such as designer clothing and fancy accessories). Since the peer group itself largely comprises people who value high-end consumption, a large section of youth are compelled to engage with consumerism as part of collective endeavour or, as they put it, 'doing things together'. Some of them admitted that while they did not support the practice of consumption personally, they felt pushed into it by the peer group. As Mazzarella (personal communication) puts it, this suggests a tension between a kind of dutifully articulated moral position emphasizing the idea that consumption should not be accorded undue importance and a desire to participate. Also, it relates with ambivalence of the youth about approval: they know that the people whose approval they want are not necessarily 'superior' to them in any way, yet they still look forward to it. Further, they believe that since consumerism, in effect, governs mainstream lifestyle, keeping away from it would lead to their marginalization. Admittedly, prominent display of and easy accessibility to tangible aspects of consumerism (e.g. shopping malls, global brands, credit cards, commodities for physical comfort and convenience with discount offers and package deals) draws them a great deal (Mathur, 2010). Ritzer (2007: 163) explains, 'In a consumer culture, people act out and affirm that culture by engaging in the process of consumption and in displaying, sometimes conspicuously, what has been consumed.' There are a wide range of acts that involve acting out consumer culture. In the Indian situation, examples include occasional vacation to domestic or overseas destination[15] and frequent visits to the shopping malls, restaurants, pubs. The percentage of youth who visit malls regularly is 76. For most of them, going to the malls instils a sense of being well informed of latest trends in fashion. Responding to the question regarding major reasons for going to the malls, only 20 per cent youth said that they went to the malls with the intent of making purchases; other reasons for going to the malls are: remain informed of the latest trends in fashion; move in 'cool environment' and just chill[16]; look for competitive deals over stylish and fashionable goods; spend time in the absence of targeted gaze of family members; entertain friends; and try different cuisines. Despite the fact that the percentage of youth who visit the mall regularly is fairly high, more than 64 per cent of them prefer to shop from traditional market places; only 30 per cent stated their preference for shopping from malls over traditional market places; 6 per cent did not have any clear-cut preference. On an average an individual spends about ₹800 per visit to the mall; the major head of expenditure being clothing which accounts for 36.8 per cent of spending per visit to the mall.[17]

The practice of consumer culture manifests, as pointed out earlier, through consumption of especially those commodities that accentuate youth's status in society. A fairly large number of youth mentioned that brand value of a commodity enhanced their status in society and that most of the time they preferred to buy branded commodities. Only a few maintained that in the 'present age of changing fashion and style, it is foolish to waste money on buying a branded item'. Interestingly, 43 per cent admitted that they would buy an unbranded item if it looked exactly like the branded one and they were convinced that the peer group would not be able to make out the difference.[18] Brand values of commodities play an important role in establishing and display this distinctiveness.

An important means of establishing and displaying distinctiveness is possession of credit cards and flashing them in the peer group. The commercial banks' offer of debit cards with every savings account has made plastic money easily accessible to and popular with the youth. Many argued that they preferred credit cards because it accorded freedom from the responsibility of carrying and taking care of large sums of cash. Also, they were free to buy commodities for which they had not provisioned earlier. Credit cards empowered them to make purchases even when they were not carrying enough money to make the payment. The subtle message is that youth do not want to be constrained by the limit of cash they carry at a time. Youth's perceptions about credit cards are: 'credit cards make the user feel modern, empowered and confident; credit cards provide a sense of identity to the user; and credit cards are convenient and easy to use'. While people did project the advantages of credit cards, not many used them frequently for the reason that use of credit cards encouraged them to spend more than they could envisage. This was opposed to the traditional ideology of self-sufficiency and judicious spending on which they have been fed in the process of socialization.

Consumer culture acquires impetus from its coercive power which, in operational terms, refers to recognition and rewards to those who conform to its demands. Those who actively indulge in consumerism join the mainstream while others are marginalized. The term of informal reference to the latter category is *bhaiya* (for boys) and *behanji* (for girls) literally meaning brother and sister respectively but implying inadeptness of the person to participate fully in 'modern society'. A *behanji* who is able to meet the demands of consumer culture inadequately and inappropriately is often ridiculed by peers who refer to them as 'BTM' (i.e. *behanji* trying to be modern or *behanji* turned modern).[19] Youth acknowledge that they are increasingly becoming fashion conscious and tend to buy only those commodities that are synchronous with contemporary style. A large number of them foreground their choice of commodities in fashion and style value, and for display in the peer group rather than in their utilities.[20] Not surprising then, youth use the new commodity as soon as possible to ensure that it has not grown out of style or become common in the peer group as it reduces the net worth for the buyer because his/her distinctiveness as the sole owner or one among few owners gets jeopardized (Mathur, 2010).

The hedonistic framework of aspiring for 'high life' may be interpreted as debased materialism in which youth seek self-realization or self-expression through possession of commodities. Those lower down the economic scale strive to appropriate the referents of consumer culture in a way that they are able to project higher social status. While some confine their choice to branded items, a few others are more discretionary and tend to pin brand value only on those items (e.g. electronic goods, clothes, shoes, jewellery, etc.) that are subject to gaze of the peer group, yet others derive satisfaction from 'look-alikes' of branded items. This is also true of availing services that have characterized the upper class [see Mathur (2007) for a discussion on this aspect]. The youth have two options before them: to display their penchant for such services and leisure time activities as buying original brands or close imitations, or to make do with learning about them from print and visual media and from the experiences of others who deal with them directly so as to be able to be part of the conversations centring around these topics. This becomes possible because the market is flooded with differentiated products and services priced variously targeting the spending capacity of people belonging to various strata in society. The ownership and display of sought-after commodities in a way enhances self-esteem, and instils confidence of sorts and a sense of empowerment as they go about their daily lives with renewed rigour.

Consumer culture feeds on people's search for meaning in their lives through the practice of consumption. This may be appreciated in light of the fact that several youth in the present day accord greater value on consumerism than on community, religion and other elements that have for long provided succour and meaning to life. Evidently then, they tend to optimize the gains from perusal of consumer culture. Traditional occasions for celebrations (e.g. religious festivals) witness ever increasing levels of consumption. In addition, some days of world-wide celebration (e.g. Christmas, first day of a new year, Valentine's Day, Father's Day, Mother's Day and many others) afford opportunities for display of affection through consumption. The number of greeting cards, flowers and gifts purchased on such occasions is stupendous.[21]

Consumption, particularly conspicuous consumption enfolds competition for status-based lifestyle notwithstanding social isolation that commonly accompanies it. The predominant benchmark of assessing people is material possessions. This evaluation, it could be said, is a cliché, especially so in India where people can readily draw on ideals of asceticism and Gandhian principles in counter posing Orientalist categories of the 'spiritual East' against the 'materialist West' as an easy critique of the advent of modern consumer culture. However, what makes urban middle-class discourse on materialism interesting is that people present consumption as central to their own social lives yet deny its legitimacy and, as many of them put it, 'real significance' for the constitution of their individual selves. Modern consumption is accepted, but this acceptance is morally ambivalent. In the interpretations of their lives and society, people draw on collective ideological resources, familial and network of kinship relations and other social formations that connect them with society at large while individually dissociating from consumer culture which is taken as immoral. The youth want, sometimes even pressurize, their family members, particularly those older to them, to approve their indulgence. Interestingly, most of them maintain that indulging in conspicuous consumption in spite of opposition from the family, takes away the joy and thrill from it, hence, they want the family to somehow agree and be happy about.

Modernity, Disembeddedness and the Transformation in Day-to-Day Lives

I asked the youth, what 'being modern' meant to them, the bases on which they classified people into 'traditional', 'modern' and 'ultra-modern', who were the people they considered to be modern and what were the attributes that made them so. What I got was a long list of people who were identified as modern (largely Indian celebrities and politicians) but a small list of qualifying attributes. The youth consider modern people as those who have a facility with use of new technology and gadgets, are active on social networking sites, and are adept in making use of, what Giddens (1991) refers to as, expert systems, among others, along with dressing well, being humble, respectable, foresighted, virtuous and industrious. A remark that came up repeatedly in conversations and seemed particularly significant in understanding the construction of modernity at the grassroots was that modern people are not the ones who completely give-up on tradition, rather they recombine it with modernity in different ways. This is consistent with the common discourse in India since the nineteenth century. Chatterjee (1993) discusses how Indians separated an 'inner' (cultural) from an 'outer' (modern) sphere that prepares ground for the articulation of a conception of modernity in which Indians are not always going to be 'behind' a standard set exclusively in the West. Two significant points emerge from close reading of youth's projection of modernity. The first is that the meaning of modernity is produced through social, economic and cultural contexts, which is generated out of different ways in which tradition and modernity get juxtaposed with each other. For this reason, the notion of modernity in the singular is challenged as that of multiple modernities gains ground.

The second is that modernity is reflexively constructed. A person's ideas about what it is to be modern and what modernity *per se* obtains largely from the process of socialization, personal experiences and interactions with the peer-group. Modernity presents new ways of casting and interpreting tradition.

Importantly, modernity creates localized hybridities that are sensitive to both local values system(s) and nostalgia for traditional ways of being and people's craving for 'good and modern life' which it promises: consider some examples. The fundamental ideology at the root of, for example, Chowki Dhani Village (representing a sample of villages and lifestyle in the state of Rajasthan for tourists) and Pind Balluchi Restaurant (serving cuisine from the state of Punjab in a village setting) draws on the fond memories and reminiscences of older people and familiarizes the youth with what it was to be in the village. The Chowki Dhani village set-up in 1989 at the outskirts of Jaipur is spread over 10 acres of land. It started as a restaurant serving traditional food of the state. Over a period of time, it incorporated elements of local culture in its architecture, infrastructure and service. One of the dining halls known as *Chaupad Jeeman Ghar* is in the shape of a *Chaupad* comprising four perpendicular rows each with seating capacity of 20 persons meeting at the centre. Another dining hall is in the shape of crease of the *ghagra* (which is a kind of loose long skirt worn by the local women). Folk artists performing on raised platforms much as they do in villages, fortune tellers, magic and puppet shows, acrobatics on bamboos, and camel, elephant and bullock cart rides as also temples, huts, lake and wells enliven the memories of village life. In order to bring authenticity to the experience, local people from adjoining villages are trained to cook, serve and perform in a way that domestic and foreigner customers are able to experience the village life in absolute comfort of amenities and luxuries they are used to and certainly away from the tribulations and anxieties that are an inseparable part of village life in real.

Similarly, Pind Baluchi restaurant set up in 2004 in New Delhi celebrates village life in the state of Punjab. The words *pind* and *balluchi* in Punjabi mean village and food, respectively.

The entrance is conspicuous by the mascot-a middle-aged man sitting on a traditional cot with a bamboo stick in his hand that is a common sight in villages of Punjab. A man in Western suit stands at the counter by the side of the mascot presenting a distinct combination of tradition and modernity. People who visit the restaurant say that the presence of the mascot adds value to their experience. The village ambience is created by incorporating landscape of mustard fields, glass bangles, traditional motifs in Phulkari embroidery (a distinguishable feature of Punjab villages), mud coated walls, water mills, wells, mannequins and service crew dressed in traditional attire. What is significant to note is that the restaurant has regulated the quantity of butter and ghee in a way that while the richness and authenticity of the food is not compromised, it is not too heavy and difficult to digest. In effect, both Chowki Dhani village and Pind Balluchi Restaurant as also other similar enterprises represent touristically reconstructed notion of Indian village. They seek to recreate the countryside ambience of which the urban youth are familiar through reminiscent narratives the older generation.

Social networking sites have completely transformed the way youth interact with each other and with generations preceding and succeeding them. Emotions, empathy, happiness, anxiety and empathy are electronically communicated as the youth interface with the machine rather with friends and relatives in person. As Nayar (2009: 142) has pointed out, 'Such networked bodies are cyborgs. Bluetoothed, networked and implanted (in some cases), the humans of today are cyborgs. They are cyborged because they extend their bodies, consciousness and themselves into different domains (virtual) and time zones across geographical spaces'. Two processes are operative: first, re-contextualization of social relations in new situations of space and time and second, commodification of wistful desires of people to return in thought or in fact to a former, cherished time in one's home or homeland. Consumer culture, in fact, presents people's nostalgia as a package on the shelf that is available for purchase. The decision to buy it over the counter or to live it as real life lies in the ideology and mind-set of the people.

The markers of tradition-specific practices and motifs are picked up and recombined with entirely different context of consumer culture that makes them appear more relevant and amenable to the youth. As another illustration consider the newly founded provision of online rendering of rituals of worship and the newly founded yoga[22] schools that have mushroomed in many parts of the different cities. A Hindu believer should go to the temple, ideally, everyday or once a week, a fortnight or at least once a month. Furthermore, certain rituals can be performed only in temples with the help of pundits who are well-versed with the intricate details. Rendering such rituals online is embedded in the overall belief that performing rituals has many consequences such as fulfilment of one's wishes, negation of evil effects on one's life accruing from other people's jealousy, one's own un-*dharmic* (i.e. against the moral order) activities and bringing in all-round prosperity and happiness. Performing rituals is a part of spiritual discipline and journey; the more intricate and difficult to perform is a ritual, the more is the spiritual merit associated with it. The facility of online rituals is offered by specific temple sites, a sample from which are the following calls for online rituals or what a few websites refer to as 'long distance pujas'.

No need to be physically present.
Pujas performed by expert priests.
Pujas performed for your specific requirements.
Pictures of the ritual in progress. (http://www.indiayogi.com)

Best Hindu services to perform rituals since 2002. Dedicated team to execute poojas personally. Delivery of prasadham[23] worldwide, proof for execution almost for all services, special worships on all Hindu events of a year…. Our speciality is, every homam[24] is performed by highly qualified Hindu priest … with great care. A portion of homam is filmed and a VCD of it will be shipped along with a yantram and prasadham. (http://www.pariharam.com)

A few websites claim to send their own volunteers to perform pujas for the believers (here treated as clients or customers) to temples far and wide. One such website states:

Most other websites offering puja … in different temples, depend just on temple 'pujari' with whom they fix a financial agreement for making and sending puja…. By changing hands after hands in this way ultimately in many cases when your puja ultimately reaches temple then the man who bring your puja to the temple forget the actual purpose of your puja….

In our case, even just for a single puja in many cases our men travel even thousands of miles to make your puja authentic, proper mannered and personalized. Even they wait for several hours in the queue to go in front of the temple deities offering your puja personally with the help of main priest. Standing in front of the temple idols they pray for your desires to be fulfilled. They are less professional minded…. (http://www.kalighat.net)

The offerings are placed before deities, rituals are conducted by the pundits and the *prasadham* is shipped or sent through surface or air mail to those who had commissioned the performance. Such convenience of offering prayers in absentia and bypassing the hardship(s) of travel to and accommodation in a new village or city and all the uncertainties that come along with are availed not just by non-resident Indians who are unable to reach a temple but also many people staying inlands. Websites such as the http://www.eprarthna.com serve an additional purpose of mailing pictures of deities and *prasadham* by post to devotees registered with them. The following are a few responses from a virtual community of extremely satisfied devotees drawn from the website.

Most of our Bank employees being devotee of Lord Ganesh start their work after doing Pooja for Ganapathy which they had downloaded from eprarthana. Hats off to the team. Great effort. (name of the sender: Sumathi, India)

I am a registered user of your site "eprarthana.com". Just a few days back I received a letter from you obtaining the prasadam. I am highly grateful to you for the same & am sending this mail to thank you for the same. (name of the sender: Harish Shrupali, India)

Hi … Really very impressive … I was in India. I used to go to temple every day before I start my work. But now I am in London. Using your virtual pooja I am getting that satisfaction now ... (name of sender: Siva, London). Such a beautiful site. As we are in overseas, if we browse through the site, really feels that it brings us back to India.... (name of sender: Balasubrmaniyam Surekha, United States)

The time–space distanciation created by distinct improvisation in transformation of old ways of viewing 'visiting' temples and performing the rituals through the computer has generated a virtual community of devotees who, in a practical sense, are faceless for each other, operate through the abstract systems but connected with each other through, as they say, the 'spirit'. They share experiences and expectations through the Internet. A run-through of the comments suggests how online worship is re-embedded in new social relationships that characterize anonymous settings of modernity. This demands renewed assessment of the cultural context of religion in the present age. In the words of Herman,

> The internet is a "cultural context in its own right"[25] that bridges the distance between the devotee and the deity in new ways: the digital image is inches away in the virtual realm, its tangible referent miles away or even nonexistent. (2010: 152)

In the same vein, more youth, both in India and abroad, than ever before are involved with yoga as practitioners. Young people have much more enthusiasm and the energy to engage with yoga that a large number of yoga schools have mushroomed in the cities. In all of them, yoga is taught by trainers rather than spiritual masters much in the same way as those in gymnasiums who train young enthusiasts to perform exercises on machines and otherwise. Over time, the mental and spiritual inputs to yoga have eroded greatly and to such an extent that the scope of yoga has come to be restricted to health gain and physical well-being. Yoga schools are marketing solutions to more and more physical and emotional problems under the banner of traditional curative system founded by Indian saints and sages with deep wisdom and insight. For large number of youth, yoga (in whatever and whichever form available) is a means to connect with the wisdom and insights of sages of the yore. Many are convinced that the yoga schools are doing a great service by adapting and adopting most important aspects of yoga to the modern times for them. The yoga training session serves as, what Giddens (1991) refers to 'access point' of abstract systems in that it revolves around facework and faceless commitments. In his words, 'At access points the facework commitments that tie lay actors into trust relations ordinarily involve displays of manifest trustworthiness and integrity couples with an attitude of "business-as-usual" or unflappability'.

Disembeddedness permeates all major aspects of daily life, yet the project of modernity is not autonomous even as it is confronted by apparently unflinching ideas about, among several others, the most common example of symbolic token, that is, money. While Giddens (1990) treats money as example of symbolic token that contributes to disembedding mechanisms associated with modernity, the Indian situation provides insights that suggest people's ambivalence towards wealth. Richness is both coveted and eschewed. The ambivalence lies rooted in Indian, predominantly Hindu, tradition embodying the ways in which ideas about and practices associated with wealth *per se* are played out. Money has been an inherent part of the social life even before the precursors of modernity matured in India. The Hindu mythology is replete with prayers and chants for wealth and richness. Most of them are directed towards two major deities. The first is Kuber—the immortal, Vedic lord of gold, silver, gems and treasures of the earth—who roams around in a bejewelled, self-propelled aerial car. The second is Lakshmi—the goddess of wealth, prosperity and fortune. She is depicted as a beautiful woman with four hands of which the upper two hold a lotus flower each; of the remaining, one is in the posture of blessing the devotes while the other points downwards with several gold coins flowing out of it [for details of symbolism associated with the lotus flower, see Walker (1983)].

Following the Hindu scriptures, human life (of men) is divisible into four periods or stages (*asramas*): *brahmacharya* (the period of studentship in which he remains celibate), *grihastha* (the period in which he establishes household), *vanaprastha* (the period of intense religious practices and retirement from worldly life) and *sanyasa* (the period of renunciation of all possessions and relationships). Of these, the second, that is, the *grihastha asrama* is one in which an individual is sanctioned to accumulate and use wealth (albeit through and in legitimate ways) and simultaneously prepare himself or herself to surrender it all at the onset of the next stage in life. There is plethora of teachings on how wealth should be acquired and how it should be used but not many of them state that pursuit of wealth is inimical to ordinary Indian way of life. What they all caution is the accompaniment of vices with wealth that should be kept under control. Additionally, money is believed to camouflage deficiencies and disorder; it is most sought-after, however, primarily for its capacity to fulfil desires, provide comfort and a sense of security in, what in sociological parlance is referred to as, risk society. As an offshoot, it is constitutive of social identity, status and power. It is interesting to note alongside that between a wealthy and poor wo(man), while the former is paid honour and feted, the latter is largely trusted. There are proverbs and anecdotes that reinforce the choice. Also, it is believed that money itself should not be lusted for and trusted, for its fluid nature that it comes and goes in the hands of people of its own accord; also because it cannot buy happiness and peace that are the ultimate objectives of human life.

A general consensus found among youth on the notion of money is that it is a source of independence making them feel confident of themselves and empowered to take decisions in life; though it is not without limitations. In nearly all the interviews about money, youth spoke about the importance of money in people's lives and linked it up with how some portion of it should be used for making provisions for the poor and infusing hope in them. Youth's perception of money and its importance in their lives was found to be influenced by the overall philosophy that surrounds it as the following remarks of two informants reveal:

Money is meant to fulfil needs. It is important to move in society with respect and with one's own identity. Money does provide both of these. To this extent money is something but it is not everything in life. (19-year-old woman)
Money can change people's quality of life. It has the power to give them hope or make them depressed. Money makes for having a

comfortable life and doing all that one wants to. Some part of it should also be spent on charity and providing good life to others. (29-year-old man)

Conclusion

The urban Indian youth, belonging largely to the middle class, are cosmopolitan and global in their outlook, lifestyle and aspirations, and expectations from life. The shift in the ideology of the younger generation[26] from idealism, stronger allegiance to general welfare over individual concerns, and national pride to personal gains is conspicuous and is accompanied with contestation between the ideologies of socialism and emotional identification with the poor (which their parents refer to on many occasions) and flamboyant consumerism (which they frequently engage with). Many of them regard material prosperity, newly acquired freedom to choose commodities and realization of aspirations of consumption as clear benefits of economic liberalization in the country. The rush for newly acquired lifestyle juxtaposed with comforts' display of economic well-being and style seemingly challenges the socially integrative character of the youth community. Fashion and style spring up as crucial basis of understanding distinctions in society. Understandably, the commodities lose their utility function and assume position of signifier of personal identity that sets an individual apart from others. Virtues of humility, self-restraint and nurturance are overrun by conspicuous indulgence in consumption and display of materialist possessions. Consumer culture and renewed lifestyle are now in the stage of providing fresh profiles to the youth. The body of youth as a 'consumer community' recognizes certain limits within which the status of a person is assessed. Those who fall on either side of the subjective limits of consumption suffer from a sense of exclusion and marginalization.

The daily lives of urban Indian youth are transformed as they adapt to and adopt the elements of consumer culture.

Households and professional bodies are transformed into spaces for manifestation of consumer culture. For the youth, in operational and more practical sense, the project of modernity transforms social transactions as 'activities are successfully routinized through their recombination across time–space' (Giddens, 1991: 134). A prominent feature of consumer culture is its potential to mingle with local cultures in a way that they are largely transformed. The transformation does not, however, generate or usher in a new culture altogether but re-positions the elements of the local culture with those of consumer culture. This has at least four prominent manifestations. The first is the rise of local consumer culture that accommodates some elements of both local and consumer culture and dispenses with a few others. In the process, 'original' contexts in which elements of local and consumer cultures obtained distinctiveness are transformed too, which disembeds them and relocates them in new contexts. The second is the standardization of social activities and the inescapable intrusion of abstract systems into all critical aspects of modern life which largely erodes the 'original sentiment' of the local cultural practices that are getting recombined with global consumer culture. This is a major adaptation that the process of recombination calls for. The third is the operation of global consumer culture simultaneously at multiple levels as Smith (1990: 176) puts it succinctly,

> … as a cornucopia of standardized commodities, as a patchwork of a denationalized ethnic or folk motifs, a service of generalized human values and interests, as a uniform, 'scientific' discourse of meaning, and finally as the inter-dependent system of communication which forms the material base for all other components and travels.

The fourth is the standardization of social activities and the inescapable intrusion of abstract systems into all critical aspects of modern life. Youth tend to see meaning in relationships in terms of what they get and what they give out in turn. As the grip of consumer culture tightens, youth feel distanced from their kin group, in many cases from parents and siblings, even as friends with similar consumption patterns gain importance. Some of them admitted that such 'consumerism-based relationships' are temporary but they nurtured them because they provided meaning in their lives.

Disembedding is, in effect, an inevitable consequence of modernity operating as a part of dialectic with re-embedding relocates youth's identity[27] as they interrogate tradition and struggle to stabilize themselves in new social order that is increasingly acquiring a global character. To this extent, Giddens's projection of disembeddedness in particular and modernity in general is illustrative of urban youth's situation in India, however, not uncritically. Kaspersen (1995: 169) writes:

> His analysis of self-identity, life-political choices, and the transformation of intimacy does not specify the constraining aspect of structures.... Some actors might have more resources, with more opportunities as a consequence. The well educated doctor can, better than a single mother with three kids, choose to live a healthy life. By possessing a higher level of cultural and economic capital, the doctor has easier access to high-quality organic food, a healthy house, a better job, etc.

The urban youth in India experience and deal with differential conditions of disembeddedness that derive from the nature and level of constraints that structures impose. It is a herculean task to present different kinds of disembeddedness in India more so because of the multiplicity of cultural and social conditions that individuals negotiate with. It is, however, appropriate to obtain an overall understanding of disembeddedness in the framework of similar social and cultural situations within which modernity and consumer culture are articulated and individuals create their identities.

Acknowledgement

I am grateful to Professor Lars Bo Kaspersen for going through this chapter with much care and interest and to William Mazzarella for a painstaking review and critical inputs. I have benefitted greatly from their insightful comments. Usual disclaimer applies. I extend my gratitude to the University Grants Commission (UGC), New Delhi as well for funding the project on which the present chapter is based.

Notes

1. The United Nations General Assembly uses the term 'youth' to include those persons between the ages of 15 and 24 years (available at www.un.org.youth accessed on 15 July 2009). In India, however, much like several countries in global south, people in the age group of 15–35 are categorized as youth by the Ministry of Youth Affairs and Sports, Government of India (available at http://yas.nic.in, accessed on 14 February 2012) for which reason, people in this age bracket are considered as youth in this chapter.

2. Marx refers to this as 'commodity fetishism'. In being related to the satisfaction of needs, use value of a commodity serves as an expression of the relationship between a person's need and object satisfaction. The exchange value, however, serves as an expression of rate and ratio at which a commodity gets exchanged with another. In monetized societies, this exchange gets mediated by money, and presents itself in the form of price of the commodity. Marx explains that since a commodity enfolds human labour in production, relation between different commodities is, in effect, a relation between different acts of human labour. He refers to the social relation between men themselves that finds expression in relations between things as 'fetishism'. Marxian perspective employs fetishism as a heuristic concept to explain the role that commodities play in the domain of consumption.

3. In weberian writings, 'disenchantment' refers to a world in which magical and/or supernatural element(s) find no place. Disenchantment arises from rationalization of society.

4. 'Intellectualized culture' is one in which religion does not serve to provide meaning to people's lives and does not foster solidarity among them. This happens when culture denigrates religion and is itself denigrated by it.

5. Roots of consumer culture are traced to eighteenth century industrialization in England.

6. So long as industrialism is not viewed solely as an institution.

7. The condition making articulation of social relation possible across space–time is explained by Giddens (1991) as 'separation of space and time'. Pre-modern modes of reckoning time–space and the tendency

to keep them together closely are given up in favour of formal methods of calculating time and ordering of space in the modern era. There is 'distancing' or separatedness of time from space making articulation of social relations possible across space–time.

8. Development of disembedding mechanism refers to the 'lifting out' of the social activity from specific, local contexts and their recombination across indefinite time–space distances.

9. By 'reflexivity', Giddens (1991) refers to the reworking of the social activity and material relations to new-age information and knowledge. This leads to major shift in social life from former principles and practices governed by tradition to those governed by modern information and knowledge.

10. Money as a form of symbolic token, for example, brackets time (since it is a means of credit) and space (since its standardized value makes transactions between spatially separated individuals possible).

11. Giddens clarifies that expert systems could well be in the form of both technological expertise, for example, banking and social relations and intimacies of the self. This implies that doctors, engineers and other specialists are crucial to expert systems of modernity.

12. Here the student has used the word 'man' to mean people in a general sense.

13. Bourdieu (1984) explains how commodities serve to mark differences and distinction among people in society.

14. Youth use the term 'coolness' to refer to a combination of stylish, social adeptness and informality. A cool person has all of these and is with no cares.

15. The fact is that there has been a significant bulge in the number of such trips with more and more people struggling to vacation abroad. The preferred destinations for those who can afford are in the United States while looking at Dubai, Malaysia and Thailand.

16. Youth use the word 'chill' to mean relax, keep away from cares and concerns and enjoy the given moment.

17. Other heads of expenditure are: accessories: 18.3 per cent; entertainment: 13.9 per cent; electronic goods: 17 per cent; food: 14.7 per cent; cosmetics: 5.2 per cent.

18. About 32.52 per cent youth, however, said that they would buy branded items in any case even while 24.27 per cent youth were indifferent between branded and unbranded look-alikes.

19. I could not find similar abbreviation for *bhaiyas* trying to be modern.

20. Percentage of youth who say that they are increasingly becoming fashion conscious and tend to buy only those commodities that are in style is 59.05 per cent.

21. Stores such as Archies Galleries introduce new range of products and target sales of ₹7 crore on such occasions. See Das in the *Hindu Business Line*, 10 February 2007, e-paper.
22. Yoga is the centrepiece of physical and mental discipline aimed at attaining a state of spiritual insight and peace. The term 'yoga' is derived from the root word *yuj* which literally means 'yoke' or the 'act of harnessing' referring to control over negative emotions (anger, jealousy, disgust, etc.), excessive excitement, and mood disturbances, distractions, fickle, maddens that would deter the mental condition of tranquillity. Put positively it means that yoga is geared to develop a sense of self-determination, sharp focus and awaken and sensitize the mind to transcend daily battles and concerns for material things embroiled in mundane things.
23. *Prasadham* refers to the remains of a puja, often treated as blessings from the god(s).
24. Homam is the form of worshipping a particular god by invoking fire (which is one among the five basic elements of which the entire universe is made; other elements in this category are: earth, air, water and ether).
25. Herman indicates that the expression 'cultural context in its own right' is borrowed from Smith (1995: 46).
26. Especially of the middle class since it constitutes the largest section of society.
27. Inasmuch as it relocates the identity of people in different age groups.

References

Barber, B. 1995. All economies are 'embedded': The career of a concept and beyond. *Social Research, 62*(2), 388–413.

Basi, Tina J.K. 2009. *Women, Identity and India's Call Centre Industry.* London and New York: Routledge.

Beckert, J. 2007. The great transformation of embeddedness: Karl Polanyi and the new economic sociology. MPIfG Discussion Paper 07/1.

Beilharz, P. 2009. *Socialism and Modernity.* Minneapolis and London: University of Minnesota Press.

Berman, M. 1983. *All That Is Solid Melts into Air: The Experience of Modernity.* London: Verso.

Bijapurkar, R. 2007. *We Are Like That Only: Understanding the Logic of Consumer India.* New Delhi: Penguin.

Block, F. 2003. Karl Polanyi and the writing of the great transformation. *Theory and Society*, *32*(3): 275–306.

Bourdieu, P. 1963. *Travail et Travailleurs en Algérie: Etude Sociologique.* Paris: Mouton.

————. 1984. *Distinction: A Social Critique if the Judgement of Taste* (translated by Richard Nice). Cambridge: Harvard University Press.

Campbell, C. 1987. *The Romantic Ethic and the Spirit of Modern Consumerism.* Oxford: Blackwell.

Chatterjee, P. 1993. *The Nation and Its Fragments: Colonial and Postcolonial Histories.* Princeton University Press.

Das, D. 2007. Cos gearing up for valentine's sales. *The Hindu Business Line*, 10 February (e-paper http://www.thehindubusinessline.com, accessed on 24 November 2008).

DeSouza, P.R., Kumar, S. & Shastri, S. 2009. *Indian Youth in a Transforming World: Attitudes and Perceptions.* New Delhi: SAGE.

Fehér, F. & Heller, A. 1983. From red to green. *Telos*, *59*, 35–44.

Giddens, A. 1990. *The Consequences of Modernity.* Stanford: Stanford University Press.

————. 1991. *Modernity and Self-Identity: Self and Society in the Late Modern Age.* Cambridge: Polity Press.

Goodman, D.J. & Cohen, M. 2004. *Consumer Culture: A Reference Handbook.* Santa Barbara: ABC-CLIO.

Granovetter, M. 1985. Economic action and social structure: The problem of embeddedness. *Journal of Sociology*, *91*(3), 481–510.

Herman, P. 2010. Seeing the divine through windows: Online darshan and virtual religious experience. *Online-Heidelberg Journal of religion on the Internet*, *4*(1), 151–178.

Insiya, I. 2009. No worries for Youngistan. *The Times of India*, 5 July.

Jenkins, R. 1996. *Social Identity.* London: Routledge.

Kaspersen, L. Bo. 1995 (trans. 2000). *Anthony Giddens: An Introduction to a Social Theorist.* Oxford and Massachusetts: Blackwell.

Marcuse, H. 1986. *One Dimensional Man.* London: Ark.

Mathur, N. 2007. *Consumerism. Alternative Economic Survey: India.* New Delhi: Daanish Books.

————. 2010. Shopping malls, credit cards and global brands: Consumer culture style of India's new middle class. *South Asian Research*, *30*(3), 211–231.

Nayar, P.K. 2009. *Packaging Life: Cultures of the Everyday.* New Delhi: SAGE.

Polanyi, K. 2001. *The Great Transformation: The Political and Economic Origins of Our Time*, 2nd edition. Boston: Beacon Press.

Ritzer, G. 2007. *The Globalization of Nothing 2.* Thousand Oaks: Pine Forge Press.

Seidman, S. 1983. Modernity, meaning, and cultural pessimism in Max Weber. *Sociological Analysis*, *44*(4), 267–278.

Shilling, C. & Mellor, P.A. 1998. Durkheim, morality and modernity: Collective effervescence, homo duplex and the sources of moral action. *The British Journal of Sociology*, *49*(2), 193–209.

Shukla, R. 2010. *How India Earns, Spends and Saves: Unmasking the Real India.* New Delhi: SAGE.

Sinha, P. 2008. Indian fashion needs a new consumption code. *Economic Times.* 1 April.

Smith, A. 1990. Towards a global culture. In M. Featherstone (ed.), *Global Culture: Nationalism, Globalization and Modernity*, pp. 171–192. London: SAGE.

Smith, H.D. 1995. Impact of 'God Posters' on Hindus and their Devotional Tradition. In L.A. Babb & S.S. Wadley (eds), *Media and Transformation of Religion in South Asia*, pp. 24–50. New Delhi: Motilal Banrsidass.

Smith, T. 1993. *Making the Modern: Industry, Art and Design in America.* Chicago: University of Chicago Press.

Walker, B. 1983. *Hindu World: An Encyclopedic Survey of Hinduism.* New Delhi: Munshiram Manoharlal.

Wood, E.M. 1997. Modernity, postmodernity or capitalism? *Review of International Political Economy*, *4*(3), 539–560.

Zukin, S. & DiMaggio, P. 1990. Introduction. In P. DiMaggio & S. Zukin (eds), *Structure of capital: The Social Organization of the Economy*, pp. 1–36. Cambridge: Cambridge University Press.

http://www.eprarthna.com, accessed on 21 October 2011.

http://www.indiayogi.com, accessed on 21 October 2011.

http://www.kalighat.net, accessed on 21 October 2011.

http://www.pariharam.com, accessed on 21 October 2011.

5

Imagining Identity in the Age of Internet and Communication Technologies

Robert Rattle

Introduction

Consumer culture has emerged as a defining feature through the twentieth and into the twenty-first century. The rapid diffusion of communication technologies has enabled consumer culture to influence a diversity of people, places and practices with rich opportunities and themes to define and construct identity. At the same time, Internet and communication technologies offer a wealth of different opportunities to express identity, and many of the inherent features of Internet and communication technologies make them contrary to many of the underlying values and trajectories consumer culture has manifest. This has established a dynamic state in which 'consumer' culture is transforming towards more fluid and virtual expressions of identity while shifting away from materialism and individualism and, indeed, potentially even consumerism.

This chapter considers the role of Internet and communication technologies in consumer culture and identity formation. It will begin with an overview of the various outlets enabled by Internet and communication technologies for imagining identity in the consumer culture, and how these reinforce prevailing themes and trajectories. It will then review some of the trends in consumer culture and identity formation manifest through Internet and communication technologies, consider some paradoxes of the more dominant trends and discuss the role Internet and communication technologies perform in transforming dominant themes or introducing new trajectories of consumer culture and identity formation.

Internet and Communication Technologies and Consumer Culture

Identity formation is an important social process that helps us define our individuality and is closely linked with our values. Internet and communication technologies have rapidly evolved to satisfy consumer culture and strengthen traditional themes of identity formation through new media by unleashing a torrent of opportunities and strengthening prevailing value structures. Materialism has performed and continues to perform an important role in consumer identities. Materialism has served as an important outlet for increasing individualism and individual self-expression (Baudrillard, 1988; Klein, 2000; Penaloza, 2001). Advertising, marketing, branding and promotional messages help fuel materialism and have become fundamental to identity formation through the growth of material artefacts.

At the production end of consumer culture, Internet and communication technologies unlock and expose new opportunities for marketing and advertising, provide a rapidly expanding arsenal of tools and processes to advance prevailing material values, and supply an ever growing variety of means to access the consumption of goods and services available through the (expanding and redefined) global market space. At the consumption end, Internet and communication technologies facilitate access to a new universe of opportunities to satisfy the consumer culture: online shopping, access to information that can be used to imagine identity through trends, fashions and new outlets, and a vast universe of personal, professional and social contacts that can be used to enhance and express identity.

Internet and communication technologies open a global world of material artefacts, instantly accessible and readily available. Enormous pass through facilities—massive airport hubs dedicated to the global transport of e-goods—enable the instant gratification and satisfaction of consumer purchases. Internet and communication technologies are magnifying and amplifying the material opportunities for identity formation and the satisfaction of accommodating demands in an efficient, increasingly convenient and effortless manner. For example, multiple devices that serve the same function, such as a computer that allows portability, one for the kitchen, one for the family room and one for personal use are adopted to manage across an individuals' multiple domain roles and needs for identity (Ropke, 2001). Conflicts between family members for their use of products, services and spaces are resolved by the expansion of Internet and communication technology products for each family member, in some cases reflecting a right of passage. Families, for instance, often had a single telephone when land lines were prominent. Today, each member of the family may have their own mobile telephone and as well as a land-based phone line. These phones are typically replaced on very short cycles with newer varieties and options, such as the smartphone or iPad, with expanded features and functions. The individual personalization of devices—from peripherals to applications—also lends to the identity formation process.

Internet and communication technology devices and their ability for self-expression and identity formation have come to form, whether through strategic marketing or genuine desires, an important sense of identity in themselves. This may be derived from the purchase of new models, multiple varieties of the same device, regular upgrading and stylizing devices to express certain fads, fashions and experiences. The short-life expectancy of many of these devices requires a constant upgrading for the expression of identity. Interest in new devices and applications, and an expanding arsenal of opportunities for which consumers can exploit their services help drive the renewal process. In the electronics world, devices—and the identities associated with them—become antiquated after as little as 18 months, and many are discarded long before this time to make way for the most updated, popular, interoperable, fashionable and advanced versions, along with the identities they represent or could be imagined.

Despite the challenges that come with incorporating the adoption of a new technology, once adopted, they form an integral component of an indispensable set of services and products that help define and develop identity. This process of technological lock-in reflects a portion of the more general expansion and deepening of commodification processes. It should come as no surprise that both absolute spending on and the proportion of household expenditure directed at Internet and communication technologies have increased (Statistics Canada, 2006). However, the depth of commodification is revealed only once one realises that this spending pattern occurred during a period when prices for Internet and communication technology products and services tumbled, while computing power exploded. The importance of this trend will be explored briefly in the following section.

Internet and communication technologies also generate a new level of commodification in identity formation. Unpacking and expanding upon the role of Internet and communication technologies in resolving domain conflicts and contributing to identity formation, their enormous growth originates from combinations of habituation, technological lock-in, planned obsolescence and creative destruction, group association, symbolism, a perceived level of time savings, multi-tasking and efficiencies and multiple varieties of the same devices to serve different time and place settings. The appeal of Internet and communication technologies has generated a self-reinforcing adoptive process. Internet and communication technologies contribute to the commodification process at the individual level to produce many effects now apparent: instant gratification, excessive entitlement and material profligacy.

Identity formation through Internet and communication technologies can be incredibly material intensive. Internet and communication technologies enable commodification and the material through the optimization, induction, supplementation and creation of new products, services and processes, and may be offset through substitution and optimization (Rattle, 2010). However, optimization functions more to enable commodification through the rebound effect than it does to offset commodification (Ayres, 2002; Heinonen et al., 2001; Heiskanen and Jalas, 2000, 2003; Jevons, 1866; Mills, 2000; Saunders, 1992). Each of these can satisfy certain imaginings of identity.

Instant gratification, for instance, is widely apparent across the entertainment sector, where music, videos, movies, books and photographs may be created, downloaded, manipulated, stored, shared and viewed in the blink of an eye. These options enable new, emerging, novel and important outlets for identity formation. So too do their processes, these themes and trajectories will be further discussed in later sections. E-commerce and selling and reselling website hubs facilitated by electronic cash and other transaction options enable this world of instant gratification and excessive entitlement for both consumers and retailers alike, buyers and sellers, where any product can be delivered door-to-door by 747's traversing massive pass-through facilities—dedicated airport hubs—constructed exclusively to accommodate the explosive growth of Internet and communication technology–induced trade (Murphy, 2000).

While this represents the more traditional modes of consumer identity formation from advanced communication devices, Internet and communication technologies also accelerate these conventional modes of identity formation. No longer are consumer identities restricted to local spaces. Internet and communication technologies offer the global space of possibilities as a forum for both expression and association of identity. It is from this perspective that Internet and communication technologies offer a significant boost to how people imagine identity in consumer culture.

Imagining Modernity and Identity through Internet and Communication Technologies

While the new communication technologies offer enhanced outlets for traditional consumer culture, they also accelerate and deepen the processes that lend themselves to the consumer culture. As productive forces separated craftsmanship and artistry from the creation of identity, a monied economy replaced the production of individual identity and expanded the reach of individual self-identity formation.

Internet and communication technologies have accelerated that monied economy and continue to transform it in ways that strengthen consumer culture through the focus of the monied economy on growth and materialism. While Internet and communication technologies expand the opportunities for complex trades throughout the global marketplace, their roles in intensifying the treadmill of growth (Schnaiberg, 1980) and the materialism of consumer culture can be quite profound (Rattle, 2010).

Internet and communication technologies enable direct access to financial trading, and income and revenue generating mechanisms previously unimagined for consumers. Through these outlets, millions of individuals make decisions to maximize profits from complex market trades which can then serve the material needs of identity. Their decisions generate transactions that slosh around in the electronic financial ethernet—all weighted by the incredible amount of opined and scripted information that increasingly forms the backbone of consumer identity.

At the same time, easier access to liquidity has been accommodated to stimulate economic growth and satisfy the material needs of more traditional identity formation themes. As new money is created faster than actual goods and services circulating in the economy, the value of money declines—it requires more fiat currency to equal the same value of a good or service (Daly and Cobb, 1994; Hoogendijk, 1993; Schnaiberg, 1980). The inevitable result is the relentless pressure for consumers to grow their incomes to maintain the material needs of identity formation. This growth compels economic expansion and commodification, and collectively generates an incredibly powerful normalizing growth force (Clark, 1995; United Nations, 1998).

Complex computer algorithms and communication protocols automate these practices down to the millisecond, where tiny fractions of time set in motion large pools of financial transactions. Investment firms and financial agencies operate in this new realm of faster, bigger and swifter triggers and volumes. Transaction and edging out huge profits in tiny fractions of time have become the focus. Fundamentals need not apply. Such imaginings of identity in consumer culture could not be possible without the electronic autopilot modes Internet and communication technologies enable. Internet and communication technologies have moved beyond craft and market logic where identity formation rested on consumer culture themes linked with the individual and group association. They have shifted the trajectories of consumer culture into the dark realm of chrematistics represented by bits and bytes as a metaphor for the individual and group associations of identity formation.

High-frequency trading is the practice of using computerized trading strategies characterized by unusually short position-holding periods. These strategies are identified by computer programs that analyze market data to exploit trading opportunities that may exist for mere fractions of a second to a couple hours. Traders that employ high-frequency trading compete on the basis of speed, and involve extraordinarily expensive investments in computers and programming. In so doing, the focus is on profits and investments in technology. The process inverts the long standing investment principles of buy and hold for value. High frequency trading has been implicated for injecting considerable volatility into the markets, mostly due to the limited to non-existent regulation placed on these traders that enables them to drive down values by rapidly withdrawing considerable amounts of liquidity from capital markets in very short order. As though to drive home the speeds and separation that complex high-speed trading has generated, recent advances now seek to overcome relativistic barriers where trading speeds exceed the 500 microsecond threshold (Wissner-Gross and Freer, 2010). At

these speeds, light propagation between geographically separated trading exchanges becomes relevant. Relativistic statistical
arbitrage, by altering the spatial distance data must travel before
a decision can be made, enables the trading of hedge funds in
which portfolios of hundreds of securities are monitored and
traded simultaneously across transcontinental communications
networks between exchanges where the time for data transmission—typically about 50 milliseconds—is longer than for computer algorithms to execute the trade. Relativistic statistical
arbitrage using complex computer algorithms and telecommuni-
cations may be possible with spatially optimal trading locations
around the planet located to minimize these relativistic delays.
Similarly, dark liquidity, another financial trading mechanism,
could not exist without the Internet and communication technologies that make them possible. Dark liquidity pools are market
liquidity that cannot be seen by other potential market participants for which its existence is accounted for in a manner that
retroactively changes the actions or status of the actions committed or relationships that existed prior to the trade.

These practices and tools could not exist without modern
Internet and communication technology tools, processes and
adaptations. The aforementioned text represents only a small
sample of the trading opportunities and financial instruments
unleashed by Internet and communication technologies, and
new adaptations and adoptions will undoubtedly be developed.
Consumers connected to Internet and communication technologies both directly and indirectly contribute to these activities
through their activities manifest through the social tapestry that
affects the very fibre of consumer culture and identity formation.

If we take as a general definition of commodification the economic selection pressures that drive and preference profit seeking
in the investment of resources, and the systematic discounting of
nonmarket goods and services (Manno, 2010), it becomes apparent that the efficient allocation of resources in financial markets
is a key to this selection pressure. The application and adaptations of Internet and communication technologies to global
financial transactions reveal a potent and deeply profound force
driving commodification for the consumption and construction

of the modern consumer identity. The ever more efficient transactions of abstract wealth through the algorithmic application of
computer programs operating across continents in the blink of
an eye to squeeze profits out of global markets represents what
could only be described as the pinnacle of commodification—
supracommodification. The process is not concerned with social
or ecological impacts, but merely the profit is derived from the
manipulation of massive pools of abstract wealth in tiny fractions
of a second. Subsequently, the results both fuel and provide outlets for consumer culture and re-imagining identity. Internet and
communication technologies have thus come to be an important
determinant in how consumers view identity by laying down
and cementing the values and structures that advance consumer
culture—competition, individualism and growth.

These mechanisms and processes support, reinforce and sub-
stantiate values that characterize consumer culture in both direct
and indirect ways. However, the evolution of these practices
that have given rise to the consumer ethic, growth economics
and commodification germinated and thrived under hierarchical structures. Internet and communication technologies invert
those structures, and it is from this perspective that Internet and
communication technologies may be a key ingredient transforming the trajectories, and evolving new themes, of consumer
culture and how people now imagine identity.

New and Evolving Ways to Satisfy Consumer Culture and Identity

Internet and communication technologies also satisfy consumer
culture through a variety of new and emerging mechanisms and
processes. They enable the creation and expression of identity
through new processes and outlets—websites, blog sites, social
media to volunteerism, microlending and crowdsourcing. Consumers can now also form and express identities in online games,
mutlimedia platforms such as YouTube videos, and they can
associate these and different identities with a much expanded

variety of actors. In so doing, consumer identity is expanding into both the material and virtual.

In many ways, Internet and communication technologies facilitate consumer identity formation based on a competitive process—the number of website hits, friends on Facebook, revenues generated through advertising or the latest and newest consumer trophies acquired through the global marketplace. New to these processes are the (initially) low access costs to employ the technologies for identity formation. As a result of the distributive nature of Internet and communication technologies, access is more egalitarian and open, where historical, material or cost barriers have been reduced. The result is a much more fluid and adaptable approach to imagining and redefining identity in consumer culture.

Conversely, many of the new and emerging ways to satisfy consumer culture and identity formation through Internet and communication technologies are collaborative and cooperative. This is in contrast to the formation of consumer culture that has been premised to a large extent on a competitive and individual focused set of values.

The empowering nature of Internet and communication technologies and their increasing ubiquity have generated a flood of new applications, innovative adaptations and creative ways of adopting the technologies. Moreover, as a result of the commodification for and by Internet and communication technologies, there has been enormous motivation to expand them to new users. ICT4D is the growth of Internet and communication technologies for developmental purposes, an attempt to raise the living standards of billions of potential consumers and coax them into the global economy. Still closely aligned with the material, these strategies view identity formation in consumer culture equivalent to economic growth. Across and between nations, there has been a rise in the distribution of free and very low cost computers. National goals have been established to ensure universal broadband access, and national programmes are being rolled out to increase the number of people online (Department of Business Innovation and Skills, 2010). Although in many cases the motivation for these approaches is to reinforce material consumer culture and contribute to formal measures of economic performance, they do ensure the increasingly diverse penetration of Internet and communication technologies and the release of their distributive empowerment (Race Online, 2010). The contagion of declaring the Internet as a basic right in many countries and the creeping potential that the Internet will shortly be declared a fundamental human right demonstrate the importance people around the world attribute to this tool (BBC, 2010). As the events in Egypt unfolded in February 2011, the Human Rights Defenders Mechanisms issued a statement through the United Nations High Commissioner for Human Rights expressing alarm 'at increasing limitations on the right to freedom of expression and information imposed by Governments actively seeking to suppress the rising number of voices who wish to be heard' and that they are 'disturbed at the major disruptions in communication networks and transmissions of news so essential to the modern world' (Human Rights Defenders Mechanisms, 2011). In this we see new themes of association in consumer culture and identity formation emerging which will be discussed here.

While many formal networks and actions have been undertaken at global, continental, national and subnational levels, it is, in many cases, the informal and private initiatives that have proven most remarkable. Facebook, a social networking website, began in 2004. By 2010, the financial market valued this initiative at $50 billion, and the number of users had grown to over 500 million (Facebook, no date). Facebook and numerous other social media tools including Twitter, for example, have been used by millions of users to connect to others, build relationships, share their passions and interests and re-construct identities. YouTube, another distributive media tool, allows almost anyone—with the necessary interface tools and skills of course—to both make and instantly publish videos and movies. It is a free platform that enables the creativity, and interactions, of millions of users daily, forming, redefining and expressing identities.

There is also a dramatic rise in open access to a diverse community of information, and open data from government departments and agencies around the world. A tremendous increase in community portals is helping disenfranchised, poor, developing and wealthy communities alike increase the opportunities for all citizens to engage in the Internet and its services. Community informatics—the 'investigation and practice concerned with principles and norms related to information and communication technology (ICT) with a focus on the personal, social, cultural or economic development of, within and by communities' —is blossoming around the world. These platforms and opportunities are opening vast repositories of new and adaptable ways in which people might imagine modernity and identity in the consumer culture.

New tools and applications are continuously being developed to help create, manipulate, assess, share, communicate and respond to data and information. Tools such as real-time analytics—the real-time analysis and reporting of data—enable a vast repertoire of opportunities.

Practices such as crowdsourcing, micro-volunteering and micro-credit are facilitated through Internet and communication technologies to share the informational, technological, social, economic and cultural burdens of all types of work while forming online and physical identities. These practices are leading to more community-based or participatory design and the shared compiling and analyses of data to solve complex problems and to nurture relevant and fresh ideas. In turn, these fluid and evolving opportunities act as a spring board for new ways to imagine and define identity. Spreading across the Internet and connected by the growing collection of tools, Internet and communication technologies throw wide open the potentials and realities of free software (wherever a commodified version exists, several free versions will also be available), free operating systems, free publishing and free photographic, video, music and entertainment platforms for sharing, storing, and manipulating data and information and for connecting communities, sharing ideas and information and cross fertilizing ideas.

Despite the apparent virtualization these tools may and do manifest, they may and do also contribute to commodification and the material in consumer culture. The tools that nurture these informational activities, connections and relationships are deeply embedded in the commodification and growth process through their physical artefacts, the motivation to have the latest and newest devices with their expanded functionalities, and the messages and signals they transmit—both subtle and overt—that support and intensify material consumer culture. Indeed, the events in Egypt in February 2011 are a direct response to continental dissent ongoing from the lack of economic growth, and the various global debt crises continue to be couched in the context of economic recession. Internet and communication technologies have expanded to the virtual realm new and constantly emerging themes of identity formation in consumer culture, yet remain securely anchored in the material. In other words, both the virtual and the material remain profoundly and firmly connected in consumer culture.

In this manner, these platforms only weakly severe the bonds between consumer culture and the material in identity formation. Indeed, they may in fact expand the material desires of identity formation through such practices and mechanisms as the purchase of the tools, exposure to vastly expanded sets of communities, communications of many more advertising messages and a growing set of opportunities for generating revenues. On the surface, the new themes and trajectories that Internet and communication technologies advance represent a curious echo to conventional themes of identity formation. Below the surface, however, may be poised a very different account.

Consumer Culture and Internet and Communication Technologies: The Joneses Paradox

Through the application of Internet and communication technologies, consumer culture and identity formation is shifting to new outlets and processes, revealing new and emerging themes. One of these is the perceived shift from the material to the virtual. Another is the shift from the individual to the group. While there are other trends evident, it is instructive to consider these two. Although these are acutely related, in terms of consumer culture, the latter may be more compelling as it posits a transformation to the very basis of what substantiates consumer culture and, increasingly, how identity is being expressed.

Consumer culture has evolved in an environment that covets competition, individualism, growth, greed and hierarchy. Amplified and reinforced with the advance of a monetary economy, class social structure and growth-biased civilization (Mead, 1963; Naiman, 1997), consumer culture exploited these traits and secured a firm grasp on identity formation. Consumer culture came to adopt and adapt these developments, exploiting the increasingly individual, material and competitive nature of society to define and re-define identity. Internet and communication technologies are transforming that environment to one in which distributive power sharing, cooperation, collaboration and egalitarianism are becoming more common. This posits a radical transformation to the form and function of consumer culture, and how people imagine modernity and identity in consumer culture.

Simultaneously, Internet and communication technologies have created a rapid, almost instantaneous, global movement of data and information, laying the groundwork for a globally connected consumer culture. Identity is becoming caught in the updrafts of these global communication ebbs and flows, as information sloshes into and out of the material. Livingston (1994) describes how other species groupings, a flock of birds or school of fish for example, have an innate ability to communicate seemingly effortlessly and instantaneously. 'The flashing angles, turns, slants, starts and stops are too swift, too fine-tuned—indeed, too erratic—to be executed by the synchronized separate movements of hundreds of individuals' (Livingston, 1994: 106). The movements of these groupings can only be explained as a form of group consciousness. Naturalists, Livingston argues, are unable to imagine this higher level beyond the individual because material-driven, technologically anchored societies are so ingrained in the cultural baggage of individualism, the prosthetic ideology of technology and the mechanistic reductionism of modern science. The synchronous movements, speed and extraordinary maneuverability—their 'oneness'—can only be marvelled at.

Could Internet and communication technologies generate a similar 'group-consciousness' affecting consumer culture and how people imagine modernity and a renewed sense of identity? Have Internet and communication technologies given birth to an emerging global consumer culture capable of functioning not as a mere aggregation of individual consumers each imagining, defining, constructing and re-constructing identity, but as a self-aware, globally synchronized consumer culture?

This phenomenon can be seen in the financial sector, where Internet and communication technologies can trigger rapidly cascading effects that ripple around the globe in mere seconds revealing debt 'crises', housing bubbles or market failures. It can be witnessed in social media, where comments made can be instantly transmitted from a single user to enormous groups of users (or vice versa), generating followers, fashions or rebuttals that define and redefine identities. The phenomenon can be detected in discussions of privacy, security, open data or the actions of large scale gatherings, protests and revolutions from Wikileaks to the Arab Spring to the Occupy movements. It can also be observed in larger trends such as micro-volunteering, micro-lending, open access and multimedia platforms where new themes and manifestations of consumer culture are emerging and consumers are redefining identity. In all these situations, real tangible developments occur in the material world that affect consumers and influence identity.

Conversely, might the individual consumer become immersed in a sea of competing individuals, making the construction and deconstruction and reconstruction of identity an increasingly competitive battle? Despite the cooperative nature of many of these platforms, their outward expressions remain largely confined to the social environments in which consumer culture emerged—competition, individualism and hierarchies, for instance.

This has two possible implications. The first is that competition and thus the outlets for which consumers may define and create identity, will strengthen. This might suggest that Internet and communication technologies will enhance certain prevailing themes, such as the material as they serve to satisfy the role of markets in identity formation. The result would be a layering of a cooperative sharing egalitarian model onto the competitive global market model that must grow to survive and seek to commodify ever greater resources and processes in the production of identity. However, using the idea of getting ahead of the Joneses as a metaphor for growth economics leading to the processes of commodification in identity formation and renewal, the emerging distributed egalitarian networks of Internet and communication technologies may generate a message internally contradictory to historical processes of identity formation that sought material accumulation to satisfy identity.

That suggests a second implication: the creation of identity may become immersed in a 'cloud' of highly data intensive computational platforms. New themes of consumer culture may emerge in which identity becomes enmeshed in a haze of swift, erratic, unpredictable complex relationships that form a global group consciousness, modifying and correcting frequently and swiftly. New themes such as the immaterial may displace the focus of consumer identity on the individual and material as relationships, communities and connections come to more strongly define identity.

Emerging are platforms and applications that reflect distributed egalitarianism, sharing and cooperation—properties that militate against the Joneses getting ahead. Could these be grafted onto a hierarchical economic paradigm and set of values that advocate competition, growth, and wealth accumulation—properties that encourage the Joneses to get ahead—as a central theme of identity formation? This is the twenty-first century Joneses Paradox.

Despite the proliferation of distributed cooperative networks, they continue to be fused onto the old competitive hierarchical structures intended for continued economic growth and commodification, and service identity in this manner. How will identity formation react to a sharing cooperative global village that operates with competitive wealth accumulating tools that seek commodification for defining identity in consumer culture? Will the basis of consumer culture be redefined by these emerging platforms and applications, challenging existing values and institutions and, indeed, consumer culture as Internet and communication technologies contribute to a sense of renewed identity?

Conclusion

Many different themes and trajectories of consumer culture have contributed to identity formation. Of these, both the material and the individual have performed important roles. Internet and communication technologies both enhance and dissolve these, lending credibility to new themes that focus on the virtual, immaterial and relational as well as the group association themes of identity formation.

Out of this we see emerging new and evolving themes of identity formation. In particular, there is cross-fertilization and deepening of the relationships between the material and the immaterial means of identity formation. While in some cases (such as social media or gaming) there is an emerging trend towards the virtualization of identity formation, it bears mentioning that there remains little evidence for the virtualization of the production and consumption of consumer identity formation. The virtualization trend has only distanced and shaded materialism (Princen, 1997) in some cases, augmented or enhanced materialism in others.

Moreover, the basic values of consumer culture remain, if not enhanced. Blog sites, online presence and social connections emphasize in many respects competition—be the first with the connections, toys, technologies, compete for the most social connections, hits on your website, comments on the blog sites, etc. The result may be a sanitized version of consumerism and identity production—easier, simpler, more convenient, technologically mediated and 'cleaner' for all intents and purposes, yet at the same time, far more resource intensive and physically manifested through people, communities, cultures and distant places.

There seems now to be emerging, a greater emphasis on the process outcomes of identity formation—the 'how' rather than 'what'; the relationships rather than the physical manifestations that facilitate those relationships. But there should be no illusions—this virtualization has very material aspects to it, and in this manner, reinforces many of the traditional forms of identity formation in consumer culture. However, the material is becoming less the objective and more the means in identity formation.

This suggests a shift towards building communities, relations and networks rather than creating identity through individualism. But it is more than group associations, a form of group consciousness. It is from this perspective that new themes and trajectories of consumer culture and identity formation may be emerging and to which a Joneses Paradox is emerging.

Internet and communication technologies perform key roles in defining consumer culture and identity—from the deeply value laden anchor of the material to the superficial materialism of conspicuous consumption. On the other hand, the same technologies have unleashed a powerful set of tools and practices, processes that are redefining how the consumer can identify with their cultures and the world around them. However, paradoxically, this latter evolution is conflicting with the former in the fundamental roles and states in which consumers can inhabit physical and consumer space.

Through the mediating technologies of communications, consumer culture has established a firm and perhaps simultaneously, a more tenuous grip on identity formation that should prove most rewarding for the astute and attuned observer.

References

Ayres, R.U. 2002. Exergy flows in the economy: Efficiency and dematerialization. In R.U. Ayres & L.W. Ayrfes (eds), *A Handbook of Industrial Ecology*, pp. 185–201. Cheltenham, UK: Edward Elgar.

Baudrillard, J. 1988. The mirror of production. In *Selected Writings* (Translated by Mark Poster). Pala Alto, CA: Stanford University Press.

BBC. 2010. *Internet Access Is 'a Fundamental Right*, http://news.bbc.co.uk/2/hi/8548190.stm, accessed on 5 February 2011.

Clark, M.E. 1995. Changes in Euro-American values needed for sustainability. *Journal of Social Issues*, 51(4), 63–82.

Daly, H.E. & Cobb, J.B. Jr. 1994. *For the Common Good: Redirecting the Economy toward Community, the Environment, and a Sustainable Future*. Boston: Beacon Press.

Department for Business Innovation and Skills. 2010. *National Plan for Digital Participation*. United Kingdom. March 2010. http://webarchive.

nationalarchives.gov.uk/tna/+/http://www.bis.gov.uk/uploads/ plan-digital-participation.pdf/, accessed on 5 February 2011.

Facebook. no date. Statistics. http://www.facebook.com/press/info. php?statistics, accessed on 6 February 2011.

Heinonen, S., Jokinen, P. & Kaivo-oja, J. 2001. The ecological transparency of the information society. *Futures, 33*(3–4), 319–337.

Heiskanen, E. & Jalas, M. 2000. *Dematerialization through Services: A Review and Evaluation of the Debate.* Finland: Ministry of the Environment.

———. 2003. Can services lead to radical eco-efficiency improvements? A review of the debate and evidence. *Corporate Social Responsibility and Environmental management, 10*, 186–198.

Hoogendijk, W. 1993. *The Economic Revolution: Towards a Sustainable Future by Freeing the Economy from Money Making.* Utrecht: Jan van Arkel.

Human Rights Defenders Mechanisms. 2011. *Governments Must Pay More Attention to People's Voices—UN Experts.* http://www.humanrights-defenders.org/2011/02/governments-must-pay-more-attention-to-people%E2%80%99s-voices-%E2%80%93-un-experts, accessed on 5 February 2011.

Jevons, W.S. 1866. *The Coal Question: An Inquiry Concerning the Progress of the Nation and the Probable Exhaustion of Our Coal Mines,* 2nd ed. London: Macmillan.

Klein, N. 2000. *No Logo: Taking Aim at the Brand Bullies.* Canada: Vintage.

Livingston, J. 1994. *Rogue Primate.* Toronto: Key Porter Books Limited.

Manno, J.P. 2010. Commoditization and oppression: A systems approach to understanding the economic dynamics of modes of oppression. *Annals of the New York Academy of Sciences, 185*, 164–178.

Mead, M. 1963. *Sex and Temperament in Three Primitive Societies.* New York: William Morrow.

Mills, M.P. 2000. *Kyoto and the internet: The energy implications of the digital economy. Testimony of Mills, before the Subcommittee on National Economic Growth, Natural Resources, and Regulatory Affairs, U.S. House of Representatives,* 2 February 2000. Available at http://www.tech-pundit. com/page.html?pageid=42

Murphy, T. 2000. Developers rush to meet demands of e-commerce. *New York Times.*

Naiman, J. 1997. *How Societies Work; Class, Power and Change in a Canadian Context.* Irwin Publishing.

Penaloza, L. 2001. On institutional perspective on the study of consumption. *Consumers, Commodities and Consumption Newsletter of the American Sociological Association, 3*(1), 4–5.

Princen, T. 1997. The shading and distancing of commerce: When institutionalization is not enough. *Ecological Economics, 20*: 235–253.

Race Online. 2010. *Strategy for the Champion for Digital Inclusion and the Digital Inclusion Task Force.* United Kingdom.

Rattle, R. 2010. *Computing Our Way to Paradise? The Role of Internet and Communication Technologies in Sustainable Consumption ad Globalization.* New York: Altamira Press.

Ropke, I. 2001. New technology in everyday life: Social processes and environmental impact. *Ecological Economics, 38*(3), 403–422.

Saunders, H. 1992. The Khazzoom-Brookes Postulate and Neoclassical Growth, *Energy Journal, 13*(4), 131–148.

Schnaiberg, A. 1980. *The Environment, From Surplus to Scarcity.* Oxford: Oxford University Press.

Statistics Canada. 2006. *Our Lives in Digital Times.* Connectedness Series. Research Paper. Catalogue no. 56F0004MIE—no. 014 Science, Innovation and Electronic Information Division (SIEID).

United Nations. 1998. *Measuring Changes in Consumption and Productions Patterns.* Department of Economic and Social Affairs, Populations Division, New York.

Wissner-Gross, A.D. & Freer, C.E. 2010. Relativistic statistical arbitrage. *Physical Review E, 82*(5).

PART II

Global Markets, Local Needs: Fashion and Advertising

6

Structural Changes Rather than the Influence of Media: People's Encounter with Economic Liberalization in India

*Steve Derné, Meenu Sharma and Narendra Sethi**

Introduction

When I did my first research in India in 1987, I was struck by Hindu men's sociocentrism; they tended to see themselves as part of a group more than as individuals (Derné, 1995). I was also struck by Hindu men's unified gender culture that emphasized men's control of the women in their lives, partly by restricting them to the home (Derné, 1995). In those years, India was a closed media landscape. The middle-class men I interviewed had no access to cable television or Hollywood

---

* Over the years, my long-time research assistant Narendra Sethi has become a co-investigator. Meenu Sharma contributed immeasurably to this chapter by helping me interviewing women. Thus, I have recognized Narendra Sethi and Meenu Sharma as co-authors of this chapter. While Derné wrote the first draft, they have provided helpful comments. Because it is Derné's impressions over the years that drive this chapter, the chapter is written from his perspective; it is a co-authored chapter.

films—Bollywood and one state-run television channel were the extent of their media consumption. In 1991, the pace of globalization in India suddenly accelerated, as the Indian economy opened. Within a decade, satellite television and Hollywood movies became widely available. Many commentators expected that exposure to new cultural models would lead to changes in cultural patterns in India. However, the interviews I conducted in India in 1991, 2001 and 2007 revealed few changes in non-elite middle-class men's sociocentrism and oppressive gender culture. Despite a transformed media world, which now celebrates cosmopolitan lifestyles, including more freedom for women and increased autonomy for young people in choosing careers and spouses, changes in the cultural orientation of non-elite, urban, Hindi-speaking men have been relatively modest. This suggested that institutional realities, more than cultural innovations, shape thinking.

My impressions on returning in 2011—two decades after economic liberalization and 25 years after I first began researching in India—to the same Indian city in which I had worked in 1991, 2001 and 2007—suggested changes—especially relating to women's employment and women's increased freedom in the public realm. But these changes appear to be brought along more by changing structural realities—the growing availability of credit and increasing employment opportunities for women—thus, confirming the importance of structural rather than cultural changes, in driving transformations in India following globalization.

In this chapter, I argue that the changes following 25 years of economic liberalization in India were driven by changes in structural opportunities (for employment, especially for women and for credit) more than by the new imaginations introduced by global media. New opportunities for women, rather than new thinking about women introduced through transnational television and films, changed their position. It wasn't new advertising of global products that introduced consumerist culture into India but new opportunities for consumption, introduced by credit and decreased trade restrictions.

Studying the Effects of Cultural Globalization in India

India pursued autonomous economic development with limited global entanglements until the mid-1980s, when the Rajiv Gandhi administration began a process of economic liberalization. When the oil price rose, associated with the 1991 Gulf War, it led to a foreign-exchange crisis; thereafter, the Indian government turned to the IMF for a bailout. In the summer of 1991, the Indian government accepted conditions for an IMF loan, reducing restrictions on investment, devaluing the rupee and lifting foreign-exchange controls. Within five years, imports more than doubled, exports more than tripled and foreign capital investment more than quintupled (e.g. Shurmer-Smith, 2000: 21–25).

Cultural globalization—the transnational movement of media—followed economic liberalization, as cable television offerings suddenly competed with state-run television and Hollywood films competed with local Hindi films. Until 1991, Indian television and film constituted one of the world's most protected media markets; however, deregulation transformed the media landscape. Fuelled by the desires of advertisers to reach the newly open Indian market, the number of television channels grew from one state-run channel in 1991 to more than 70 cable channels in 1999. Access to television increased from less than 10 per cent of the urban population in 1990 to nearly 75 per cent by 1999. In 1991, cable television reached 300,000 homes; in 1999, it reached 24 million homes. India remains the world's largest producer of feature films but with the easing of foreign exchange restrictions Hollywood captured 10 per cent of the market. In 1991, only a few foreign films were showed in the most metropolitan cities, but by 2001 foreign films were dubbed into Hindi and screened widely (e.g. Thussu, 2000).

Many commentators anticipated that cultural globalization would transform life around the world. Appadurai (1996: 52) famously argued, for instance, that because of transnational cultural flows associated with migration, tourism and mass media, people now consider 'a wider set of possible lives than they ever did before'. Because of this, Appadurai (1996: 44) argues, culture has become 'less what Pierre Bourdieu would have called a habitus (a tacit realm of reproducible practices and dispositions) and more an arena for conscious choice, justification, and representation'. Many observers of the Indian scene suggested that new media would transform family arrangements and gender in India by encouraging dating (e.g. Jain, 1998) or helping men accept women as superiors in the work force (e.g. Chandran, 1996). Yet we have few systematic studies examining the extent to which such changes have in fact occurred.

During what enthusiasts of globalization call the 'golden summer' of 1991 (Das, 2001: 213), I was in India, doing research with young male Indian filmgoers in the city of Dehradun. Although I mostly interviewed educated men, with good jobs or good job prospects, none had access to television beyond the one state-run channel and few had seen even one Hollywood film. Like the broader cross-section of Indian men whom I interviewed in the 1980s (Derné, 1995), the men whom I interviewed in 1991 focused on Indianness as the cornerstone of their identity. They often associated Indianness with what they saw as distinctive family systems that included arranged marriages and limitations on women's movements outside the home (Derné, 2000). Like the broader cross-section of Indian men whom I interviewed in the 1980s (Derné, 1995), the men whom I interviewed in 1991 had a sociocentric orientation: young men saw themselves as entangled in webs of relationships within a group. To understand how globalization had affected the lives and understandings of ordinary Indians like these young men, I returned in 2001 to replicate the study conducted a decade earlier.

As in 1991, I interviewed young men in their teens and twenties—a useful focus since the young are heavy consumers of new media. As LiPuma (2000: 63) rightly states, an understanding of changes in thinking and ways of being should focus *especially* on 'those who are coming of age' who are often, after all in the throes of 'forging their identity'. By focusing on men in their teens and twenties in each era, I tried to examine whether new media had affected men's cultural orientations towards family and gender as they entered adulthood.

As in 1991, I interviewed men with good standards-of-living but who didn't speak any (or very much) English. They were professionals or successfully self-employed people (23 per cent in 1991; 16 per cent in 2001), undergraduate or postgraduate students (41 per cent in 1991; 50 per cent in 2001), successful labourers or holders of lower-middle class jobs such as office clerk (36 per cent in 1991; 34 per cent in 2001). Their families owned scooters or televisions, but they could barely dream of owning automobiles or travelling abroad and they purchased few global products. Ordinary middle-class Indians like these constituted about 16 per cent of households across India in 2000, with 40 per cent of the urban population. They see themselves as 'middle-class' Indians—below the position of the rich jetsetters—the 3 per cent of Indians (10 per cent of urban ones) with high incomes, college degrees, English-language skills and global connections—but well above the position of the destitute 53 per cent of Indians who earn less than US$500 annually (Shurmer-Smith, 2000). For these non-elite middle-class Indians, economic globalization provided greater access to some goods, like televisions, which had previously been difficult to obtain due to foreign exchange restrictions. But because they lacked English-language skills and global connections, new high-paying jobs linked to global markets were beyond the reach of such people, and their middle-class incomes kept them from fully entering the utopia of consumption trumpeted in new media.

While in 2001, the effect of economic liberalization on non-elite Indians' job prospects was limited, the cultural globalization that took place in the 10 years between the two studies dramatically changed the cultural landscape for ordinary Indians. In 1991, no Hollywood film was screened in the three months while I was working in Dehradun; however, in 2001 dubbed Hollywood films were the main fare at the city's two most elite theatres. Audience could watch Hollywood films about adventurers traversing dangerous snowy peaks (*Vertical Limit*), B-grade films aiming at sexual titillation (like a dubbed version of the low-budget Hollywood film *Sexual Intent*) and action films with spectacular special effects like Arnold Schwarzenegger's *Arnold Ka Mukabla* (*The Confrontation of Arnolds*, a dubbed version of

Hollywood's *Sixth Day*). In 1991, none of the men whom I asked had seen Hollywood films; however, nearly 60 per cent of the men whom I interviewed in 2001 had watched such films—half watched dubbed films regularly. Nearly a quarter (7/32) of the men I interviewed were so charmed by foreign films that they claimed to be watching very few Hindi films.

Also, growing access to television and, especially, cable is quite significant. In 1991, few of the men whom I interviewed had access to television and even those who had televisions were limited to state-run Doordarshan programming (as satellite TV was completely unavailable). In 1991, Doordarshan's hits were family serials, serialized Hindu mythologies, and (biggest of all) a weekly Hindi film and a weekly programme devoted to Hindi-film songs. By 2001, television had rapidly expanded so that nearly 88 per cent (i.e. 28 out of 32) of the men whom I interviewed had access to television. The expansion of cable was dramatic. While none of the men whom I interviewed in 1991 had access to cable television, by 2001, about 69 per cent (i.e. 22 out of 32) had at least some access to cable television.

Attachment to Existing Family Arrangements in a Globalizing World, 2001

As I detail in *Globalization on the Ground* (2008), men's orientation in 2001 had not changed much despite the onslaught of new media. By 2001, the advent of globalization has intensified the celebration of autonomy and individual choice. The idea that young people's love for each other should be the basis for marriage is reasserted by cable television's American serials (e.g. *Santa Barbara*), which shows young people in pursuit of the 'right one'. Influenced by global media, Hindi-film hits now emphasize the search for the right partner (while in earlier eras they focused instead on overcoming parental opposition). The big 1997 hit *Dil To Pagal Hai* famously opens with the female actor voicing her certainty that 'someone somewhere was made for me and that I'll meet him'. The hero scoffs at the 'nonsense' of having a 'soulmate', but the heroine remains firm: 'When I meet my soul-mate, I will recognize him. He will speak to me and give me a sign and my heart will realize ... this is love.' In the increasingly cosmopolitan media world, love as a basis for marriage is the celebrated goal.

Yet despite the transformed media landscape and the increased celebration of cosmopolitan lifestyles, the men whom I interviewed in 2001 remain as committed to arranged marriages as the men whom I interviewed before the global media deluge. Vinod, an unmarried 22-year-old high school graduate, enjoys cable television and Hindi film love stories, but remains committed to arranged marriages: 'Love marriages are only stories in films. In real life, they are not possible. I haven't given a thought to marriage, but I know I'll marry according to my parents' wishes'. This mantra was voiced by the range of ordinary middle-class men whom I interviewed. Virendra, 22, is a Hindu, Jat, in a postgraduate engineering programme, living in a family headed by his father who is with Indian Police and a house wife mother. Virendra likes to copy the 'smart (*sunderta*) dress' of his favourite film stars and enjoys Hindi film love stories, yet he too remains committed to arranged marriages: 'In reality, love marriages are not successful. In actual life, a love marriage is not possible. I'll marry with my parents' wishes'. Another 19-year-old upper-caste Hindu student living in a joint family headed by a father with a good service job similarly said that while the films he likes are love stories, it wouldn't be possible in real life. Although his favourite film, *Mohabbatein,* features a school teacher who encourages his students to pursue love, this student remains certain that 'any girl I could find for myself would not be as good as the girl my parents will find for me'. Despite a decade of cultural globalization celebrating the search for love, similar percentages of men voiced an on-balance disapproval of love marriages (68 per cent in 1991 and 66 per cent in 2001). The percentage of men voicing an unqualified support of love marriages also changed little in a decade (14 per cent in 1991 and 19 per cent in 2001).

While in affluent circles (and in the media that cater to them), there has been a widespread belief that globalization has encouraged dating and love marriages, my study's systematic comparison showing little change in ordinary middle-class Indians' attitudes towards marriage is confirmed by a number of other studies. Systematic, geographically extensive evidence is lacking, but most sober commentators from the end of the 1990s (e.g. Srivastava, 2011; Uberoi, 1998: 307) see little increase in love marriages and the few systematic local studies we do have show little change in attitudes about marriage and family. A 1998–1999 study found that 65 per cent of 15–34-year-olds in Delhi, Mumbai, Kanpur and Lucknow said that they would obey their elders 'even if it hurts' (Page and Crawley, 2001: 176). A mid-1990s study of urban college students found that 68 per cent said they wanted to have their parents arrange their marriage (Pathak, 1994). Abraham's (2001: 149–151) 1996–1998 study found that a 'majority' of low-income students in Mumbai thought that love marriages were unsuccessful. The students Abraham interviewed 'preferred an arranged marriage for its stability and security'. In the absence of change in structural realities of family life or economy, a decade of cosmopolitan celebration of love has apparently done little to change men's views.

While transnational media intensified favourable images of independent women who often work in the paid economy (e.g. the popular Ally McBeal), by 2001 ordinary middle-class men seemed no less attached to gender arrangements that limit women's public activities and freedom. In 1991, men were the primary consumers of action movies and even at screenings of the more respected social films (where women might make up one-third of the balcony audience) there are few women in the cheap floor seats. Men enjoyed homosocial bonding in this all-male world. In 2001 (as in 1991), they shout out to greet friends both in the hall and while waiting outside. Men enjoyed putting arms around each other or playfully batting each other. They joke, dance and roughhouse together. Some men seemed to enjoy their exclusive use of cinema hall public spaces, while emphasizing how this contrasts with women's home-based lives. Tahsin, a married 25-year-old male, describes his compelling attraction (*chaska*) to Hindi film as so strong that he watches at least two movies a week, but he proudly relates that his wife is so 'home loving (*gharelu*) that she even objects to seeing movies with her own husband'. For Tahsin, the cinema hall is a place that men enjoy, while women should remain at home. Tahsin said he rarely watches television at home. 'It's for women and children', he says.

In both 1991 and 2001, men's discussion of their favourite heroine showed a focus on women's home responsibilities. Tahsin doesn't like many of today's heroines; he says that they expose too much of their bodies. Tahsin's favourite heroine is Kajol because of her innocence (*bholapan*). A 25-year-old who likes satellite television and American movies such as *Titanic* and *Godzilla* similarly told me that Aishwarya Rai was his favourite Hindi film heroine because of her generosity, referring to her widely reported willingness to donate her eyes to science after her death. This man likes women who are willing to sacrifice for the broader society. Other local surveys showed ordinary middle-class men's ongoing attachment to gender arrangements that make women primarily responsible for home duties. Abraham's (2001: 142) interviews showed that college-going men want women to be 'simple', 'home-loving' and in possession of a 'compromising nature' that makes them 'respect elders'—views which closely parallel men's views in previous decades.

Men's attachment to existing gender arrangements may be one reason that so many ordinary middle-class men were uneasy with new media that appear to challenge these arrangements. Virendra, the postgraduate engineering student who often watches cable television, is committed to arranged marriages and joint-family living. Although he likes 'smart dressing' of cosmopolitan heroes, he complains that 'satellite TV is making younger people too mature'. Umesh, a civil draftsman whose marriage has just been arranged, likes Hollywood movies and television, yet is disturbed by programming that gives the message 'that a brother should allow his sister to go with her boyfriend to watch a movie. These are not good things', he says, 'so they shouldn't be shown on television'. This unease with global media sometimes generates protests against globalization's effect on local gender arrangements. For several years protesters have responded to Valentine's Day, by attacking couples in restaurants and burning Valentine Day cards (Sengupta, 2001). Other protesters targeted discotheques for 'spoiling the minds of youth' (India Abroad, 1999) and the 1996 staging of the Miss World pageant in Bangalore for threatening Indian womanhood (Fernandes, 2000: 625; Oza, 2001). Although often orchestrated by political elites, these protests resonate with ordinary middle-class men.

By 2001, transnational media had not led ordinary middle-class men to experiment with new gender arrangements. If it had made them aware of a 'wider set of possible lives', cultural globalization has only increased their vigorous defence of local family lives and gender culture.

Non-elite Indian men's attachment to arranged marriages and to limiting women's public freedom reflects the economic and family structures that ordinary Indians face. Without expanded economic opportunities, young men rely on parental support in the early years of marriage. Often living in joint households in the first years of marriage, men want a wife to embrace an attitude of compromise given competing demands within a family. Because ordinary Indian women lack the connections and strong English-language skills that would allow them to compete in the global economy, most men want women to work in the home rather than at jobs that don't pay very well. Despite the media celebration of love, the institution of arranged marriages and limitations on interactions between unmarried men and women remain obdurate structural realities. These institutional realities— and men's interest in maintaining gender arrangements—press against ordinary Indian men's acceptance of love marriages and women's freedoms that are celebrated in the media they enjoy from Hollywood movies to local productions that have been influenced by cosmopolitan media.

Changing Social Structures and Elite Transformations, 2001

While my work in 2001 focused on continuities in non-elite men's gender culture, transformations in elite Indian culture demonstrated the role of institutional change in leading individuals to embrace new cultural meanings. First, the growth of consumerism over the first decade of liberalization was driven more by the new availability of goods than new cultural celebration of consumer lifestyles. The affluent Indians whom Fernandes (2000: 614) interviewed in 1998 saw 'new choice of commodities as a central indicator of the benefits of economic liberalization'. They talked about how access to goods in early times was limited to those who had the financial means to travel abroad to purchase goods. But today, as one person told her, 'abroad is now in India', a statement that shows that affluent Indians' 'aspirations of consumption' can 'now take place within India's borders'. Referring to the desire for cellphones and holiday homes, the editor of a print magazine told Fernandes (2000: 614) that previously 'people would feel a sense of guilt—that in a nation like this a kind of vulgar exhibition of wealth is contradictory to Indian values. I think now consumerism has become an Indian value.' Hindi films have been participating for many years in this process of encouraging consumerist desires. In 1985's super-hit movie, *Ram Teri Ganga Maili*, the elite hero's uncle who has returned from a foreign trip presents the hero with an 'alpine hat from Switzerland, a leather jacket from France and a polaroid camera' the novel operation of which he explains excitedly. But in the days of licensing and regulation, such items were novelties, the result of a foreign trip. Indians only really embraced the culture of consumerism when the economic structures changed to open markets, making global goods readily available to those with cash.

Even by 2001, affluent Indians were more likely to embrace new cultural imaginations of gender and family trumpeted in transnational media precisely because globalization has transformed their structural realities. By 2001, 3 per cent of Indians (10 per cent of urban ones) with high incomes, college degrees, English-language skills and global connections have been able to draw on new high-paying jobs (from computer programmer to operating call centres) oriented to the international market and can now buy international products, which had previously been restricted by foreign-exchange controls. Affluent Indian women move about elite shopping arcades more because of new possibilities for consumption than new celebrations of women's independence. Those affluent Indians who embrace women's paid labour do so because of high-paying opportunities that can help usher in the utopia of consumption more than because of global media's positive portrayals of women in the public sphere. It is because of new opportunities for economic independence rather than new cultural inculcation that affluent Indians increasingly embrace dating and love marriages as real possibilities. Non-elite Indians are exposed to the same global celebrations of consumerism, women's public freedoms, love marriages and cosmopolitan identity as elite Indians, but non-elite Indian men reject these new cultural maps because globalization has failed to transform the structural realities non-elites face.

This description of the new consumerism in India and the transformed family and gender arrangements of affluent Indians shows that a change in the material world has been accompanied by a change in the mental world of thoughts and feelings: by the late 1990s, increasing opportunities for global employment and consumption had led the affluent to a consumer orientation and wider acceptance of cosmopolitan gender arrangements.

Living with Transnational Media, 2007

Although my comparison of non-elite men's culture in 1991 and 2001 suggested continuities, it is of course possible that the long-run effect of new possibilities suggested by global media would be greater than the immediate effect. In 2007, I was in Dehradun doing interviews to understand Indians' conceptions of well-being. My limited work in Dehradun in 2007 confirmed that absent changes in social institutions, purely cultural, media-introduced changes have little impact.

The 2007 interviews were not aimed at replicating my 1991 and 2001 studies, but I did interview 17 men aged 18–26—a group that parallels the bulk of filmgoers whom I interviewed in 1991 and 2001. With the aim of reflecting on changes since 2001, I also did at least one participant-observation session in five of the seven theatres operating in Dehradun in 2007. This consideration of subsequent changes and continuities, 2001–2007, confirms the primary significance of structural factors in rooting culture, class and gender.

The largest structural change between 2001 and 2007 is the improving economic position of the local middle class in Dehradun. At the national level, India has experienced robust economic growth and a surging stock market. Credit, nearly impossible for the local middle class to obtain in 1991, has greatly expanded. At the local level, in 2001 Dehradun was made the (temporary) capital of the newly formed state, Uttarakhand, introducing more economic prosperity and growth into the region. The effect of this economic growth has been to improve the situation of the local middle class. With credit available, the age of homeownership has declined from the higher forties to the mid-thirties (*Pioneer*, 2007a), and purchases of motorcycles and even automobiles have entered the possibilities of the local middle class. Thus, local middle-class people may feel increasingly secure. For instance, my Dehradun research assistant, now working for a satellite news channel, is comfortable with his position in the Indian economy. Of men whom I interviewed with jobs tied to the local economy, only one retired individual expressed a lack of well-being stemming from his economic position (and his discontent stemmed more, I think, from having gifted his wealth to an ungrateful family).

But the position of the poor has not much changed. Citing government reports, Uttarakhand's Chief Minister B.C. Khanduri reports that for the bottom 30 per cent of the population there has been no perceptible improvement in cereal and nutrient intake in both urban and rural areas (Khanduri, 2007). Improving middle-class status has reached relatively few. In 2007, only 14 per cent of India's population earned more than ₹8,000 per month (*Indian Express*, 2007a). Only 24 people in 1,000 have a personal computer and fewer than three have broadband connection (*Newsweek*, 2007). Especially significant is that infrastructural improvements have not reached many poor and rural Indians: forty per cent of India's population still lacks access to electricity (*Indian Express*, 2007b: 1) and two-thirds still lack access to toilets (Aiyer, 2007).

There has not been much improvement in the structural conditions that disadvantage women in India. In 2007, Indian women's labour-force participation remained low—just 36 per cent, compared to 84 per cent of men. Thus, the World Economic Forum ranks India as one of the ten worst countries in the world in terms of the gender gap in economic participation and opportunity (Ramasubbu, 2007). A UN agency reports that because of prenatal sex selection and aborting of female foetuses, the sex ratio increasingly favours men: in 2001, 108 boys were born per 100 girls; in 2007, 120 boys were born per 100 girls—a problem that is worse in urban areas (*Pioneer*, 2007b.)

As a result, perhaps, I did not observe very much that suggested substantial changes in gender arrangements. Systematic counts in markets showed roughly 10 times as many men as women in public places and that roughly 10 times as many women wear saris and salwar kameezes, rather jeans and pants (although jeans and pants are now more prevalent at some cinema-hall screenings). A local middle- and upper-middle-class housewarming party I attended had an exclusively male guest list and was gender segregated: women were inside the home, while men remained outside, eating snacks, in a tented enclosure— the space where not a single woman entered during my several hours being there. I heard preachers in gurdwaras railing against 'micro-minis' and jeans for young women. While there are many women in balconies in cinema halls presenting movies aimed at attracting large numbers of dating couples (e.g. *Jab We Met*) or attracting middle-class audiences (e.g. *Om Shanti Om*), cheaper seats are still overwhelmingly filled with men. While I observed more young couples dating in cinema halls and two of the men whom I interviewed (as of this date) were in or had been in a dating relationship with a woman, more often young people were having their marriages arranged. The largely working-class audience at the Kanak theatre still responded enthusiastically to male violence, whistling as a heroine is tied up, or clapping as women are slapped or a villain displayed a revealing photo he was using to blackmail a woman. More than 150 cases of eve teasing—public sexual harassment and threats—are reported each month in Dehradun and few of the perpetrators are brought to justice (Shukla, 2007). While all of the 52 men whom I approached in public places or workplaces agreed to be interviewed, only 9 of the 18 women I asked were willing to be interviewed, perhaps reflecting the continuing threat to reputation that could arise from being seen with unrelated men, a lack of ease interacting with unrelated men due to often segregated schools and workplaces and/or the continuing pressure of women's disproportionate housework responsibilities.

Finally, perhaps because economic opportunities of children of the local middle class remain uncertain (even as the economic position of those with local-middle-class jobs improve) and because joint-family living remains common, the sociocentric cultural orientation remains firm. Eleven of the 17 young men whom I interviewed were largely raised in families that included more than one couple of their parents' generation or older. Five men in this age group were labourers or in jobs below local middle-class status (e.g. seller of jaggery, cook). While the other 12 men in this age group were of local middle-class background, a large number were students who had not yet themselves obtained middle-class jobs. Perhaps because of the common joint-family background and the continued existence of economic insecurity, all but two of these men expressed views consistent with a cultural focus on the group over the individual—an orientation I first noted in the wide-ranging interviews I conducted in 1987.

A 19-year-old male Punjabi student, living in Dehradun for his studies, speaks English well, sports cosmopolitan fashion and enjoys riding a motorcycle. Although embracing a consumer lifestyle, his discussion of well-being shows a strong sociocentric focus on others: When I asked him his purpose in life, he describes his motto as to 'enjoy living for others. Even while you do your own work, the taste in doing another person's work is the best taste'. Snapping his fingers, he describes how he immediately helps out his friends, even if they call him at 2 in the morning. Growing up in a joint family that included his parents and his grandparents and describing his family as facing economic insecurity despite his prosperity, this young man was living with the family and economic structures that support a sociocentric cultural focus. A 21-year-old working in Dehradun as a news reporter and pursuing a college degree hails from a large family that he describes as fully joint. While he takes pride in his news reporting—and especially aims to combat pre-modern superstitions—his main purpose, he says, is to always help others: 'I should never do any work that causes unhappiness to anyone. Any work I do should be selfless. I am not concerned about my own happiness. But whatever I am doing must deliver happiness to the person standing next to me'. An 18-year-old scheduled-caste student, from a large joint-family with 30 members, has come to Dehradun to study. While he describes recognition of his personal academic achievement at an assembly as a source of well-being, his main cultural orientation is clearly sociocentric: When I ask him about his aim in life, he says that 'it would be easy to enjoy the money sent by the parents, to be self-centred and think about myself. But real happiness lies in fulfilling the dreams of my parents'. An 18-year-old who sells jaggery outside a theatre came to Dehradun at the age of 13, having only passed fifth standard. His orientation to well-being also focuses on society rather than self. When I ask him what well-being means, he says that he is happy when everyone is happy. 'When people talk well to each other, I gain happiness', he says. He describes the festival period as good for sales, but still connects his happiness during this period to the joys of others: 'A festival is associated with being happy with each other and greeting the customers with cheer. This leads me to experience happiness'. A 22-year-old student, in Dehradun for studies, lives in such a large joint family that he has to pause to count its members on his fingers. He describes Bollywood films as his hobby, yet he doesn't focus on individualistic joys saying that 'the meaning of well-being for me is to see my parents happy and make them happy because they've done a lot of things for me until now'. Continuities in structures of family living and economic opportunity militate against the fundamental change in the sociocentric orientation.

The *Hindustan Times* calls Dehradun one of India's 'new boom towns' (Parashar, 2007). The seat of the capital and possessing elite educational institutions, Dehradun has experienced more economic prosperity than other cities, rising with India's economic growth. Still, even in this city, placed well to benefit from globalization and India's economic growth, in 2007, there were significant continuities in the cultural orientation and gender culture of the young labourers and local-middle-class men whom I interviewed in the fall of 2007—continuities rooted in persistent economic and family structures that include gender arrangements that disadvantage women.

Structural Changes and Gender Transformations in India, 2011

Four years later in 2011, 20 years after the golden summer in which India's economy liberalized, I was again in Dehradun completing further interviews on well-being. At this point, my impression is that women are enjoying growing freedoms of movement outside the home. Eleven periods of observations of public interactions show that while men still occasionally outnumber women in public by ten to one, more often they only outnumber women two to one and sometimes it is even closer than this. Eight periods of systematic observation show that while women are still more likely to wear salwar kameezes and saris than jeans, wearing jeans, especially for middle-class youth, has become acceptable. Women wearing such clothing no longer face catcalls, at least in Dehradun, as would have been common in 1987 or 1991. Certainly, women are rarely present in tea stalls, cheap eateries and cheap theatres and are much outnumbered even in the most prestigious cinema halls. Most run-of-the-mill protests against corruption in 2007 had few if any women participating, but women sometimes participated in the more celebrated protests.

A number of personal observations confirm this change. In early October 2011, while trekking to Har Ki Dun, I met a group of women brought together by a travel supplier called Women on Wanderlust. The women, with jobs in journalism and industry, came from all over India—Jharkhand, Delhi, Mumbai and

Lucknow. One of them commented to me that 20 years ago, it wouldn't have been possible for a woman to leave her 9-year-old child and go trekking. Indeed in 1987, one man said to me that a child needs his mother 24-hours a day (Derné, 1995). In early October 2007, three women began patronizing the cheap eatery at which I took my meals. Until then, this had been an almost exclusively male sphere, although women would sometimes accompany a male family member who was visiting Dehradun. As I write this, they had been present for three of my four most recent meals there (two breakfasts and one lunch). They were dressed in neither modern clothes, like jeans, nor once-in-a-season special saris (with a brightly made-up face) as you sometimes see for women who go out on special occasion, but simple neat salwar kameezes. The men in the dhaba were respectful, providing them with their own table. Anand Patwardhan's film *Father, Son, Holy War* showed men in the 1980s complaining that women who go outside the home have one man in the morning, another with lunch and another at dinner. What was notable about the reaction of the lower-middle-class men in the dhaba was the lack of titter or comment after the women left the dhaba. Even for the lower-middle-class men eating at the dhaba, women's public presence had become normal.

Indeed, women themselves confirm the greater opportunities for freedom of movement, especially in employment. In 2011, I asked the men and women I interviewed who were above 35 years of age to reflect on the changes in women's condition that they had witnessed in recent decades. In 1987, men commented that women were not allowed to go outside the home, even to shop, unless taking another family member with them. A 68-year-old Hindu woman who had spent her life as a housewife reflected that:

> During our time, we were only inside our houses and our whole lives were spent working according to the husband and in laws. All the talent in us was kept down (*dabna*). Nowadays, women are getting the opportunity to show their talents and they are serving both their responsibilities to the house and the outside.

Another 60-year-old Hindu housewife agreed that

During our time, we were supposed to stay at home and do the household work no matter how qualified we were. But now every woman wants to do the job according to the requirements and according to their education. Now, parents are educating their girls equally as their sons.

And an 80-year-old Hindu housewife reflected that

During our time, women were only to give birth to children and look after their families. They were confined within the boundaries of their home. But now things have changed a lot. Now women are educated and are working and are financially independent.

I have often observed families who are happy with daughters, as well as sons, and educate daughters equally to sons, even refraining from teaching their daughters household skills.

It is worth noting, too, however, that women are now faced with a second shift (Hochschild, 1989)—getting no relief from household work, despite taking up earning. I have observed many women in paid employment who nonetheless do all, or nearly all, of the house's work. I often see women walking very young children to school—and I only rarely (indeed, only once) have seen men performing this household work. A 33-year-old Muslim housewife complained that the conditions of the women have worsened because women today have too much of the workload on them. A 63-year-old male Muslim lawyer emphasized the that 'employment of women is seen in almost every department', but he nonetheless felt that:

woman are exploited because there is a lot of burden on them. They have to look after both the home and office or whatever their workplace. This is creating a lot of burden on the women and it is bringing the bad impact on their health.

In 1987, an executive household head would have often had servants to do housework. Shurmer-Smith (2000: 32) states that in the late 1990s a full-time live-in servant cost less than a take-out pizza. The costs of these servants have gone up and men are reluctant, in any event, to have food 'cooked by maid servants', suggesting the increasing burden of the second shift on women in the paid labour force. Thus, a 2011 *Hindustan Times* survey conducted in eight metros found that '87 per cent of women say they feel stressed most of the time' and 82 per cent say 'they have no time to relax' (Ghosh, 2011).

Globalization's Transformations and the Centrality of Institutions

The impression of changes in 2011 that I have just described serves to highlight the importance in changing social structure in transforming the Indian society. The celebration of women's movements outside the home in media and news accounts pre-dates by more than a decade the changes I observed in 2011. This suggests that the changes are more the result of changing social structures and opportunities for women, rather than new ideas introduced by transnational media. The growth of coeducation has made men and women increasingly comfortable interacting together. In 1991 and 2001, Indian women's employment oppor-tunities were limited, so men preferred to restrict women to the household labour. But in 2011, women's employment could con-tribute substantially to household income—and the benefits of higher income have been intensified by the increasing availabil-ity of credit. It is these transformations, rather than new cultural ideas, that have increased women's freedom of movement and participation in the paid labour force. At the same time, the struc-tural reality of male dominance in the family continues to impose a second shift on women. As other studies have shown (e.g. Wolf, 1994), within patriarchal social structures, greater employment opportunities for women have only increased the burdens men place on women.

Acknowledgements

The US Department of Education provided a Fulright–Hays Doctoral Dissertation Abroad grant that supported the 1986–1987 research and a Faculty Research Abroad grant that supported the 2011 research. The American Institute of Indian Studies supported my research in India in 1991 and 2001. SUNY—Geneseo provided a sabbatical that allowed me to conduct the 2001 and 2007 research. The sociology department at Delhi University sponsored my 1986–1987, 1991, 2001 and 2011 research. I am especially thankful to my advisors there, Andre Beteille, Veena Das and Radhika Chopra, as well as Satendra Kumar, Sanjay Srivastava and Janaki. Abraham. A Rockefeller fellowship at the Office of Women's Research at the University of Hawaii in 2002 provided the time to analyze the data and think about the issues I present in this chapter. In 1991, 2001, 2007 and 2011, Narendra Sethi was a fantastic research assistant who helped me conduct and translate interviews. Meenu Sharma helped me conduct and translate interviews in 2011.

References

Abraham, L. 2001. Redrawing the Lakshman Rekha: Gender differences and cultural constructions in youth sexuality in urban India. *South Asia*, 24(2), 133–156.

Aiyer, Y. 2007. No toilets, please, we're Indian. *Indian Express*, 20 November, p. 11.

Appadurai, A. 1996. *Modernity at Large: Cultural Dimensions of Globalization.* Minneapolis: University of Minnesota Press.

Chandran, P. 1996. Target: The Indian male. *India Today Plus*, Third Quarter, pp. 69–78.

Das, G. 2001. *India Unbound: A Personal Account of a Social and Economic Revolution from Independence to the Global Information Age.* New York: Knopf.

Derné, S. 1995. *Culture in Action: Family Life, Emotion, and Male Dominance in Banaras, India.* Albany: SUNY Press.

———. 2000. *Movies, Masculinity, and Modernity: An Ethnography of Men's Filmgoing in India.* Westport CT: Greenwood Press.

———. 2008. *Globalization on the Ground: Media and the Transformation of Culture, Class and Gender in India.* New Delhi: SAGE.

Fernandes, L. 2000. Nationalizing 'the global': Media images, cultural politics and the middle class in India. *Media, Culture and Society, 22*(5), 611–628.

Ghosh, P. 2011. Sexist, boorish, misogynist, and this must change now. *Hindustan Times,* 18 September, p. 12.

Hochschild, A. 1989. (With Anne Machung) *The Second Shift: Working Parents and the Revolution at Home.* New York: Viking.

India Abroad. 1999. Ban sought on discotheques. March 19, p. 11.

Indian Express. 2007a. Hands of India's rich as dirty as west: Greenpeace. 14 November 2007, p. 8.

_____. 2007b. 60 mn Indians still without power by 2030 warns global energy agency. 8 November 2007, pp. 1–2.

Jain, M. 1998. Romance: Move over, cupid. *India Today International,* 16 February, pp. 42–43.

Khanduri, B.C. 2007. If we cannot help poor, we cannot save rich. *Pioneer Panorama,* 9 November, p. 1.

LiPuma, E. 2000. *Encompassing Others: The Magic of Modernity in Melanesia.* Ann Arbor: University of Michigan Press.

Newsweek. 2007. November 10. Cited by 'What the World is Reading'. *Indian Express,* 12 November 2007.

Oza, R. 2001. Showcasing India: Gender, geography, and globalization. *SignsI, 26*(4), 1067–1095.

Page, D. & Crawley, W. 2001. *Satellites over South Asia: Broadcasting, Culture, and the Public Interest.* New Delhi: SAGE.

Parashar, U. 2007. Dehradun's Derring-do. *Hindustan Times,* 28 October, p. 15.

Pathak, R. 1994. The new generation. *India Today,* 31 January, pp. 48–60.

Pioneer. 2007a. Homeowners' Go Younger by 20 Years. 5 November, p. 6.

_____. 2007b. UNFPA warns India to check female foeticide. 31 November, p. 6.

Ramasubbu, K. 2007. India Matches Pak in women's economic rights, *Indian Express,* 19 November, p. 17.

Sengupta, H. 2001. Incidents of violence, vandalism Mar valentine's day. *India Abroad,* 23 February, p. 24.

Shukla, Shikha. 2007. Police stand mute spectator as eve teasers go scot free. *Pioneer, 28*(November), 2.

Shurmer-Smith, P. 2000. *India: Globalization and Change.* London: Arnold.

Srivastava, S. 2011. The choices of Karva Chauth. *Indian Express,* 15 October, p. 15.

Thussu, D.K. 2000. The hinglish hegemony: The impact of western television on broadcasting in India. In D. French & M. Richards (eds), *Television in Contemporary Asia*, pp. 293–311. New Delhi: SAGE.

Uberoi, P. 1998. The Diaspora comes home: Disciplining desire in DDLJ. *Contributions to Indian Sociology*, *32*(2), 305–336.

Wolf, D. 1994. *Factory Daughters: Gender, Household Dynamics and Rural Industrialization in Java*. Berkeley: University of California Press.

7

Fashion, Advertising and Identity in the Consumer Society

Douglas Kellner

Introduction

For decades, billions of dollars have been spent on advertising in contemporary capitalist societies, often more than on education. When one considers that an equal amount of money is spent on design, packaging, marketing and product display, one sees how much money is squandered on advertising and marketing. For example, only eight cents of the cosmetics sales dollar goes to pay for ingredients; the rest goes to packaging, promotion and marketing. Consequently, a tremendous amount of resources, talent and money is invested in advertising.

The expansion of marketing and advertising was a necessary consequence of the system of mass production developed in modern capitalist societies. By the early years of the twentieth century, industrial capitalism had already perfected techniques of mass production. The assembly line, scientific management of the labour process and the emergence of the modern corporation revolutionized production and made possible the creation of new mass consumer goods. New modes of advertising, marketing, packaging and design helped produce mass consumption and consumers who would purchase and utilize the new world of commodities. The result is the now familiar consumer society within which most of us were born and in which we work, consume, amuse ourselves and suffer.

Advertising and fashion are two of the dominant mechanisms in the production and reproduction of the consumer society and construction of contemporary identities. Advertising attempts to produce consumer needs for commodities that will allegedly solve a wide range of our personal problems and which will supposedly provide a large number of gratifications. Advertising tells us that new commodities will make us happier, more popular and more successful. Advertising helps construct idealized masculine and feminine identities and provides role models for emulation.

Fashion in turn provides the constant cycle of new products, styles and images that keep consumer demand at a high level. Advertising tells us that to be 'with it' and up to date, we must be fashionable, and buy and exhibit all the latest products and fashions. Both advertising and fashion, therefore, work together to manage consumer demand and thus to reproduce the consumer society and consumer-oriented identities.

Hence, advertisement and fashion not only play a crucial role in consumer demand management, but they also promote a view of the world complete with an ethics, politics, gender role models, identities and sense of appropriate and inappropriate daily social behaviour. Advertising and fashion thus have crucial economic and socializing functions in shaping behaviour and inducing people to participate in the consumer society.

In this study, I will first discuss identity in modern and postmodern societies and then how advertising, fashion and the consumer society play key roles in constructing contemporary identities. In conclusion, I will go beyond constructing identities in consumer society in terms of fashion and style, arguing for alternative strategies of constructing individual selves.[1]

Identity in Modern and Post-modern Societies

According to anthropological and sociological folklore, in traditional societies, one's identity was fixed, solid and stable. Identity was a function of pre-defined social roles and a traditional system of myths that provided orientation and religious sanctions to define one's place in the world, while rigorously circumscribing the realm of thought and behaviour. One was born and died as a member of one's clan, of a fixed kinship system, and of one's tribe or group with one's life trajectory fixed in advance. In premodern societies, identity was unproblematical and not subject to reflection or discussion. Individuals did not undergo identity crises, or radically modify their identity. One was a hunter and a member of the tribe and gained one's identity through these roles and functions.

In modernity, identity becomes more mobile, multiple, personal, self-reflexive and subject to change and innovation.[2] Yet identity in modernity is also social and other related. Theorists of identity from Hegel through G.H. Mead have often characterized personal identity in terms of mutual recognition, as if one's identity depended on recognition from others combined with self-validation of this recognition. Yet the forms of identity in modernity are also relatively substantial and fixed; identity still comes from a circumscribed set of roles and norms: one is a mother, a son, a Texan, a Scot, a professor, a socialist, a Catholic and a lesbian—or rather a combination of these and multiple other social roles and possibilities.

Identity in modernity is a function of multiple subject positions with relevant positions accordingly multiplying as nation, class, ethnicity or race, gender, sexual preference, job and other constituents of identity become relevant factors in defining who one is. In modernity, one must thus choose which factors in the matrix of identity positions define who one is. Choices become more complex and conflicted as new possibilities emerge. That is, at one time national identity might have been salient: with an American, British, French, and saw oneself and the world through the prism of national identity. In the nineteenth century class became an important constituent of identity, as workers and capitalists both attempted to develop political organizations to promote class-consciousness and solidarity. With the rise of widespread emigration in the nineteenth century, especially to countries such as the United States or Australia, or to the metropoles of the major empires, race and ethnic identity became important (it was also central in different ways in the United States before the Civil War that left a legacy of racial discrimination, still ongoing). And with the rise of feminism gender became important, as gay liberation movements promoted sexual preference as a key constituent of identity.

In modernity, identities are thus still relatively fixed and limited, though the boundaries of possible identities, of new identities, are continually expanding. Indeed, in modernity, self-consciousness comes into its own. It becomes possible to continuously engage in reflection on available social roles and possibilities and to gain a distance from tradition (Kolb, 1986). One can choose and make—and then remake—one's identity as one's life-possibilities change and expand—or contract—and new constituents of identity are defined by social movements as important (i.e. gender or sexual preference). Also, a prevailing ideology of individualism in modernity challenges individuals to create their own unique identities out of the multiple subject positions that constitute their matrix of social indicators and markers.

Modernity also increases other directedness, however, for as the number of possible identities increases, one must gain recognition to assume a socially validated, recognized identity. In modernity, there is still a structure of interaction with socially defined and available roles, norms, customs and expectations, among which one must choose and reproduce to gain identity in a complex process of mutual recognition. In this way, the other is a constituent of identity in modernity and, consequently, the other directed character is a familiar type in late modernity, dependent upon others for recognition and thus for the establishment of personal identity (Fromm, 1955; Riesman et al., 1950).

In modernity, identity therefore becomes both a personal and a theoretical problem. Certain tensions appear within and between theories of identity, as well as within the modern individual. On one hand, some theorists of identity define personal identity in terms of a substantial self, an innate and self-identical essence that constitutes the person. From Descartes' cogito, to Kant's and Husserl's transcendental ego, to the enlightenment concept of reason, to some contemporary concepts of the subject, identity is conceived as something essential, substantial, unitary, fixed and fundamentally unchanging. Yet other modern theorists of identity postulate a non-substantiality of the self (Hume), or conceive of the self and identity as an existential project, as the creation of the authentic individual (Kierkegaard, Marx, Nietzsche, Heidegger and Sartre). The existential self is always contingent and fragile, and requires commitment, resolve and action to sustain, thus making the creation of identity an existential project for each individual.

Anxiety also becomes a constituent experience for the modern self. For one is never certain that one has made the right choice, that one has chosen one's 'true' identity, or even constituted an identity at all. The modern self is aware of the constructed nature of identity and that one can always change and modify one's identity at will. One is also anxious concerning recognition and validation of one's identity, by others. Further, modernity also involves a process of innovation, of constant turn-over and novelty. In some formulations, modernity signifies the destruction of past forms of life, values and identities, combined with the production of ever new ones (Berman, 1982). The experience of modernité is one of novelty, of the ever-changing new, of innovation and transitoriness (Frisby, 1985). One's identity may become out of date, or superfluous, or no longer socially validated. One may thus experience anomie, a condition of extreme alienation in which one is no longer at home in the world.

By contrast, one's identity may crystallize and harden such that ennui and boredom may ensue. One is tired of one's life, of who and what the one has become. One is trapped in a web of social roles, expectations and relations. There appears to be no exit and no possibility of change. Or, one is caught up in so many different, sometimes conflicting, roles that one no longer knows who one is. In these ways, identity in modernity becomes increasingly problematical and the issue of identity itself becomes a problem. Indeed, only in a society, anxiousness about identity could raise the problems of personal identity, self-identity and identity crises, and be subject to worry and debate. Theorists of self-identity are often anxious (Kierkegaard, Heidegger and Sartre) concerning the fragility of identity and analyze in detail those experiences and social forces that undermine and threaten personal identity.

Identity in modernity was also linked to individuality, to developing a uniquely individual self. Whereas traditionally, identity was a function of the tribe, the group, or a collective, in modernity identity was a function of creating a particularized individuality. In the consumer societies that emerged after World War II, identity has been increasingly linked to style, producing an image and how one looks. It is as if everyone has to have their own look, style and image to have their own identity, though, paradoxically, many of the models of style and look come from consumer culture; thus, individuality is highly mediated in the consumer society of the present.

Thus, in modernity, the problem of identity consisted in how we constitute, perceive, interpret and present our self to ourselves and to others. As noted, for some theorists, identity is a discovery and affirmation of an innate essence that determines what I am, while for others identity is a construct and a creation from available social roles and material. Contemporary post-modern thought has by and large rejected the essentialist and rationalist notion of identity and builds on the constructivist notion that it in turn problematizes. Consequently, one of the goals of this chapter will be to explicate how identity is formulated in post-modern theory and is constructed in contemporary cultural forms. At stake is whether identity is fundamentally different in so-called post-modernity and whether a distinction between modernity and post-modernity, and modern and post-modern identities, can be sustained.

From the post-modern perspective, as the pace, extension and complexity of modern societies accelerate, identity becomes qualitatively and extensively more and more unstable, more and more fragile. Within this situation, the discourses of post-modernity problematize the very notion of identity, claiming that it is a myth and an illusion. One reads both in modern theorists like the Frankfurt School, and in Baudrillard and other post-modern theorists, that the autonomous, self-constituting subject that was the achievement of modern individuals, of a culture of individualism, is fragmenting and disappearing, due to social processes which produce the levelling of individuality in a rationalized, bureaucratized, mediatized and consumerized mass society.[3] Post-structuralists in turn have launched an attack on the very notions of the subject and identity, claiming that subjective identity is itself a myth, a construct of language and society, an overdetermined illusion that one is really a substantial subject, that one really has a fixed identity (Coward and Ellis, 1977; Jameson, 1984, 1991).

It is thus claimed that in the post-modern culture, the subject has disintegrated into a flux of euphoric intensities, fragmented and disconnected, and that the decentred post-modern self no longer experiences anxiety (with hysteria becoming the typical post-modern psychic malady) and no longer possesses the depth, substantiality and coherency that was the ideal and sometimes achievement of the modern self (Baudrillard, 1983c; Jameson, 1983, 1991). Post-modern theorists claim that subjects have imploded into masses (Baudrillard, 1983b), that a fragmented, disjointed, and discontinuous mode of experience is a fundamental characteristic of post-modern culture, of both its subjective experiences and texts (Jameson, 1984, 1991). It is argued that in a post-modern media and information society one is at most a 'term in the terminal' (Baudrillard, 1983c), or a cyberneticized effect of 'fantastic systems of control' (Kroker and Cook, 1986). Deleuze and Guattari (1977) celebrate schizoid, nomadic dispersions of desire and subjectivity, valorizing precisely the breaking up and dispersion of the subject of modernity. In these theories, identity is highly unstable and has in some post-modern theories disappeared altogether in the 'post-modern scene' where:

> The TV self is the electronic individual par excellence who gets everything there is to get from the simulacrum of the media: a market-identity as a consumer in the society of the spectacle; a galaxy of hyperfibrillated moods ... traumatized serial being. (Kroker and Cook, 1986: 274)

Many of the post-modern theories privilege media culture as the site of the implosion of identity and fragmentation of the subject, yet there have been few systematic studies of media culture from this perspective. With the exception of the work of Jameson (see Kellner, 1989), few of the major post-modern theorists have carried out systematic and sustained examination of the actual texts and practices of popular media culture. For instance, Baudrillard's few references to the actual artefacts of media culture are extremely sketchy and fragmentary, as are those of Deleuze and Guattari (while Deleuze has written extensively on film, he does not theorize it as post-modern). Foucault and Lyotard have ignored media culture almost completely. And while Kroker and Cook carry out detailed readings of contemporary painting, they too neglect to carry out concrete studies of mass-mediated culture in their explorations of the post-modern scene (though, à la Baudrillard, they ascribe tremendous power to the media in the constitution of 'the post-modern scene').

In this study, I examine some mass-mediated artefacts to see what they tell us about the construction of identity in contemporary consumer societies in terms of advertising and fashion. My focus in on cigarette ads, since banned, which demonstrate the extent to which the consumer society went to construct gender and individual identities in terms of consumer products. To begin, I want to sketch out the historical role of images, fashions and commodities in the construction of contemporary identities, raising some questions about what advertising does and how it can play important roles in identity construction.

Advertising and Fashion as Channels of Desire

Today we are constantly bombarded by the messages and images of the consumer society. We wake up and turn on the radio, television or a record player. We go to school or work and observe the styles of clothes those around us, talk about and perhaps admire people's possessions, enjoy household gadgets and products and are assailed on all sides with advertising messages to buy, consume and possess the wonders of the commodity society.

Yet we rarely raise such questions as: When, where and how did the consumer society arise and why did it become such a central force in our lives? Does consumption make us happier, freer and better off than we were in a less consumer-oriented environment? How are our attitudes, behaviour and values shaped by advertising, fashion and all the institutions of the consumer society? What roles do advertising, fashion and consumerism play in legitimating the current socio-economic system, and in making us compliant players in the capitalist game of competition, success and material consumption? How are our very identities shaped by advertising and fashion? How can we become more rational consumers and free ourselves from media manipulation and advertising indoctrination?

Probably few of us raise these questions. Most of us have grown up in a society populated by magazines, television and radio with their ubiquitous ads. Most of us go to shopping malls or stores and are confronted with slickly packaged goods and a wealth of services—all for the right price of course. We are used to everything from medical to sexual services having a price tag and are told that there is no free lunch: everything in the society is a commodity and we are led to believe that consumer capitalism in the best socio-economic system in the world. Is this so? How did consumer capitalism come to play such an important role in our lives?

In *Captains of Consciousness*, Stuart Ewen tells of how corporations, advertising agencies and market research organizations began planning ways to produce consumers and to promote consumption as a way of life in the United States during the 1920s (Ewen, 1976). Individual resistance to new products had to be broken down and individuals had to be convinced that it was 'good' to consume, spend money and gratify their desires. Previously, a work ethic and puritan savings ethic prevailed which held that getting what you wanted, when you wanted it, and enjoying the process were immoral; advertising had to convince individuals on the contrary that consumption was a new route to happiness and satisfaction. Advertising also attempted to create fears that unless individuals bought products to combat bad breath, body odour, oily or tangly hair, they would not be socially acceptable. Thus, advertising attempted to create problems and fears to which commodities were offered as a solution and desires for new products. In this way, a commodity self emerged in which different products allowed individuals to develop or present different aspects of 'their' personality that could be produced or shaped by using the right products and producing the right image.

To keep a high level of consumer demand in place, individuals also needed to be constantly persuaded that they continually needed new products to be fashionable and up to date. The advertising and fashion industries thus had to persuade consumers to throw away old products and to continually buy new ones. The fashion industry began to accelerate the turnover of models, trends, styles and products. While formerly individuals purchased products for durability, now style and fashion began to dictate consumer choices. Previously, automobiles, for instance, followed more or less the same design and style and one presumably bought an automobile for life. In the consumer boom after World War II, however, new automobile styles, fashion styles and constant refashioning of products and styles promoted a frenzied orgy of consumption in which individuals bought, borrowed and stole to constantly purchase the latest models and fashions which the fashion and consumer industries set out to promote.

Advertising and fashion combine individuality and conformity in curious ways. Individuals consume and pursue fashion to individuate them yet do so in order to be socially accepted, to fit in, to be popular. Moreover, it is mass produced goods and fashion that are used to produce individuality. Such a commodity self and presentation of 'individuality' in terms of fashion and mass goods could only emerge in a society controlled by 'image'. How did such a social order emerge, and what role did mass images play in the production of the consumer society and commodity self?

As Elisabeth and Stuart Ewen tell us in their important history of consumer culture, consumerism and Americanism were promoted by mass images beginning in the nineteenth century

when newspapers began selling advertising and when corporations attempted to impress their brand name and product's
image on the consumer (Ewen and Ewen, 1982). Ewen tells the
story of how a young Czech girl, Anna Kuthan, was fascinated by
the labels on bales of cotton and the products she handled as a
servant girl in Vienna; these 'channels of desire' promised a new
world of commodity paradise, happiness through consumption
and a new identity as a consumer. She eventually immigrated to
the United States where the reality of the 'American dream' was
a life of hard work and suffering compensated by a few brand
name products that she had always dreamed of. Was she, in fact,
better off leaving her home and traditions to toil in a New York
ghetto? Was the possibility of enabling her children to own a
house in the suburbs worth her own life of toil? Is consumption
the way to happiness?

By the 1920s, corporations, advertising agencies and market
research organizations began planning ways to produce consumers and to promote consumption as a way of life in the United
States (Ewen, 1976). Individual resistance to new products had to
be broken down and individuals had to be convinced that it was
acceptable to purchase goods that they had previously produced
themselves and that it was morally justifiable to consume, spend
money and gratify desires. Previously, a work ethic and puritan
savings ethic prevailed which held that getting what you wanted,
when you wanted it, and enjoying the process were immoral;
advertising had to convince individuals on the contrary that consumption was a new route to happiness and satisfaction.

Advertising also attempted to create fears that unless individuals bought products to combat bad breath, body odour, oily or
tangly hair, they would not be socially acceptable. Thus, advertising attempted to create problems and fears to which commodities
were offered as a solution and desires for new products. In this
way, a 'commodity self' emerged in which different products
allowed individuals to develop or present different aspects of
'their' personality that could be produced or shaped by using the
right products and producing the right image.

The consumer society evolved into the dominant form of
American society after World War II and by the 2000s had

become a global phenomenon. It had its origins in the big department stories (Macy's, Gimbel's and Marshall Field's) and the mail order houses (Sear's and Ward's) that began in the nineteenth century (Ewen and Ewen, 1982). It was promoted by the advertising agencies and corporate campaigns of the 1920s but was postponed first by the Great Depression of the 1930s which dramatized the failures of capitalism to provide a rational society without state intervention (Ewen, 1976) and World War II which dramatized the darker side of twentieth century drives for power and profits. After World War II, returning servicemen came home with large amounts of back pay and the corporations tooled up to make the consumer society a reality. New goods, services, shopping centres and marketing techniques appeared, and the move towards the suburbs and rise of television helped promote the consumer society (Jezer, 1982).

The era from the 1950s to the present might be seen in retrospect as the age of consumption. But how do advertising, fashion and consumption socialize us into being compliant participants in the dream world of consumer culture? What sort of identities does advertising and the consumer society offer? On one level, advertising and fashion function to manage consumer demand, to get us to buy products, but on a deeper level what is significant about advertising and fashion is not the fact that they sell us this or that toothpaste, shampoo or car, but that they sell us consumerism as a way of life and promote the belief that happiness is to be found through consumption.

Advertising implies that a solution to every problem can be found through the commodity purchased, and thus offers commodity solutions to all the problems of life. Fashion tells us that products, styles and trends are constantly changing and that one must keep up with fashion and all the new products to be with it, to be popular, to make it. You're not getting enough dates. Buy the proper mouthwash, deodorant, perfume or after-shave lotion and all will be well. You're not successful sexually? Buy a new car, better clothes, more up-scale alcohol and toys and you'll score. This sounds crude but it is the clear message of most fashion ads, and a large percentage of magazine ads that use sexual desires and insecurity to sell their products—and sometimes includes blatantly subliminal sexual imagery as well (Key, 1972).

Advertising also promises commodity solutions to health problems. You're not feeling well? Just take Geritol for tired blood; XY and Z for headaches; A or B for heartburn or indigestion; or eat Wheaties, the breakfast of champions, or Total or K or whatever, and you'll supposedly be bursting with vim, vigour and vitality.

Advertising also plays on fears that one is either not attractive enough or is not properly playing one's role in life. Do you want to be a good housewife and mother? Buy X soap to eliminate ring-around-the-collar; brand P frozen pizza to bring your family to quasi-orgasmic ecstasies; and Q bathroom deodorant and sweetener to give your toilet more appetizing smells and colours. Want to have a happy family life: go to MacDonald's, pig out on Big Macs and enjoy the pleasures promised to all good Americans (and be sure to have plenty of stomach remedies at home to deal with the aftermaths of junk food orgies).

Do you want to have fun then enjoy community, and social acceptance. Join the Pepsi generation, or be a Pepper, or drink Coke, or the uncola, 7-Up (and be sure to have a good dentist for when your teeth start rotting). And girls, do you want to be a Total Woman? Easy, just buy a 24-hour perfume so you can work your ass off at the office or school; come home and fix dinner and clean up house, and still be sexy and sweet smelling for husband or boyfriend. And do you want to be really respected and desired, boys? Just get a new luxury car, read Playboy or Hustler to see what you need for your pad, and just wait for the bunnies to come running over (and hope that they don't bring any sexual diseases with them).

The point that I am trying to make is that ads offer commodity solutions to all problems, and present consumption as the route to happiness. Therefore, advertising not only sells products but tries to sell consumerism as a way of life, the American way of life. It provides role models showing us how to be a proper man or woman, and sells specific values such as romance and sexuality as crucial values of fundamental importance. In turn, it uses desires for sex and romance to sell specific products.

Advertising also sells institutions like the family, and American values like individuality, gratification through consumption and the joys of ownership. As Robert Goldman has argued, certain ads promote an idealized version of American history and the institutions and values of corporate capitalism as they try to huckster their products (Goldman, 1984). For instance, McDonalds' ads frequently contain images of small town America, family life, middle-class affluence and integrated Americana that surround the images of the Big Macs and McMuffins that they are trying to sell.

Other ads promote consumerist ideology by equating consumerism with 'Freedom of Choice' (i.e. between their light and regular beer) or tell you to be an 'individual' by buying this or that product, or dousing yourself in this or that perfume or aftershave lotion. And note that 'individualism' here is defined in terms of possession, consumption and style—as opposed to thought, action, dissent, rational behaviour and autonomy, which were previous definitions of individualism in earlier stages of modern societies.

Advertising, Images, Identity and Mythologies

Like film and television narratives, advertising too can be seen as providing some functional equivalents of myth. Like myths, ads frequently resolve social contradictions, provide models of identity and celebrate the existing social order. Barthes (1972; orig. 1957) saw that advertising provided a repertoire of contemporary mythologies, and in the following discussion I depict how cigarette ads contribute to identity formation in contemporary society. The following analysis is intended to show that even the static images of advertising contain subject positions and models for identification that are heavily coded ideologically. As in the previous discussion, I argue here that the images of media culture are important both in the mode of their formal image construction and address and identities which they help construct, as well as in terms of the meanings and values which they communicate.

Accordingly, I discuss some print ads that are typical of hegemonic forms of advertising and which lend themselves to critical analysis.

Print ads are an important sector of the advertising world with about 50 per cent of advertising revenues going to various print media, while 22 per cent is expended on television advertising. Let us look first, then, at two cigarette ads: a 1981 Marlboro ad aimed primarily at male smokers and a 1983 Virginia Slims ad which tries to convince women that it is cool to smoke and that the product being advertised is perfect for the 'modern' woman (see Figures 7.1 and 7.2).[4] Corporations like the tobacco industry undertake campaigns to associate their product with positive and desirable images and gender models. Thus, in the 1950s, Marlboro undertook a campaign to associate its cigarette with masculinity, associating smoking its product with being a 'real man'.

Figure 7.1:
1981 Marlboro ad

Source: http://i.ebayimg.com/t/1981-Marlboro-Cigarettes-Ad-2-Cowboys-1-White-Shirt-/06/!B+rVFnwCWk~$(KGrHqQOKiIEzS11)pB9BN!YUqyoG!~~_3.JPG (accessed on 4 April 2012).

Figure 7.2:
1983 Virginia Slims ad

Source: http://www.flickr.com/photos/chanadaal/431990861/ (accessed on 4 April 2012).

Marlboro had been previously packaged as a milder women's cigarette, and the 'Marlboro man' campaign was an attempt to capture the male cigarette market with images of archetypically masculine characters. Since the cowboy, Western image provided a familiar icon of masculinity, independence, and ruggedness, it was the preferred symbol for the campaign. Subsequently, the 'Marlboro man' became a part of American folklore and a readily identifiable cultural symbol.

Such symbolic images in advertising attempt to create an association between the products offered and socially desirable and meaningful traits in order to produce the impression that if one wants to be a certain type of person—for instance, to be a 'real man' —then one should buy Marlboro cigarettes. Consequently, for decades, Marlboro used the cowboy figure as the symbol of masculinity and the centre of their ads. In a post-modern image culture, individuals get their very identity from these figures; thus advertising becomes an important and overlooked mechanism of socialization, as well as manager of consumer demand.

Ads form textual systems with basic components which are interrelated in ways that positively position the product. The main components of the classical Marlboro ads are the conjunction of nature, the cowboy, horses and the cigarette. This system associates the Marlboro cigarette with masculinity, power and nature. Note, however, in Figure 7.1 how the cowboy is a relatively small figure, dwarfed by the images of snow, trees and sky. Whereas in earlier Marlboro ads, the Marlboro man loomed largely in the centre of the frame, now images of nature are highlighted. Why this shift?

All ads are social texts that respond to key developments during the period in which they appear. During the 1980s, media reports concerning the health hazard of cigarettes became widespread— a message highlighted in the mandatory box at the bottom of the ad that 'the surgeon general has determined that cigarette smoking is dangerous to your health'. As a response to this attack, the Marlboro ads next features images of clean, pure, wholesome nature, as if it were 'natural' to smoke cigarettes, as if cigarettes were a healthy 'natural' product, an emanation of benign and healthy nature. The ad, in fact, hawks Marlboro Lights and one of the captions describes it as a 'low tar cigarette'. The imagery is itself 'light', white, green, snowy and airy. Through the process of metonomy, or contiguous association, the ad tries to associate the cigarettes with light, natural, healthy snow, horses, the cowboy, trees and sky, as if they were all related 'natural' artefacts, sharing the traits of 'nature', thus covering over the fact that cigarettes are an artificial, synthetic product, full of dangerous pesticides, preservatives and other chemicals.

Thus, the images of healthy nature are a Barthesian mythology (Barthes, 1972) which attempt to cover over the image of the dangers to health from cigarette smoking. The Marlboro ad also draws on images of tradition (the cowboy), hard work (note how deeply in the snow the horse is immersed; this cowboy is doing some serious working), caring for animals and other desirable traits, as if smoking were a noble activity, metonomically equivalent to these other positive social activities. The images, texts, and product shown in the ad thus provide a symbolic construct that tries to cover over and camouflage contradictions between the 'heavy' work and the 'light' cigarette, between the 'natural' scene and the 'artificial' product, between the cool and healthy outdoors scene and between the hot and unhealthy activity of smoking, and the rugged masculinity of the Marlboro man and the light cigarette, originally targeted at women. In fact, this latter contradiction can be explained by the marketing ploy of suggesting to men that they can both be highly masculine, like the Marlboro man, and smoke a (supposedly) 'healthier' cigarette, while also appealing to macho women who might enjoy smoking a man's cigarette which is also 'lighter' and 'healthier', as women's cigarettes are supposed to be.

The 1983 Virginia Slims ad (Figure 7.2) attempts in a similar fashion to associate its product with socially desired traits and offers subject positions with which women can identify. The Virginia Slims textual system classically includes a vignette at the top of the ad with a picture underneath of the Virginia Slims woman next to the prominently displayed package of cigarettes. In the example pictured, the top of the ad features a framed box that contains the narrative images and message, which is linked to the changes in the situation of women portrayed through a contrast with the 'modern' woman in the following. The caption under the boxed image of segregated male and female exercise classes in 1903 contains the familiar Virginia Slims slogan 'You've come a long way, baby'. The caption, linked to the Virginia Slims woman, next to the package of cigarettes, connotes a message of progress, metonomically linking Virginia Slims to the 'progressive woman' and 'modern' living. In this ad, it is the linkages and connections between the parts that establish the message which associates Virginia Slims with progress. The ad tells women that it is progressive and socially acceptable to smoke, and it associates Virginia Slims with modernity, social progress and the desired social trait of slimness.

In fact, Lucky Strike carried out a successful advertising campaign in the 1930s which associated smoking with weight reduction ('Reach for a lucky instead of a sweet!'), and Virginia Slims plays on this tradition, encapsulated in the very brand name of the product. Note too that the cigarette is a 'Lights' variety and that, like the Marlboro ad, it tries to associate its product with health and well-being. The pronounced smile on the woman's face also tries to associate the product with happiness and self-contentment, struggling against the association of smoking with guilt and dangers to one's health. The image of the slender woman, in turn, associated with slimness and lightness, not only associates the product with socially desirable traits, but in turn promotes the ideal of slimness as the ideal type of femininity.

Later in the 1980s, Çapri cigarettes advertised its product as 'the slimmest slim!', building on the continued and intensified association of slimness with femininity. The promotion of smoking and slimness is far from innocent, however, and has contributed to eating disorders, faddish diets and exercise programmes, and a dramatic increase in anoxeria among young women, as well as rising cancer rates. As Williamson (1978) points out, advertising 'addresses' individuals and invites them to identify with certain products, images and behaviour. Advertising provides a utopian image of a new, more attractive, more successful, more prestigious 'you' through purchase of certain goods. Advertising magically offers self-transformation and a new identity, associating changes in consumer behaviour, fashion and appearance with metamorphosis into a new person. Consequently, individuals are taught to identify with values, role models and social behaviour through advertising which is thus an important instrument of socialization as well as a manager of consumer demand.

Advertising sells its products and view of the world through images, rhetoric, slogans and their juxtaposition in ads to which tremendous artistic resources, psychological research and marketing strategies are devoted. These ads express and reinforce dominant images of gender and position men and women to assume highly specific subject positions. Two 1988 and 1989 Virginia Slims ads, in fact, reveal a considerable transformation in its image of women during the 1980s and a new strategy to persuade women that it is all right and even 'progressive' and ultramodern to smoke. This move points to shifts in the relative power between men and women and discloses new subject positions for women validated by the culture industries.

Once again the sepia-coloured framed box at the top of the ad contains an image of a woman serving her man in 1902; the comic pose and irritated look of the woman suggests that such servitude is highly undesirable and its contrast with the Virginia Slims woman (who herself now wears the leather boots and leather gloves and jacket as well) suggests that women have come a long way while the ever-present cigarette associates woman's right to smoke in public with social progress. This time the familiar 'You've come a long way, baby' is absent, perhaps because the woman pictured would hardly tolerate being described as 'baby' and because women's groups had been protesting the sexist and demeaning label in the slogan. Note, too, the transformation of the image of the woman in the Virginia Slims ad. No longer the smiling, cute and wholesome potential wife of the earlier ad, she is now more threatening, more sexual, less wifely and more masculine. The sunglasses connote the distance from the male gaze which she wants to preserve and the leather jacket with the military insignia connotes that she is equal to men, able to carry on a masculine role, and is stronger and more autonomous than women of the past.

The 1988 ad (Figure 7.3) is highly anti-patriarchal and even expresses hostility towards men with the overweight man with glasses and handle bar moustache looking slightly ridiculous while it is clear that the woman is being held back by ridiculous fashion and intolerable social roles. The 'new' Virginia Slims woman, however, who completely dominates the scene, is the

Figure 7.3:
1988 Virginia Slims ad

epitome of style and power. This strong woman can easily take in hand and enjoy the phallus (i.e. the cigarette as the sign of male power accompanied by the male dress and military insignia) and serve as an icon of female glamour as well. This ad links power, glamour and sexuality and offers a model of female power, associated with the cigarette and smoking. Ads work in part by generating dissatisfaction and by offering images of transformation, of a new personal identity. This particular ad promotes dissatisfaction with traditional images and presents a new image of a more powerful woman, a new life-style and identity for the Virginia Slims smoker. In these ways, the images associate the products advertised with certain socially desirable traits and convey messages concerning the symbolic benefits accrued to those who consume the product.

Although 'Lights' and 'Ultra Lights' continue to be the dominant Virginia Slims types, the phrase does not appear as a highlighted caption in the 1988 ad as it used to and the package does not appear either. No doubt this 'heavy' woman contradicts the 'light' image and the ad connotes instead power and (a dubious) progress for women rather than slimness or lightness. Yet the woman's teased and flowing blonde hair, her perfect teeth which form an obliging smile, and especially her crotch positioned in the ad in a highly suggestive and inviting fashion code her as a symbol of beauty and sexuality, albeit more autonomous and powerful.

The 1989 Virginia Slims ad, by contrast, depicts a more conventional image of woman, but one that is significantly different from the earlier, more traditional images of women in the ads. At the top of the 1989 ad, there are, once again, two vignettes in black and white that connote the bad old days for women. On the left, a working woman lights up a cigarette and angers her boss. Below, however, the beautiful Virginia Slims woman confidently and happily holds the cigarette in her hand. The ad as a whole connotes the standard message of progress, linking Virginia Slims to the 'modern woman' who has progressed from oppressed servant of men to independent subject of her own life.

The appearance of the 1989 Virginia Slims woman contributes to this message. Her hair is teased, her make-up is perfect, her smile is dazzling, and her clothes are flamboyant. Indeed, the woman could easily be a model for a fashion ad: she wears long, phallic ear-rings to connote her (quasi-masculine) power; the ear-rings are also mismatched, connotating her independence, style and non-conformity. The 'loud' red hat, carelessly strewn over her shoulder also connotes her individuality while the bright red shirt, which exposes both her shoulders and part of her stomach, connotes daring and sexuality. The gold bracelet on her wrist connotes luxury and fashion, while the belt with the silver buckle and the exotic short shirt connotes colourfulness and creative individual fashion. Thus, the Virginia Slims cigarette is not only associated with modernity and progress, but also with individuality, sexuality, fashion and style.

The point I am trying to make is that it is precisely the images that are the vehicles of the subject positions and that therefore critical literacy in a contemporary image culture and consumer society requires learning how to read images critically and to unpack the relations between images, texts, social trends and products in commercial culture (Kellner, 1995). My reading of these ads suggests that advertising is as concerned with selling life-styles and socially desirable identities, which are associated with their products, as with selling the product themselves or rather, that advertisers use the symbolic constructs with which the consumer is invited to identify to try to induce her to use their product. Thus, the Marlboro man (i.e. the consumer who smokes the cigarette) is smoking masculinity or natural vigour as much as a cigarette, while the Virginia Slims woman is exhibiting modernity, thinness or female power when she lights up her 'slim'.

This sort of reading of advertising not only helps individuals to resist manipulation, but it also depicts how something as seemingly innocuous as advertising can depict significant shifts in modes and models of identity. For example, the two Virginia Slims ads suggest that at least a certain class of women (white, upper-middle and upper class) were gaining more power in society and that women were being attracted by stronger, more autonomous and more masculine images. Advertising campaigns attempt to incorporate such images to associate their products with the socially desired traits that are then further promoted with the ads' attempts to promote their products.

While the Marlboro ads once centred on the 'Marlboro man', and in the early 1980s continued to feature this figure, curiously, by the late 1980s, human beings disappeared altogether from some Marlboro ads that projected pure images of wholesome nature associated with the product. The caption 'Made especially for menthol smokers', the green menthol insignia on the cigarette package, and the blue and green backdrops of the trees, grass and water in the ad all attempt to incorporate icons of health and nature into the ads, as if these menthol Lights would protect the buyer from cigarette health hazards. Undoubtedly, this transformation in the Marlboro ads points to growing concern about the health hazards of cigarettes which requires even purer emphasis on nature. Yet the absence of the Marlboro cowboy might also point to the obsolescence of the manual worker in a post-industrial information and service society where significant sectors of the so-called new middle class work in the industries of symbol and image production and manipulation.

The prominent images of the powerful horses in the 1990 Marlboro ad (Figure 7.4), however, point to a continued desire for power and fantasies of virility and masculinity. The actual powerlessness of workers in contemporary capitalist society makes it in turn difficult to present concrete contemporary images of male power that would appeal to a variety of male (and female) smokers. Eliminating the male figure also allows appeal over a wider range of social classes and occupational types, including both men and women who could perhaps respond more positively to images of nature and power than to the rather obsolete cowboy figure. Further—and these images are clearly polysemic, subject to multiple readings—the new emphasis on 'Great refreshment in the Flip-Top box' not only harmonizes with the 'refreshing' images of green and nature, but points to the new hedonist, leisure culture in post-modern society with its emphasis on the pleasures of consumption, spectacle and refreshment. The refreshment tag also provides a new legitimation for cigarette smoking as a refreshing activity (building on the famous Pepsi 'pause that refreshes'?) which codes an obviously dangerous activity as 'refreshing' and thus as health promoting.

Moreover, the absence of human figures in mid-1980s Marlboro ads could be read as signs of the erasure of the human in post-modern society, giving credence to Foucault's claim that in a new episteme the human itself could be washed away like a face drawn on sand at the edge of the sea (Foucault, 1970: 387).

Figure 7.4:
1990 Marlboro Lights ad

Yet the human cannot so easily be wished away and lo and behold in 1989, not only human figures, but the Marlboro man himself returned in a new ad campaign. The 1989 Marlboro ad provides an example of a new advertising strategy that requires the consumer to produce the meaning herself, much like a modernist text. This fully two-page ad portrays giant hands (presumably those of the Marlboro man himself) holding a pair of gloves, with a cigarette held between two gnarled and weather-beaten fingers. The only caption—besides the federally mandated list of ingredients and warnings to one's health—says: 'Come to where the flavour is'. There is no Marlboro cigarette box portrayed nor any caption stating the brand name. Instead one has to look quite closely at the small brand name inscribed on the cigarette itself to discern precisely what brand is being advertised.

Half of the two-page ad is buried in darkness with only the caption and difficult to decipher fragments of images emerging. The other half of the ad centres on the gnarled hands, perhaps projecting the subliminal message to those concerned with the health risks of smoking that it is possible to smoke and survive. For the heavily lined hands are obviously those of someone who has lived life to the full, whose vicissitudes and experience are etched into the very skin of his hands, whose deeply textured skin attests to a long-lived life. In this way, the cigarette is associated with survival and a full life, thus assuaging worries that smoking constitutes a serious risk of cancer and other dread diseases and providing subliminal functions of anxiety reduction—a typical task of contemporary advertising.

This Marlboro ad is one of a genre of contemporary ads which forces the consumer to work at discerning the brand being sold and at deciphering the text to construct meaning. The minimalism of product signifiers appeals to readers jaded with traditional advertising, tired of the same old stale images, and bored with and cynical towards advertising manipulation. To the cool post-modern reader, the association of masculinity with smoking Marlboros might be laughable, yet even such minimalist ads utilize product differentiation and use new images while building on old cues. In addition to appealing to a survivalist urge in the contemporary smoker, the 1988 Marlboro ad invites her to 'Come to where the flavour is'. The emphasis on flavour appeals to hedonist tastes, to enjoy the flavour, to light up for pleasure. Such appeals interpellate contemporary individualist–hedonist impulses to have fun, to do what one wants and pleases at all costs—even the destruction of one's health.

The textual system of the ad addresses its reader as an individual, as someone able to read the complex ad and to choose their own pleasures as they will. There is thus a subliminal appeal to the individual's freedom and creativity which invites the reader to interpret the ad as one chooses and to light up the cigarette when one pleases in disregard of the obligatory government warnings linking cigarettes to health risks. The gnarled hands as well are those of an individual who takes charge of his life and who makes his own decisions, so the text as a whole is structured to associate smoking Marlboro with individuality and power. Interestingly, this ad and the other Marlboro ads that erase human subjects play down gender identity and one might read this as a de-centring of gender identity in contemporary society, as a disassociation between the product and gender, as a bracketing of the centrality of gender in the constitution of identity. The appeal here is directly to use-value, to the pleasure and flavour that the cigarette produces rather than the sign value of masculinity, or the appeal to power.

Moreover, this text works to get the reader to identify with the product and to produce a pleasurable feeling from the feat of producing meaning, from reading the ambiguous text, that is presumably then transferred to and associated with the product, so that the image of Marlboro is associated with free choice and creativity. And yet the highly paid cultural interpreters who work for advertising agencies were hedging their bets concerning the Marlboro ads of the late 1980s. These ads featured a return of the previous realist ads which centre on the old Marlboro cowboy, along with production of a new type of ad just analyzed, as well as a new series of pure nature imagery.

In the post-modern 1990s, Marlboro returned to recycling old images, especially of the famous cowboy and nature. The 11–17 December 1993, *TV Guide* back cover ad, for instance, features the cowboy riding a horse, followed by another horse which he has roped and is leading through a snowy field. The white snow is blowing behind the cowboy deploying the images of nature. Thus, the image combines power and control with images of nature, implying that if you want to be a natural man and in control, smoke a Marlboro. Curiously, however, although the corporate insignia 'Marlboro' is featured in bright red script there is no pack of cigarettes, or even a single cigarette, shown, nor is the cowboy, pictured hard at work, smoking. It is if Marlboro is embarrassed by their product and can only sell the qualities of nature and masculinity—and death, as the Surgeon General's Warning, boldly emblazoned in a letter box in the bottom right-hand corner notes.

The multiplicity of strategies in cigarette ads shows that the advertising agencies of contemporary capitalism are not at all sure as to what will attract consumers to their products, or with what images consumers identify. For, as I have been arguing, one of the features of contemporary culture is precisely the fragmentation, transitoriness, and multiplicity of images, which refuse to crystalize into a stable image culture. Thus, the advertising and cultural industries draw on modern and post-modern strategies, and on traditional, modern, and post-modern themes and iconography.

Traditional, Modern and Post-modern Identities and the Consumer Society

The Marlboro cigarette advertising campaigns just explored suggest that the highly paid and often sharp interpreters of the contemporary scene in the employment of corporate capital see the continuing existence of traditional identities, where masculinity is still important, combined with a modern concern for power and enjoyment as a continuing social force and matrix of contemporaries values and identity. These ads show that traditional and modern culture coexists with a post-modern culture whereby new forms of images are needed to catch the attention of a jaded and cynical consumer. If post-modernity were the cultural totality that some of its celebrants claim, one imagines that the most highly paid and sophisticated image producers would inundate its denizens with post-modern imagery, but, no, contemporary advertising and media culture suggests that instead the contemporary culture is highly fragmented into different taste cultures which respond by producing quite different images and values.

A megacorporation like Marlboro goes after all of these audiences, thus one sees a certain heterogeneity in its image productions with different appeals sent out to different audiences according to market segmentation: the old Marlboro man for readers of *TV Guide*; horses and nature for the health and vitality conscious readers of fashion magazines like *Elle and M*; and more complex aesthetic spectacles for the gourmet hedonists who read *Vanity Fair* and the like. The multiplicity of advertising strategies pursued by the Marlboro folks also points to the immanent contradictions of commodity culture. Advertising attempts to produce identities by offering products associated with certain traits and values. And yet the inexorable trends of fashion and the new advertising campaigns undermine previously forged identities and associations to circulate new products, new images, new values and new identities.

To be sure, there have been ad campaigns that adopt postmodern strategies of image construction to sell their goods. Robert Goldman describes one Reebok campaign that failed (1992) and in 1993–1994, Levi's ran an ad campaign that showed disconnected fragments of images and words of the contemporary scene with the product logo submerged in the text as just another fragment, forcing the viewer to figure out what was being advertised—which is, one supposes, an effective way to get the brand name in the viewer's mind which is a major function of the advertisement, though as failed post-modern ad campaigns indicate, the strategy of deploying post-modernism in the aesthetics of advertising is risky.

Advertising, fashion, consumption, television and media culture constantly destabilize identity and contribute to producing more unstable, fluid, shifting and changing identities in the contemporary scene. And yet one also sees the inexorable processes of commodification at world in this process. The market segmentation of multiple ad campaigns and appeals reproduces and intensifies fragmentation and destablizes identity that new products and identifications are attempting to restabilize. Thus, it is capital itself which is the demiurge of allegedly post-modern fragmentation, dispersal of identity, change and mobility. Rather than post-modernity constituting a break with capital and political economy as Baudrillard and others would have it, wherever one observes phenomena of post-modern culture one can detect the logic of capital behind them.

This argument suggests that much post-modern theory is excessively abstract in bracketing political economy and capitalism from the phenomena that it describes and thus occludes their economic underpinnings. Furthermore, such theory tends to overgeneralize, taking examples from new emergent trends that it conflates into a new cultural dominant. Some post-modern cultural theory also abstracts from ideological content and effects, focusing merely on formal structures or image construction. Against such positions, I have argued that rather than advertising and the other images of media culture being flat, one dimensional and without ideological coding, as some post-modern theory would have it, many ads are multi-dimensional, polysemic, ideologically coded, open to a variety of readings and expressive of the commodification of culture and attempts of capital to colonialize the totality of life, from desire to satisfaction.

My analyses thus suggest that in contemporary image culture, the images, scenes, stories and cultural texts of media culture offer a wealth of subject positions that in turn help structure individual identity. These images project role and gender models, appropriate and inappropriate forms of behaviour, style and fashion, and subtle enticements to emulate and identify with certain identities while avoiding others. Rather than identity disappearing in a post-modern society, it is merely subject to new determinations and new forces while offering as well new possibilities, styles, models and forms. Yet the overwhelming variety of possibilities for identity in an affluent image culture no doubt creates highly unstable identities while constantly providing new openings to restructure one's identity.

It is difficult to say whether on the whole this is a 'good' or 'bad' thing, and it is probably safer to conclude with Jameson that the phenomena associated with post-modernity are highly ambivalent and exhibit both progressive and regressive features.

There does seem to be more of an acceptance of multiple and unstable identities in the contemporary cultural mileux than was the case previously. Modern identities—however multiple and subject to change—appeared to be more stable, whereas there currently seems to be more acceptance of change, fragmentation, and theatrical play with identity than was the case in the earlier, heavier and more serious epoch of modernity.

On one hand, this increases one's freedom to play with one's identity and to dramatically change one's life (which may be good for some individuals), while, on the other hand, it can lead to a totally fragmented, disjointed life, subject to the whims of fashion and the subtle indoctrinations of advertising and popular culture. Against a totally dispersed, fragmented and disconnected identity, one might want to valorize certain features central to modern identity, such as autonomy, rationality, commitment, responsibility and so on, or one might want to reconstruct these concepts, as, for instance, Habermas has attempted to do with rationality. In any case, identity continues to be the problem throughout modernity, though it has been problematized anew in the current orgy of commodification, fragmentation, image production and societal, political and cultural transformation that is the work of consumer capitalism.

Indeed, the quest for identity is arguably more intense than ever in the present moment. There has been something of a rebellion against producing identity solely as an individual achievement in the contemporary era, with increased emphasis on tribal, national, group, and other forms of collective identity. In many parts of the world, there has been a return to tribalism, to past forms of collective identities—national, religious or ethnic—and one finds parallel projects in so-called identity politics whereby individuals gain identity through membership in groups and affirmation of a collective identity (i.e. as a woman, a black, a gay or some combination thereof).

Yet the quest for individuality and particularity in one's look, image, style and life continues apace. Media figures such as Michael Jackson, Madonna and Lady Gaga show that identity is a construct, that it can be constantly changed, refined and fine-tuned, that identity is a question of image, style and looks.

Michael Jackson, for instance, erased the boundary between black and white, male and female and adult and youth in his image constructions. In some of his music videos, he appears black, in others white and in yet others indeterminate; sometimes he appears highly masculine, sometimes more feminine, sometimes androgynous. At times, he appears as an adult, firmly in control of his career as King of Pop, and other times he appears as a youth, as a lover of children who is more comfortable with kids and being a kid than with adults.

Madonna and Lady Gaga constantly changed identities, looks and fashion, creating outrageous alternatives to standard feminine identities and becoming role models for their fans. While it is fine to produce one's own look and style, identity is more complex and differentiated than through image alone, as Madonna and Lady Gaga themselves reveal in their clever constructions of their careers and changes of fashion and musical style in different periods [on Madonna, see Kellner (1995)].

The point is that many icons of media culture suggest that identity is a matter of individual choice and action and that each individual can produce their own unique identity. In any case, the issue of identity is more pressing and contested than ever before in contemporary societies. Against the globalization of culture, there are intense struggles to preserve and enhance national identities; against the forced identities of modern nationhood (often a product of imperialism), individuals and groups are constructing identities in terms of religion, ethnicity and region against former national identities; against all collective identities, other individuals are attempting to construct their own personal identities, which often are, however, highly mediated by collective forces.

Personal identity is thus fraught with contradictions and tensions. Many individuals, for often different reasons, are indifferent to national or other collective identities and wish to construct their identities through their own life-styles, looks, and image. Others passionately embrace identity politics and construct their identities, their deepest sense of who they are, by affirming their membership in various groups or collectivities (i.e. women, blacks, gays or whatever). Some have labelled this form of identity politics 'post-modern', but interest group politics and even gaining identity through political and group affiliation is also a modern phenomenon.

In response to the attempts of advertising and the consumer society to construct identities in terms of consumption and look, individuals need to learn to read and decipher advertising, learning to see through the hype and puffery and to be able to analyze and criticize its manipulative techniques. One should learn to protect oneself against domination by advertising through becoming aware of how ads are constructed; of what techniques are being used; of what devices are used to manipulate you; and of what general social messages you are receiving. Finally, despite propaganda from corporations and advertising agencies to the contrary, one should see advertising itself as a parasitical industry dedicated to manipulation, and not providing information as advertisers claim—at least this is true of most television and magazine advertising. Advertising is a tremendous social drain that a rational society would either eliminate or radically restructure from an instrument of manipulation into solely an instrument of socially necessary and beneficial information. Arguably, advertising is a disgraceful waste of resources, talent and time (Packard, 1960), and anyone who tells you differently is deceived or is prostituting themselves. A rational society would ban advertising completely or would simply use it for informational purposes.

However, in capitalist societies, advertising is a prime manipulator of consumer demand and a source of political socialization and propaganda for the system, though it is not usually perceived as such. Moreover, advertising has come to dominate broadcasting and our media system in the United States and other capitalist societies. While it appears that television in the United States is 'free', one actually pays higher prices for goods and services because costs of advertising are passed down to consumers. Thus, one not only literally pays for the indignity of having one's television programmes interrupted but advertising dominated programming ensures that the television networks will keep providing mediocre programming that manages not to offend significant segments of the mass audience.

In the Internet era, one is finding that Google and other popular Internet sites are also using advertising to fund their activities so that as one surfs the net for information, one is increasingly being subjected to advertising messages. Eventually, citizens of advanced capitalist societies are going to have to seriously question the priorities, values, and institutions of consumer capitalism. Each individual and society as a whole need to consider the social effects of advertising and fashion and whether the consumer society provides the most rational and beneficial social order, or whether we can produce better alternatives. The many-sided failures of neo-liberalism in the 2000s provide the incentive for critical scrutiny of our current social organization and require that we find better alternatives if we wish to preserve the democracy, freedom, and individuality to which we pay lip service.[5]

Notes

1. This chapter is obviously written from the perspective of a North American living in Los Angeles in a high-consumption society. In an era of globalization, however, such mechanisms and themes that are discussed in this area increasingly appear globally. For my take on globalization, see Kellner (2002).

2. On identity in modernity, see Berman (1982), and the essays collected in Friedman and Lash (1992). On the discourses of modernity, see Hardt and Negri (2009). Following Berman, I interpret modernity here as an epoch of rapid change, innovation and negation of the old and creation of the new, a process bound up with industrial capitalism, the French revolution, urbanization and social and cultural differentiation. Following the conventions of modern social theory, I assume a distinction between modern and pre-modern societies, but it should be kept in mind that such distinctions are ideal types that highlight certain features of a social order, while sometimes covering over similarities and continuities.

3. On the Frankfurt school analysis of the decline of individuality, see Kellner (1989). On the dissolution of identity in post-modernity, see Baudrillard (1983a, 1983b, 1983c); Jameson (1984, 1991); and other texts that I discuss in the following. For my take on the discourses and problematics of the post-modern, see Kellner and Best (1991, 1997, 2001).

4. The method of reading ads and the interpretation of advertising which follows is indebted to the work of Goldman (1984, 1992) and his collaborative work with Steve Papson (Goldman and Papson,1996).
5. In 2011, what Al-Jazeera called the 'Arab Awakening' resulted in uprisings in North Africa and the Middle East, protests broke out against capitalist-induced debt crises and austerity programmes throughout Europe, and in New York an 'Occupy Wall Street' protesting against corporate greed and corruption quickly spread through the United States and then the entire world. These issues are the topic of my book *Media Spectacle and Insurrection, 2011: From the Arab Uprisings to Occupy Everywhere* (2012).

References

Barthes, R. 1957. *Mythologies*. New York: Hill and Wang.
Baudrillard, J. 1983a. *Simulations*. New York: Semiotext(e).
———. 1983b. *In the Shadow of the Silent Majorities*. New York: Semiotext(e).
———. 1983c. The ecstasy of communication. In H. Foster (ed.), *The Anti-Aesthetic*, pp. 126–134. Washington: Bay Press.
Berman, M. 1982. *All That Is Solid Melts into Air*. New York: Simon and Schuster.
Coward, R. & Ellis, J. 1977. *Language and Materialism*. London: Rutledge & Kegan Paul.
Deleuze, G. & Guattari, F. 1977. *Anti-Oedipus*. New York: Viking.
Ewen, S. 1976. *Captains of Consciousness*. New York: McGraw-Hill.
Ewen, S. & Ewen, E. 1982. *Channels of Desire*. New York: McGraw-Hill.
Foucault, Michel. 1970. *The Order of Things: An Archaeology of the Human Sciences*. New York: Pantheon Books.
Friedman, J. & Lash, S. (eds). 1992. *Postmodernism and Identity*. London: Hutchinson.
Frisby, D. 1985. *Fragments of Modernity*. Cambridge: Polity Press.
Fromm, E. 1955. *The Sane Society*. New York: Holt Rinehart Winston.
Goldman, R. 1984. We make weekends: Leisure and the commodity form. *Social Text*, *8*(winter), 84–103.
———. 1992. *Reading ads Socially*. London and New York: Routledge.
Goldman, R. & Stephen, P. 1996. *Sign Wars*. New York: Guilford Press.
Hardt, M. & Negri, A. 2009. *Commonwealth*. Cambridge, MA: The Belknap Press of Harvard University Press.
Jameson, F. 1984. Postmodernism: The cultural logic of late capitalism. *New Left Review*, *146*(July–August), 59–92.

Jameson, F. 1991. *Postmodernism, or, the Cultural Logic of Late Capitalism.* Durham and London: Duke University Press.

Jezer, M. 1982. *The Dark Ages.* Boston: South End Press.

Kellner, D. 1989. *Critical Theory, Marxism, and Modernity.* Cambridge, UK and Baltimore: Polity Press and John Hopkins University Press.

———. 1995. *Media Culture, Cultural Studies, Identity and Politics between the Modern and the Postmodern.* London and New York: Routledge.

———. 2002. Theorizing globalization. *Sociological Theory,* 20(3), 285–305.

Kellner, D. & Best, S. 1991. *Postmodern Theory: Critical Interrogations.* London and New York: Macmillan and Guilford Press.

———. 1997. *The Postmodern Turn.* New York and London: Guilford Press and Routledge Press.

———. 2001. *The Postmodern Adventure: Science Technology, and Cultural Studies at the Third Millennium.* New York and London: Guilford and Routledge.

———. 2012. *Media Spectacle and Insurrection, 2011: From the Arab Uprisings to Occupy Everywhere.* London and New York.

Key, W.B. 1972. *Subliminal Seduction.* New York: Signet.

Kolb, D. 1986. *The Critique of Pure Modernity.* Chicago: University of Chicago Press.

Kroker, A. & Cook, D. 1986. *The Postmodern Scene.* New York: Saint Martin's Press.

Packard, V. 1960. *The Waste Makers.* Baltimore and London: Penguin.

Riesman, D., Glazer, N. and Denney, R. 1950. *The Lonely Crowd.* New York: Anchor Books.

Williamson, J. 1978. *Decoding Advertisements.* London: Marion Boyers.

8

Cultural Politics of Branding: Promoting 'KamaSutra' in India

William Mazzarella

Introduction

The world of advertising, like the consumer capitalism it lubricates, has little time for the past. Driven ever onward by the almost instant obsolescence of everything it produces, its eyes remain anxiously trained on the immediate future. A great deal has changed in Indian public culture and advertising in the two decades since 1991, when a brand of condoms cheekily named KamaSutra appeared in a flurry of daring images and provocative copy. What seemed shocking then would barely raise an eyebrow in today's mediascape, saturated as it is by MMS scandals, surgically boosted Bollywood heroines and Internet porn. So perhaps the story of KamaSutra at this point can best be appreciated as a yardstick by which to measure how far we have come (or, as some would have it, how low we have sunk).

I wrote *Shoveling Smoke*, the book that contained the analysis of the KamaSutra campaign excerpted here, a decade ago—which was also a decade after KamaSutra was launched. Today, the condoms themselves have pretty much faded into the woodwork. They can still be found tucked more or less unobtrusively in among their competitors in Indian chemists' display cases. And the once-shocking ads, yellowing around the edges, now exude that peculiar quality of the recently outmoded in which everything seems at once hopelessly passé and needlessly effortful.

Of course a significant part of the KamaSutra campaign's impact in its time had to do with its clever juxtaposition of image and text, especially its cloaking of an eminently up-to-date provocation in the mantle of unassailable tradition. But it was also about much more than the product. The campaign was only on a relatively superficial level a sensation because of its bold content. At another, perhaps deeper level, its power to compel had to do with the way it registered a tectonic shift in Indian public culture during the early 1990s: a shift in relation between the politics of pleasure and the politics of citizenship, a shift that can blandly be summed up in the term 'liberalization'. While KamaSutra qua product, qua ad campaign has now grown old, the new age whose coming it made viscerally intelligible is still very much our own.

I mentioned just now that advertising has little time for the past. Let me modify this: the manifest discourse of advertising has little time for a past that has not resolutely been put in its place. As soon as a decent interval of, say, 20 years has passed, advertising mobilizes a visual shorthand for the preceding period that, with a few agreed-upon digital brushstrokes, invokes a cozy period feel. According to this 20-year rule, the 'KamaSutra moment' should itself now be just about ready to take up its rightful place in this prop room of official nostalgia. A good time, then, to revisit this moment from the perspective of a time (the time of my fieldwork, 1997–1998) when it had taken on narrative form but its questions were still not quite settled.

This stereotyping of the past happens outside the ads as well. One of the general characteristics of moments of epochal transition—and I think the early 1990s were one such moment in India—is the extraordinary amount of effort put into asserting a radical break with the recent past. It is as if, in the midst of the rapid change, such moments can only understand themselves as everything that the past was not. It would not, therefore, be altogether an exaggeration to say that the primary product of liberalization in India was not all the new brands, not all the clamorous advertising, not the new retail environments, but rather a simplified *Gestalt* of the pre-liberalization period that, again, could be conjured with a few brush-stroke words—'socialist', 'Nehruvian', 'permit-license raj' and so on. These words operated not as invitations to reflection, but rather as indexical icons of a past that would make the present intelligible as long as they were not examined too closely.

Looking back at the book, *Shoveling Smoke*, now, my major criticism of the version of me that wrote it would be that I was too taken in by this liberalization gestalt. If I was able to render visible something important about the 1990s, then it was at the cost of a deeper sense of the less obvious yet crucial continuities between liberalization and what went before. It is as if while I understood the need to explore the slower structures that subtended the fast-moving surface forms of the KamaSutra campaign, my perspective on the broader historical shifts that produced liberalization remained too defined by the ideological discourse of liberalization itself. Still, surely every reasonably attentive ethnographic project also has a chance of exceeding, in surprising ways, the limited intentions of its author.

Something opens up in a retrospective view of the relation between a historical moment and the investigations it produces: a sense of the structural affinity whereby both the time and the work are, in a determinate relation to each other, blind the better to see. If there was a critical impulse in *Shoveling Smoke*, then it was an intimate one: a critique that started from, and dwelled within, the immanent contradictions of its time and place. There are costs and benefits to this kind of object intimacy. On one level, the work remains as much of its time as the object to which it is tightly tied. But by the same token, its object intimacy can also disclose immanent potentials whose historical significance may only come alive decades later. This, then, may be the unsolicited, untimely gift with which the ethnographer repays the generosity of informants whose professional concerns remain firmly fixed in the present. As Adorno observes in *Minima Moralia*: 'Thought waits to be woken one day by the memory of what has been missed' [Adorno, 2005 (1951): 81]. The following are excerpts from Chapters 3 and 4 of *Shoveling Smoke: Advertising and Globalisation in Contemporary India* (Mazzarella, 2003).[1]

In the autumn of 1991, a 'premium' brand of condoms called KamaSutra was launched in India. My first encounter with the brand came by way of a later instalment of its advertising campaign, which I came across during my first visit to Bombay in January 1997. At that time, I had no knowledge of the notoriety of the brand, nor of the multiple narratives that surrounded it. What struck my eye most forcefully about the ads was their coupling of a brand name and quotations from Vatsyayana's *Kamasutra*, with images that were nothing if not contemporary in styling and intent. At first, this juxtaposition made me wonder about the commercial and cultural politics of what one might call 'trademarked tradition.' What did it mean for a contemporary Indian consumer product to be marketed to Indians through the use of an ancient[2] Indian treatise on the science of the senses? Could comparisons be drawn between Vatsyayana's intended audience, the *nagaraka*—roughly, the well-to-do man-about-town[3]—and the figure of the affluent urban Indian premium-brand consumer— crudely, the 'Indian yuppie'—that was being delineated in advertisements, press commentaries, and corporate conference rooms all around me? [...]

In October 1991, the Mumbai-based glamour magazine *Debonair* sold out its print run in a matter of days. That month's issue quickly became a collector's item, changing hands at premium prices. But it wasn't the editorial content that sparked this enthusiasm. Nor did it appear to be a direct result of the magazine's customary photo-features of half-naked women, inserted in between a characteristically eclectic assortment of literary efforts, surveys and social commentary.[4] What was happening was a marketing man's dream come true: by all accounts, readers were actually buying the magazine for the advertisements it contained. That month, a company called JK Chemicals (JKC)[5] had launched a new product—a self-proclaimed 'premium condom' called KamaSutra. And as part of the attendant media blitz, their ad agency, Lintas: India, had taken out every single page of advertising space in *Debonair*.

The ads that were featured in *Debonair* that month were in part the same ads that ran elsewhere: blue-tinted photographs of a half-clad couple, clutching each other in a variety of urgently passionate poses. The aesthetic parameters were clearly derived from the visual repertoire of Western fashion shoots and the glossier end of pop videos, suggesting candidly captured yet carefully stylized moments. The man was invariably positioned in a supporting role as the ardent source of the female model's pleasure. Both of them had closed eyes, the man's face usually half-hidden, while the woman's head was thrown back, suggesting submission to a pleasure heightened by the discerning deployment of a KamaSutra condom. By way of guidance for the sophisticated lover, each ad featured one of a series of quotations from the text of the *Kamasutra* itself. In at least one case, the text directly implied that the acquisition of the product might be the key to a woman's desire: '… The man should do whatever the girl takes most delight in, and he should get for her whatever she may have a desire to possess.' Invariably signing off with the baseline 'for the pleasure of making love', the copy of the ads specifically sought to position the condoms themselves as a source of enjoyment.

But the centrepiece of the issue amounted to a veritable KamaSutra advertising supplement, in the form of a multi-page photo-essay entitled '… and then came KamaSutra (or the beginnings of a new sexual revolution sparked off by a condom)'. In addition to the ads that also ran elsewhere, the text of the copy was interlaced with glamour shots of the female model featured in the main ads, Pooja Bedi, as well as topless pictures of two other women. Several of these images were published in the fold-out format that *Debonair* used for its regular photo-features, but differed from the usual fare in that they echoed the smooth production values of the main KamaSutra ads, thus giving the impression that KamaSutra could bring a whole new level of gloss to erotic objectification. Lest the process remain at the level of looking, the text of the copy suggested that the refinement connoted by the brand in turn offered nothing less than self-realization. First, a quasi-history was evoked, which would allow the brand to appear as a contemporary rediscovery of a timeless truth:

Over 3000 years ago, the Egyptians used linen sheaths. Casanova used condoms made out of animal intestines. World Wars I & II saw condoms issued in standard service kits for men in the armed forces. The Beatles and Rock'n Roll and the sexual revolution ignored the condom to the dark side of the moon [sic]. And for years, there was an uncomfortable silence. And then came KamaSutra. The condom. Dedicated to the partners of love-making. And their pleasures.[6]

One might note, in passing, the manner in which the passage used stereotypical images of Western postwar popular culture to cue the period which in the Indian context tacitly refers to the post-Independence years, here a time, apparently, of 'uncomfortable silence'. The body of the text went on to explain that KamaSutra condoms were specifically designed to enhance pleasure, that they were in themselves objects of desire, inseparable from sex and to stress that it was up to the consumer to take the initiative:

The fact is that KamaSutra condoms are created for lovemaking. Pure fact. And that KamaSutra condoms are especially textured. Contoured. Dotted. On the outside. Also ultra-thin. And that the attraction begins with the aura around the KamaSutra condom itself. However, a lot will depend on you. And the ambiance in which you open the pack. And the manner in which you decide to wear KamaSutra. Or let someone else put it on for you. It's just the beginnings of the desire called KamaSutra.

The final lines presented the decision to purchase the condom as the first step in the consumer-citizen's duty to inaugurate a national erotic revolution: 'The stage is set. The location is upto [sic] you. The fires have been on low for too long. KamaSutra condoms have been launched in October 1991, all over the country. It's your revolution. It's your condom. It's KamaSutra.'

Amrita Shah was at that time the editor of *Debonair*. In November 1997, I asked her about the public stampede for the issue. She told me

I was completely taken aback. I couldn't work out why this was happening. I mean, it wasn't as if we were featuring anything more explicit than what we had run before. But it got to the point where we were actually considering a second print run. The models in the launch campaign were girls that we had already featured in *Debonair*. So what was the big deal?

As I amassed more information about the campaign, I continued to ask myself this same question. Unquestionably, KamaSutra had been a 'big deal': *Debonair* had flown off magazine-sellers' racks at an unprecedented velocity, but the impact of the campaign had also been articulated in ways that, at first sight, appeared less commercially desirable but ultimately all added to the publicity that surrounded the event. There were complaints to the Advertising Standards Council of India (ASCI), questions raised in parliament, a ban on Doordarshan (DD, the state-administered national television network), and a flurry of letters to the press. At this early stage, all I could surmise was that the *hangama* surrounding the launch had less to do with the selling of erotica than with the eroticization of selling in a wider sense. As Wolfgang Fritz Haug puts it: 'Here it is not the sexual object that assumes commodity form, but instead the entirety of useful objects with commodity form tends to assume in some way a sexual form' (Haug 1987, 120). Such, then, were the outlines of KamaSutra's public debut. But what were the origins of this infamy?

Origins

Gautam Singhania was the 24-year-old scion of one of the most prominent industrialist families in India. 'The condom project', as KamaSutra was referred to in the beginning, offered him a chance to stretch his entrepreneurial wings.[7] JKC, which was run by his father, had been casting around for a small investment opportunity for him, something on the order of five or six million US dollars. It was the end of the 1980s, and several factors had conspired to make the condom market an attractive proposition. Under the Board of Industrial and Financial Reconstruction, ailing industries, many of them in 'backward' areas, could qualify for grant money and tax incentives from the government. A factory site in the depressed city of Aurangabad[8] appeared ideal for the project, particularly since the Singhanias had been able to strike a deal with a South Korean supplier for some hi-tech condom-manufacturing equipment. Condoms seemed a promising bet both for the domestic market, where free government distribution required a supply of 700–800 million pieces a year, and for export, where the labour-intensive nature of condom production put India at a comparative cost advantage.[9] Finally, the contemporaneous emergence of AIDS as a major issue seemed set to give the previously stagnant commercial condom market a fillip.[10]

Knowing next to nothing about the condom market, Singhania and his associates at JKC entrusted the promotion of the entire project to Lintas: Bombay, a large advertising agency that had already done work for the Park Avenue line of suiting, a division of the prestigious Raymond brand, one of the most visible companies under the JK Group umbrella. Lintas found itself faced with a not entirely thrilling prospect: the billings for the account were rather meager (at least by its standards as one of the top two agencies in India),[11] and there was a widespread impression that the free and subsidized condoms distributed by the government under the brand-name Nirodh had been instrumental in creating a great deal of popular resistance to the product category as a whole.

Here, then, was the marketing problem: how to stimulate desire for a brand within a product category that was more or less universally thought to be an anti-aphrodisiac?

From Anathema to Accessory

The official hero of the KamaSutra story was Alyque Padamsee, then close to the end of his reign as CEO of Lintas: India. In this guise, he appeared as the Legendary Adman, routinely, almost casually revolutionizing the very basis of marketing through inexplicable flashes of inspiration. When eventually I got a chance to meet him, he told me:

[the government condom, Nirodh] acted as a deterrent to sex, because as soon as you thought of Nirodh, you lost your erection! If you lose your erection, you can't put on a condom. The logic is simple, but nobody seemed to have stumbled upon it. So I said, 'how can the male think of the condom as a pleasure-enhancer?' Nobody wants to sit down to a sumptuous meal, and then be told that you have to take medicine before it. Kills your appetite.[12]

By the time I got my audience with Padamsee, however, I had already spoken to a number of the other key players in the KamaSutra story. And in the process I had discovered that the 'attraction [that] begins with the aura around the KamaSutra condom itself' had a complex and in some respects contradictory parentage.

Adi Pocha, now the head of a film scripting and production company called Script Shop, was the creative director on the KamaSutra account. He told me that the idea for a pleasure-enhancing condom had come to him in the course of brainstorming in preparation for a pitch for a different condom account at Lintas: Calcutta where he was at that time creative head, about 18 months before the JKC project landed at his new job in the Bombay office.[13]

I'll explain what the exact thinking was. If a guy is into sex, and he doesn't wear a condom, chances are he's doing it for a child. Or, just because he can't care less. But if a guy wears a condom, that means he's only into sex for the pleasure. Right? [...] But a condom is perceived as inhibiting pleasure. So we said 'why don't we turn that around on its head, and see if we can associate some amount of sexiness with a condom. So that a guy who's considering buying a condom says 'OK, if I've got to wear a condom, why don't I at least go for the sexier one?'[14]

In Pocha's narrative, Padamsee appeared as the mediator between an inspired creative idea and the cautious company-minded instincts of 'the suits' at the agency:

All these guys said 'you're crazy! How can you position a condom as an aphrodisiac?' To Alyque [Padamsee's] credit, when I surfaced it at the brainstorm, Alyque said [in expert impression of theatrical Padamsee cadences] 'yes, my boy! That's brilliant! Just go with it!' And then of course everybody just piled onto that. Then in Bombay, when this whole KamaSutra thing—of course it was just a piece of rubber at the time—when the whole thing came up, again there was a lot of resistance from servicing [the account executives]. There was a lot of … I won't mention names, but there was a lot of people who went into, you know 'let's water down the position a bit, let's make it love instead of sex,' and 'let's have this woman reading poetry' and, you know, stuff like that. And again to Alyque's credit, he stuck by me right through and said 'nooo! It will be sex!' And that was it. Once Alyque had spoken, everybody just kind of fell into line.

From a perspective several years down the line, with KamaSutra an established success, Pocha—true to creative mythology—was still stressing the intuitive 'leap' that had produced an irresistible idea for a particular campaign. [Account Executive Jayant] Bakshi, on the other hand, had extended the lesson of KamaSutra beyond the product itself. Whereas Pocha and Padamsee narrated the triumphant eroticization of an inherent anti-aphrodisiac, Bakshi's exegesis capitalized upon the association between condoms, family planning, and the anti-erotics of government discourse. In effect he extended the dramatic reversal of the brand (anathema to accessory) from the product itself to the entire mode of communication that it exemplified. 'The understanding of what will work for KamaSutra, the brand as we now know it, started off as a learning in 1976, which is a good 15 years before the brand was finally launched.'[15]

Bakshi had formed part of a task force, drawn from several agencies, to work in consultation with the Government of India on a project to devise more effective methods for the communication of family planning messages to urban and semi-urban populations:[16]

> … in fact one of the biggest problems that family planning had was that we used to call it 'family planning.' After successive representations by the advertising field, we began to call it 'family welfare.' We started positivizing it. […] The moment you said 'family planning' people said 'don't talk to me about it!' So when we were launching KamaSutra it was [with] that understanding.

Family planning was one of the paradigmatic projects of modernization and development within the dispensation of post-Independence Indian state planning. Bakshi was suggesting that one of the government's greatest problems in this area was a lack of legitimacy grounded in an insufficient understanding of what made people 'buy into' a particular venture. One of the cruellest manifestations of this legitimacy crisis was the authoritarian resolve of the Emergency declared by Indira Gandhi in 1975–1977 with its ubiquitous and infamous sterilization camps. Doctors with quotas to fill left scars on the collective memory as well as on citizens' bodies.[17] The method advocated by advertising and marketing interests, conversely, posited a form of communication that would not simply disseminate information to passive recipients, but rather engage its audience aesthetically, with promises of pleasure and self-realization. In such a manner, a dialectic of reciprocal exchange—rather than force and refusal—might be created between citizen and state.

Condom publicity during this period, Bakshi and others argued, had similarly not made any concessions to seducing its audience; rather the emphasis was on getting across an unequivocal message, through slogans like '*do ya teen bachche bas!*' ('two or three children are enough!') or 'You have two, that will do!' The stern tone of these communications, Bakshi implied, was a symptom of the government's distance from the sensate lives of the people. The understanding that the advertising and marketing industries could bring to the task, on the other hand, was apparently based upon an empathy borne of direct experience. This experience was all the more profoundly attuned to the embodied preferences of its audience in that it was motivated not out of a desire to regulate, but rather to sell, and therefore to seduce. As Brian Barton, co-founder of US-based advertising agency BBDO, once put it, 'If you want to find out about people, try selling them something' (quoted in S. Fox 1990, 308). Conversely, even the name of the government product, Nirodh, a Sanskrit-derived word meaning 'restraint' or 'control', seemed detached and admonitory.[18] Bakshi said,

> […]What we attempted to do was position KamaSutra for the pleasure of making love. Trying to tell couples that this was going

to enhance sexual pleasure, and therefore they should use it. Not keep talking about the fact that 'it's for your own good, therefore do it'.

Nirodh metonymically represented the government as a whole ('as soon as you thought of Nirodh, you lost your erection'—and, as Bakshi suggested, if you listened to the government, you could well stand to lose more than that), while KamaSutra stood for the pleasures of the consumer's market. Impotence and humiliation led to stagnation and alienation; virility and sensuous self-assertion to responsive and inclusive sociality.

Adi Pocha, the creative director, had stressed that the affective power of the images used for KamaSutra, channelled through the desirable connotations of a 'premium' brand, was intended first and foremost to steal market share away from the closest competitor in the product category (then, as now, a brand called Kohinoor). But Jayant Bakshi's perspective was quite different. Certainly he was proud of the precise manner in which the KamaSutra brand, as an identifiable set of graphic and stylistic conventions, had been able to 'take ownership' of—not to say domesticate—a particular area of consumer desire.[19] But if KamaSutra was to be made a symbol of the wider social possibilities of marketing, then the relative exclusivity of its pricing and brand image had somehow to be made congruent with its universal significance. Family planning, as the quintessential government planning project, provided the crucial link between the supposed universality of sexual activity and the shared experience of subjection under an allegedly incompetent polity. Therefore, it could also provide the strategic point of intervention for an advertising industry bent upon reconfiguring the very terms of public communication.

Liberated by KamaSutra, the masses throw off the shackles of prudery: 'It's your revolution. It's your condom. It's KamaSutra'. Suddenly the aesthetic positioning of the product appears progressively inclusive. As Bakshi framed it,

> ... quality suffered in this country. Service suffered in this country
> [...] I think a *latent* desire was always there with people to try and
> express it [dissatisfaction], and I think one of the expressions was

this case [the KS campaign]. And coming as it did on the heels of this liberalization movement, I think it just fitted. It seemed that, at a very large level, the time was just right for somebody to say 'hey, I'm going to express myself—I need a condom!'

Here, then, was the apotheosis of the consumer citizen: the civil franchise of the 'right to choose' triumphs serenely over the arduous, contradictory and messy procedures of representative democracy. In this version, the story of KamaSutra was the story of the present, that is, the story of liberalization: how the consuming energies of the people had been liberated from the paternalist grip of the state. The eroticized images contributed by advertising appeared primarily as facilitators, mediating between individual desires and the collective rationality of the market. The instant gratification promised by the consumerist dispensation looked like the direct antithesis of the perpetually deferred realization of the dream of development. The gleaming surfaces of the world according to marketing seemed a million miles from the grubby habitat of the bureaucrat.

But the problem of pleasure remained a formidable aporia to the linkage between consumption and public service. The pleasures of seduction and the indulgence of desire that drove consumer goods advertising were quite simply absent from exhortations to public service, much as the latter might otherwise demonstrate the ability of the well-deployed image productively to harness self-interest.

This is where KamaSutra was able to provide the crucial connection. Qua condom, KamaSutra provided a unique connection between the critique of government communications and the metaphorical equation of the universality of the sexual activity with the inclusiveness of consumer desire. In this capacity it supplied the missing link in the campaign to eroticize not simply consumer goods, but public speech in general. Precisely the government's family planning initiatives continued, well into the 1990s, to provide the material for morality tales about the price of being prudish about public service.

In 1993, for example, it was discovered that the Madras branch of the Family Planning Association of India had simply been burying vast numbers of government condoms in ditches and elsewhere, in order to avoid owning up to the fact that they were unable to interest their constituency in them and thus risk losing their funding. On the defensive, local medical authorities ended up blaming the government for not providing adequate resources with which to educate the people in the proper usage of condoms.[20] Two years later, another story described a solution that was at once more bizarre and more creative. A reporter in Uttar Pradesh found that the State Health Directorate was selling off its supply of Nirodhs to, of all things, toy manufacturers, who were apparently only too happy with this cheap supply of high quality rubber.

For KamaSutra, on the contrary, there was apparently no contradiction between acknowledging, along with one journalist, that the brand was 'selling the notion that sex is fun, safe, and somehow upmarket to young, high income yuppies' (Sengupta, 1991) and at the same time making public service claims on behalf of the product.

The fiction that high-end consumerism could comfortably be aligned with public service was of course never going to be a stable one. Indeed, one price of the union was the inability of the advertisements to overtly refer to any social 'issues' since these would have been perceived as 'negatives', dampening the erotic potential of the brand. Adi Pocha, the creative director, suggested to me that AIDS wasn't yet 'big enough to position a brand on' in India in 1991. But Aniruddha Deshmukh, executive director at JKC, conceded that the cultural politics of branding precluded such options, couching his explanation in terms of a concern for public propriety. I asked him why they had not chosen to market KamaSutra on an anti-AIDS platform, given that growing awareness of the epidemic had been one of their reasons for getting into the condom business in the first place. While conceding that condoms as a generic category could, indeed should, be marketed on such a platform ('so it's there in the back of the mind that all condoms are good against AIDS'), he opined that the lifestyle connotations of someone choosing a particular brand on the basis of its protection against AIDS—and thus himself being identified with that ('it would be a giveaway to his life-style')—would not be socially acceptable.[21]

If you have a condom, which you're promoting saying that this is

> very good as a prevention against AIDS [...] saying that it has got nonoxynol-9 or something like that, and if you have consumers buying that, it's a very strong indication that here's a person who's promiscuous or is visiting commercial sex workers. Now that's not accepted over here as yet. So you would have a highly very limited segment for that [...] We don't believe that there is a segment that you can market a condom to on those lines.[22]

The reporter who interviewed Gautam Singhania at the time of the KamaSutra launch, however, came to his own succinct conclusion: 'Gautam Singhania has discovered an erogenous place in the market which, when stimulated, he hopes, would yield pleasurable results' (Menon *op cit*).

The Brand Name

Once the Big Idea of the sexy condom had been arrived at, the name KamaSutra seemed particularly fortuitous to the agency team because it instantly satisfied three crucial requirements: maximum reach/intelligibility, an erotic connotation, and cultural legitimacy. As Aniruddha Deshmukh, executive director of JKC (now JKC-Ansell) recalled

> See, the advantage of KamaSutra as a brand name, if you look at it simply as a brand name, is that it cuts across all language barriers. It's a brand name which is understood very clearly in south, in north, in east, in west. So that was a distinct advantage. It cuts across all income barriers. [...] everyone in India was aware of Kamasutra as a cultural heritage.[23]

The form of this awareness, moreover, was ideal. It was vague enough to permit a great deal of creative intervention. [...] Jayant Bakshi:

... when we took Kamasutra within the Indian ethos and the Indian context, it was because we knew that in its expanded form mentally it would mean a lot more than we would ever say. That was the joy of it. We said less but we meant more.[24]

The third part of the equation, the cultural acceptability of the name, functioned as the perfect foil to its suggestive capacity, particularly when coupled with the startlingly bold images that came to define the campaign. Even beyond legitimation *per se*, JKC and Lintas' appropriation of the name KamaSutra implied a kind of cultural restoration through consumption. Although strategically the name was above all useful as an 'alibi', it also played perfectly into the critique of the alienating agency of centralized planning, and enabled the impression that a more authentic, more sensuous, Indian identity might be accessible through its mediation.[25] Adi Pocha explained,

> We thought that if we do something as radical as this, because in the Indian context that would be very radical, we'd need ... something that would prevent people from jumping down our throats. So then we came up with the idea of using 'KamaSutra' as the brand name, since that's part of Indian heritage and Indian culture. It legitimated it. See, Indians are very hypocritical about sex, OK? We have a population of some nine hundred million people; we must be knowing something about sex. But we don't like bringing it out in the open; we don't like talking about it. It's not considered good to be sexy. I think it's just a phase that our civilization is going through. Because at one time we were extremely sensual and erotic. I mean, if you look at the *Kamasutra*, it's as erotic and as advanced in sexual thinking as you can get. So all we said was 'let's just go back to the fact that that's what we genuinely are. Let's use that. Put the name KamaSutra on the condom, and then let the hypocrites try and attack us'.

The sanctity of one reified collective (that of the 'official' cultural heritage) was mined on behalf of another (that of aspirational consumer spectacle). As a result, bold images were legitimated, and it was this relation that most commentators focused upon. But the connection between the legitimation bestowed by the idea of a collective heritage and the fact that the *Kamasutra*

itself was, after all, a text historically aimed at defining aristocratic behaviour was just as important. This second connection
contained, on the one hand, the populist implication that consumption might help restore to the masses an identity and a set of
possibilities that had hitherto jealously been guarded by national
elite. On the other hand, it was important that the aristocratic
connotations of the *Kamasutra* not be in any way 'diluted', that
they should become part of the aspirational identity of the brand,
lending it, as Alyque Padamsee put it to me, 'a touch of class'.

> You see, the Kamasutra is not a pornographic book. It's a sexual
> manual written, you know, hundreds and hundreds of years ago.
> And it talks about sex as an art and as a science. It doesn't talk
> about sex as, you know, the f-word, OK?

Vatsyayana's text, then, combined aesthetic distinction with
the idea of a collective heritage. Strategically, the effect of this
combination was that it was not the direct means for the realization of the good life, but rather the 'authentic' cultural basis for
the aspiration to do so, that was available to all. The brand profile,
moreover, was coupled with a highly contemporary and visually
oriented eroticization. Padamsee offered the following vignette as
an illustration of this equation. To avoid point-of-sale embarrassment, 'KamaSutra' had been given the alternate name 'KS'. Each
ad bore joint baselines: the brand-conceptual 'for the pleasure of
making love', and the more practically oriented 'Just ask for KS'.
'KS', it seemed, had become a kind of shorthand for desirability
('and if it's desirable, then it's buyable') among students in elite
Bombay colleges: 'we had tape recordings. We did a kind of *vox
populi* in colleges, and we found that girls would describe a man
as "he's quite KS", which means "he's quite sexy"'.

On one level it would seem that the campaign visuals simply
brought an arresting contemporary execution into tension with
the 'high-cultural' and 'traditional' backbone of the brand name.
On another, as we shall see in the following section, the production of the KamaSutra images involved an entirely separate elaboration of the double field of the aesthetic, one that was brought
into temporary alignment with the parallel elaboration already
developed around the name.

The Image

As I have suggested, aesthetic politics always involve a double claim about the 'natural'. On one hand, the 'first nature' of visceral bodily response; on the other hand the 'second nature' of 'good taste'. In the story of the making of the images that would announce KamaSutra, we can follow this duality as it was mediated by the photographer's camera.

The campaign would be addressed, first and foremost, to heterosexual men; hence, the client and the agency agreed that the weight of its erotic power would have to come from a strongly foregrounded female model.[26] Alyque Padamsee remembers his young client, Gautam Singhania, during early meetings intoning a scopophiliac mantra: 'I want you to make my eyes dance with delight'. Eventually, and after extensive negotiations, an up-and-coming young actress and tabloid celebrity called Pooja Bedi (daughter of the prominent stage, film, and television actor Kabir Bedi, with whom Alyque Padamsee had professional connections) signed on to deliver the requisite hard-hitting sex appeal. In Padamsee's words, she was 'quite a bit of a starlet, and something of a sex bomb'. Jayant Bakshi remembered that the agency hoped to capitalize upon the 'buzz' created by her tabloid notoriety: 'She had a fairly amorous existence, and in fact one of the reasons when we took her as the right choice was to do with being able to get a rub off from her personal life'.[27] Having already established the charge attached to her image in the public sphere, the decisive test for the agency was to gauge Bedi's erotic efficacy in person. Adi Pocha was dispatched to meet her, and was not disappointed. 'I really liked her, because she really kind of exuded sexuality. She's talking to you and, you know, you can see it and feel it'.

Pooja Bedi, then, seemed ideally suited to fulfil the promise of the Big Idea: namely, to make something as regrettable as a condom seem desirable. The intensity of her physical presence promised to generate the kind of attention that the client and agency hoped would be convertible into exchange value. Nevertheless, the aesthetic calculus was not quite so straightforward. For purposes of legitimacy as well as market positioning, this visceral surge had to be regulated, made subordinate to the reproducible regularity of a brand narrative. This constraint was not simply a matter of containing an apparently wild current, but also of sublimating it into a more refined form. Adi Pocha remembered,

> [W]hile we had borrowed from the book, the Indian book, our imagery was all very Western. [...] That was deliberate, because what we felt was that people at that stage looked up at Western imagery, OK? And we wanted to position the brand slightly higher. [...] Indian imagery was considered, you know, a little down-market. For whatever reason.

The project of refining the erotic energy embodied in Pooja Bedi was at once geared to the articulation of an upmarket brand image and to the question of maintaining 'good taste'. This was a matter of legitimating the intensity of the images, or in Pocha's words, 'how to make these pictures erotic, without crossing that line of accepted social decency'. In one sense, this project was self-consciously artificial: the agency imposed an aesthetic boundary on the campaign. In another sense, it was crucial that this imposition would appear guided by 'objective' and 'natural' parameters.

Lintas called in the man they thought would be ideal for the job: a Delhi photographer called Prabuddha Das Gupta, who was becoming well known in the industry for his monochrome work in a number of genres, including calendars, 'art' photography, fashion and advertising. Das Gupta's own recollections of his first meeting with the Lintas team suggest that the desired 'Western-aspirational' styling of the campaign was conceived in a kind of the verité mode:

> They had a brief and, I mean, they even had some pictures which they had pulled out of some Western magazines. Because there wasn't anything in India that was like that. They wanted this whole feeling of, kind of, spontaneity and sensuality [...] not the carefully created, beautifully lit kind of thing, but more of a kind of shot-from-the-hip and caught-as-they're-doing-it kind of thing. [... A]gain you come back to 'the blossoming middle

classes'—that's where it was targeted at. And for these guys, for this set of middle class people, for aspiration they would immediately turn their heads Westwards. So that was decided, that 'we are going to make it Western-aspirational,' as in ... what was happening at that time? Calvin Klein, maybe.[28]

Indeed, for Adi Pocha, choosing Prabuddha Das Gupta as the photographer for the KamaSutra campaign meant bringing in someone whose aesthetic talent seemed to be at once 'natural' or 'intuitive' and highly eroticized.

> You know, the thing about Prabuddha is that he's not cluttered by technology. [...] I think what was great about Prabuddha was that he is a very sexual person himself. I think he enjoys sex! [...] More than that, he enjoys being a voyeur. I think that's what he brought to the whole thing. He was able to ... er, really bring some amount of sexiness to the pictures. Very subtly. He'd just be waiting for the right moment ... and boom! That was it. [...] So he was literally just a voyeur capturing things on film. [...] Like I remember when I saw the contact sheets, he shot very little. [...] Most other photographers would go through this motor-drive thing like *ta-ta-ta-ta-ta!* [mimes machine-gun camera shutter action]. No, he would just find an image, he let that image happen. He allowed the people to find their own image and then he'd just capture it.[29]

The 'documentary' role of the solitary camera provided the physical means; Das Gupta's 'natural' aesthetic sense—itself driven by a powerfully erotic gaze—provided a universalizing moral justification for a set of stylistic parameters that were at the same time consciously geared towards capturing the aspirations of a particular imagined audience, 'the blossoming middle classes'. In parallel, the 'unmediated' quality of Das Gupta's photographic craft served as a kind of ontological guarantee for these same preferences.

And yet—crucially—it wasn't just a matter of opposing 'down-market Indian' to 'up-market Western' or 'repressed past' to 'liberated future'. Rather, the ur-Indianness of KamaSutra as a label and as a set of historically embedded connotations suggested that the aspirational, cosmopolitan Indian consumer of the future would enjoy, at one and the same time, a return to an ancient and authentic Indian self.[30]

Yet this, paradoxically, was a sexual liberation that depended upon the strictest aesthetic discipline: upholding the boundaries of 'good taste'. Here is the exact point at which we can see the intersection of two tensions. First, the ambivalence of an aesthetic discourse that simultaneously appeals to nature and refinement. Second, the ambivalence of a commodity image that relies on a visceral, visual concretion that its discursive elaboration can never quite contain. For Das Gupta, the man who had been hired to oversee the aesthetic parameters of the campaign, this double tension manifested itself in the form of his initial concern that the images of Pooja Bedi's body would introduce a dangerous element of excess, overflowing the boundaries of good taste:

> I do remember at one point I wasn't particularly comfortable with the idea of Pooja Bedi. [... B]asically I think it was ... well, Pooja Bedi is a very voluptuous sort of woman. Big breasts, wide hips. I mean, she, if anybody fits in more with the traditional notion of an 'Indian woman.' [...] It didn't have anything to do with personal preferences, but I just thought that at that point - maybe I was wrong, because the pictures worked - was that that sort of voluptuousness might tend to lead it more towards a sort of vulgarity, you know? I wanted someone with a less obviously [...] voluptuous body. Which would, to my mind, keep it well on this side of what would be called ... I guess, 'good taste.' For want of a better phrase.

'The pictures worked', it seems, in spite of—or, perhaps, because of—this tension. The public life of KamaSutra, like that of any advertising campaign, was about the management of affect. Most obviously, this management was intended to generate commercial value. But as I have suggested, the possibility of controllable commercial value depended upon the elaboration of a particular aesthetic idiom. Nor was that project confined to the internal machinations of the agency and the client. Rather, given the boldness of the campaign and the explosive publicity that it generated, the affect-managing effort was necessarily extended into wider public spaces.

The Public Field

Most people I talked to in Bombay remembered KamaSutra as a virtuosic publicity stunt, a textbook example of the high contrast between the persuasive agility of the new marketing and the alienating rigidity of government regulation. Between the lines of this story of heroes and villains, however, I discerned a more complicated set of negotiations. Among the most obvious of these negotiations was the struggle over the acceptability of the campaign itself, a struggle that was of course a direct response to the brashness of its entry into the public arena. But as I gradually reconstructed the public cultural field of the 'KamaSutra moment', I began to suspect that this debate was itself the visible face of a larger process. To be specific, if somewhat technical: what was at issue was the legitimate authority to manage, through a normative-aesthetic discourse, the extraction of commercial value from the public circulation of affect-intensive images.

Let me illustrate. First there was the matter of anticipation. Lintas—the agency in charge of the KamaSutra account—keenly fanned the flames of controversy even before the campaign had been released. Teasing 'leaks' were offered to the press; Pooja Bedi, apparently, had demanded a 'no-nipple' clause in her contract. And, as Jayant Bakshi pointed out, a great deal of advance 'buzz' had been generated through media circuits, the publicity industries.

Nor were Lintas disappointed by the publicity generated by critics of the campaign. One of the first to strike was the Women and Media Committee of the Bombay Union of Journalists, who lodged a complaint with a subcommittee of the Advertising Standards Council of India (ASCI), the Consumer Complaints Council (CCC),[31] calling the campaign 'highly irresponsible, voyeuristic, and sexist' (Pillai 1992).

Meanwhile, a Member of Parliament in the Rajya Sabha (the 'Council of States' or upper house) called Dinesh Trivedi complained about the campaign in a 'special mention' to the then Minister of State for Social Welfare, Margaret Alva, requesting that she call for a ban.[32] Arguing that ads like those for KamaSutra involved the 'portrayal of women as sex objects',

Trivedi and his parliamentary associates also sent a complaint to the Press Council, which alleged that 'the ads sought to promote "sex itself" instead of family planning and prevention of sexually transmitted diseases' (Prakash 1993). Doordarshan (DD), the national television network, had provisionally approved the storyboards for two KamaSutra spots in September 1991, and, according to Jayant Bakshi, the finished films were given a 'verbal nod' in November. But in the wake of the parliamentary stir, DD informed Lintas in early 1992 that permission to screen the spots had been withdrawn, pending a review of all relevant materials by then Information and Broadcasting Minister Mahesh Prasad (Koppikar 1992).

In March 1992, the ASCI/CCC issued a ruling, informing JKC and Lintas by letter that the campaign was indeed both 'objectionable and sexist', attempted to satisfy 'voyeuristic sensibilities which exceed common decency', and offered material that served 'more to titillate than to sell' (Pillai, *op cit*). Apparently, it took the Press Council another year to reach a decision; in March 1993, it issued a statement decreeing that KamaSutra was guilty of

> titillating the sex feelings of adolescents and adults. [...] The photographs of the models and the postures in which they have been shown are no doubt obscene, because these are vulgar and indecent in the context of an Indian morality.

Finally, in April 1993—a whole seventeen months after his complaint—Dinesh Trivedi received a letter from the Information and Broadcasting Minister pleading helplessness because 'the Department of Women and Child Development, which administers the Indecent Representation of Women (Prohibition) Act of 1986, had failed to respond' (Prakash *op cit*).

All the uproar amounted to very little in the way of action but a great deal of free publicity. The ASCI/CCC reprimand merely required that Lintas 'amend' the existing advertising. This they did, re-arranging the existing pictures, writing some new copy, and publishing them as a legally 'new' ad, triumphantly entitled 'The Complete Unabridged KamaSutra'. The 'alibi' function of the brand name effectively served to screen Lintas and JKC from accusations of violating Indian morality. The government's hapless and ineffectual response seemed only to prove everything that the free market ideologues had been arguing all along about bureaucratic inefficiency. And DD's ban was not much of a strategic blow (although it did cost Lintas a handsome percentage of the hefty national television advertising rates), since KamaSutra's intended consumers could in any case be more efficiently targeted through cable television and cinema.

Aftermath

Other notorious campaigns followed; Tuffs Shoes and Calida 'innerwear', to mention only two (incidentally, Prabuddha Das Gupta was the photographer on both of these campaigns). Increasingly, particularly in the wake of the arrival of satellite television and the onslaught of advertising for global brands, the case for bold images was made in terms of 'keeping up with globalization', a process whose dizzying dynamics could not be regulated on a national basis. And yet in some ways, precisely the constant escalation of the visual stakes may have been one of the reasons why, by the time of my fieldwork in 1997–1998, KamaSutra—the brand that, more than any other, had inaugurated the bold commodity image in India—was thought by many in the advertising industry to have 'lost the plot'.

These critiques pointed precisely to the two central problems in the commercial management of affect: brand control and aesthetic legitimation. Like stamping an insignium on a herd of livestock, consumer goods branding proclaims ownership of, and control over, a productive resource. But in the latter case, the productive resource comprises the evanescent symbolic and affective elements of public culture. On the one hand, this means that claims to brand ownership always entail a kind of 'cultural enclosure', a private arrogation of a public resource (Coombe 1998; Mazzarella 2002). On the other hand, this work of enclosure is locked in a perpetual struggle with the ever-accelerating transformation of public cultural meanings. In a sense, branding is akin to a puppy chasing its own tail, since this perpetual acceleration is itself partly caused by the relentless drive for differentiation that competitive marketing brings about.[33] In short, the textbook example of a successful brand parries a dual command: keep abreast of changing times, but maintain a continuous identity.

The custodians of KamaSutra were quite forthright about the balancing act involved. The continuity of the brand was a matter of maintaining certain 'key ingredients', as Aniruddha Deshmukh of JKC put it—visual markers and conceptual foundations. Its adaptability, conversely, depended upon Jayant Bakshi's ability to integrate a constant attention to changing public discourses on sex with the overall structure of the brand, to 'freshen the expression' of its 'core Idea'. At the same time, this affect-managing project was not simply about maintaining a formal balance between structure and change. The transcendent legitimation of the 'truth' of the brand had, from the beginning, been an aesthetic one. KamaSutra had to be tastefully erotic, or it was nothing.

Adi Pocha and Alyque Padamsee had both once been close to the brand, and had observed its development after their own respective departures. Interestingly, their critiques of latterday installments of the campaign spoke precisely to the dual foundation—structural and aesthetic—that I have just described. Pocha, for his part, deployed a classic creative critique of the executive's unimaginative preoccupation with structure over impact. 'They're *suits*', he told me.

> You know what I mean? They're suits, they're gonna think that way, OK, because they're scared. […] I still see the same kind of shots. Just because the original campaign had blue photographs doesn't mean you continue with blue photographs, OK? There's a certain sameness, it's lost the surprise. It's lost the unpredictability of a good fuck [laughs]! Which is what sex is all about. […] Nobody gets turned on by sameness. You see a woman nude once, twice, thrice, four, five times. After that you're not scrabbling over each other to take her clothes off anymore. You know what I mean? It's OK. You want to see something else. […] What they've done is they've kept all the elements but forgotten what

worked for them. I mean, who cares? Throw away the blue pic-tures! Who cares?! Throw away the little wiggly sperms and throw away the quotes from the *Kamasutra*. None of that is important. What is important is that when I see a KamaSutra ad, I should feel just a little bit sexier. [...] They've lost that.

Padamsee, for his part, felt that the all-important aspirational aesthetic positioning of the campaign—its class—had become confused:

[The campaign] went to HeartBeat and my good friend, who was looking after it anyway at Lintas, Jayant Bakshi, took over the account. I think then he went a little off the rails and thought that what we were doing was selling sex. We were not. We were selling sensuality, which is not the same as sex. [...] It was a bit too explicit. You know, the girl was half undressed, and big boobs, and you know the whole thing became a kind of ... not even Playboy ... I'll say Hustler. You know? [...] So I think it needs to get back a little of its class. It needs also a model who is today's epitome *not* of Monica Lewinsky,[34] but let's see ... I wouldn't mind Sharon Stone, to tell you the truth, hm? Because from her ... what was that movie? Basic Instinct. She's moved up the ladder a bit, you know. Just as Marilyn Monroe did. So I'd like that sort of image. Someone who's sex-u-al, but not cheapo-sexy. You know? Not someone you'd find in a porno palace.

My point here is not to evaluate the 'truth' or otherwise of these judgements, but rather to point to how important these two sets of considerations were to perceptions of the efficacy of the campaign: on the one hand, the tension between the need to formalize and 'own' a particular image-identity relationship, and, on the other, the need to give this relationship—the brand—an aesthetic legitimation.

Looking back over the statements I have collected here, a par-ticular discursive binary emerges with some regularity: a 'classy' campaign versus a 'vulgar' campaign. The way in which this ter-minology speaks to an aesthetically grounded politics of social distinction is obvious enough. Over the course of my discussion over KamaSutra, I have repeatedly stressed the importance, for the whole consumerist dispensation in India, of emphasizing its populist credentials. I have already shown how this was a matter of offering a mode of universal address that would be a credible alternative to citizenship in the developmentalist dispensation of the post-Independence Indian state. But it was also a response to the particular machinery of affect-management that had been put into place during the Nehru years. Indian broadcasting and film censorship policies were based, quite overtly, on an aesthetic paternalism according to which male viewers with low incomes and little education were thought to be particularly susceptible to the unpredictable effects of affect-intensive images (Ghosh 1999; Vachani 1999). So if the consumerist dispensation promised to extend the healing properties of the mass-mediated image to each and every Indian, was there not something contradictory in using the word 'vulgar'—which, after all, literally designates the 'common' people—to dismiss unacceptable ads?

Perhaps it was nothing more than a matter of a professional elite habitually and unreflectingly perpetuating the aesthetic paternalism that it had inherited. But against the background of the argument concerning the category of the aesthetic that I have offered in this chapter, I think we might also explore some subtler connections. Immanuel Kant suggested that aesthetic judgement might provide the true basis for the good society. In his *Anthropology*, Kant in fact defines the vulgus, or 'rabble', as those who are separated or excluded from the civil union of the gens, or the 'nation' [Kant 1978 (1798), 225]. 'Taste' or the ability to bring reasoned judgement into harmony with aesthetic experience is the condition for entry into the fellowship of the gens. Once again, we may read Kant's terminological distinction simply as a justification for social distinction, a connection that may easily be traced down to the present-day cultural politics of globalizing consumerism. But such an interpretation would also miss a parallel, but this time generative, affinity: the promise of the aesthetically grounded realization of the fullness of the good social community. And it was in this register that KamaSutra, once more, provided a crucial means of transition.

Calling the product KamaSutra, as I have shown, offered both a means of legitimizing the bold content of the campaign and the promise that aspirational consumerism, more than simply providing a long-awaited outlet for pent-up libidinal energies, could channel those energies into a higher purpose: the future rediscovery of a more authentic 'Indianness'. A culturally specific *sensus communis*, then, but one that depended on a coordination with the global sweep of history rather than the specifically national time of development.

To be sure, the aesthetics of KamaSutra belonged to a moment immediately preceding the globalization of consumer goods markets in India. But insofar as the campaign pointed towards the possibility of the eroticization of cultural identity through aspirational consumerism, it also prefigured one of the most important problematics of the 1990s, namely the ambivalent commercial value of 'Indianness' in advertising.

Notes

1. Originally published in Chapter 3: 'Citizens Have Sex, Consumers Make Love: Kama Sutra I,' pp. 59–98 and Chapter 4: 'The Aesthetic Politics of Aspiration: Kama Sutra II,' pp. 99–148 in *Shoveling Smoke: Advertising and Globalisation in Contemporary India*, William Mazzarella, Copyright, 2003, Duke University Press. All rights reserved. Republished by permission of the copyright holder. www.dukeupress.edu. The present version is excerpted from these chapters. For the complete text, see the original.

2. The Kamasutra was originally compiled by the fourth-century scholar Vatsyayana, and has, like most major 'Hindu' texts, since then spawned a vast supplementary literature of commentaries and interpretations. Its introduction into nineteenth-century European Victorian society through Richard Burton's selective English translation contributed to its popular and prurient reputation as an 'oriental sex manual', a reputation which persists among contemporary Indian middle-class professionals, the intended audience of the KamaSutra ads. Although much of the text of the Kamasutra is indeed concerned with sexual practice, the refinement of sensual pleasure (*kama*) through sex is to be pursued in relation to the other major goals of life—*dharma* (a famously complex term which is often translated as righteous or ethical action, in relation to one's position in life) and *artha*, the management of material interests. Consequently, the Kamasutra, before launching into its famous sequence of sexual recommendations, dwells in detail on interior decoration, education, leisure, and care of the body.

3. Alain Danielou offers the following characterization of the *nagaraka*: 'a wealthy, cultivated bourgeois male who is an art-lover and either a merchant or civil servant living in a large city' (Danielou, 1994: 7). Doniger and Kakar (2002) is a superior translation of the text itself. In contemporary usage, as Chatterjee (1995: 102) reminds us, *nagarik* is in fact used to denote 'citizen'.

4. The juxtaposition of 'high' literary content with 'low' imagery was, from the beginning, a conscious move on the part of the founders of *Debonair*, and one of the ways in which the magazine sought to carve out a 'progressive' aesthetic agenda. Without denying the tremendous differences between the two publications, both in terms of content and socio-historical role, it should not be forgotten that Playboy, at the time of its inception, involved a similarly novel combination.

5. JK Chemicals is one of the main companies of the JK Group, named after its founder, the late Juggilal Kamlapat Singhania. In 1988, the JK Group was divided into three separate corporate entities, each headed by one of JK Singhania's sons—Padampat, Kailashpat and Lakshmipat—and *their* sons. The three family groupings were given control of, respectively, JK Synthetics along with cotton, jute and iron companies; Raymond (leaders in high-end men's suitings and body-care products); and JK Industries, which included JK Chemicals.

6. This and all subsequent quotations from the launch ads are taken from the KamaSutra advertising supplement that appeared at the centre of the October 1991 issue of *Debonair* magazine.

7. In April 1998, I attempted to schedule an interview with Mr Singhania. His secretary, however, was of the opinion that since I had already spoken with Aniruddha Deshmukh, the executive director of JKC, I had 'the whole story'.

8. Incidentally, the name Aurangabad would, upon reflection, also have seemed auspicious: the Persian word *aurang*, from which it is derived, combines the meanings of 'emperor's throne' with 'building for manufacture' and 'warehouse'.

9. At the time of the KamaSutra launch there were two large-scale producers: Hindustan Latex (HL), a public sector company—and the largest manufacturer of condoms in the world—and TTK-LIG, a private operation, which had evolved out of the earlier London Rubber Co. The commercial market amounted to a total of around 400 million pieces annually, including the subsidized government brand Nirodh (which commanded 56 per cent of the market by volume, primarily supplied by HL). There was only one substantial non-subsidized branded player, a TTK brand called Kohinoor (20 per cent of the market at that time) which was being marketed on a relatively conservative family planning platform. Another TTK brand called Fiesta had acquired a

five per cent market share with a campaign that had been quite risqué for its time (the mid-1980s), in which the theme had been 'different colours for different days of the week,' thus to some extent preparing the ground for a more eroticized approach. These figures on market share are from Annuncio (1993) and Irani (1991).

10. Lobo (1991) estimates that the AIDS 'scare' had caused a 12 per cent per annum growth in the Indian commercial condom market in the late 1980s and early 1990s.

11. In fact, the launch campaign ended up wildly overshooting promotional budgets, although accounts of the original budget vary. Alyque Padamsee, then CEO of Lintas: India, told me that it was ₹3.3 million; in Doctor and Sen (1997), Jayant Bakshi, the executive in charge of the account, estimates it at ₹6–7 million, and suggests that around ₹11.9 million was actually spent.

12. Interview with Alyque Padamsee, Bombay, February 1998. All subsequent quotations from Padamsee, unless otherwise referenced, are from this conversation. The market research that Lintas conducted around this time confirmed their hunch: it showed that although awareness and even one-time trials of condoms among members of the target group (at the time of launch, defined as urban middle-to-high income males, 25–40 years old) were as high as 80 per cent, continued use was a dismal two to three per cent.

13. This other condom account, which Lintas did not win, was for a brand called Adam.

14. Interview with Adi Pocha, Bombay, February 1998. All subsequent quotations from Pocha are from this conversation.

15. Interview with Jayant Bakshi, Bombay, November 1997. All subsequent quotations from Bakshi, unless otherwise noted, are from this conversation.

16. Bakshi told me that this particular group of professionals went out and did field interviews in cities and towns with populations of more than 50,000 people. At no point during this initiative, and the one that followed in 1979–1980 (unlike earlier advertising industry involvements in government family planning initiatives), was there a serious move to engage the advertising industry in communicating with people in rural areas.

17. The frequent brutality of Emergency-period sterilization initiatives is widely discussed but thinly documented. A powerful fictionalized account appears in Mistry (1995). For relevant references, see those cited in Krishnaji (1998). While the sterilization camps came to be identified with the authoritarian excesses of the Emergency, the period was not without its own moments of tragicomedy, especially for those not directly affected by it. Raj Thapar remembers in her memoirs:

Little decorated vasectomy plants sprang up on every street, adorned with tins of cooking oil as giveaways—this, which had disappeared from the market—and armed with loudspeakers throwing out suggestive film songs. [...] At the Irwin Road camp one evening there was a macho looking man at the mike singing a little ditty - in English, with a broad Punjabi accent: 'Come have yourself vasectomised, make your family systematized', whatever that may mean. I realized that it could only be aimed at me—certainly none of the fruit-sellers around were familiar with English, so who else, thought I, as I looked up and down the street. No one. (Thapar, 1991: 419)

18. Ardashir Vakil, in his fictionalized memoir of a Bombay childhood in the early 1970s, describes the scenario:

I walked back to the corner of Carmichael Road, where the *paan-wala* on the corner still had his shop open. I had forty paisa in my pocket. I thought I might find something to eat. In the front of his shop I saw a box of Nirodhs. I had no idea what they were though I had seen the advertisements saying, 'Hum do, Hamare do' (The two of us and our two children), which the round cartoon faces of mummy, daddy, smiling son and pig-tailed daughter. The model family. (Vakil, 1998 [1997]: 124)

19. In the course of my November 1997 interview with him, Jayant Bakshi explained:

[W]e launched 'For the pleasure of making love,' and the delightful part of it is that now when we do our attitude surveys, there is an actual position that comes through from the consumer, which says 'what do you use a condom for?' 'Birth prevention?' 'STD and AIDS prevention?' And then there is one for 'pleasure.' And every time we see that we're delighted because we say, 'KamaSutra will live for a few more years'.

20. In fact, one doctor interviewed at the time made it sound more like a problem of ballistics than of reproductive health: Says Dr Narayan Reddy, Consultant in Sexual Medicine, 'Because people do not know how to use condoms, the failure rate is high through the tearing of a condom, because during ejaculation semen is expelled at 40 to 90 km/h' (Bhagat, 1993).

21. Alyque Padamsee, in his published account of the campaign, is even more forthright:

There was a very spirited defence put up [at Lintas] against going the sex route. And instead opting for the safe route. As protection against AIDS. But we found that it was the wrong button to press. If you scare the devil out of people for having unprotected sex, they get turned off. They don't read your advertisement. They don't want to think about AIDS. If you want to sell a condom, don't tell your target audience, 'Unless you wear a condom, you'll get AIDS and die'. (Padamsee, 1999: 274)

22. Interview with Aniruddha Deshmukh, Bombay, January 1998. All subsequent quotations from Deshmukh are taken from this conversation.
23. Interview with Aniruddha Deshmukh, Bombay, January 1998. All subsequent quotations from Deshmukh are taken from this conversation.
24. Interview with Jayant Bakshi, Bombay, January 1998.
25. In fact, one might argue that there are structural parallels between Vatsyayana's exhaustive enumeration of sensual possibilities and the multiplication of possibilities for high-end consumer gratification through the profusion of product variants offered under a brand umbrella: one of the more recent KamaSutra ads, from the 6–97 phase of the campaign, seemed explicitly to play on this correlation. The ad presented the range of products as a kind of mirror for sexual self-understanding. The layout showcased the entire KS range, which by that point included eight different packages of variously textured and 'scented' condoms. There was by now even a bumper pack of 15 for the insatiable. Beneath a headline demanding 'What kind of lover are you?' the viewer could follow arrows through a flowchart linking the various packs, thus arriving at the product that was perfectly matched to his predilection: 'Are you the moody type? Do you keep it simple, stupid, flowing with the tide, or do you occasionally swim against it? Are you fussy? Are you flexible? Are you driven by wild fantasies? We believe your condom choice can help come up with an answer'.
26. As it happens, the male model in the original campaign, Marc Robinson, at that time virtually unknown, has since become one of the leading male models in India, in addition to attempting a move into cinema. At the time, however, in Adi Pocha's words: 'Very frankly, Marc was ... at that stage, he was a prop'. The photographer, Prabuddha Das Gupta, who recommended Robinson for the job, elaborated: 'Marc was relatively unknown. Pooja was a star. Pooja was getting a huge amount of money. Marc was getting like a piddly ... some ₹20,000, whatever'.
27. See Moeran (2001) for a discussion of such promotional synergies.
28. Interview with Prabuddha Das Gupta, Bombay, April 1998. All subsequent quotations from Das Gupta, unless otherwise noted, are taken from this conversation.

29. Note that Ansel Adams distinguished the serious photographer on the basis of a rigorous avoidance precisely of such 'machine-gun photography' [see Sontag (1989) (1977): 117].

30. As a protest against the temporal scheme of the developmentalist state, we can read mass consumerism in the postcolony in Benjaminian terms: against the empty, homogenous and linear time of the modernist project of national development, the consumerist vision held out the vision of a blinding flash of simultaneity—past, present and future redeemed in one great 'now'.

31. The ASCI and the CCC were set up in 1985, and conclusively incorporated in 1986.

32. The complaint was lodged on 28 November 1991. Trivedi, who belonged to the Janata Dal party, was supported in his mention by a broad coalition of members, including Deputy Chairperson Najma Heptullah, M.A. Baby, Bhubaneshwar Kalita, Mira Das, Murli Bhandare, and Mohammad Afzal.

33. Daniel Miller reflects: '… could it be that one of the major appeals of brands is that they represent a kind of bedrock stability in a world of rapidly changing social structures and social relationships?' (Miller, 1997: 57). No doubt this is accurate on an experiential level. And nothing would please the professional advocates of marketing more than such a proposition. But we might also propose that the 'stabilizing' effect of branding—quite apart from its political economic functions—represents a palliative response to anxieties brought about, in no small part, by the relentless pace of consumer marketing itself. There, in a nutshell, is the dialectical movement of the cultural politics of consumer capitalism.

34. My interview with Padamsee took place just as the Lewinsky-Clinton scandal had taken over the news media of the world.

References

Adorno, T. 2005. *Minima Moralia: Reflections on a Damaged Life.* London and New York: Verso.

Annuncio, C. 1993. A barren market. *Advertising and Marketing,* November.

Bhagat, R. 1993. Where condoms are buried in ground. *Indian Express,* 28 January.

Chatterjee, P. 1995. The disciplines in colonial Bengal. In P. Chatterjee (ed.), *Texts of Power: Emerging Disciplines in Colonial Bengal,* pp. 1–29. Minneapolis: University of Minnesota Press.

Coombe, R. 1998. *The Social Life of Intellectual Properties: Authorship, Alterity, and the Law*. Durham, NC: Duke University Press.

Danielou, A. 1994. *The Complete Kamasutra*. Rochester: Park Street Press.

Debonair. 1991. Kama sutra advertising special. October issue.

Doctor, V.V. & Sen, S. 1997. A tough, rough and risque market. *Business World*, 7 September.

Doniger, W.W. & Kakar, K. 2002. *Kamsutra*. Oxford: Oxford University Press.

Fox, Stephen. 1990. *The Mirror Makers: A History of American Advertising and Its Creators*. Champaign, IL: University of Illinois Press.

Ghosh, S. 1999. The troubled existence of sex and sexuality: Feminists engage with censorship. In C. Brosius & M. Butcher (eds), *Image Journeys: Audio Visual Media and Cultural Change in India*, pp. 233–260. New Delhi: SAGE.

Haug, W.F. 1987. *Commodity Aesthetics, Ideology, and Culture*. New York: International General.

Irani, M. 1991. What is your brand? *Times of India* (Bombay), 8 December.

Kant, I. 1978. *Anthropology from a Pragmatic Point of View*. Reprint. Carbondale: University of Southern Illinois Press.

Koppikar, S. 1992. Lintas to serve notice to Doordarshan on KamaSutra. *The Independent*, 11 April.

Krishnaji, N. 1998. Population policy. In T. Byres (ed.), *The Indian Economy*, pp. 383–407. New Delhi: Oxford University Press.

Lobo, A. 1991. Marketplace: Condom marketing has come a long way. *Times of India*, 21 October.

Mazzarella, W. 2002. Cindy at the Taj: Cultural enclosure and corporate potentateship in an era of globalization. In D. Mines & L. Sarah (eds), *Everyday Life in South Asia*, pp. 387–399. Bloomington: Indian a University Press.

———. 2003. *Shoveling Smoke: Advertising and Globalisation in Contemporary India*. North Carolina: Duke University Press.

Menon, R. 1991. Condom courage. *Island*, October.

Miller, D. 1997. *Capitalism: An Ethnographic Approach*. Oxford: Berg.

Mistry, R. 1995. *A Fine Balance*. Toronto: McLelland and Stewart.

Moeran, B. 2001. Promoting culture: The work of a Japanese advertising agency. In B. Moeran (ed.), *Asian Media Productions*, pp. 270–290. London: Curzon.

Padamsee, A. 1999. *A Double Life: My Exciting Years in Theatre and Advertising*. New Delhi: Penguin.

Pillai, A. 1992. KS Ad found objectionable. *The Pioneer*, 10 April.

Prakash, A. 1993. Ignoring strictures, KamaSutra ads are back with a bang. *The Pioneer*, May 16.

Sengupta, R. 1991. Who's the boss, anyway? *Indian Express,* 15 September.

Sontag, S. 1989. *On Photography.* New York: Noodan Press.

Thapar, R. 1991. *All these years: A memoir.* New Delhi: Penguin.

Vachani, L. 1999. Bachchan-alias: The many faces of a film icon. In C. Brosius & M. Butcher (eds), *Image Journeys: Audio-Visual Media and Cultural Change in India,* pp. 199–230. New Delhi: SAGE.

Vakil, A. 1998. *Beach Boy: A Novel.* New York: Charles Scribner.

9

Shopping for Fashions in Post-socialist Russia

Olga Gurova

Introduction

The American sociologist Sharon Zukin has observed that 'shopping has come to define who we, as individuals, are, and what we, as society, want to be' (Zukin, 2004: 8). What has this meant for people and society in Russia, which, in only 20 years, passed shortages, food coupons and queues at the beginning of the 1990s to consumer abundance, relative freedom of choice and a variety of retailers in the early 2000s? Today, the retail is one of the fastest growing markets in Russia; it contributed to 19.7 per cent of GDP in 2009 in comparison to 8.1 per cent in 2001.[1]

This chapter focuses on the fashion retail as an indicator of the transformation of consumption in Russia in the last 20 years. It discusses the following questions: How has the fashion retail changed? How were these changes perceived by the consumers? What kinds of consumers emerged in the context of the new retail environment? In order to understand these processes, I use St. Petersburg, the second largest city in Russia and its so-called cultural capital to answer these questions by using data collected from a combination of sources. These sources include ethnographic observation and interviews with consumers between 18 and 66 years of age[2] and various documents, such as data from the Russian Statistical Agency, reports from consulting and real estate agencies, local newspapers and online sources.

I begin by presenting a brief overview of the scholarship on the retail and its transformation in post-socialist states. Then I continue with empirical evidence of the transformation of the retail business in Russia in the 1990s and the beginning of the 2000s. Finally, I suggest a typology of consumers that formed in the new retail environment and its culture of consumption.

The Retail Trade and Post-socialism: An Overview

The retail trade and shopping in post-socialist countries have recently been the focus of academic research, given that retail has been one of the leading sectors of post-socialist economies in the 1990s and the first decade of the new millennium scholars talk about a 'retail revolution' (Radaev, 2007). Scholars have explored how new spaces of consumption have proliferated while old spaces have been restructured in post-socialist cities such as Zagreb, Croatia; Warsaw, Poland; Zagora, Bulgaria; and St. Petersburg, Russia (Garstka, 2009; Jakovcic, 2010; Kreja, 2006; Zhelnina, 2009).

There are certain commonalities in the retail development in post-socialist countries as well as distinctive features. Both Kreija and Jacovcic discuss how large-scale retail has changed the urban landscapes of East European cities. In the 1990s bazaars were popular places for daily shopping, especially in large Polish cities, whereas in the second half of the 1990s the massive construction of new forms of retail, including shopping centres, changed the habits of Poles: 'today bazaar traders struggle not only with the administrative constraints, but also with the outflow of customers who prefer modern retail developments' (Piskiewicz, cited in Kreja, 2006: 261). Kreja mentions several old and new retail formats in Poland: the bazaars, department stores, superstores, supermarkets, hypermarkets, shopping centres, retail parks and metro shopping centres as well as the hybrids intrinsic to post-socialism including topical arcades and topical shopping centres. The latter are maintained by local entrepreneurs and represent a civilized form of the bazaar, whose number meanwhile has gradually shrunk (Kreja, 2006: 260). Kreja considers the contemporary development of retail to be a 'success' arising from the diversity and variety of retail formats that have appeared in the past 20 years. Jakovcic (2010) explains this success from the point of view of the regeneration and gentrification of urban spaces.

Zhelnina, on the other hand, views a similar situation differently. She talks about the 'transition to civilized retail' in Russia and draws particular attention to the unsuccessful fate of the 'uncivilized' retail format, namely, open-air markets in St. Petersburg. Markets today are characterized as 'dirty' and 'not safe'. This rhetoric reflects a particular view of the middle class in large cities, which have experienced relative prosperity lately. For the middle-class consumers shopping is 'no longer a question of getting the cheapest goods, but of convenience, comfort and safety and also enjoyment' (Zhelnina, 2009: 62). At the same time, as Zhelnina demonstrates, 'there remain a fairly large proportion of people, for whom shopping or selling on the clothing market is still a daily practice' (Zhelnina, 2009: 62); demolition of the open-air markets thus directly affects their lives.

Several explanations for the transformation of retail trade, which can be relevant to post-socialist context as well, have been proposed. Ritzer demonstrates that McDonaldization has become the key principle of contemporary consumer culture. By McDonaldization, he means the domination of efficiency, rationality, predictability, calculability and non-human technologies that control people (Ritzer, 2011: 25). In comparison to bazaars and peddlers, newer forms of retail such as shopping malls are much more rationalized, controlled and efficient, that is, McDonaldized. Hence, we can observe the growing rationalization of the retail. Ritzer also talks about the irrationality brought on by McDonaldization: 'shopping centre capitalism' is seen as 'totalizing and ubiquitous, destroying traditional forms of economic activity' (Crewe and Beaverstock, 1998: 290). In other words, shopping malls are considered as intrinsically the servants of evil capitalism (Chaney, 1990; Crewe, 2003; Goss, 1993; Ritzer, 2011).

Featherstone discusses globalization as an ongoing process related to the transformation of consumer culture and retail. He shows that '(t)he world becomes assimilated into a common culture' (Featherstone, 1995: 6), resulting in a 'global consumption' in which certain forms of retailing, marketing and selling techniques have rapidly proliferated around the world (Featherstone, 1995: 7). The contemporary expansion of international retailers and key retail formats, such as shopping malls, are symptoms of globalization.

However, to consider a shopping mall as a hegemonic form of retail is to simplify the reality. The tendency to localization illustrates the growing plurality of the retail milieu (Crewe, 2000: 277). Localization refers to the 'marginal consumption spaces' (Crewe and Gregson, 1997) that give consumers independence from multinationals, retail chains, shopping malls and other features of the global consumer culture. These channels, 'alternative retail channels' (Williams, 2002), 'unconventional consumption space' or 'inconspicuous retailing' (Crewe, 2000) include all informal and/or second-hand modes of acquiring goods (Williams, 2002: 1898), such as market stalls, second-hand shops and so on. These forms have meanings of sociality, creativity, distinction and fun, on the one hand and economic necessity, on the other hand (Williams, 2002: 1907–1908). The rise of technology, above all, the Internet, has introduced many new forms of retail and shopping practices. Online bargains, design markets and the like bring the conventions of the marketplace as well as unfixed, unpredictable, varied and negotiable activities into retailing (Crewe and Beaverstone, 1998: 291). The alternative retail channels are often considered a 'space of resistance' to the dominant rationalized order of exchange (Crewe and Gregson, 1998: 40) and the McDonaldized culture of consumption (Ritzer, 2010).

The development of retail corresponds to the particular changes in social structure. There is a significant symbolic relationship between forms of retailing and particular social groups (Crewe and Beaverstock, 1998: 291). Shopping malls celebrate the consumer culture of the middle class, in which money, status and class matter. The malls are seen as 'cheerleaders of new forms of consumerism' (Crewe and Beaverstock, 1998: 291). Through their surveillance and control of consumption, such seemingly public, but actually private spaces strengthen the boundaries between the consuming and the non-consuming public (Crewe and Beaverstock, 1998: 291). At the same time, alternative consumption spaces create emancipatory potential and enable those from differing social groups as well as those who seek a unique and more individualized consumption to fit into this space.

Transformations in the retail trade and consumer culture are not limited to changes in organizational formats; they are also reinforced by individual attitudes and practices. Garstka explores how consumers' attitudes, opinions and actions shift in relation to new and old places of retail in Bulgaria. She argues that there is an increasing 'pluralism of urban postmodern consumer groups' and that the city dwellers 'actively work to support, produce and reproduce changes in the built urban environment' (Garstka, 2009: 38). Linking changes in urban environment with individual practices and experiences, she separates several 'consumer profiles'. In the analysis as follows, I pose a similar question and suggest a typology of consumers in St. Petersburg, Russia. Before doing this, I will discuss developments in the retail trade as a general context for the transformations in the consumer environment in Russia over the past 20 years in order to link the consumer profiles with retailing formats in further analysis.

Transformations in Retailing: Evidence from Russia

The purpose of this section of the chapter is to review the development of the retail trade in Russia since the 1990s. In order to analyze the transformation, I rely on the idea suggested by Aspers, who has sought differences among sellers through the views of consumers (Aspers, 2010: 14). Thus, besides organizational transformation, the consumers and their perceptions are the focus of my analysis. This review is schematic rather than systematic and is undertaken for the purpose of exploring the dominant retail formats related to clothing, as well as to understand the general logic of the consumer transformation in Russia. In order to reconstruct the history of the retail trade in detail, further research is needed.

I identify four stages in the development of the retail since the beginning of the 1990s: from 1992 to the mid-1990s; from the mid-1990s to the beginning of the 2000s; the years 2003 to 2008; and from 2008 to the present.

In the first stage, from 1992 to the mid-1990s, following the collapse of the Soviet Union, the state withdrew from economic planning and management processes and declared its intention to move the country towards a market economy. In 1992, the Decree on Freedom of Trade was introduced, which guaranteed rights and new opportunities for collective and individual entrepreneurs to develop their businesses in the clothing production and fashion retail. The retail was mostly privately localized in the hands of peddlers who were involved in the international trade called the 'shuttle trade' or the 'suitcase trade', whereby individuals purchased merchandise abroad in small quantities and sold it domestically on the local market (Mukhina, 2009: 341). Clothes were sold in open-air markets, in street and subway stalls and kiosks, from folded beds and sometimes directly 'from the seller's hand'. Clothes were also sold in the former state-owned stores and department stores, which had passed from the state to small-scale business owners. Joint venture stores appeared. Second-hand stores and consignment shops were also in demand. Luxury fashion items were overpriced and sold in boutiques. A large number of people were involved as individual entrepreneurs in the 1990s in all these types of trade. As Mukhina shows, by the mid-1990s nearly 30 million people in Russia were directly involved in the shuttle trade, which provided 75 per cent of all consumer goods in Russia (Mukhina, 2009: 341). This stage was a period of prosperity for individuals and small-scale retail businesses.

The major open-air markets in the 1990s in St. Petersburg included the Okkervil' market at the Ladozhskaia metro station, where almost everyone the entire city purchased clothing;

the Udel'nyi market, where old objects were sold 'from hand to hand', and the enormous Sennoi market on Sennaia square. As Zhelnina describes Sennoi at the time, 'all imaginable means of selling (from hand, from improvised stands, and permanent booths), all imaginable goods (food, clothes, technology, antiques) and all imaginable types of vendors (dossers, pensioners, criminals, entrepreneurial start ups) were juxtaposed on this one patch of urban space' (Zhelnina, 2009: 51).

Besides the markets, the peddlers could sell clothes through networks of family and friends (almost everybody knew someone who was involved in this business); hence, interpersonal connections as part of this activity were extremely important. The shuttle traders also acted as commercial agents and approached offices or businesses, offering anything from food to clothes. Bringing in clothes to Russia, mostly produced in Turkey and China, the shuttle traders were the major sellers of clothing in the 1990s:

Interviewer: Where did you buy clothes [in the 1990s]?

Alexei (born in 1944): At the open-air markets, and shuttle traders brought them to us. Well, I had a friend who used to go to Turkey. He brought various goods—jeans, jean suits, women's leggings. Sometimes he brought them to the place where we worked and sold them.... At the end of the 1990s all department stores, (such as) Gostinka (the Gostinyi Dvor department store) and the Passage were transformed into (a number of) little boutiques. Well, in Gostinka, it was possible to buy something decent; there was a good choice in the Sadovaya wing, especially in men's suits. But outerwear, such as coats or jackets, was expensive. And for shirts the prices were all right.... Open-air markets opened everywhere (in St. Petersburg). We used to go to Kupchino (a metro station) because there was a great choice in the local market. You could find at least something there.

After experiencing the empty shelves caused by the progressively unravelling, centrally planned economy, people in Russia were initially both fascinated by the emerging consumer abundance and enjoyed what this new reality had to offer:

Elena (born in 1945): First, we ran after these Turkish goods. Bright blouses, everything was bright ... on the markets! And eventually it became so monotonous and uniform; everyone wore the same things.... First, everyone was seduced, but eventually....

Eventually the attitude to the open-air markets and other forms of retail from the 1990s changed, largely due to state and local policies and to changes in the fashion retail market.

In the second stage, from the mid-1990s to the beginning of the 2000s, three major tendencies must be emphasized. First, the St. Petersburg authorities fought with the small-scale traders in order to take control of their business. In 1996, authorities implemented the so-called kiosk war aimed at moving the peddlers off the streets.[3] However, the major event to affect the shuttle traders was the economic crisis of 1998 and the collapse of the national currency, the Russian ruble. Since transactions depended on the US dollar exchange rate, many small businesses suffered such massive losses that they never recovered. For this reason scholars treat the year 1998 as a turning point in the dynamics of the shuttle trade and point to the much smaller numbers of traders at the beginning of the 2000s. Another reason for the decline of the shuttle traders was the new customs regulations and in particular, the rule that lowered the duty-free limit for individual travellers from 35 to 50 kilogramme (Mukhina, 2009: 353). Up until then, small-scale retail had flourished not only in the open-air markets and on the streets, but also in small independent stores, which occupied every imaginable space, such as former drycleaners, Laundromats, repair shops, pram storage rooms and basements.[4]

The second tendency was the extensive reconstruction of department stores. One of these was Moskovskii, redone in 1996. According to the local newspaper, an international partner participated in rebuilding the store, which guaranteed a high quality of 'civilized' retail trade and 'European service'. The discourse of a civilized retail trade became a major discourse related to retail and shopping in the second half of the 1990s. By contrast with the 'uncivilized' open-air markets, the department stores paid taxes, and therefore prices for consumer goods were higher. Department stores also implied 'pleasant' shopping 'in comfort' and 'warm conditions' (meaning a friendly atmosphere as well as a pleasant temperature) instead of 'hustling through the stalls'.[5] These were safe environments; hence, a customer did not worry about the safety of his or her bag as was the case in the poorly controlled open-air markets, and on the streets. Renovated department stores promoted a style of service with 'European' standards: the salespersons were supposed to be 'nice' and 'polite', 'with smiling faces', not 'bleak guardians'.[6] Yet in reality it took time to achieve these standards: 'Service changed (in the 1990s) and became better. But sometimes sales persons were too obtrusive.... Sometimes they were slightly uppity' (Larissa, born in 1945).

The third tendency took place in the second half of the 1990s, when newly built shopping malls opened their doors to consumers. In St. Petersburg one of the first shopping malls of the so-called first generation was Balkanskii, opened in 1998. This new mall was advertised as a luxury construction made of glass and steel: 'a magnificent passage (about 20,000 square metres) with 6-metre-high passageways, gently sloping stairs, galleries, escalators, where there were always sunny places, thanks to roof lights and special illumination.'[7] Retail spaces, generally rented by private entrepreneurs, were spacious and light with open, self-service shelves and comfortable chairs for clients. The malls introduced new kinds of activities to consumers—spending leisure time in entertainment zones and food courts. A local newspaper report devoted to Balkanskii claimed in slightly exaggerated tones that in this store, the consumer is the main actor: 'Balkanskii is an enterprise, in which the most important and respected person is not the head of the store, the back office or a sales person but "his majesty" the consumer.'[8] The prices in shopping malls, in contrast to the open-air markets, were perceived to be higher, not only because private entrepreneurs had to pay rent, but also for symbolic reasons: this was 'civilized' trade, with indoor fitting rooms (at the open-air markets, people tried on clothes outdoors all year round, no matter what the weather was), fixed prices and price tags, guarantees, the possibility to return goods and the chance to buy everything under one roof. There was also an additional symbolic meaning: shopping in malls indicated a certain level of well-being, not accessible to the majority of city dwellers. One interviewee recalled:

> Larissa (born in 1945): I remember, in the mid-1990s, I liked to go to the malls, with better design, better doors, no matter what they sold. But they were so beautifully illuminated, magnificent, stylish, despite the fact that I could not afford to buy anything there because I did not have enough money. It was really pleasant for me just to come and see how everything was arranged. And it was pleasant that a salesperson run up immediately with the question: 'Do you need help?'

In the second half of the 1990s international retailers operated through intermediate sellers who developed their chains (Benetton, Adidas, Reebok) as well as through domestic retailers (OGGI, SELA). Hence, clothing was sold at their stores, at the markets, in department stores, shopping malls and multi-brand stores, in the independent designers' salons and factory stores as well as at boutiques selling luxury brands for well-off clients. At this stage the discourse on 'civilized' trade was popular; therefore, the criticism of uncivilized trade as well as the changes that occurred since the mid-1990s gradually forced peddlers, one-man kiosks and the like from the public space, squeezed out the open-air markets, which, however, were housed in proper buildings from then on, and initiated the era of the large-scale retail (Zhelnina, 2009).

A new turn in the consumer sphere in Russia occurred at the third stage, from 2003 to 2008, with the proliferation of a 'second generation' of shopping malls considered 'urban cathedrals' and the dominant form of retail in contemporary consumer culture (Crewe, 2000). Built according to the latest international standards, they featured spacious retail zones, 'anchor' stores (stores generating huge streams of customers), food courts and entertainment zones. These new malls enhanced new retail strategies, such as Western technologies in making sales, the wide acceptance of credit cards, loyalty programmes and 'real' sales (earlier, clothes had gone on sale if they had flaws, which explained why the price was reduced). They also facilitated the exchange and return of unwanted items.

The proliferation of shopping malls was looked on favourably by the city authorities[9] and peaked in the city in 2006. The economic recession of 2008–2009 severely affected large-scale retail trade; however, the number of shopping malls in St. Petersburg is still increasing. At the beginning of 2011, there were 159 large-scale retail properties in St. Petersburg, 68.8 per cent of which were shopping malls. Throughout 2011 a further increase in the share of shopping malls in the overall structure of the large-scale retail trade, up to 70–75 per cent, is expected.[10]

The majority of retailers in the new malls were global retail chains, and domestic sellers had an opportunity to join them in the malls' highly competitive milieus. Among the domestic retail chain stores selling fashionable clothes were Concept Club, Glance and Zolla. Global retail chains were represented by ZARA, Topshop, Mango, Camaieu, Sëppala and many others. For consumers it was not always easy to tell domestic retail chains from global ones. The domestic retailers copy the strategies of the global retailers by using foreign names and rarely present themselves as a 'made in Russia brand'. The retail chains opened their stores in the main shopping districts of St. Petersburg (Nevskii prospect, the Bolshoi prospect at Petrogradskaya storona), thereby contributing to development of street retail in the city.

Various types of shopping malls, including those outside of the city (Mega), in remote districts (Nord, Rumba, Raduga, Grand Canyon, Frantsuzskii bul'var), and in the centre of St. Petersburg (Galeria) were mentioned in the interviews. Several classifications of shopping malls are in use, but the major retail format in St. Petersburg is a retail-entertainment centre.[11] Maxim (born in 1976) gives his impressions of the newly-built shopping mall Galeria, opened in 2010:

> I like this shopping mall because, as it seems to me, it blends with the architecture around it by comparison with what else was built earlier in the city. It does not look aggressive in the architectural milieu of St. Petersburg. And I like the entrance. There are statues, antique-looking…. And I like how everything is arranged; it is clear where to go. And it has a pleasant atmosphere.

The enthusiastic attitude to shopping malls proves that these newly built shopping centres perfectly suited with the consumers, who were mostly from the middle class. The environment of large newly built shopping malls reminded that everything, from streets and benches to cafes, playgrounds' cinemas and bowling alleys, was available for consumers. Malls facilitate practices that were not widespread before, such as family shopping, weekend shopping and suburban shopping.

However, malls were also criticized for being out of place in the architecture of St. Petersburg, for instance, like the mall 'Pik on Sennaia square'. Besides, the interviewees said that instead of leisure, shopping had become a hard job: they complained that it was not always easy to get to the malls outside of the city; shopping 'eats' up too much time; it made people exhausted; there were still lines, no matter what size the mall is; it is not always easy to find what you are looking for; and some malls were awkwardly planned. The stores at the malls, the most popular ones in particular, were 'a mess' with clothes scattered around. This mess made a sharp contrast with the 'external' chic and general order of the malls. Besides, malls 'kill originality' and individuality, as they were not usually selling unique clothes, but rather the uniform brands offered by global and domestic retail chains.

Among other forms of the fashion retail at this stage were luxury brand boutiques, outlets selling brand garments for discount prices; discount stores, which usually belonged to brand-name retail chain stores and sold garments from past collections; and hypermarkets, which provided generic garments at cheap prices (such as Auchan, O'KEY, Lenta). The open-air markets had decreased in number and were largely considered a retail channel for the lower classes.

This period of the retail trade development enforced the trend of a decreasing number of participants in the market, thanks to the proliferation of large-scale retailers and retail chains. This proliferation was supported by the city authorities, who tried either to remove or to civilize the clothing markets. As a result, the retail trade became more depersonalized and standardized as the new practices related to service appeared and people became used to them. The large-scale retailers and the big shopping malls were warmly welcomed by consumers, but with certain reservations.

The 'fourth stage' began during the economic recession of 2008–2009. At the beginning of 2010, the state authorities introduced a new federal law entitled 'On the foundations of the state regulation of the retail trade in the Russian Federation'.[12] With this legislation the state intended to control the further proliferation of large-scale retail chains. The law has been problematic for large-scale retailers, because it prohibits the opening of new stores for chains occupying more than 25 per cent of the market in any particular region. Although these activities affected food rather than fashion retailers, the public discussion of this law has included consideration of the harmful consequences of large-scale retail domination and has led to greater criticism of neoliberalism as well as a re-examination of the effects that large national and transnational actors have on the market.

During the recession, along with the further development of the large-scale retail, various kinds of small-scale sellers for niche shopping have developed. For example, new forms of clothing markets have appeared, such as designer markets, an event that takes place in a designated art space on weekends every few months. An example is the Sunday Up Market, '[the] sophisticated experience of a fashion weekend that brings together unique hand-made goods and collections by fledging designers'.[13] Among the participants in this type of markets are more established designers as well as recent graduates from textile academies who have a chance to present themselves to consumers. These markets intend not only to sell consumer goods, but also to create a community of people—most of whom are younger—with similar lifestyles and preferences in fashion, music, literature and so on.

The so-called dematerialized retail formats, such as Internet shopping, or more generally e-commerce (Ritzer, 2010: 13), has been growing thanks to proliferation of the Internet in Russia. In addition, various types of online sellers, maintained by independent individuals or small groups of entrepreneurs, have emerged. Among them are Click-boutique, Epotaje and Boutique-online. These online vendors are another retail format through which local designers can sell their clothes. These online retailers supply fashions that are unique and different from what large-scale retailers have. Since only a single copy if an item is often produced, prices may be high.

The new informal market of sellers on social networks, such as Vkontakte.ru and Livejoirnal.com, has recently enjoyed rapid development. These are individuals or small groups of people who create accounts through which they sell clothes. The goods sold can come from the following sources: first, the wardrobe of the owner of the account or his/her family and friends; second, flea markets and second-hand stores; third, various online sellers, mostly from Asia. The owners of the accounts themselves must find the clothes to sell. As for used clothes, they sometimes do not go online immediately, but may be modified to make new pieces, and only go on sale after that. In such markets the sellers play the role of producer as well as consumer; hence, they act as 'prosumers, 'creative consumers' or 'craft consumers'—those who are engaged in the production and consumption of garments simultaneously (Beer and Burrows, 2010; Ritzer, 2010).

The attitude to these type of retail forms, as well as to e-commerce in general, among my informants differs and ranges from positive—'I use all of them' (Valeriya, born in 1981)—to negative—'why do you need stuff that others want to throw away?' (Alexei, born in 1978). However, whereas malls introduced 'civilized' shopping and abundance, these small-scale retailers delivered diversity, helped to increase the number of participants in the marketplace and revived non-standardized trade. Small-scale retailers as well as online vendors—and this may sound like a paradox—brought face-to-face interactions, informal contacts and indeed, personality, back to the retail trade. The retailers went to their 'roots', evoking small-scale formats—more convenient, less time-consuming and more personal (Ritzer, 2010: 191).

Thus, the development of retailing in Russia in the 1990s and the early twenty-first century went through various stages, each of which brought new retail formats to the market and contributed to the creation of a pluralistic consumer milieu. Open-air markets and peddlers were major channels for getting clothes in the first half of the 1990s; 'old' and 'new' shopping malls proliferated from the mid-1990s, and by the end of the first decade of the

2000s e-commerce was experiencing growth contributing to the diversification of consumer identities.

A Typology of Consumers

Consumers may be identified by their preference for particular forms of retail trade and their attitudes to these forms. Based on the interviews, I identified the following types of consumers, which I discuss in detail in the following: the advanced consumer, squanderer, socialist consumer, alternative/creative consumer and the convenience consumer. These types of consumers were identified on the basis of a number of criteria, namely the preferred retail format, their level of adjustment to current culture of consumption, demographic characteristics, the volume of economic and cultural capital (in this research equivalent to income and education respectively). Besides attitudes to retailing, I was interested in a broader set of shopping patterns related to clothing consumption, mostly in the first decade of the 2000s.

The group of 'advanced consumers' belongs to the middle class or higher. They have managed to succeed as consumers largely due to their adaptability to the current consumer culture and retailing milieu. They recognize the importance of consumption in today's life, enjoy it and express an interest in shopping.

Advanced consumers, as the interviews show, generally prefer to shop in recently-built shopping malls, since 'it's the level of the middle class or sometimes a bit higher. I can name ... the Mega [shopping mall]. It's convenient to buy everything under one roof' (Ilya, born 1977). The majority of these individuals are 'family consumers' in their 30s or 40s, and they prefer to shop on weekends and get to the malls by car. Therefore, the availability of parking lots is a significant reason why they are attracted to the newer shopping malls and also the reason they avoid the old-style department stores, first-generation shopping malls and open-air markets.

In general, advanced consumers may shop in all types of retail formats and thus behave like omnivorous consumers. They do not mind going to open-air markets if there is a need for something other than status goods or just out of curiosity.

> Ilya: I don't see any reason to go to an open-air market nowadays because you can buy everything in stores and the quality is guaranteed. But I have bought stuff at the market, too. Once I needed a cap, and in the stores, nothing worked, so I went to the market and found what I was looking for. (Ilya, born in 1977)

> Interviewer: Have you shopped in second-hand stores?

> Ilya: Yes, once. We hadn't gone for a really long time, but our friends, they go from time to time, and I said: 'Just out of curiosity'. So we decided to go there too and we'll go back ... I didn't buy anything for myself; the men's department was small. But my wife found several interesting things.

Thanks to sufficient economic capital, for the advanced consumers price is not the first and foremost factor in making purchasing decisions. However, they are knowledgeable consumers and are aware of the prices at different sellers including outside the country. Nor do they scorn sales. In general, the advanced consumers are open to new things—loyalty programmes, new retail formats and so on—and the new possibilities that the retail market may offer.

As for the characteristics of the clothes, that are important for these consumers' purchasing decisions, the garments should be comfortable, durable, functional and of high quality. Advanced consumers are usually well acquainted with brand names, since this kind of knowledge is part of their cultural capital.

Unlike the next group, the squanderers, and thanks to their higher cultural capital, the advanced consumers try to avoid wasteful behaviour, the latest trends and style risks, preferring a smart casual style of clothing. They criticize conspicuous consumption:

> Ilya: A class of people has appeared who wear fashionable, expensive clothes. [They] change their clothes very often whereas the other class has adopted a European, or Scandinavian style, in where everyday outfits consist of quiet and completely

comfortable clothing, not high-end brands. This means you're not dressed from head to toe in Prada and Hugo Boss.

Nevertheless, advanced consumers recognize the symbolic meaning of consumption and talk about positional goods; as Ilya says: 'I know that if I buy [these shirts], people will perceive me differently; my social status will rise in their eyes.'

The 'squanderers' are also well integrated into current consumer culture. They belong to the middle- or upper-middle class and possess middle to high volume of economic capital and a low to middle level of cultural capital. Squanderers consider shopping a pleasure, are usually emotionally involved in the process and make no moral judgements about spending money on clothes. On the one hand, this model of consumption is based on Colin Campbell's notion of romantic consumerism and hedonism (Campbell, 1987): 'When you shop, it produces serotonin, and you feel happy. You feel excited. Buy something—and you feel great' (Anna, born in 1990). On the other hand, not only does the process of shopping create pleasant feelings, but also the symbolic power of purchasing gives social status. It is important for squanderers to communicate their status through clothes; it gives them a sense of stability and well-being. Anna says: '[Consumer goods] give you a feeling of stability; no, not of superiority, but you get something, you get status. Consumer goods help your self-actualization. Perhaps this is an illusion … but you buy it to bring it (status) to people's attention.'

Squanderers are careful in choosing consumption sites since these also signal status. Shopping locations as well as the clothes themselves are considered an important means of cultural and social distinction, which is why squanderers choose the newly built shopping malls with their global brands and avoid open-air markets and second-hand stores, which they see as 'for the lower classes'. They also choose brand garment retailers, including luxury brands, which have stores in the main shopping districts in St. Petersburg (Nevskii prospect, Bolshoi prospect of Petrograd side). In terms of demographics, squanderers are often singles or young couples; hence, shopping in the centre of the city suits their lifestyles very well:

Interviewer: Do you shop in shopping malls?

Anna: Yes, it's easier than going from one store to another. I like Atrium (a mall at Nevskii prospect), and also Bolshoi prospect; I really like Petrogradka [Petrograd side]. There are lots of stores, and [they are] very close to one another. There is a huge gallery; I don't remember the name. [I shop at] Mega [a shopping mall outside the city] as well, but OK, I haven't been there for a long time.

Normally, squanderers do not try to save on clothes. The amount of money they spend may vary greatly, from 1,000 rubles (about $33) to $3,000 per month. The number of clothes in their closets is often characterized by the expression 'more than enough but nothing to wear':

Interviewer: Do you have lots of clothes?

Anna: Yes, I do. I have even more clothes than I need, to be honest. My parents often say this. Although my mom has even more stuff than me. And she tells me: 'I have nothing to wear!' She opens her closet, [and] stuff just falls out on you. I understand that I have enough clothes to wear, but I want more.

Unlike the advanced consumers, the squanderers refuse to wear smart casual clothes and choose symbolic value over use value in their clothing. Squanderers are relatively skilled consumers in terms of brand names, which are important for immediately signalling status. They prefer luxury big-name brands as well as well-known mass market brands. Furthermore, they are fond of conspicuous consumption: Anna says 'I like Guess; I have a whole lot of Guess. I love Armani. Well, I just bought Louis Vuitton [a purse] in Milan, [and am] so excited about that. I like Escada Sport and, in general, Escada'.

Brand names of clothes suggest a higher price, which, in the perception of consumers, means higher quality. Despite fashionability, style and fit as major reasons for a purchase, squanderers expect clothes to be of high quality and thus last longer:

Interviewer: Why do you choose these brands?

Anna: They fit my style. I like their design. Calvin Klein, you can buy for everyday use. If you buy a nice expensive purse, nothing will happen to it, even if you use it for long time. And a T-shirt. See, just a black T-shirt. Why should I spend 3,000 rubles on it? You'll be wearing this black T-shirt five years from now wherever you want: to the beach or anywhere. And nothing will happen to it. It will not lose its colour or fit; it will not turn into garbage in two days.

'Socialist consumers' belong to the middle or lower classes, are older (45 plus), were born and socialized in a socialist consumer culture and see today's situation from the point of view of their past experiences. They are rational about their clothing choices, and they do not often follow the latest trends. However, due to their higher volume of cultural capital, they are relatively interested in being contemporary and dressing with style. They are relatively knowledgeable about modern consumer culture and express a desire to participate in it. But at the same time they experience certain difficulties with the availability of suitable clothes. Thus, shopping for them is the opposite of pleasure and hedonism, as is the case with the squanderers. Instead, they talk about irritation, dissatisfaction and frustration when shopping and a lack of real interest in it.

Socialist consumers assign a high value to clothes and do not have many. They use clothes thoughtfully, carefully and for as long as possible ('I have had this coat for 20 years') in accordance with the attitude to clothes in a socialist society. Since their economic capital is not high, socialist consumers do not splurge on clothes, usually have no specific clothing budget and prefer to buy clothes when a replacement is needed; in other words, out of necessity rather than fashion:

Interviewer: Do you have many clothes?

Larissa: I don't. Of course, I would like to have more, but, on the one hand, there is no need; I don't have many places to go to wear them anyway, and I don't have any motivation to show them off. On the other hand, perhaps I've gotten used to asceticism, so you wear what you have and buy clothes every once in a while, maybe

once a year, once in two years, just to replace something. But
it's mostly for summer clothes because in the summer you spend
more time outside the house.

When socialist consumers were younger, they had to shop in a
context of scarcity. Having had this experience, they should have
welcomed the transformations in retailing that have occurred in
post-socialist times. In fact, they appreciate the new retail formats, but prefer to shop at the old-style department stores, such
as Moskovskii, and in the individual stores of domestic producers and retailers such as the factory store Pervomaiskaia zaria,
the owner of brand names Zarina and befree for women and
FOSP for men. These producers existed in St. Petersburg back in
socialist times and in the 1990s changed their names; however,
socialist consumers recognize the old companies under the new
names. Socialist shoppers also try to avoid second-hand stores,
largely because of their assumptions about used clothing being
'unhygienic' or 'for poor people', or they just said they were 'too
old to wear old clothes'.

As for the new retailers, socialist consumers appreciate them,
as I mentioned, but at the same time they express regret and dissatisfaction over the clothes on offer:

> Larissa: I don't like the stuff sold in these stores. If I need some-
> thing and am going shopping, I am easily disappointed. The
> designs are not for me; I don't like them, since they are clothes
> for kids, not adults. And if there are clothes my size, then they are
> old-fashioned, so [there is] nothing interesting. You go shopping,
> find nothing and get into a bad mood. Recently, I haven't been
> able to find anything at all....

The problem that socialist consumers face is the target market
of the shopping malls. The majority of international and domestic retail chains proliferated in the 1990s and the early 2000s are
targeted at young people. Thus, people over 45 years of age are
largely ignored by the retailers; this older clientele must deal with
difficulties such as poor availability of suitable styles and designs.
The interviewees point to 'naked bellies and low-cut trousers' as
well as 'glitter and sequins' among other things:

Larissa: Everything is dreadful. To buy something to go out in is, in fact, almost impossible for me. Everything [they have in the stores] is either cheap or the completely wrong design. All this glitter and sequins; all those styles.... They don't suit my spirit.

Not only are the styles and designs problematic, but also these consumers question the quality of the clothes: 'In today's fashion, you know, there is so much sloppiness ... strings everywhere, bad stitching' (Larissa, born in 1945).

Socialist consumers are critical of the attitude to clothes in the new retail chain stores, where merchandise is just scattered around. They also do not appreciate the long lines at fitting rooms, which they experienced during socialist times and hoped never to experience again. They are critical of other changes, too, such as service, pointing to a lack of professional qualities in sales persons:

Larissa: The service varies. Sometimes it's OK, good and unobtrusive; yes, but sometimes.... There are many stores, I would say, in which the sales persons lack professional skills—sales persons with no skills to communicate with consumers. The service [maybe] is rather obtrusive when they follow you around all the time, especially if it is an expensive store, and you feel like a beggar. Or, on the contrary, [you feel] a complete lack of attention. Thus, to find a good sales person who would understand you and be genuinely happy to assist you is as difficult as finding good clothes.

'Alternative or creative consumers' are aware of the novelties of the current culture of consumption; they are well socialized, but sometimes deliberately choose to exclude themselves from particular forms of consumption. Most creative consumers are young adults between 18 and 30 years of age. They often rely on green values and are engaged in second-hand and flea-market shopping.

Creative consumers often serve as both consumers and producers of merchandise; they develop and participate in new alternative forms of retailing and shopping. Campbell (2005) described the emergence of what he refers to as the 'craft consumer', who purchases principally out of a desire to engage in creative acts of self-expression—s/he already has a clear and stable sense of identity (Beer and Burrows, 2010: 4; Campbell, 2005: 24). The most important characteristic of creative consumers is that they participate in the production of what will be consumed (Beer and Burrows, 2010: 4). Creative consumers prefer various kinds of alternative shopping that give them opportunities to participate actively in producing, selling and shopping, for example, at flea markets and in self-established online groups in social networks through which they exhibit and sell clothes:

> Alina (born in 1984): I mainly use the spb.barakholka.com.ru website. There are plenty of groups and many accounts. I check them, and there are girls participating in this form of retail and exchange; they put the pictures of the clothes online. If you like something, you can buy or if you really like it [but do not want to buy], you can exchange it for something else.

Creative consumers are the major clients of the alternative retail formats: the previously discussed small-scale operators who have recently emerged in St. Petersburg. As the interviewees stated, they do not buy and sell professionally, but confess that it is a temporary activity. Like the socialist consumers, the creative consumers criticize the mass market and are not satisfied with it. However, they criticize it for different reasons.

The most valuable for the creative consumers is not the novelty of a thing but the story behind it; therefore, they often prefer to shop for used clothes—vintage, retro, and the like. The meaning of shopping for them is buying unique clothes and enjoying the process of looking for something that is not standard, meanwhile valuing the process of communicating while shopping. For younger people, the 'coolness' of second-hand shopping lies in the resisting of predictable mass-market shopping.

Although price is not their major reason for buying cheaper clothes, the creative consumers often do not have significant amounts of money; many are students, for example, who are not usually very well-off. Hence, money can be an important issue, and sometimes they prefer to exchange rather than buy clothes: 'You give [an item] to me, I give something to you, and we all are happy…. Therefore, you saved money for your budget, which is a good thing' (Alina, born in 1984).

Brand names are important to creative consumers; however, unlike squanderers, they criticize the mass market and luxury brands and choose brand names from the past—socialist brands— first, and second, local names. Socialist brands and Soviet symbols get a second life in the wardrobes of creative consumers, which may be a sign of nostalgia. However, since these consumers are of a younger age, their perception of socialist culture lacks the experience of actually living in a socialist world. This is why socialist brands, which for the older generation symbolized something else, signify 'uniqueness' and 'coolness' for these young adults. At the same time, being interested in the history of clothes, they more or less know the meanings of the clothes in the socialist system and are able to understand the value of garments from the past.

Unlike other types of consumers, creative consumers do not always care about quality, preferring style and design. If they talk about quality, for example, in reference to used clothes, they mean an absence of conspicuous holes or unremovable stains.

Creative consumers do not completely ignore mass market stores, but they limit their shopping in such places to items related to personal hygiene rather than to personal identity. Sometimes they also shop for shoes in regular stores for the same hygienic reasons. They also try to avoid open-air markets, unless it's a flea-market. Although the markets work for them in terms of cheap prices, they do not meet their expectations in terms of unique clothes.

The last type of consumer is the 'convenience type'. Of varying ages, this consumer's financial resources range from low to mid-level as does the cultural capital. As with creative shoppers, convenience consumers are not very well integrated into the contemporary consumer culture, but unlike the creative shoppers, it is not always their own choice. There are two reasons that they are excluded: first, a lack of economic capital, and second, a feeling that the current consumer culture does not fully suit their identity; thus, they prefer to stick to habitual consumer venues and past practices.

In general, the convenience consumers articulate a preference for shopping in stores that are 'close to where they live'.

For the older interviewees, the number of stores that have suddenly sprung up has been overwhelming. They often perceive the growth as 'trading noise' and do not remember the names: 'Stores? There are so many stores, I don't remember the names. I go to the ones on the square (close to where I live)' (Olga, born in 1964).

The younger consumers express interest in the newer retailers, such as discount stores that sell brand garments for less. They are interested in sales, loyalty programmes, and any other activity that allows them to shop in an inexpensive way:

Ksenia (born in 1990): I go shopping when there are sales—in winter, around December, and in summer. In summer, it seems to me that there are permanent sales. I don't even know when they start. In July, perhaps, and they last until September....

Interviewer: Do you go to discount stores?

Ksenia: Yes, I do.

Interviewer: Which ones?

Ksenia: Vero Moda, InCity, Romashka.... I go there because there may be a piece from a new collection for half the price, maybe with a minor defect on the inside of a coat, where nobody will ever see it.

Along with discount stores and old-style shopping centres, convenience consumers were one of the few groups to articulate their relatively recent choice of shopping at open-air markets.

Interviewer: So, you gave up shopping at the open-air markets, right?

Ksenia: Well, you know, [not completely,] sometimes I still go there, to buy a sweater. Sometimes you have to find something to wear—a jacket, a jeans, a trousers, a shirt, a nice blouse, a skirt or a sweater. They have prices that may be less expensive than in the stores [nowadays]. I think I [almost] gave up markets a couple of years ago when the sales appeared.

The older generation has replaced open-air markets with shopping at hypermarkets, such as O'KEY, Auchan and Lenta, which sell groceries as well as lower quality general merchandise at cheap prices.

Price and quality are the main imperatives for convenience consumers in choosing clothes. They do not much care for brands, mostly expressing in their narratives categories from socialist times—'Finnish boots', 'Belorussian knitwear', 'Baltic clothes': 'I may like something, but if the combination of price and quality is not satisfactory, then I will put it back, grinding my teeth. It's just painful to pay for something that will fall apart in a week' (Olga, born in 1964).

In sum, five types of consumers have been identified—these are the main ideal types—and their characteristics discussed. It was not rare to see a combination of more than one type of consumption and shopping in the same interview. However, the clear connections with a particular set of sellers make these types relatively consistent.

Conclusion

This chapter has presented an analysis of the transformation of the fashion retail and of consumption in Russia over the past 20 years and discussed how these were perceived by consumers. During this period, the country survived a retail revolution during which the retail became one of the fastest growing markets. The process of developing retailing was not linear, as this research has shown. It started off at the beginning of the 1990s with legislation that gave a large number of people the opportunity to become involved in different kinds of entrepreneurial activities, including shuttle trading for clothes. By the middle of the first decade of the 2000s, the number of individual actors in the market had significantly decreased as the dominant retail formats eliminated more and more the peddlers and open-air markets in favour of large-scale retailers, including shopping malls, the latter of which civilized, standardized and depersonalized the process of acquiring consumer goods. By 2010, the recession had necessitated the development of small-scale retail business, such as showrooms and design markets, which, in contrast to the mass fashions in shopping malls, provided individualized fashions and personalized service.

By the end of the first decade of the 2000s, consumers found themselves in a new environment with very different shopping conditions. These new conditions facilitated the creation of various types of consumers, defined by their preferred retail formats and other characteristics. The present research has enabled me to identify five types of consumers: the advanced consumer, the squanderer, the socialist consumer, the alternative and creative consumer, and the convenience consumer. Retailer preferences and shopping practices depend on demographic and social characteristics and vary according to the degree of cultural and economic capital.

In general, this analysis of the transformation of retailing and shopping in Russia shows how the country has reacted to the many challenges and issues that have arisen in the past twenty years, for example, the free market versus state control, globalization versus localization, standardization versus personalization and the proliferation of transnational companies and neoliberal ideology versus local initiatives, all of which affect consumers and consumer culture, thus making the country an interesting object of study in the context of the development of global consumerism.

Notes

1. The Russian Statistical Agency; see http://www.gks.ru, accessed on 2 August 2013.
2. The interviews were conducted in 2010–2011 in St. Petersburg. The majority of the interviewees were well educated. Approximately two-thirds were women, who usually have a higher level of competence in fashion and clothing than men. All the participants were living at St. Petersburg when the interviews were conducted with exception of two, who had recently relocated to Moscow. Among the interviewees were small business owners, engineers, museum employees, managers, accountants, economists, clerks, teachers, university professors, students and retirees.

3. Sankt-Peterburgskie vedomosti. 17 October 1996. 199 (1375).
4. Sankt-Peterburgskie vedomosti. 1 April 1997. 60 (1485).
5. Sankt-Peterburgskie vedomosti. 26 October 1996. 246 (1422).
6. V nashikh stenakh shirpotrebom ne torguiut // Sankt-Peterburgskie vedomosti. 4 July 1998. 43 (1422).
7. Takogo, kak Balkanskii, bol'she net // Sankt-Peterburgskie vedomosti. 7 February 1998. 24 (1698).
8. Ibid.
9. The state and the city authorities facilitated the development of the large-scale retail trade by introducing the programme known as the Conception of development of the consumer market in St. Petersburg, 2005–2007 (Kontseptsiia razvitiia potrebitel'skogo rynka Sankt-Peterburga na 2005–2007 gody), which claimed that the chain principle of retail trade organization was favourable. This programme stimulated the growth of retail chains in St. Petersburg.
10. An overview of the retail market in 2010, see: http://www.colliers. spb.ru/images/analitika/pdf/Colliers_International_Overview_2011_ SPB.pdf, accessed on 2 August 2013.
11. A retail-entertainment centre is a group of retailers coherently integrated, located in a particular zone and operated by a developing company. A retail-entertainment centre usually includes stores, entertainment areas (cinemas, bowling alleys, etc.) and food courts. In Russia the word 'mall' is usually used as a synonym for a 'retail-entertainment centre'.
12. Ob osnovakh gosudarstvennogo regulirovaniia torgovoi deiatel'nosti v Rossiiskoi Federatsii, see http://www.rg.ru/2009/12/30/torgovlya-dok.html
13. Sunday Up Market, see http://en.sundayupmarket.ru/

References

Aspers, P. 2010. *Orderly Fashion: The Sociology of Markets*. Princeton, NJ: Princeton University Press.

Beer, D. & Burrows, R. 2010. Consumption, prosumptions and participatory web cultures. *Journal of Consumer Culture*, *10*(1), 3–12.

Campbell, C. 1987. *The Romantic Ethic and the Spirit of Modern Consumerism*. Oxford: Basil Blackwell.

———. 2005. The craft consumer: Culture, craft and consumption in a postmodern society. *Journal of Consumer Culture*, *5*(1), 23–42.

Chaney, D. 1990. Subtopia in gateshead: The metro center as a cultural form. *Theory, Culture and Society*, *7*(4), 49–68.

Crewe, L. 2000. Geographies of retailing and consumption. *Progress in Human Geography, 24*(2), 275–290.

———. 2003. Geographies of retailing and consumption: Markets in motion. *Progress in Human Geography, 27*(3), 352–362.

Crewe, L. & Beaverstock, J. 1998. Fashioning the city: Cultures of consumption in contemporary urban space. *Geoforum, 29*(3), 287–308.

Crewe, L. & Gregson, N. 1997. Tales of the unexpected exploring car boot sales as marginal spaces of contemporary consumption. *Transactions of the Institute of British Geographers. 23*(1), 39–53.

———. 1998. Tales of the unexpected: Exploring car boot sales as marginal spaces of contemporary consumption. *Transactions of the Institute of British Geographers, 23*(1), 39–53.

Featherstone, M. 1995. *Undoing Culture: Globalization, Postmodernism and Identity.* London: SAGE.

Garstka, G.J. 2009. Social pluralism in the postsocialist city: Diverging consumer groups in the consumption landscape of Stara Zagora, Bulgaria. *Anthropology of East Europe Review, 27*(1), 37–50.

Goss, J. 1993. The 'magic of the mall': An analysis of form, function, and meaning in the contemporary retail built environment. *Annals of the Association of American Geographers, 83*(1), 18–47.

Jakovcic, M. 2010. New spaces of consumption in postsocialist city: Example of the city of Zagreb, Croatia. http://bib.irb.hr/datoteka/403403.P12-Martina_Jakovcic.pdf, accessed on 2 August 2013.

Kreja, K. 2006. Spatial imprints of urban consumption: Large-scale retail development in Warsaw. In *The Urban Mosaic of Postsocialist Europe: Contribution to Economics,* pp. 253–272. Heidelberg: Physica-Verlag HD.

Mukhina, I. 2009. New loses, new opportunities: (Soviet) women in the shuttle trade, 1987–1998. *Journal of Social History, 43*(2), 341–359.

Radaev, V. 2007. *Zakhvat rossiiskikh territorii: novaia konkurentnaia situatsiia v roznichnoi torgovle.* Moscow: HSE Publishing House.

Ritzer, G. 2010. *Enchanting a Disenchanted World: Continuity and Change in the Cathedrals of Consumption.* Los Angeles: SAGE.

———. 2011. *The McDonaldization of Society—6.* Los Angeles: SAGE.

Williams, C.C. 2002. Why do people use alternative channels? Some case-study evidence from two english cities. *Urban Studies, 39*(10), 1897–1910.

Zhelnina, A. 2009. From Barakholka to shopping mall: Transformation of retail spaces in St. Petersburg. *Anthropology of East Europe Review, 27*(1), 51–64.

Zukin, S. 2004. *The Point of Purchase. How Shopping Changed American Culture.* New York & London: Routledge.

10

Sales Tours or How Czech Seniors Learned to Love Capitalism

Marketa Rulikova

Introduction

This chapter examines how seniors in the Czech Republic have coped with the invasive entry of consumerist choices since the collapse of socialism in 1989–1990. While younger generations have eagerly embraced consumerism, it might be expected, in line with what has been termed continuity theory (Atchley, 1999), that seniors, who are most habituated to the old ways and more marginalized from an economically productive life, would struggle most dramatically with accepting new and unfamiliar norms. The demand conditioned under socialism for intergenerational solidarity within the family, in the form of pooling resources and providing in-kind assistance (mostly by seniors) to their offsprings' families, has been gradually disappearing. Persistent efforts by seniors to remain helpful to their children and grandchildren are encountered with lukewarm support or even open hostility, often leading to intergenerational conflict. In addition, the socio-economic status of the elderly population has declined significantly due to their reliance on state pensions, which have been disproportionately degraded relative to salaries

in the emerging private sector. As a result, the inevitable diminution in expectations and intergenerational misunderstandings in
the family led to disappointment and depression among seniors.

Current research, however, reveals some positive shifts in
lives of seniors who have managed to find meaningful pursuits
in retirement in a surprisingly innovative way. In the context of
studying the leisure of seniors after retirement in Western societies, Roberts (2006) noticed that people in their later years have
generally—compared to younger people—less control over their
life events, given uncertainties regarding their physical and mental capacities, as well their dependence on their children. In the
case of Czech seniors, it is therefore even more unexpected to
discover their newly asserted agency that has developed despite
the double obstacle of their own physical aging and the systemic
transformation in their country. As will become clear in this
chapter, new market opportunities have provided seniors an
arena not merely for satisfying consumers' needs and desires, but
also and more importantly for constructing new identities and
groups. The research focus here is on seniors, but the findings
extend beyond this age category and give testimony to one of
the most profound social changes in the Czech family since the
collapse of socialism.

The research for this chapter was undertaken between 2008
and 2009, when I participated in *předváděčky*,[1] or what I call here
sales tours, direct sales events designed for senior customers. In
the overall economy, sales tours constitute a marginal enterprise
utilizing techniques of direct sales, but in the world of seniors
they often play a central role, around which they organize their
weekly activities.[2] The sales tours I observed typically involve
day long bus excursions to attractive, nearby tourist destinations.
Organized by retail companies, the trips require their participants to spend a significant part of their time listening to marketing pitches and product demonstrations. For an ethnographer,
these trips serve as an ideal venue for studying one relatively
marginal but revealing area in which the old *habitus* of socialism
(embodied in the responses of seniors) collides with new market
habitus of capitalism (represented both by the salesmen who pitch
their products to the seniors and the children and grandchildren

waiting back at home to rebuke their elders for the purchases they have made). The intimacy of sales trips, especially lengthy bus rides with participants, provided invaluable insights into seniors' ideas about consumption, as well as their more general thoughts on the meaning of life, relations with their offspring, and many other themes. During these friendly conversations, I also had an opportunity to ask seniors to comment on developments in their lives over the past 20 years. I participated in six such events and in several product demonstrations (a more modest, but related form of marketing) before this period of concentrated research. I conducted 14 in-depth interviews with people living in different parts of the Czech Republic who participated in sales tours and had several dozen conversations with middle-aged and young people whose relatives have engaged in sales tours. Additionally, websites where Internet users debate their experience with sales tours were also useful sources, even though comments appearing on these sites could not be controlled for any socio-demographic characteristics.[3] References to *předváděčky* in the national media were especially useful to get a better sense of the controversy, which surrounds this seemingly innocent and marginal market enterprise.[4]

Sales Tours Sell Well among Seniors

Sales tours evolved from formerly home-based or locally organized product demonstrations that were popular among many Czechs in the early 1990s, a period of pioneering and often primitive forms of retail marketing. As younger cohorts abandoned direct sales for a more competitive or simply broader assortment of retail options found in department stores, 'big box' stores, specialty boutiques, shopping malls and direct marketers were compelled to reorient their businesses and focused their attention on potentially more promising (because more malleable) customers for whom they coined the formula of sales tours. Sales tours are explicitly targeted at retired people. They take place during workdays and virtually all participants are equal to or above 60 years of age. This peculiar 'capitalist business' builds on notions and practices of 'socialist consumerism', which results in a unique symbiosis of satisfied predatory vendors and similarly satisfied older customers who enjoy a comfortable environment that reproduces in a modified form many practices of 'old times'.

Seniors are most often invited to participate in 'free-of-charge' or low-fee bus trips through leaflets that appear in their mailboxes. Comfortable buses bring groups of seniors from different parts of the country together to a selected destination[5] where, typically in an old-fashioned local restaurant or pub, participants—usually numbering between 70 and 150—spend the bulk of their time sitting through product demonstrations, which culminate in strong-armed efforts by sales personnel to sell the featured goods. Featuring products of mostly collective consumption (e.g. dish sets, induction hotplates, vacuum cleaners, multifunctional steam irons) to be purchased for the good of the whole family rather than to meet one's own individual consumption desires reflect a marketing appeal based on older patterns of consumption that emphasized the survival and success of the group over those of the individual. Limited financial resources and, even more profoundly, restrained consumer supply compelled people prior to 1989 to seek long-lasting commodities. In this sense, seniors' favouring 'the durable' over 'the fashionable' does not relate so much the frugality of the elderly as to deeply rooted routines developed in times when buying a colour television or washing machine, those longstanding symbols of status and achievement, was for a family the event of a decade. Offering previously unknown and in former socialist countries widely 'fetishized' Western goods (Drakulic, 1993; Merkel, 1998; Rausing, 2002)—for which, consumers had 'no experiences but high expectations' (Gurdon et al., 1999: 5)—was an obvious way for companies, many of which are branches of Western corporations, to tap into the Eastern European market.

After the official marketing and sales part of the programme, customers are offered a free or subsidized lunch, followed by entertainment that might range from a brass band concert to visiting a medieval castle or zoo, going on a boat trip, or attending a garden show. The incorporated cultural events are intended to increase the attractiveness of the trip. A similar function can be attributed to the gifts that are distributed to every participant at the end of product demonstrations, regardless of whether a person purchased anything. These 'tokens' are presented, in the words of one salesman, as 'an expression of the company's respect for its valued customers'. They, however, seem to be intended to induce sufficient guilt in seniors so that they will make purchases. In line with the logic of direct sales, gifts reinforce advertisements and are expected to spread positive word of mouth.

Providing 'free travel' exploits the pattern whereby customers, habituated under socialism to paying for goods, were unwilling to pay for services. In this sense, it is more useful to consider seniors' old expenditure habits rather than measure their actual financial situation in order to understand the seeming absurdity of seniors being drawn by the prospect of free travel to participate in sales tours, during which they will be forced to listen to interminable sales pitches and sometimes coerced into spending the equivalent of hundreds, and occasionally even thousands, of Euros. The popularity of sales tours over regular tours is due to the assumption of participants that they will not have to disburse money for the trip they are taking, which thereby keeps intact, at least in a nominal sense, their habitual disdain for paying a fee for service.

As a leisure time activity and segment of the service sector, travel had a distinctive position in the state socialist setting. Privately, travels were sought-after by a largely urban population as a means of social and physical escape, but prior to 1989 options and destinations of travel were controlled and extremely limited. Consequently, in order to escape from their clogged block apartments and gain some release from the pent-up resentments at their lack of civil freedoms, city dwellers set off every available weekend and vacation for their own, their relatives', or their friends' rural bungalows and country houses, known as *chatas* and *chalupas*.[6] Typically reachable within a 30–60 minute drive, these 'getaways' represented the dominant mode of private travel,[7] since the high cost and limited availability of gas, inadequate accommodations, and closed borders stifled other forms of individually initiated travel.[8]

To the extent that people took other, more ambitious theme trips, they favoured collectivized state-sponsored travel (overseen by state enterprises through union organizations, the most important of which was ROH,[9] and often dispensed as a reward for achievement in the workforce) over commercial tourism due to their low cost (Williams and Baláž, 2000). In order to join heavily subsidized ROH trips that often took them to attractive destinations, participants were willing to tolerate the propaganda that was invariably part of such trips or that provided the ostensible organizing framework for particular trips (e.g. sightseeing excursions whose theme might be the 'glories of communist architecture' or visiting factories in a partner foreign city). In this light, sales tours can be understood as a capitalist re-invention of socialist era tours in a number of senses. In both the prior socialist and contemporary capitalist contexts, tourists, under the pretext of receiving a 'free' reward, are required to pay for their reward by enduring hours of indoctrination. Likewise, tourists on both socialist leisure and capitalist sales tours often had to accept without complaint humiliating treatment at the hands of their 'guides'. Finally, in both situations, participants, as will be discussed in the following, find quiet ways to sabotage, or at least deflect, the programmatic aspirations of the tour leaders, whether they are related to instilling communist precepts or making sales.[10]

Intergenerational Conflict over Consumption

While sales tours provide a window into some of the ways that older Czechs preserve the socialist *habitus* of consumption under the new conditions of market capitalism, these half-shopping-half-entertainment excursions also delineate points of tension and confusion at the very core of Czech society—the family unit itself. In analyzing these contemporary social strains, it is critical to acknowledge that what happens around sales tours is as perplexing and anthropologically meaningful as what happens on them. While the decision to go on a sales tour ostensibly relates to a senior's personal and independent action, its 'consequences' often affect others. Simple conversations between family members about the value and legitimacy of sales tours can turn into arguments over priorities and responsibility within the family, but even more intense conflicts arise when seniors return from trips after having made unexpected purchases that might seem extravagant and wasteful to other family members.

In making sense of the intergenerational conflicts associated with sales tours, it is important to emphasize the novelty that post-retirement travel represents in Czech society. Travel after retirement was uncommon, not only because of financial and health concerns (Williams and Balá, 2000), but also because seniors were enmeshed in the ongoing web of family life through the variety of services they provided, including cooking, home-production of clothing, house repair, babysitting for grandchildren and vegetable gardening. Strong intergenerational solidarity was an indispensable advantage in an economy of shortage and was at the centre of a set of socially expected and unquestioned moral obligations binding seniors and their offspring (Haukanes and Pine, 2003; Kornai, 1980; Smith and Stenning, 2006; Verdery, 1996). For the post–World War II generation, disposable labour and wealth, which seniors were generally eager to share, brought this first 'affluent' generation high social status and a strong sense of personal meaning.[11]

The times and family dynamics, however, have changed. As I demonstrated elsewhere (Rulikova, 1998), Czech families' economic and social strategies dramatically shifted after the advent of the free market. With the immediate influx of goods of many kinds, it became more reasonable and desirable to engage in cash-generating activities, for example, moonlighting, working overtime, taking second jobs, or starting one's own business. The epicentre of economic activity for most families was pushed from the domestic sphere to the public labour market, with a consequent erosion of shared family time and ties. While practical expressions of family support remain rather strong within Czech families compared to Western European standards, expectations of material and emotional support from home are in decline, especially among the youngest generation (Možný et al., 2004).

According to findings from an extensive quantitative research study on intergenerational solidarity in the Czech Republic, the youngest cohorts operate increasingly as autonomous individuals who '... demarcate their private life independently from their family' (Možný et al., 2004: 21). Longitudinal demographic and sociological data further testify to increased individualization and diversification in the intimate lives of the young (Možný, 2008; Tomášek, 2006). Most significantly, for the youngest cohorts, new lifestyle opportunities—pursuit of career, international travel, and an inexhaustible variety of entertainment and individualized consumption options—provide attractive alternatives to family life, and many young adults are choosing—as in the West—to postpone starting families of their own or even foregoing marriage and raising children altogether (Chaloupková and Šalamounová, 2007).[12] In a discussion of contemporary household arrangements among youth, Tomášek (2006) introduced the concept of 'urban tribes' to the Czech context, as he registers a growing number of roommates sharing apartments and socializing with peers, forming thus a kind of families of choice.

While productive cohorts were compelled to adapt quickly to the new social and economic order following the collapse of the socialist order, seniors have sailed the wild waters of transition at a different, slower pace. Shut out from their traditional role as active and productive family contributors, seniors often feel left behind and left out. 'I don't blame (my children and grandchildren) for not having time for me', one informant confessed, with understanding and resignation simultaneously in her voice. 'Today, everybody has to take care of themselves. And in these times, it is not easy'. This family nuclearization as a result of 'cultural preference to westernize and, at least for some, (declining) economic pressure' has also been observed in other post-socialist countries [Ahmed and Emigh in Smith and Stenning (2006: 199)].

Seniors responded by shifting the cultural imperative of assisting their offspring from providing more common labour, time and home produced objects to providing purchased goods. And so, where retired women had previously knitted sweaters or plucked feathers in order to make comforters for their daughters' and granddaughters' dowry, they set off on sales tours with the intention of purchasing sets of knives, dishes or anti-allergic blankets with the same aim of building their offspring's dowries or helping them with purchases they might not otherwise, according to the seniors, be able to afford. Indeed, the vast majority of my informants confessed that they shop primarily for their children or grandchildren. As one informant noted, 'I buy only for my children. I don't need such fancy dishes. I am happy with the set I have. And it's been with me since my wedding!' Whereas the shift from providing labour, production and care to endowing commodities can be interpreted in terms of 'cooling intimacy' (Illouz, 2007) or 'purchasing intimacy' (Zelizer, 2005) in the sense that it represents an intrusion of commodity relations within the family unit, it can also be seen as an example of seniors' perhaps futile attempt to retain their traditional resourceful role while recognizing new ways in which it can be demonstrated.

While a sense of duty is often the motivation for sales tour purchases, the feeling of having fulfilled that duty gives way to remorse or confusion, as young relatives make it clear that they do not appreciate the presents received from their elders:

> I have bought this anti-electro-smoke blanket for all my grandchildren. But my oldest granddaughter L. [who is 33] is not grateful at all. And I was buying this blanket with her in mind because she is seriously ill.... You know, they don't appreciate your care. They don't know what is good for them. They don't appreciate health as we, seniors, do. But one day they will realize ... I just hope it won't be too late.... (A 73-year-old woman, retired clerk)

Not surprisingly, making unasked-for purchases for absent family members collides with the consumption choices of younger generations who, as 'beneficiaries', disapprove of or look down on the 'practical' product choices of their (grand)parents, and who want to make their own individual decisions on purchases in accordance with their personal style and brand loyalties:

> I told my mother not to buy me anything—that I simply don't want it. And I won't discuss the issue any more. And we stopped talking about sales tours. We know it always ends up in an argument. (A 50-year-old woman, bio-grocery-store owner)

We are so unhappy with our mother! She never tells [us] anything, goes on those trips, and then comes back with all that junk which she is so excited about. I told her we don't want it. You know you can buy the comforters in any specialized store these days, and for much cheaper. But she says that it is not the same quality. I don't know what to do with her. I would like her to spend her pension money on herself, enjoy life. But no, no, no.... (A woman in her mid-forties, distance-learning student)

They are old. You cannot really change their mind. They are stubborn. I only hope that they don't buy stuff that is too expensive, because they don't have the money for it. And we warned them against buying on crooked credit. We told them they would have to pay back way more. But I cannot prevent them from buying gifts for their grandchildre.... (A man in his early fifties, plumber)

The aftertaste of disagreement between relatives over sales tour purchases is especially bitter for the beneficiaries given the steady pauperization of seniors. In the context of the changing balance of purchasing power between the younger and older generations, it is both awkward and guilt-inducing in the younger generation to see seniors, currently the poorest social group in the country, keep buying overpriced goods for their professionally active and better-off younger family members. The problem is exacerbated by a communications gap as increasingly seniors seem to have only a vague understanding of the financial condition of their relatives. The old practice of talking about money within families, often in the form of complaints at its absence, has been disappearing in a re-stratifying society, as the discussion of wealth becomes taboo. Given this lack of discussion, one explanation for seniors carefully saving their low pension incomes[13] in order to purchase appliances for their young kin is that they are unaware of the financial condition of their offspring (also illustrated in the following quote).

Aware of their elders' efforts to help, beneficiaries find themselves at an impasse: on the one side, they feel guilty that their elderly relatives deprive themselves in order to purchase expensive, low-quality and undesired appliances; on the other side, they do not want to offend their benefactors by rejecting presents:

We don't really talk about money with my granny or uncles and
aunts anymore. Not that it is a secret or that we are rich and want
to hide it from others, but each one is doing differently and we
don't want to bring up what separates us. My granny always asks
me if I have enough money. And I say, 'Yes, granny, you don't
need to worry'. But then she still goes and brings me 500 crowns
so that nobody sees it. She tells me to buy what I need. And it's
so hard. I know I will please her when I accept the money, but
you know … it's embarrassing to know that she saves so hard
for a moment like this … [pause]…. And then I go and pay 1500
crowns for my haircut…. (A 27-year-old student from Prague
whose grandmother lives in a small town in Moravia)

I just accept those gifts. I pretend that it might be useful. But I
emphasize that I don't want [my folks] to buy any of those dishes
or vacuum cleaners. I told them I may accept only what they bring
as free gifts. And you know … then you start using those knives
and they last for three cooking times and break…. (A woman in
her late forties, kindergarten teacher)

Several middle-aged informants disclosed to me that it took
them years before they finally intervened and ordered their parents not to buy them any more stuff, or even made them return
purchases. In some cases of this sort, seniors were relieved to
have to return items, because they realized with regret that they
had been tricked or had acted impulsively in making a purchase.
Purchase returns are by and large carried out with the assistance
of the offspring (which can, only half facetiously, be interpreted
as an inverted form of intergenerational solidarity, helping diso-
riented seniors adapt to affluent consumer society).

Seniors themselves are generally not knowledgeable about
their customers' rights and are also not as assertive in expressing their dissatisfaction. Age difference in voicing or not voicing consumer complaints suggests that this tendency might also
be explained in relation to the senior generation's early life
experience under state socialism. According to Kolarska and
Aldrich (Gurdon et al., 1999), in their extended application of
Hirschman's exit-loyalty-voice theory, people under state socialist regimes have tended to react passively—that is with 'silence'—
to the abuse that they suffered at the hands of authorities and

retailers alike. Whether out of fear or resignation, people tended to articulate complaints only within the safe confines of home and not in public. This attitude of passive acceptance at being a victim, and of writing off mistreatment on the part of manufacturers and retailers as simply 'bad luck', or 'the way it is' began to disappear soon after the demise of the centrally dictated economy (Gurdon et al., 1999). However, while younger cohorts might feel confident in expressing their dissatisfaction with mistreatment or shoddy products, the active expression of such complaints is still difficult for most seniors. Similarly, just as seniors tend to avoid complaining, they also sometimes seek to avoid domestic arguments about wasteful shopping by storing or hiding the expensive appliances in a garage or at the bottom of a dresser (where are already stored yet to be presented dowry gifts for grandchildren yet to be married).

In making sense of the intergenerational tensions that the study of sales tours reveals (and the still preliminary, though suggestive evidence of changing family relations generally), Hochschild's concept of an economy of gratitude involving 'misgiving' and 'misreceipt' of gifts is especially useful (Hochschild, 2003).[14] She understands 'gift' in the broader sense of any given object or action that extends regular expectations (of a donor and a benefactor) as regards social exchange. In her words, a gift is something 'extra', even though in double-earner families it might include something as trivial as washing a dog or performing other domestic chores. Drawing on Hochschild's analysis of the difficulties faced by husbands and wives in negotiating a balance between traditional gender roles and the new pressures brought about by women's participation in the labour market and the disparity in how men and women interpret their separate contributions to the household, it can be argued that the transformation of the socialist economy has led to the principal axis of tension to be across generational rather than gender lines. Hochschild argues that the misunderstandings that cause difficulties in marriages in the United States are the product less of individual traits than of more profound social forces, that is, the mounting gender gap in expectations about division of labour at home, career sacrifices, and the like. Men in a modern capitalist society only unwillingly surrender their power and prestige to market-achieving women and often interpret the compromises they make to the household economy as a 'gift' to their wives, so that when—from their perspective—that 'gift' remains unappreciated, resentment and misunderstandings ensue. In an analogous fashion, one can see in the often tense relations between generations in the Czech Republic a similar 'gratitude clash' resulting from each side trying to 'help out' family members across the generational divide but failing to understand which help is most appropriate or desired by family members whose actions are based on motivations and cultural assumptions that the other side increasingly is unable to understand.

Sales Tours as an Arena of Search for New Lifestyle

The *a priori* supposition that the popularity of sales tours simply demonstrates the sad reality of seniors' vulnerability to manipulative and predatory merchants who use 'the old logic of things' as their weaponry, distorts the more complex and indeed colourful, dimension of sales tours. In order to fully explain the phenomenon and longevity of sales tours in the Czech Republic, it is critical to realize that, as sales tours evolved, they have helped seniors fill in the gap that sprung up as a result of their disconnected contacts with children and grandchildren and their feeling of marginalization in the majority society. In this context, sales tours are opportunities for seniors, often widows or widowers, to renegotiate their identity and group.

As disclosed to me during scattered conversations on the bus, many elderly neighbours and acquaintances set out on tours jointly, notifying each other about upcoming events, registering together, debating about the quality and desirability of products, and most recently also providing each other with tips on how to resist salesmen's attempts to force unwanted purchases on them. All of these activities contribute to creating new informal support groups, and sometimes, even friendships. It should be noted that while this late modern, mostly urban, trend of supplementing or compensating family with a network of friends has been observed among young Czechs (Možný, 2008; Tomášek, 2006, 2008) or Western seniors (e.g. Allen et al., 2011; Finchum and Weber, 2000; Stevens and Van Tilburg, 2011), a proper study of friendships among seniors in the Czech Republic has been missing. Observations from my fieldwork seem to suggest that a similar trend of substituting family with friends and acquaintances takes place among seniors. It needs to be emphasized though that when directly asked about their openness to meeting people, seniors usually seemed embarrassed to admit their attraction to new groups. My informants by and large downplayed the quality and intensity of these contacts. As one woman in her early sixties remarked to me, 'Oh yes, we've known each other for quite some time. You know, there are always the same people coming to sales tours. But we never really keep any contacts with one another outside of our trips'. While I do not have sufficient evidence to offer a definitive explanation for this (rather common) type of response, I would argue that guilt over reorienting their affection from family kin, dictated by old habits of family-centred assistance, might be one reason why seniors downplay the importance of these connections.

Another obvious sense one acquires on a sales tour is that the rhetorical style of product demonstrations and the interactions accompanying them resembles the atmosphere of a social club. Thus, while doing their best to convince the audience of the merits of Teflon pans or super-efficient induction hotplates, salesmen also offered recipes that promote healthier nutrition and economical meal preparation. Seniors are likewise encouraged to share their own examples of culinary magic. When cleaning products are featured on the programme, the salesmen quiz the audience on how to get rid of certain kinds of stains, and arguments break out in the room over the best techniques, along with discussions on how to enhance sleep or treat a particular illness or pain. These salesmen-led discussions are a true pell-mell, ranging from 'granny's old-fashioned' cures to learning about the virtues of new technologies, and remind one of invented multifunctionality of objects under socialism which Drakulic (1993) sarcastically compared to 'enforced environmentalism'. To my amazement, I learnt that lanolin, originally designed to soften cloth, can also rejuvenate an aging leather coat; what is more, it can also alleviate psoriasis and varicose veins.

According to my informants, sales tours, over their 15-year history, have gradually turned from straightforward trade ventures between friendly salesmen and unsophisticated senior customers into intensive efforts by overbearing marketers to convince ever more hesitant and impoverished customers to buy goods that they neither need nor desire. At the same time, seniors have not been without leverage in these transactions, and both the marketers and their potential customers mobilize a set of strategies that keeps sales tours sufficiently lucrative for the companies sponsoring them. The unwritten law of both retailers and seniors is to keep balance between commerce and entertainment. Originally this equation was easily achievable. Seniors, hungry for Western durable goods of superior quality, were shopping in droves, regardless of steep prices. In exchange, they enjoyed luxurious bus drives, free lunches, and—as my informants nostalgically recalled—the attention of smiling, caring vendors. Product demonstrations were brief and untiring because seniors had no doubts about the quality of the merchandise.

As their supply of goods expanded, and facing disapproval from their families, along with shrinking savings, seniors gradually abandoned extravagant expenditures. Still, drawn especially by the cultural programme and the desire for social contact that was offered, seniors have not refrained from registering to attend free sales tours, even when they had no intention to make any purchases. On their end, when profits began to decline, retailers stiffened up their marketing strategies. Interactions between retailers and seniors became a chase to outsmart the other side. Seniors are aware of the fact that in order to keep sales tours alive, they cannot always be saying 'no', at least not straightforwardly and *en masse*, and somebody from the crowd has to purchase the products. Hence, they have creatively developed a variety of 'maybe' and 'maybe later' responses to the salesmen's strong-arm tactics in order to prolong retailers' hope for future profit:

I love the iron. It's so smart that you can get steam into it from the vacuum cleaner and it's great that it irons curtains while they are hanging. It's awesome. But it's also expensive. Hm … 30,000 CZK. It's a lot of money. I really will have to consult with my husband. (A woman in her mid-sixties)

We already have six of these blankets. They are extraordinary, we know. And we are thinking about getting a pair for our daughter and her family. But you know, they have their own taste.… Why don't you give me your 'internet mail' and they will get in touch directly with you. But we will tell them that the blankets are superb. I mean, they have already seen them in our place. But we will remind them.… (A retired couple in their late sixties)

While many excuses were carefully prepared at home, last minute alibis are sometimes plotted jointly with friends in restrooms during coffee breaks. This 'customer solidarity' is, however, extended only to the close circle of 'friends'. Realizing that sustaining sales tours is conditioned by effectuated sales, participants oftentimes encourage newcomers or undecided acquaintances on trips to buy appliances with the hope that the retailer's continuing profits will lead to their offering future trips. And thus, what might be called viral marketing, that is, informal 'chitchat' about popular products, is skewed by self-interest in making sure that sales tours continue. While the immediate objective is inverted, the logic of this behaviour is similar to consumer practices under state socialism, for while the socialist reality of deficiencies required competition among customers (not retailers) and the winner (of a commodity) had to outsmart other customers to win the prize, sales tours in this declining capitalist niche feed competition between customers. In this case, however, the object is not to win the coveted object, but to convince other customers into buying goods one is not interested in so as to mollify the salesmen and perpetuate the event.

Despite increased sophistication in marketing, seniors often resist the entreaties of sales personnel to purchase big-ticket items. As a consequence, salesmen, who are salaried on a commission basis, become distressed and aggressive towards the participating seniors (and often towards each other as well).

In 'uncooperative' groups, seniors are occasionally locked in the presentation hall, and demonstrations are extended for long durations, even 7–8 hours in a row, with minimal breaks and lunch being postponed until late afternoon. When seniors protest these conditions, salespeople sometimes threaten to make the 'excursionists' travel home in a taxi (an extravagant service that most seniors have never used in their lives), or they will refuse to allow seniors to get into the bus for the return trip to home until a designated number of customers have bought a particular appliance. There are always more than two salesmen and they watch us so that we don't fall asleep. They act like 'slave bosses' (*raubíři*), but how cannot you sleep if you've heard the same rubbish so many times? An 83-year-old widow commented with laughter. 'They also shut us up when we comment that the price is not as competitive as they claim. And they can be pretty rude. They quickly turn from refined gentlemen into jerks, I'm telling you', complained another. At the end of an unsuccessful sales session, I have seen seniors humiliated by being forced to wait outside in the rain in a long line to receive their promised gifts, all the time being subjected to taunts from the sales staff that they are abusing the good will and hospitality of the company by coming only to pick up their free gifts. 'You guys here in Prague are pretty dirty, I must say', commented one salesman when no one in the group was willing to buy a CZK 30,000 vacuum cleaner. 'Hope that at least this washing powder improves your cleanliness', he added sarcastically. Nearby seniors pretended to miss the comment and hastily packed their gifts into their bags.

It is remarkable that despite this discomfort and humiliation many seniors are still willing to put up with such behaviour. The reason, it seems, is that maltreatment is calculated as a 'necessary price' for having the opportunity to enjoy an active social life. Besides this pragmatism, the legacy of uncivil shopping experiences under socialism makes the entire venue feel less outrageous to seniors who well remember, and perhaps have been conditioned by, the constant humiliations that were an inevitable part of the process of acquiring goods (Kornai, 1980; Merkel, 1998). Waiting in long lines, sometimes overnight, and bribing shop assistants, who—in compliance with the socialist mentality—were usually brusque, if not rude, in their dealings with customers were everyday realities. Today's seniors are still accustomed to the rule that they have to suffer before they acquire goods or—even more so—obtain a free gift. As a result, there is almost an expectation that, in order to buy high-tech desirable goods, they will have to endure such behaviour. They are not happy with this state of affairs and resent the rudeness they are subjected to, but as under state socialism, they sleep it off and sign up for the next trip as soon as the opportunity is available (the same way as they sleep off the criticisms of relatives who are critical of their willingness to go along with the rudeness of sales personnel).

Conclusion

Current seniors in post-socialist countries in Eastern Europe are often referred to as a lost generation, or transformation losers. This 'unfortunate' generation experienced practically overnight the devaluation of their socio-economic status and, even more importantly to them, saw their offspring rush off to participate in the new opportunities afforded by capitalism. While seniors appreciated that their children and grandchildren were able to find gainful employment, self-realization, and ever more bountiful consumption, they lamented the loosening of extended family ties and the diminution of their own status within their families.

Ironically, relief from frustrations over the erosion of family ties has been sought for at least some seniors within the realm of consumerism. Seniors initially looked to the market for commodities, which could serve as substitute for previously self-produced goods and which their old habits dictated they should provide to their offspring. Given frequent faux pas in gifting, along with the exhaustion of savings spent on these mismatched purchases, seniors partially retreated from buying. At the same time, however, seniors have not given up the shopping arena overall. As demonstrated here, declining to participate in sales tours would cause them to lose one of their few chances for socializing in light of diminished opportunities for spending time with their ever more over-extended and scattered families. My field research indicated that, despite their initial bitterness and reluctance to participate in new societal forms, seniors have come to accept and even enjoy opportunities associated with the new world of consumerism. While this development is perceived by many as the pitiful plight of a manipulated, vulnerable part of the population, this study proved almost the opposite: seniors' agency and resourcefulness becomes apparent in situations when they mobilize what might be called a 'free-riding' strategy in order to obscure their lack of financial wherewithal and sustain the illusion of their status as customers who deserve market (or any) attention.

While old habits might occasionally cause them to feel guilty for enjoying rather than labouring in their leisure, seniors justify their embrace of this new lifestyle as a way to reconnect with the majority of society. In the same vein, seniors have discovered new opportunities for redefining identity and group, and even friendship. While more thorough research on non-kin relations among Czechs in later years is needed, the current study suggests the emergence of a new phenomenon. The advent of non-kin support groups and friendships devoted to sharing leisure activities among Czech seniors seems to go along with trends observed in other European countries. Modernization theories try to explicate such tendencies by arguing that more developed countries undergo more significant structural change in primary groups while secondary groups play a more pronounced role in social support networks (Hollinger and Haller, 1990).

In all likelihood, this 'one of a kind' generation won't be reproduced in the same manner in future cohorts, given that newer seniors will represent more socially and economically diverse populations shaped by their experiences under capitalism during their productive years. Predictably, sales tours in their current form will not persist, and that by the time new cohorts of seniors retire, more sophisticated leisure and travel opportunities marketing to seniors will have emerged. However, sales tours can be seen as an historic milestone of an important stage in profound social change that has occurred in recent years in Czech family and Czech society generally.

Notes

1. In this chapter, I use the idiom 'sales tour' to translate the popular term *'předváděčka'* (sg.)—or *'předváděčky'* (pl.)—which is a shortened form of *'předváděcí akce'*, that is, demostration events. The English phrase, 'sales trip', is thus slightly inaccurate, because 'demostration event' has a more generic meaning, referring to any type of direct sale ventures. However, the travel component will be critical for the current analysis, and therefore I decided to employ this more loaded term.

2. The level of seniors' participation on sales trips is hard to estimate. In an attempt to compensate for this the lack of data, I requested students in several of my courses (totally around 60 people) to investigate the topic among their grandparents. Roughly two-thirds of these students' grandparents had participated at least once in a product demonstration or sales trip. About a fifth of them confessed to regular participation. During my own participation on sales trips, I naturally encountered a biased sample of those interested in them. Yet, I also witnessed several events at which more potential participants remained outside of a bus or presentation hall than those who managed to enter due to limited seating, from which I infer the general popularity of these trips.

3. For example: zpovednice.cz (transl. confession), orbion.cz, christnet. cz. larry.cz, and many others. Thematically, these websites range from travel agencies' discussion forums, to Christian community sites, to students' diaries. The most common contributions are complaints about Beck International Ltd. and Beck Reisen Ltd. companies, their fraudulent practices, and the tricks they use to coerce people to buy products. A portion of discussions also contains lay-legal advice and requests for people to join lawsuits-in-preparation as witnesses.

4. Criticism stems from violating customers' rights, for example, overpricing products; insufficient translation of instructions; not abiding by stated return policies; and enforcing obscure and misleading credit conditions. In addition, and as will be discussed, seniors have been harassed and threatened, especially when sales have declined. Presentations become inhumanely long, and seniors have sometimes been forced to remain listening to product demonstrations without breaks, creating unbearable conditions, especially for elderly people, many of whom suffer from various medical problems, including incontinence. It is even not unheard of for salespersons to threaten seniors by denying them return transportation. Harassment is also often accompanied by rude language. Numerous cases of customers' rights violation and maltreatment on sales trips have been reported in the Czech media and via other public institutions (e.g. ČT, 2007, websites of ČOI and SOS).

5. Most trips take place locally, though a recent trend is to offer sales trips abroad. While these novelty trips abroad require some prepayment, organizers appear to calculate that this pre-selection or filtering will attract a wealthier clientele (including younger cohorts), and thus more and bigger sales will be realized. The most recent innovation of Beck Reisen Ltd. has been to turn theme tours into an actual object of sales on local, in-country sales trips; a conventional 'free' gift provided on this type of sales trips is a set of travel suitcases. The strategy of advertising theme tours instead of household appliances, however, is only a more sophisticated attempt to promote and sell the usual product assortment. Internet discussions divulge the rest of the story: vacationers with Beck Reisen tourist agency, besides 'enjoying' their tour, are also made to sit at (surprise!) product demonstrations. Theme tours as a new commodity might be also read as a new, yet cautious attempt at addressing more 'Western-minded' elderly customers who might be more interested in seeking experiences (travels) than material goods. The validity of this assumption, as well as its practical success remains to be seen.

6. Lay readers might find Burton (2009) a useful reference for learning about the phenomenon of *chatas* and *chalupas* in the Czech context.

7. In a country of 15 million inhabitants, there were reportedly 23,500 *chatas* and 54,000 *chalupas* (Williams and Baláž, 2000).

8. While the weekend houses across the communist bloc have been extensively documented as sites providing plots of land used for subsistence or source of status (see, for example, Lovell (2003) or Zavisca (2003) for the context of Russian '*datchas*'), literature on the functions and meaning of *chata's* and *chalupa's* in Czechoslovakia, however rare, supports their most crucial function as a site of recreation (Williams and Baláž, 2000).

9. ROH stands for Revolutionary Union Movement and was the central union controlled by the state and Communist Party.

10. In the atmosphere of those times, when practical jokes constituted a form of passive resistance to the regime (Caldwell, 2004), participants turned the propaganda tour into a caricature, as the cinema of the period sometimes managed to reveal. Thus, Marek Piwowski's *Rejs* (1970), a Polish film, represents an outstanding satirical comedy that focuses on this activity. In the Czechoslovak cinema, an illustration of the phenomenon of socialist collective travels, even though not up to the standard of Piworski's wit and absurdity, is Bořivoj Zeman's *Anděl na horách* (1955).

11. Devoting oneself to kin has developed into a deeply rooted cultural norm that contrasts with the Western emphasis on the quality of life

of individuals who are encouraged to consume, travel, and get more education for themselves.

12. As a result, young people in the Czech Republic do not marry and establish families at as early an age as their parents or grandparents. In 1989, the average age at first marriage was 21.8 for women and 24.6 for men. In 2008, the age of first marriage increased to 28.7 for women and 31.4 for men. Average age at which women had their first child similarly shifted from 22.5 to 27.3. In the age category of 25 to 29, 78 per cent of men were single (compared to 28 per cent in 1991) and 60 per cent of women were unmarried (Český statistický úřad, 2008, 2009).

13. For the structure of Czech seniors' household expenditures between 1990 and 2000, see Večerník (2008). The widely-shared impression of seniors' frugality in their everyday consumption (and spending a significant amount of their leisure hunting for the best bargains) was documented in a film *Czech Dream* by Vít Klusák and Filip Remunda (2004).

14. Hochschild understands gift in a broader sense of any given objects or actions that extend regular expectations (of a donor and a benefactor) as regards social exchange. In her words, gift is something 'extra', even though in a double-earner families it might include as trivial offers as washing a dog or other domestic chores.

References

Allen, K.R., Blieszner, R. & Roberto, K.A. 2011. Perspectives on extended family and fictive kin in the later years: Strategies and meaning of kin reinterpretation. *Journal of Family Issues, 32*(9), 1156–1177.

Atchley, R.C. 1999. *Continuity and Adaptation in Aging.* Baltimore: The John Hopkins University Press.

Burton, R. 2009. *Prague: A Cultural History.* Northampton, MA: Interlink Books.

Caldwell, M. 2004. *Not by Bread Alone: Social Support in the New Russia.* Berkeley, LA: University of California Press.

Český statistický úřad. 2008. Složení obyvatelstva podle věku a rodinného stavu. Downloaded from: http://www.czso.cz/csu/2009edicniplan. nsf/t/1D00355EB5/$File/400709a1.pdf (accessed 14 October 2010).

———. 2009. Česká republika od roku 1989 v číslech. Downloaded from: http://www.czso.cz/csu/redakce.nsf/i/cr_od_roku_1989#01 (accessed 14 October 2010).

Chaloupková, J. & Šalamounová, P. 2007. Postoje k manželství, rodičovství a k rolím v rodině v České republice a v Evropě. *Sociologické studie* 04. Praha: Sociologický ústav.

Drakulic, S. 1993. *How We Survived Communism and Even Laughed.* New York, NY: Harper Perennial.

Finchum, T. & Weber, J.A. 2000. Applying to continuity theory to older adult friendships. *Journal of Aging and Identity, 5*(3), 159–168.

Gurdon, M., Savitt, R. & Pribova, M. 1999. Consumer activism in the Czech Republic: The role of exit and voice in a changing economy. *The Journal of Socio-Economics, 28*(1), 3–19.

Haukanes, H. & Pine, F. 2003. Ritual and everyday consumption practices in the Czech and polish countryside: Conceiving modernity through changing food regimes. *Anthropological Journal on European Cultures, 12*, 103–130.

Hochschild, A.R. 2003. *The Commercialization of Intimate Life.* Berkeley, LA: California University Press.

Hollinger, F. & Haller, M. 1990. Kinship and social networks in modern societies: A cross-cultural comparison among seven nations. *European Sociological Review, 6*(2), 103–124.

Illouz, E. 2007. *Cold Intimacies: The Making of Emotional Capitalism.* Cambridge: Polity Press.

Kornai, J. 1980. *Economics of Shortage.* Amsterdam: North-Holland.

Lovell, S. 2003. *Summerfolk: A History of the Dacha, 1710–2000.* Ithaca, NY: Cornell University Press.

Merkel, I. (ed.). 1998. *Getting and Spending.* Cambridge: Cambridge University Press.

Možný, I. 2008. *Rodina a společnost.* Praha: Sociologické nakladatelství.

Možný, I., Přidalová, M. & Bánovcová, L. 2004. Mezigenerační solidarita. Výzkumná zpráva z mezinárodního srovnávacího výzkumu Hodnota dětí a mezigenerační solidarita. Praha: VÚPSV.

Rausing, S. 2002. Re-constructing the 'Normal': Identity and the consumption of western goods. In M. Ruth & C. Humphrey (eds), *Markets and Moralities: Ethnographies of Postsocialism,* pp. 127–142. Oxford: Berg.

Roberts, K. 2006. *Leisure in Contemporary Society,* 2nd Ed. Oxfordshire: CABI.

Rulikova, M. 1998. The impact of post-communist transformation on the economic and social behaviour of the Czech family. In D. Dornisch (ed.), *Post-Communist Transformations,* pp. 119–147. Warszawa: IFIS Press.

Smith, A. & Stenning, A. 2006. Beyond household economies: Articulations and spaces of economic practice in postsocialism. *Progress in Human Geography, 30*(2), 190–213.

Stevens, N.L. & Van Tilburg, G. 2011. Cohort differences in having and retaining friends in personal network in later life. *Journal of Social and Personal Relationships, 28*(1), 24–43.

Tomášek, M. 2006. Single a jejich vztahy: kvalitativní pohled na nesezdané a nekohabitující jednotlivce v České republice. *Sociologický časopis, 42*(1), 81–105.

———. 2008. Naše blízké vztahy a společenské demokratizační změny. K novému chápání zdrojů integrace a reprodukce společnosti po roce 1989. Downloaded from genderonline.cz

Večerník, J. 2008. Household consumption in the Czech Republic. *Polish Sociological Review, 2*(162), 153–173.

Verdery, K. 1996. *What Was Socialism, and What Comes Next?* Princeton, NJ: Princeton University Press.

Williams, A. & Baláž, V. 2000. From collective provision to commodification of tourism? *Annals of Tourism Research, 28*(1), 27–49.

Zavisca, J. 2003. Contesting capitalism at the post-Soviet Dacha: The meaning of food cultivation for Urban Russians. *Slavic Review, 62*(4), 786–810.

Zelizer, V. 2005. *Purchase of Intimacy*. Princeton: Princeton University Press.

PART III

Subaltern Concerns and Moral Subjectivities

11

Politics of Consumption, Politics of Justice: The Political Investment of the Consumer

Roberta Sassatelli

Introduction

With the advent of modernity, consumption has been insistently portrayed as a private act, untouched by power. Aligned with the market, commerce, the family has been pushed into the private sphere; it has been opposed to the public and political spheres of the state, citizenship and rights. However, it is becoming increasingly evident that both the ways in which consumption is represented and the ways in which it is organized are deeply intertwined with power relationships. Power relations inherent in consumer patterns and cultures are of different sorts, but recently it is mainly a politics of effects (on the environment) and (global) justice that has been stressed. This emphasis has gone hand in hand with mounting awareness of the ambiguities of the commoditization process.

Indeed, when they consume goods in contemporary Western societies, people essentially engage with the process of commoditization (i.e. with the translation of objects and services into commodities, exchangeable in the market through money), and they make use of meanings produced and reverberated by the promotional industry, advertising in particular. Nevertheless, consumption configures itself as a process of de-commoditization—a term with which we may indicate the re-translation of the meanings and uses of commodities through daily life, on the basis of needs that are not directly reducible to those of production, retail or promotion even if they are not entirely free and are anything but individual. However, as de-commoditization, consumption is neither reducible nor symmetrical to production or retail. This opens the space for power effects and strategies of different sorts, including global division of labour (with consumerist nations consuming a disproportional share of global produce) and environmental effects. A growing wealth of literature is documenting the spread of initiatives and social movements that question the limits of the market, the relationship between production and consumption and ultimately the environmental and social effects of private consumption mainly in the Western countries. Such initiatives—often dialectically intertwined with the market, occasionally looked favourably by governments, always entailing the political investment of the 'consumer' as a 'responsible actor'—are currently conveniently grouped under the banner of 'political consumerism'. Political (or critical) consumerism addresses globalization as de-territorialization, the disarticulation of production and consumption, and the separation of politics and the market. Issues of global justice and environmental sustainability are regular features of its overall narrative.

In this chapter, I try to open the black box of political consumerism, considering some of its different facets, and exploring its contradictions and dilemmas. Addressing what has been considered a transformation of politics in Western society, the chapter aims to explore the scope of the political investment of the consumer for a politics of justice. Especially among political scientists, the use of critical consumer action—as varied as symbolic protest, product boycotting or the purchase of ethically coded products, and the development of alternative provision networks—has been saluted as a development and an antidote to the individualization of politics and its vanishing into sub-politics.

What gets collected under the banner of political consumerism is nevertheless varied enough to require a problematization of a too simple equation between consumer action and voting. Moreover, if the cultural framing of the consumer as a political actor is becoming dominant it cannot be simply superimposed on the actual practices and patterns of (critical, ethical, or responsible) consumption, which in turn carry meanings and mechanism that cannot simply be reduced to the political investment of the consumer. Finally, even when (critical, ethical or responsible) consumption responds to strictly political motives, there is still the question whether individual consumer awareness of systemic, unintended effects may translate consumption into a genuine politics of justice. Indeed, the understanding of the many facets of critical consumer behaviour requires a broader view of the politics of consumption. After considering some of these issues, I shall thus conclude proposing a few analytical considerations on the different dimensions of the politics of consumption. On such background I shall re-consider the space of a politics of justice and the important role that a new definition of pleasure may have to complement a view of duty and responsibility prevalent within the dominant political framing of the consumer.

The Politics of Consumption as a Politics of Justice

Against traditional critical views considering that advertising is able to commend consumption as an alternative to political rebellion (i.e. Lasch, 1979), there is increasing awareness that the sphere of consumption can constitute itself as a space for negotiating political action. For example, as early as the late eighteenth century, English women used their consumer power to support abolitionism (Davies, 2000). Later, at the turn of the twentieth century, the National Consumer Leagues appeared in the United States and were mostly concerned with using manifestations and boycotts on the part of consumers to exert indirect pressure on specific enterprises denounced as both producers and employers. Founded by Florence Kelley and inspired by the Progressive

Movement, social justice was their utmost purpose, that is, they published 'white lists' of manufacturers who treated their workers fairly (Glickman, 1999; Strasser et al., 1998). They anticipated the sequence of mobilizations against the rising cost of living that sprang up around the First World War in many Western countries often led by housewives' organizations. The French *Ligue Sociale d'Acheteurs,* for example, was influenced by its American counterpart and was likewise created for the ethical education of consumers, with the aim of bringing about changes in working conditions by developing a sense of responsibility in buyers for the treatment of workers, portraying consumers as citizens who had the 'right to intervene in capitalism' (Chessel, 2006). Broadly speaking, these movements were successful in inspiring changes in legislation regarding work or price control, and they effectively offered women a possibility to speak out and act in the public sphere: in their capacity as 'consumers' women claimed the responsibility and right to intervene in masculine territories such as work, trade unionism, and local and national politics. These are early examples of consumer protest that clearly go beyond standard consumer defence, such as that represented by the consumerist and product-testing organizations that developed especially after the Second World War and became consolidated with the adoption by various international bodies of 'consumer rights'. This blend of consumerism, that is largely internal to existing market relations being mainly concerned with value-for-money and information transparency, is clearly not the only way for consumers to associate.

Indeed, much more recently, and especially after the WTO 1999 protests in Seattle, the political investment of the consumer has become more explicitly aimed at critically addressing globalized capitalist relations using notions of (global) democracy, justice, and social and environmental sustainability. This politics of consumption clearly aims to be a politics of global justice, whereby global refers to a characteristically post-colonial world and to the planet as a living, finite, common resource. A new hybrid actor, the citizen–consumer is being increasingly relied upon as the constituency and the agency for political and economic transformation. Global capitalism has tended to raise local hackles, provoking resistance in many different forms, including fundamentalist ones. As globalization proceeds, it is especially large multinationals that have become the targets of growing critical attention, both within environmentalist organization and for the alter-global movement. Economic globalization has highlighted a number of external diseconomies that derive from market expansion as currently managed (such as pollution, the inequality between consumers, the widening gap between North and South, food scares, etc.). In introducing innovations that alter the routines of consumption, expanding the relevant human community, disarticulating economic from socio-cultural processes, globalization creates a space to bring into question the naturalized boundaries of the market. A number of grass-roots movements have organized not only boycotts of particular products, but also powerful symbolic protests.

The spread of McDonald's on the world scale, for example, has stimulated numerous hotbeds of resistance that have often taken on global dimensions but press for local control of resources. In particular, since 1985 the London-based group of the international environmental movement Greenpeace has promoted an anti-McDonald's campaign, a boycott day that is held every autumn in a growing number of countries. The growing success of this initiative is also due to the massive public resonance of the libel case that McDonald's brought against two Greenpeace activists, for their distribution of protest leaflets. The leaflet maintained that the American giant exploited children with its advertising and its employees with low pay, promoted unhealthy eating, damaged the environment through encouraging the deforestation of Amazonia to produce low-cost forage, and treated animals in inhumane fashion. The so-called McLibel case, still the longest running case in English legal history (from 1994 to 1997), was a public relations disaster for McDonald's which, despite its skilful lawyers, was unable to win on all items (Vidal, 1997). Internationally, protests against McDonald's have generally been non-violent but none the less emblematic: for example, in France, McDonald's were filled with apples, occupied by farmers with chickens, ducks and geese, covered with dung, and so on. Some of these actions were guided by the farmer and trade-unionist Joseph Bové, who reached international fame destroying a barrel of his precious Roquefort cheese in front of a McDonald's during the anti-globalization protest in Seattle 1999. Bové's actions can be seen as part of the French tradition which, from the nineteenth century, has given a patriotic cast to the development of agricultural policy and ties gastronomy to the safeguarding of the national territory, and yet nevertheless transcends this to promote the local and sustainable agriculture at the international level. In the logic of Bové's protest, production and consumption are not separated: both are political questions since the counterpart to exploited workers is said to be the consumers for whom it is ever harder to find genuine products.

Well beyond these examples it is evident that a growing variety of discourses, both within the marketplace and outside it, in politics and civil society, are calling into being the 'consumer' as not only an active subject but also, and more fundamentally, as a political subject. Institutional actors at the international and supranational levels as well as anti-globalization movements are particularly vocal in addressing consumers as a constituency, called forth as a partner in checking the otherwise allegedly unhampered workings of international business. Examples abound, from the EU Green Paper on business social responsibility that places the consumer and the citizen side by side and identifies both as the main constituency for ethical business, to the wide spectrum of local, national and international organizations that are increasingly concerned with mobilizing social actors as 'consumers' (i.e. traditional environmental movements, fairtrade campaigns, anti-sweatshop boycotts, etc.). As suggested, it is not entirely new to explicitly link consumption with the pursuit of moral and political aims, still today a discourse about the 'duty' and 'responsibilities' of social actors *qua* 'consumers' has consolidated into something of a master narrative. People are increasingly and explicitly asked to consider that to shop is to vote and that daily purchases, product boycotts, and consumer voice may be the only way individual men and women across the globe have to intervene on the workings of increasingly global and disembedded markets.

These phenomena have been typically set against developments in what is defined as 'post-democracy' (Crouch, 2004).
Contemporary Western societies have witnessed a profound
change in their citizens' forms of political participation. While
traditional means of political involvement, such as voting and
party membership have declined in Western countries over the
last few decades, protest and other unconventional activities
appear to have become regular forms of political participation by
citizens. Unconventional means of participation have to a degree
become 'normalized', and the repertoire of citizen's actions has
continued to expand, and to do so especially in the 'private'
and 'cultural' domains of 'consumption' and 'culture jamming'.
Besides demonstrations, strikes, rallies, public meetings, occupations—all variants of the established repertoire of citizens' actions
(Tarrow, 1998)—in recent years a growing number of people
have started to deploy consumer choice as a means of political
participation across Europe. Deploying theories of mobilization,
political scientists have typically concentrated on refining the set
of explanations for such developments. These explanations quite
often fit a general sociological picture, whereby contemporary
societies are said to be experiencing a process of 'individualization' and people are portrayed as increasingly reflexive about
their identities, values and actions (Beck, 1997; Giddens, 1991).
The increase in individual skills, as a consequence of improved
education and of greater information availability, has arguably
given way to citizens who are more aware of social problems and
their underlying causes and who also have greater capacities and
means to articulate their dissatisfaction. New forms of participation have often been associated with growing levels of distrust
among citizens for traditional political institutions, particularly as
to the ability of governments and institutional actors to respond
to and control new uncertainties and demands emerging from
everyday life (Norris, 2002). Politics itself is emerging in places
other than the formal political arena ('sub-politics') because citizens no longer think that traditional forms of political participation are sufficient (Beck, 1997).

In this vein, Beck and Gernsheim (2001: 44) have argued
that, via the political deployment of consumer choice, 'citizens

discover the act of shopping as one in which they can always cast their ballot—on a world scale, no less'. Political scientists and sociologists have thus moved from framing to action. There is now a growing body of studies focussing on consumer action as political participation, some of which assessing the phenomena in a comparative perspective, focussing on social, cultural, and economic background of 'political consumers' and on the influence of religious affiliation and involvement in more traditional forms of political participation (Micheletti, 2003; Micheletti et al., 2004; Tosi, 2006). This reflects not only the growing relevance of a political investment of the consumer though a political vocabulary drawing on themes such as democracy, (global) justice and social and environmental sustainability (Sassatelli, 2006), but also the growing relevance of 'responsible' or 'ethical' products in Western markets. According to EFTA (2005) the sales volume of Fair Trade products grew 154 per cent in Europe between 1997 and 2004. Fair Trade Coffee has been the fastest growing segment in the US market, growing a spectacular 67 per cent per year before the financial crisis (Arnould, 2007). When considerations of justice or charity may come to conflict with shrinking budgets for European Consumers, Fair Trade coffee and Fair Trade products generally have been growing at a two-digit speed per year (EFTA, 2010) and the field of Fair Trade production and commerce is getting increasingly institutionalized (WFTO, 2012). More broadly, the European Social Survey has shown that approximately one third of Europeans have boycotted certain goods or/and have bought goods for political and ethical reasons. According to Ifoam, organic production is growing a steady 10 per cent every year and a growing number of studies on alternative food networks (from box schemes to farmers' markets) are showing their vigour in many advanced economies (Dubouisson-Quellier and Lamine, 2004; Goodman, 2003; Holloway et al., 2006).

Shopping for human rights, ethical or environmental issues more generally has been defined, notably by Micheletti (2003) as 'political consumerism'. With this label, she indicates (Micheletti, 2003: 2–3)

Actions by people who make choices among producers and products with the goal of changing objectionable institutional or market practices. Their choices are based on attitudes and values regarding issues of justice, fairness, or non-economic issues that concern personal and family well-being and ethical or political assessment of favourable and unfavourable business and government practice. Political consumers are the people who engage in such choice situations. They may act individually or collectively. Their market. choices reflect an understanding of material products as embedded in a complex social and normative contest.

Such definition portrays the 'political consumer' as a unidimensional, quite coherent, and remarkable rational being, engaged in consumption for the sole purpose of politics. On the contrary, from the sociology of consumption we know that consumption, possibly even more than other forms of social action taking place in other spheres of life, is multilayered and multidimensional: we often regionalize our preferences to accommodate different logics, we construct compromisory lifestyles, we use goods to accommodate conflicts both within ourselves and with others, and so on (Sassatelli, 2007). As it does not distinguish between the current, strongly normative political framing of the consumer and actual consumer practices and culture, but tends to impose the former onto the latter, Micheletti's definition does not allow for the fact that responsible or political products and practices are very varied and diverse, at times contradicting each other or difficult to reconcile. This is evident, for example, when we try to be both supportive of local agriculture (which might not be organic) and attentive to sustainability (which entails both supporting organic production and lowering food miles); or when we hope to be both socially fair on a global scale and support fair trade goods while supporting local female cooperative entrepreneurship. Such tensions are amplified by the sheer variety of actors (both individual and collective, economic and political, oriented towards profit maximization or towards collective goods) which are, for various reasons, contributing to shaping politically coded views of the market. This variety is reflected in the uneven resonance of political consumerist initiatives and the varying economic and political effectiveness of the attempts to approach commodities as bearers of environmental, ethical and political concerns.

Systemic and Subjective Dimensions of the Political Investment of the Consumer

While 'lifestyle politics' has come to function as a form of civic participation for a few people in the West (Beck and Gernsheim, 2001; Schudson, 1998), consumption has been framed through a political vocabulary. In other terms, consumption has been so symbolically politicized that, so it has been argued, it is no longer possible to sharply divide between 'citizenship and civic duty' on the one hand, and 'consumption and self-interest' on the other (Scammell, 2000; Soper and Trentmann, 2007). This signals a dual move. On the one hand, the commercial rhetoric of consumer choice has penetrated political discourse and inspired political reforms like the privatization of public services—such as in the case of Great Britain public health which has met with a strong resistance by citizens (Clarke, 2006). Likewise, political vocabularies, and in particular the notion of voting, are being used in commercial campaigns for rather ordinary commodities, from sanitary towels to ready-made meals. Such ads typically naturalize an interlocking of the commercial frame, working upon the notion of individual satisfaction, and of the political one, working on the idea of voting (for a greater good), which could otherwise appear as arbitrary.

Drawing on a political vocabulary, a number of voices have thus celebrated the political persona of the consumer. The consumer has been portrayed as the truly global actor who can be a counterweight to big transnational corporations, and can replace the vanishing citizen in working for a cosmopolitan democracy: today, 'citizens discover the act of shopping as one in which they can always cast their ballot—on a world scale, no less' (Beck and Gernsheim, 2001: 44). Similar claims rest on a dubious metaphor assimilating consumer choice with voting (and voting with democracy). Let us tease out what is implicit in the metaphor:

that consumer choice is like voting, that it is effective, that it is democratic. These assumptions can easily obliterate the specificity of voting and consumer choice, the fruitful synergies which can be produced by considering their mutual transformation, and, last but not least, their ambiguities. On the latter, it is useful to remember that the (rather spurious) parallel between the market and democracy, purchasing and voting, has been explicitly made by economists and marketing experts already at the beginning of the 19C, partly to legitimatize the free market as a agent of freedom and sovereignty for the population (Dickinson and Carsky, 2005). This view may indeed be seen as a development of the 18C idea that the market is a foremost civilizing force (Hirschman, 1982).

Let's explore some of the ambiguities of the current political investment of the consumer, considering both symbolic framings and practical patterns. It would indeed be mistaken systematically to attribute a deliberately political intention to all consumer choices of a critical variety. Many of the practices that come under the umbrella of critical consumerism may be conducted by consumers who have in mind meanings and objectives other than strictly political ones. For example, in the United Kingdom, alternative distribution networks, including second-hand shops, not only respond to a politically conscious middle-class consumer, but also attract disadvantaged urban groups who may not be able to afford to shop via formal channels (Williams and Paddock, 2003). Likewise, the demand for organically grown vegetables typically mixes private health concerns with some degree of environmental consciousness, and comes from diverse sources, including a large vegetarian movement as well as health-conscious or gourmet carnivores (Lockie and Kristen, 2002). The same ethically or politically coded product can be purchased by differently characterized consumers and the same consumer can purchase or refuse certain ethically coded products for a number of reasons, including but not confined to what we would define as ethical or political ones. For example, in Italy, a large proportion of those who buy Fair Trade goods do so because they 'like' the products or consider them 'better quality', or just 'by chance'; quite a few of them though mix this motive with some vague ethical aim, while others are more vocal about the ethics and politics of their choices, but would also admit that ethical coffee is better to taste (Sassatelli, 2008). As I will elaborate later, here we see that practising ethical choices may come from different sources, but it is rarely predicated on pure virtue or duty: it contains an aesthetic angle, practices of pleasure, ideas of quality through which ethical consumers may reconstruct some coherence in their often diverse motivational baggage.

More broadly, contrary to purist views, if we look at practices, it is not easy to isolate political or ethical reasons for ethical shopping as if they were both distinct and antagonist to aesthetic considerations or in fact relational ones. Indeed, through a purist eye we may easily fall into the trap of considering all alternative ways of consuming as a cultural disease or a false ideology as Baudrillard (1970) maintained in his *La société de consommation*. Baudrillard indeed focuses at the symbolic or discursive level: he maintains that consumer 'counter-discourse' is functional to the maintenance of the status quo, it 'does not afford any real distance from consumer society'. Baudrillard clearly considers that, if there is no escape from the commodity form, there is no alternative. In other terms, alternative commodities feature as a contradiction in terms that can at best be utopian. Moving to practice, he then appears to be the forerunner of those purist positions which consider that the only alternative way to consume would be either not doing it, or doing it totally outside commodity circuits. Yet, the multifaceted and multilayered nature of consumer actions, including those having to do with ethical and political products and practices, suggests that, while there may be no escape from market society and consumer choice, choices may be constructed and practised in quite a variety of ways. To be sure, cultural sociologists and geographers working empirically on alternative and responsible commodity networks have typically stressed that ethically and politically coded products such as fair trade goods are still a niche market. And one that is quite often appealing to the cultured middle-to-upper classes in the West—precisely those who are remarkably interested in the distinctive value of ethically coded goods as much as their political content (Johnston and Baumann, 2007;

Johnston et al., 2011). This observation is all the more important as we consider that the constellation of critical consumption stretches widely to reach out, for example, Slowfood initiatives that may be said to occupy the hedonic pole, the critical consumption field (Sassatelli, 2004; Sassatelli and Davolio, 2010). However, distinctive aims may nevertheless legitimatize and promote alternative commodity circuits. Some of these circuits also respond to values other than money and quantity and consider the common good, gift relations, and civic engagement as irreducible elements of not just of consumers' duties and responsibilities but also of their gratification and pleasure.

Let's take a step back and consider more seriously the sociological function of utopias and utopian goods (Levitas, 1990). Utopias can work as incitement to change, and this, I propose, is partly the function of political, ethical, or critical consumerist discourse. Discourse can typify the human action in ways that cannot be practised, the gap between a utopian discourse and practice, however, may work as a threshold for change. The sociologist should thus appreciate that radical opposition to the commodity form and commercialism in this light. Indeed, an antinomy between commercial aims and ethical aims appears to work as dialectical resource to modify views of capitalism in many critical or ethical consumerist initiatives. This is certainly the fundamental dynamic of value creation and progress within the Fair Trade field in Italy (Sassatelli, 2006, 2008). In Italy, activists who work at the commercial end of Fair Trade (shops, import organizations) place emphasis on the positive role of commercialization as 'cultural vector'; those who are concerned with labelling schemes stress the role of 'good principles'; the cultural and political entrepreneurs emphasize the risks of commercialization and the role of 'education and awareness'. The very fragmentation of the Fair Trade market in the Italian context seems to favour such a plurality of voices, which arguably results in a more democratic space.

This brings us to a systemic level and begs the question of effectiveness of ethical or political consumerism as a politics of justice. Effectiveness of ethically coded consumption initiatives can be conceived in terms of, at least, public resonance, corporate change, and ultimately political–economic change. We know that as Fair Trade goes mainstream, it has had its difficulties in always keeping its promises to help producers in developing countries. Recent work on global antisweatshop campaigns (Micheletti and Stolle, 2007) and on their appropriation by US company American Apparel (Littler and Moor, 2008) seems to point to the fact that wide public resonance, and even commercial success, may not always correspond to a real improvement in the working life of garment workers. Alternative consumer practices can easily be absorbed by the market. The marketing and advertising industries are well aware of the interest in ecological, ethical and political themes among a certain strata of Western populations and have long started to promote their own versions of the 'greening of demand' (Zinkhan and Carlson, 1995). The institutionalization of a dialogue between consumerist and environmental organizations and large multinational commercial companies may also have ambiguous effects (Barnett and Cloke, 2005; Doubleday, 2004). Codes for ethical business and for socially responsible management are becoming widespread, yet they are typically self-administered by industry itself. In response to boycotts and consumer choices in pursuit of specific causes, a variety of labelling schemes, often set up by ad hoc organizations variously linked with either business or political institutions, are playing a crucial role. This does not mean that ethical claims can easily be used in a purely instrumental fashion, for ethically oriented consumers may demand proof of standards and may push companies much further than expected. But it does suggest that the relation between consumption and production is different from the direct, symmetrical one portrayed by the twin notions of demand and supply. In particular, the reaching of global markets may imply an emphasis on efficiency and promotion that can transform green and Fair Trade products into fetishes (Hudson and Hudson, 2003; Levi and Linton, 2003).

A focus on the different aspects of effectiveness shows the importance of focussing on the systemic level, and points to the limits of simply translating the paradigm of voting into the world of consumption, however responsible it might become. In particular, it helps us considering the crucial role of intermediation, representation and governance—all aspects that are central to theories of democracy concerned with the nature of political vote. Thus, for example, while certain consumption such as the consumption of news seems to be crucial for both civic engagement and truly political consumerism (Shah et al., 2007), the presence of politically and ethically motivated cultural intermediaries and social movements appears crucial if the micro-politics of everyday life responsible consumption are to be translated into political pressure for social justice and environmental sustainability. Among the scholars involved in the analysis of political and critical consumerist initiatives there is thus a growing emphasis on issues of not only political entrepreneurship, but also governance and the regulatory frameworks that may institutionalize political consumerism (Bevir and Trentman, 2007), finally embedding considerations of justice in global commodity networks. The latter rests on the political negotiation of forms of knowledge, auditing and procedures that translate economic externalities into endogenous components of commodities and commodities networks. Clearly, an analytical shift in focus from political consumerism to the politics of commodity networks is wanting. A politics of commodity networks should acknowledge consumers' power and its limits. Such move clearly entails a focus on the role of both civil society (movements, political and cultural intermediaries) and political bodies (at local, state and supra-national levels). Indeed, in line with some of the more promising development within economic sociology, it entails conceiving of the market itself as an embedded socio-economic formation charged with normative dynamics, rather than an abstract mechanism made of individualized individuals and corporate entities operating in purely instrumental fashion. More broadly, markets are institutions that can be organized differently (see Callon, 1998; Carrier, 1997), and they can thus be put to many different ends. While there is no easy road to alternative ways to organize market capitalism, capitalist and profit-driven markets can be transformed to take into account the redistribution of resources, avoid economic polarization, and stress a new set of pleasures. While it is difficult to imagine that they can do it all, engaged consumers may be one of the levers of the transformation. A perspective on the relationship between critical consumption, democracy and ultimately justice is crucial to this end. While it is mistaken to suppose that the individual, global consumer increasingly invoked by Fair Trade and other critical consumerist initiatives can now carry on a global scale the duties and capacities of the citizen, or can transform the awareness of effects into a politics of justice, it would be foolish to deny the political potential of consumer choice. A democratic politics cannot snobbishly look at market-mediated actions as they are indeed a major form of participation to society by the vast majority of people, both citizens and not. Still, while we all consume, we do so in many different ways that are largely a function of our different resources and of the different political infrastructure that upholds different systems of consumption. In banal terms, if in contemporary democracies each citizen has a vote, consumers are notably different in terms of purchasing power and may thus have rather different degrees of influence on the market. Critical consumption does try to make the political infrastructure of our everyday consumer lives visible to us, yet different positions within that infrastructure, and different infrastructures (often still determined by national borders) make critical consumption more or less probable and viable. This double-bind construction shows that there is still a space for politics in the traditional sense; indeed, that politics and consumption can act in synergy in the transformation of the market.

Getting back to the analogy with voting, we should also consider the 'subjective' level. The discourses surrounding critical consumer practices provide a set of specific criteria of choice drawing on 'regimes of justifications' (Boltanski and Thévenot, 1991) that have been taken beyond the dominant mode of legitimating markets in Western culture. As I have suggested elsewhere (Sassatelli, 2006, 2008), themes mainly associated with the promotion of consumption as a legitimate sphere of action *per se*—'taste', 'good taste', 'pleasure', 'fantasy', 'comfort', 'distinction', 'happiness', 'refinement' and so on—are replaced (or supplemented) by themes predominantly associated with the definition of a democratic public sphere and with production. The vocabulary of critical consumerism draws either on social and political activism (to purchase is to 'vote', 'protest', 'make oneself heard', 'change the world', 'help the community', 'mobilize for a better future' and so on) or on production (to purchase here becomes 'work you do for the community', 'effort done for yourself and the other', 'creative', 'productive' and so on). Yet, we should be aware that at the level of practice, shopping ethically enables us to make choices that matter to us in ways that political voting may not, because these choices matter in themselves, empowering us in everyday life, rather than for their expressive potential or possible larger effects on macro-realities (Schudson, 2007). We thus should not equate 'genuine' critical choices with political votes, even though consumer choices can contain an implicit or explicit, unwilling or willing political component. Intrinsic pleasures are fundamental in consumption, and yet pleasure is not necessarily individualistic or alternative to the common good. Fair trade choices, participation in a basket scheme or the support of local agriculture cannot be written off as simply yet another positional option, the consumption of lost simplicity on luxury grounds. They often entail the elaboration of quite distinctive views of quality of products and of pleasure as what can be derived from the experience of quality.

The extensive narrative interviews research that I have conducted in Italy among critical consumers as well as activists from a variety of ethical and political consumerist organizations was quite telling on this. Clearly the critical consumption field is home to quite different sensibilities. Different consumers, initiatives and products occupy different spaces: some are more atoned to issues of global justice, others to issues of environmental sustainability, others still to issues of local development and territory protection (Sassatelli, 2004, 2006). Critical consumption may go hand in hand with a shift towards high-quality commodities [such as in environmentally conscious foodism or Slowfoodism, see respectively, Johnston and Bauman (2007) and Sassatelli and Davolio (2010)] or it may imply some form of general 'sobriety' or 'downshifting' in consumption, rejecting upscale spending as well as long working hours, and living a simpler, more relaxed life in order to discover new pleasures and enhance personal satisfaction, as well as to further socio-economic equality and environmental awareness (Etzioni, 1997; Nelson et al., 2007; Soper, 2008). Yet, beneath such varied repertoire of justifications, consumers attracted to different critical practices and products share some common ground. Three themes in particular emerge in varying degrees and combinations from the verbalizations produced by critical consumers about their lifestyles: equality and interdependency, collective goods and the pleasures of frugality (Sassatelli, 2008). Most of these consumers have put forward a civic vision of the market, contending that market relations thrive among equals, and indeed that to realize itself the market's social potential requires a pacified social space, which places value on redistribution. They also seemed to share the view that goods that transcend individual, exclusive enjoyment (in particular, the environment) are of the essence for consumers' quality of life, but are all too often neglected by capitalist market relations: here again, consumer choice is seen as a way to internalize environmental factors. Finally, the liberal view of the relationship between consumption and happiness has been regarded as simplistic. Italian critical consumers seem to have learnt Scitovsky's (1992 ; see also Sassatelli, 2013) lesson on the joyless result of mainstream consumerism: they often put forward alternative views of pleasure as slowness, relationally thick variety and sober refinement which clash with mere quantitative, acquisitive and ultimately obsolescence-driven versions of consumer culture. This matches a growing body of the literature in philosophy and the social sciences which argues that people's well-being might be understood in terms other than their expenditure, and which starts from notions of 'quality of life' that will often add environmental or relational depth to a short-term, individualist and private vision of individual choice (Nussbaum and Sen, 1993).

On the whole, these findings point to the relevance of a reshuffling of the notion of pleasure as a non-individualistic process of encounter between people, things and contexts which is both shaped by and shapes individual taste. A thoroughly political process though, as it constitutes subjectivities as much as expressing them. At the subjective level, we thus should be aware that the consumer who is invested by political power through political consumerist narratives, is at times tacitly constituted as an every-day political agent in practice. As I shall suggest, this implies that power dimensions of consumption such as distinction and hier-archy of taste cannot be eliminated from the critical consumption field, and must instead be monitored through a more structural politics of justice at the systemic level.

Difference, Normality and Effects: Placing Justice Back into the Politics of Consumption

Recent literature in sociology and anthropology has shown that contemporary consumer practices are characterized by a deep ambivalence that stresses various levels of politics of consump-tion (Sassatelli, 2007). In particular, consumption neither frees subjects nor is it the expression of absolute freedom outside of social norms. Likewise, it is not totally determined by advertis-ing and the culture industry, by commodities, shopping centres, theme parks, fast-food chains and such like. Not only, at the subjective level, consumer practices may be occasions for self-realization and emancipation as well as for frustration and sub-jugation, but also at the systemic level, even truly satisfying and self-enhancing consumer practices may become highly danger-ous or dysfunctional when their aggregate effects are looked at. At the systemic level we thus have to consider the effects of individual consumption on collective values and resources, from democracy to the environment.

All in all, it is because of its ambivalence that consumption is essentially a site of politics. Not to take a step back and prob-lematize the political investment of the consumer as evident in political consumerist initiatives and critical consumer practices, we should bear in mind the various dimensions of the politics of consumption. First, as a vast literature amply documents, choices of consumption are the site of what may be defined as a 'politics of difference': they are means of social inclusion as well as exclusion. To this we can add another dimension of power which has to do mostly with the 'normality', 'legitimacy', 'fairness' or otherwise of certain goods and practices and with the identity ascribed to the consumer. There is thus a 'politics of normality'. The politics of normality points to the normative view of the consumer which is conventionally sustained commercial relations and to the kind of self-realization which the consumer is expected to be after. These two dimensions of the politics of consumption are clearly intertwined, as persons belonging to different social categories are differently able to sustain what may appear a normal and legitimate image of themselves as consumers. They are also intertwined with a third dimension, the 'politics of effects'. This dimension has to do, in particular, with the effects of consumption on both at a subjective and systemic level. For example, the normative constitution of the consumer as a competitive being and of consumption as a Darwinian field of self-chosen inequalities may produce quite dysfunctional effects in terms of both individual realization and environment sustainability, as growing levels of consumer expenditure will bring forth neither more happiness, fairness nor indeed greater respect for nature. A particular aspect of the politics of effects is the 'politics of justice', something which has to do with (global) democracy and equality as well as with environmental sustainability as a token of respect for future generations worldwide. As suggested at the beginning of this chapter, the current political investment of the consumer evident in a number of political consumerist initiatives is predicated on such politics of justice. In this chapter I have shown that, rather than taking the political consumer at face value, and squarely on its role in fuelling a politics of justice, we should appreciate the dilemmas of political consumerism, considering all three dimensions of the politics of consumption.

Let me conclude reconsidering in this light some classic sources for the politics of justice in the consumption sphere. The regulation of consumption on ethical, environmental grounds has certainly been fuelled by the recognition that, in contrast to neo-liberal slogans, the common good doesn't automatically spring forth from the pursuit of individual interests. Against such celebratory stance, in his well-known work *The Social Limits of Growth*, Fred Hirsch (1977) showed that the democratization of luxuries and superfluous goods which mark status may become a dangerous and pointless game. Only recently has the great majority of the population had access to this 'positional' kind of consumption which was previously reserved only for privileged groups. The opening up of the possibility of competition within the field of consumption for the majority of the population has not, however, cancelled out social differences: for whilst the least favoured groups now consume to display, their relative positions have yet to change. This also has the complex effect of heating-up demand, leading to strong social and economic instability, as well as dangerous effects on the environment. In other terms, if not tempered by equalitarian views or checked by redistributive policies, the opening up of the competition in consumption does not bring forth a real democratization of luxuries while producing a number of unwanted externalities. Indeed, the emphasis on consumer sovereignty, on private consumption and individual satisfaction has tended to blind us to the role of what Castells (1977) has called 'collective consumption', that is consumption of public services provided by the state or political institutions to the whole population. Of course, after the crisis of the Welfare system, it is easy to fall into the illusion that everything can be privatized with excellent results in terms of economic efficiency. Nevertheless there are many who still emphasize that certain goods, those which amount to the diffuse minimum necessities in a given society (water and roads, but also education and health), cannot be efficiently produced, distributed and consumed through the mechanisms of the market alone, which in the long term generates strong economic inefficiencies (Sen, 1977, 1985). Indeed, the differences in economic, social and cultural resources between the members of the populations in the West, and even more so between Western and developing countries, are so marked that they may put the efficiency and legitimacy of the free-market under stress. They may even jeopardize the self-realization of those who can materially afford it.

The current political investment of the consumer should take stock of the discussion on the different dimensions of the politics of consumption, if justice is to be more than a fashionable catchphrase. We are becoming aware that the neo-liberal view that everyone in the consumer society is much freer to acquire the lifestyle and identity they desire runs the risk of falling into an imaginary world of endless abundance, a magi aggregate made of equal opportunities for individual, free and unfailing self-realization. Becoming aware that a normative vision of consumption, consumers and their satisfaction is implicated in mainstream consumer culture through a politics of normality, and that a politics of difference is always intertwined with the pleasures of consumption in everyday life, we become more capable of tackling the dilemmas facing justice and consumer culture.

References

Arnould, E.J. 2007. Should consumer citizens escape the market? *Annals AAPSS, 611*, 96–111.

Barnett, C. & Cloke, P. 2005. Consuming ethics: Articulating the subjects and spaces of ethical consumption. *Antipode, 27*(1), 23–45.

Baudrillard, J. 1998 (first publ. 1970). *The Consumer Society: Myths and Structures.* London: SAGE.

Beck, U. 1997. *The Reinvention of Politics: Rethinking Modernity in the Global Social Order.* Cambridge: Polity Press.

Beck, U. & Gernsheim, E. 2001. *Individualisation.* London: SAGE.

Bevir, M. & Trentmann, F. 2007. *Governance, Consumers and Citizens.* Basingstoke: Palgrave.

Boltanski, L. & Thévenot, L. 1991. *De la justification. Les économies de la grandeur.* Paris: Gallimard.

Callon, M. (ed.) 1998. *The Laws of the Market.* Oxford: Blackwell.

Carrier, J. (ed.) 1997. *Meanings of the Market.* Oxford: Berg.

Castells, M. 1977. *The Urban Question.* London: Edward Arnold.

Chessel, M-E. 2006. Women and the ethics of consumption in France at the turn of the twentieth century. In F. Trentmann (ed.), *The Making of the Consumer: Knowledge, Power and Identity in the Modern World.* Oxford: Berg.

Chessel, M-E. & Cochoy, F. 2004. Autour de la consommation engage. *Sciences de la Société, 62,* 3–14.

Clarke, J. 2006. Consumers, clients or citizens? Politics, policy and practice in the reform of social care. *European Societies, 8*(3), 423–442.

Crouch C. 2004. *Postdemocracy.* London: Polity Press.

Daunton, M. & Hilton, M. (eds) 2001. *The Politics of Consumption.* Oxford: Berg.

Davies, K. 2000. A moral purchase: Femininity, commerce, abolition, 1788–1792. In E. Eger & C. Grant (eds), *Woman and the Public Sphere. Writing and Representation, 1660–1800.* Cambridge: Cambridge University Press.

Dickinson, R. & Carsky, M. 2005. The consumer as voter: An economic perspective on ethical consumer behavior. In R. Harrison, T. Newholm & D. Shaw (eds), *The Ethical Consumer.* London: SAGE.

Doubleday, R. (2004) Institutionalizing non-governmental organization dialogue at Unilever: Framing the public as 'consumer-citizens'. *Science and Public Policy, 31*(2), 117–126

Dubouisson-Quellier, S. & Lamine, C. 2004. Faire le marché autrement. L'abonnement à un panier de fruit e de légumes comme forme d'engagement politique des consommateurs. *Sciences de la Société, 62,* 145–168.

EFTA. 2005. Fair Trade in Europe. Facts and Figures, EFTA.

———. 2010. Fair Trade Facts and Figures. A Success Story for Producers and Consumers, EFTA.

———. 2011. Annual Report on Fair Trade.

Etzioni, A. 1997. Voluntary simplicity: Characterization, select psychological implications, and societal consequences. *Journal of Economic Psychology, 19*(5), 619–643.

Giddens, A. 1991. *Modernity and Self-Identity.* Cambridge: Polity Press.

Glickman, L.B. 1999. Born to shop? Consumer history and American history. In L.B. Glickman (ed.), *Consumer Society in American History.* Ithaca, NY. Cornell University Press.

Goodman, D. 2003. The quality turn and alternative food practices: Reflections and agenda. *Journal of Rural Studies, 19,* 1–7.

Hilton, M. 2002. The female consumer and the politics of consumption in twentieth-century Britain. *The Historical Journal, 45*(1), 103–128.

Hirsch, F. 1977. *The Social Limits of Growth.* London: Routledge.

Hirschman, A.O. 1982. Rival interpretations of market society: Civilizing, destructive or feeble. *Journal of Economic Literature, 20,* 1463–1484.

Holloway, L. et al. 2006. Managing sustainable farmed landscape through 'alternative' food networks: A case study from Italy. *The Geographical Journal, 172*(3), 219–229.

Hudson, I. & Hudson, M. 2003. Removing the Veil? *Organization and Environment, 16*(4), 423–430.

Johnston, J. & Baumann, S. 2007. Democracy versus distinction: A study of omnivorousness in gourmet food writing. *American Journal of Sociology,* 113(1), 165–204.

Johnston, J., Szabo, M. & Rodney, A. 2011. Good food and good people: Understanding the cultural repertoire of ethical eating. *Journal of Consumer Culture, 11*(3), 293–318.

Kraidy, M.M. & Goeddertz, T. 2003. Transnational advertising and international relations. US press discourses on the Benetton 'we on death row' campaign. *Media, Culture and Society, 25*, 147–165.

Lasch, C. 1991 (first publ. 1979). *The Culture of Narcissism.* New York: Norton.

Leonini, L. & Sassatelli, R. 2008. *Il Consumo Critic.* Rome: Laterza.

Levi, M. & Linton, A. 2003. Fair Trade, A cup at a time? *Politics & Society, 31*(3), 407–432.

Levitas, R. 1990. *The Concept of Utopia.* Bern, Switzerland: International Academic Publishers.

Littler, J. & Moor, L. 2008. Fourth worlds and neo-Fordism: American apparel and the cultural economy of consumer anxiety. *Cultural Studies, 22,* 5–6.

Lockie, S. & Kristen, L. 2002. Eating green. *Sociologia Ruralis, 42*(1), 23–40.

Micheletti, M. 2003. *Political Virtue and Shopping: Individuals, Consumerism and Collective Action.* London: Palgrave.

Micheletti, M., Follesdal, A. & Stolle, D. (eds) 2004. *Politics, Products and Markets.* London: Transaction Publishers.

Micheletti, M. & Stolle, S. 2007. Mobilizing consumers to take responsibility for global social justice. *Annals AAPSS, 611,* 157–175.

Morris, M. 2005. Interpretability and social power, or why postmodern advertising works. *Media, Culture and Society, 27*(5), 697–718.

Nelson, M.R., Rademacher, M.A. & Paek, Hye-Jin. 2007. Downshifting consumers = upshifting citizens? An examination of local freecycle community. *Annals AAPSS, 611,* 1–56.

Norris, P. 2002. *Democratic Phoenix: Reinventing Political Activism.* Cambridge: Cambridge University Press.

Nussbaum M. & Sen, A. (eds) 1993. *The Quality of Life.* Oxford: Clarendon Press.

Renard, M.C. 2003. Fair trade: Quality, market and conventions. *Journal of Rural Studies, 19,* 87–96.

Sassatelli, R. 2001. Tamed hedonism: Choice, desires and deviant pleasures. In A. Warde & J. Gronow (eds), *Ordinary Consumption.* London: Routledge.

——. 2004. The political morality of food. Discourses, contestation and alternative consumption. In M. Harvey et al. (eds), *Qualities of Food: Alternative Theoretical and Empirical Approaches.* Manchester: Manchester University Press.

——. 2006. Virtue, responsibility and consumer choice. Framing critical consumerism. In J. Brewer & F. Trentmann (eds), *Consuming Cultures, Global Perspectives.* Oxford: Berg.

——. 2007. *Consumer Culture, History, Theory, Politics.* London: SAGE.

——. 2008. *L'investitura politica del consumatore. Modelli di soggettività e mutamento sociale.* In L. Leoninie & R. Sassatelli (eds), *Il consumo critic,* pp. 144–169. Bari: Laterza.

Sassatelli, R. 2009. *Representing Consumers: Contesting Claims and Agendas.* In K. Soper et al. (eds), *The Politics and Pleasures of Consuming Differently. Better than Shopping,* pp. 25–42. London: Palgrave.

———. 2013. Creativity takes time, critique needs space. In N. Osbaldiston (ed.),˙ *Culture of the Slow: Social Deceleration in an Accelerating World.* Basingstoke: Palgrave.

Sassatelli, R. & Davolio, F. 2010. Consumption, pleasure and politics. Slow-food ˙and the politico aesthetic problematization of food. *Journal of Consumer Culture, 10*(2), 1–31.

Scammell, M. 2000. Internet and civic engagement: The age of the citizen consumer. *Political Communication, 17,* 351–355.

Schudson, M. 1998. *The Good Citizen. A History of American Civic Life.* New York: Free Press.

———. 2007. Citizens, consumers and the good society. *Annals AAPSS, 611,* 236–249.

Scitovsky, T. 1992. *The Joyless Economy.* New York: Oxford University Press (2nd revised edn, 1997).

Sen, A.K. 1977. Rational fools: A critique of the behavioural foundations of economic theory. *Philosophy and Public Affairs, 6*(4), 317–344.

———. 1985. *Commodities and Capabilities.* Amsterdam: Elsevier.

Shah, D.V., McLeod, D.M., Friedland, L. & Nelson, M.R. 2007. The politics of consumption: The consumption of politics. *Annals AAPSS, 611,* 6–15.

Soper, K. 2008. Alternative Hedonism, Cultural Theory and the Role of Aesthetic Revisioning, *Cultural Studies, 22*(5), 567–587.

Soper, K. & Trentmann, F. (eds) 2007. *Citizenship and Consumption.* London: Palgrave.

Strasser, S., McGovern, C. & Judd, M. (eds) 1998. *Getting and Spending: European and American Consumer Societies in the Twentieth Century.* Cambridge: Cambridge University Press.

Tarrow, S. 1998. *Power in Movement: Social Movements and Contentious Politics.* Cambridge: Cambridge University Press.

Tosi, S. 2006. *Consumi e partecipazione politica.* Milano: Franco Angeli.

Trentmann, F. (ed.) 2005. *The Making of the Consumer: Knowledge, Power and Identity in the Modern World.* Oxford: Berg.

Vidal, J. 1997. *McLibel: Burger Culture on Trial.* New York: The New York Press.

Vogel, D. 2005. *The Market for Virtue. The Potential and Limits of Corporate Social Responsibility.* Washington: Brookings Institution.

WFTO. 2012. Annual Report 2012 World Fair Trade Organizations, WFTO.

Williams, C.C. & Paddock, C. 2003. The meaning of alternative consumption practices. *Cities, 20*(5), 311–319.

Zinkhan, M.G. & Carlson, L. 1995. Green advertising and the reluctant consumer. *Journal of Advertising, 24*(2), 1–16.

12

Ethical Consumption in the Global Age: Coffee's Promise of a Better World

Nicki Lisa Cole

Introduction: 'You're Not Just Buying Coffee'

In the winter of 2006, I stood in a Starbucks coffeehouse in Santa Barbara, California, and held in my hand a package of Guatemala Antigua coffee. At that time, I was a graduate student enrolled in a seminar titled 'Sociology of Knowledge', for which I had just read Edward Said's classic text, *Orientalism* (Said, 1978). Looking at the package, and taking in the images and text that adorned it, I realized that I held a contemporary travel narrative, quite similar to those Said had deconstructed in his book. With an artistic rendering of a Guatemalan woman in traditional dress, a map of coffee growing regions around the world, and a description of the *terroir* in which the coffee had been cultivated, Starbucks offered its customers a glimpse into the life of the coffee producer. Additionally, the package presented a snapshot of the relations of global capitalism. A side panel read:

> We believe there's a connection between the farmers who grow our coffees, us and you. That's why we work together with coffee-growing communities—paying prices that help farmers support

their families and improve their farms, and funding projects like a health clinic in eastern Guatemala. It's all part of our commitment to sustainable growing practices and an equitable relationship with farmers that allows us to deliver superior coffee to you. By drinking this coffee, you're helping to make a difference.

With this text Starbucks describes the basic relations of production and consumption, and places an ethical frame around them by relaying its socially responsible business practices and philanthropic endeavours in this growing region. Starbucks assures its customers that the coffee is cultivated in an ecologically sustainable manner, and that the end result is a high-quality product. Further, Starbucks interpellates the customer as an ethical actor, who by virtue of a simple consumer choice facilitates social and economic change in a distant land.

Taken together, the images and text attached to this product struck me as a modern day iteration of the colonial travel narratives that were the focus of Said's analysis. This narrative is presented through the white tourist gaze, deploys imagery that appears 'exotic' to the viewer, cultivates a sense of distinction between the American consumer and Guatemalan producers and frames the capitalist relations between a northern corporation and southern producers as a form of benevolent intervention into producers' communities. In this narrative, consumers are cast in the role of saviour, who, simply by purchasing the product, help suffering people who are seemingly incapable of helping themselves.

Shortly after my experience in Starbucks, I came across a sign in The Coffee Bean & Tea Leaf, another American coffee chain, which read 'You're not just buying coffee'. I wondered, what am I buying? The sign continued, 'A portion of this sale is donated to help children grow through education in communities worldwide'. It seems then, that those who purchase coffee branded or certified as 'the right choice' purchase a certain image of a producer, a perceived connection to that person, and moral consumer subjectivity. This phenomenon is not limited to coffee. Today there are more and more products around us that are presented as ethical options. A walk through most

American supermarkets reveals a wide variety of organic fare, free range and 'cruelty free' meat and eggs, sustainably farmed or wild caught salmon, and 'green' paper products made from recycled materials. We are inundated with advertisements for hybrid vehicles, sweatshop-free clothing and fairly traded goods of all shapes and sizes. Companies small and large, from the local independent coffeehouse, to Chevron and Walmart, tell us that purchasing their products is a vote for environmental sustainability, fair labour conditions and global economic justice.

Because of the diffusion of ethically coded goods in the American marketplace over the last decade, more and more scholars have turned their attention to the practice that has come to be known as 'ethical consumption'. I use the term to describe a set of practices that manifest at the intersection of concerns about planetary sustainability, personal health, conditions of production and quality of life of labourers. Some scholars prefer the term 'political consumption', and frame the practice as a new form of political action, while others emphasize a connection between consumption and civic responsibility, and thus favour 'consumer citizenship'. Those of us who use 'ethical consumption' emphasize the grounding of ethics in everyday consumer practices (Lewis and Potter, 2011: 10). Further, from a research perspective, I find it important to not presuppose the phenomenon to be a political act, or a form of civic engagement.

What is sociologically interesting about the phenomenon of ethical consumption is that it signals shifts in the cultural logic of global capitalism. Shifts in business practices and sourcing models, and the messaging that accompanies these, indicate that the corporate world has become hip to consumer concerns, and has re-conceptualized these concerns into a new market of opportunity. With the diffusion of ethically coded products in the marketplace came the mainstreaming of an ideology of ethical capitalism, and a discourse of ethical consumption. Ethical consumption has risen dramatically over the last decade, which signals shifts in contemporary American values, identities and consumer practices. This fact also raises questions about the reproduction of the system of global capitalism, since the practice reflects critical awareness of social, environmental and economic problems associated with the system.

With the research presented in this chapter, I offer a culturally grounded analysis of ethical consumption and its relationship to global capitalism. Through surveys and interviews with consumers of ethical coffee, I illuminate the dominant approaches to practising ethical consumption, and the personal and collective motivations that move people towards it. This research, thus, reveals the ideology that organizes the practice, and advances understanding of the contemporary cultural logic of global capitalism within the United States. While consumerist lifestyles and identities are now spreading to regions of the world where these have historically not dominated culture (Mathur, 2010), the United States, as the world's leading consumer nation, continues to be a harbinger of trends in consumerism. If the logic of consumerism is tipping towards ethics in the United States, it is important to understand why and how, and what positive or negative effects might come of this, so that social scientists and policy makers can shape the future of the practice.

Theoretical Debates Surrounding Ethical Consumption

When considering this contemporary trend, many scholars note that forms of ethical consumption have existed for nearly as long as have consumer markets. However, there is also consensus that there are differences in today's ethical consumption that render it unique, and specifically situated within our contemporary historical moment. Lewis and Potter (2011: 5) point out that the 'problematization of living' common in contemporary Western societies, and the address of it through consumer channels, is what distinguishes ethical consumption today from prior forms. By 'problematization of living', Lewis and Potter refer to popular awareness in Western nations that there are problems associated with the consumerist lifestyle that dominates social and economic life. People in these nations are increasingly aware of the harmful environmental, social and economic consequences of global capitalist production and consumption. Many now attempt to address their discomfort and anxieties caused by this twenty-first century reality by expressing an ethical agency through consumer channels. Because such concerns are addressed through consumption, Lewis and Potter emphasize the 'ordinariness of ethics' that is expressed by this practice (p. 10). Bringing ethics into consumer decisions is a sign that ethical concerns are now infused into everyday life in Western societies, and have been mainstreamed into today's consumer terrain. Given this fact, the central debate among scholars of consumption is whether the practice has any real political purchase.

The most virulent critics of ethical consumption argue that it cannot even exist, is in fact oxymoronic, in a capitalist society. Monbiot (2007) asserts that capitalism is inherently unethical because it is premised on the exploitation of labour, which negates the existence of ethical consumption. Bauman (2008) also views the practice as a contradiction in terms because he reasons that a 'society of consumers' is inhospitable to ethical subjectivities. Guthman (2008) found in her research of food politics and consumption in California that at best, ethical consumption manifests as a neoliberal subjectivity that does nothing more than provide the cultural logic for harmful neoliberal economic and development policies. Others see the radical promise of ethical consumption, yet caution against the ability of the practice to relieve liberal guilt caused by awareness of global social and economic problems through market-based solutions, without effecting any real change (Cook and Crang, 1996; Featherstone, 2011).

Some point out that what were initially 'alternative' models of sourcing and consuming have been co-opted and watered down through processes of mainstreaming that folded transnational corporations (TNCs) into the mix (Raynolds and Long, 2007). The inclusion of TNCs afforded greater marketing power to ethical goods, often with the help of celebrities, and thus raised their profile during the 2000s. However, Goodman (2010) points out that this 'celebritization of development' created so much demand for ethical goods that the shortened commodity chain, the founding hallmark of ethical trade, was sacrificed for market growth. Inclusion and growth has raised questions about the sincerity of ethical claims, and prompted concern about the potential 'green' and 'white' washing of corporate business as usual. Finally, some point out that the 'responsibilization' of individual consumers both justifies and reinforces the neoliberal dismantling of social services and of corporate regulations, which vanishes the responsibility of the state to protect human and civil rights (Littler, 2009).

Yet, for as much criticism of ethical consumption that exists, there are those who champion the practice and its potential to enact social and economic change. Micheletti (2003) argues that consumption can empower the average citizen to take responsibility for themselves and their society. Because of this, she views the practice as a reinvention of politics and democracy in the context of a 'post-political world' (p. 14). From her vantage point, ethical consumption broadens the scope of policymaking by more readily including the concerns of the general population. Viewed as political engagement, the expression of social and environmental concerns through consumption pressures TNCs to be more responsible actors on the global stage (Micheletti and Stolle, 2008).

Still, some find these claims hard to swallow. Low and Davenport point out that 'business only has to move as far and as fast as consumers want and there is little onus on business to "create" change, internally or externally' (2008: 325). Goodman (2010) critiques the model of salvation through market development on the grounds that it only works for those who can produce something of value, like a pleasant image and reassuring narrative, in the eyes of northern consumers. Further, some problematize that the logic of ethical consumption—do good by consuming—serves to more deeply entrench consumerism as the cultural dominant, as opposed to encouraging a critical dialog around its negative effects (Low and Davenport, 2008). To this end, Lewis and Potter (2011) distinguish between 'consumption' and 'consumerism' when weighing the merits of an ethical approach to purchasing. They point out that those who assert ethical consumption is oxymoronic for its relationship to capitalism are actually critiquing 'consumerism', not the practice of consumption. They conceptualize 'ethical consumption' as a term that can apply to a range of practices that can operate in alternative economic systems (p. 29).

Taking both sides into consideration, it seems that the crux of this scholarly debate is whether ethical consumption operates within the normative system of global capitalist production and consumption, or whether it operates outside of, and thus challenges, the system. The question, then, is whether ethical consumption is merely an adaptation of consumer culture to our contemporary moment, or if it is an attempt at reforming it. I see the pressing question as one of consciousness. While above-mentioned intellectual critiques and affirmations are well taken, there is, admittedly, a conspicuous lack of research that evaluates the cultural resonance of ethical products, and interrogates the universe of knowledge that surrounds the practice. To fill this void, my research with consumers of ethical coffee seeks to reveal both the personal and social significance of the practice. I pose the following questions: (i) What consumer values, desires, and identities does an ideology of ethical capitalism both respond to and interpellate? (ii) What is expressed and reproduced through ethical consumption? (iii) What is the relationship between an ethical consumer identity and the system of global capitalism?

Background: Ethical Coffee in the United States

I use the term 'ethical coffee' to encompass a variety of sourcing models now practised by coffee companies, large and small, within the United States, and to refer to any coffee that is certified or marketed as the 'right choice' with regard to environmental and social concerns. This loose definition encompasses both independent third party certification models, and internally monitored, company-specific models of ethical sourcing. Today, the most widely distributed, well known, and consumed model is Fair Trade certified (Barrientos et al., 2007). TransFair USA, now Fair Trade USA, launched the label in the United States in 1998, and since then it has become a standard bearer within the coffee industry, and a prototype for certification of other goods.

The power of its marketing campaigns has resonated with consumers to such an extent that they tend to use the term to refer to ethical coffee in general (Murray and Raynolds, 2007; Renard and Peréz-Grovas, 2007).

Beyond Fair Trade, other major ethical sourcing models include Organic certified, which is commonly coupled with Fair Trade in the United States, The Rainforest Alliance certified, UTZ certified, and 4C Common Code (Specialty Coffee Association of America, 2010). In addition, many companies, particularly multinational corporations such as Starbucks and The Coffee Bean and Tea Leaf, have their imports independently verified as ethically sourced (though not certified), and also partner with NGOs on socially responsible initiatives in producing communities (Grodnik and Conroy, 2007). Beyond certification, many smaller, independent roasters and coffee companies within the specialty coffee industry employ internal, company-specific sourcing models that are commonly referred to as 'direct trade' or 'relationship coffee'. Though not externally verified, such models feature transparent and very short commodity chains, long-term relationships between producers and buyers, use of a quality-based price scale and an emphasis on helping producers improve the quality of their product.

Coffee was in fact the first consumer good to be surrounded by a framework of ethical certification (Raynolds and Long, 2007; Renard and Peréz-Grovas, 2007), which no doubt contributes to its current mainstream status in American society. In 2007, a telephone survey conducted by the National Coffee Association found that sixty percent of American adults are aware of at least one model for ethically sourcing coffee (National Coffee Association, 2007). At its outset, ethical coffee in the United States was particular to the specialty coffee sector, which is loosely defined as dealing exclusively in coffees of exceptional quality. In 2009, this sector made 13.65 billion USD in sales, which equals about a third of total national coffee sales (Bolton, 2009). Signalling both the desire for premium coffee, and the attractiveness of ethical coding, the annual average growth rate of the specialty sector is four times greater than that of conventional coffee within the United States, and was projected to exceed 18 billion USD in sales by 2012 (Bolton, 2009). And, due to its inclusion of TNCs, sales of Fair Trade certified coffee more than doubled annually between 2000 and 2007 (Grodnik and Conroy, 2007). Industry analysts Pierrot and Giovannucci (2010) reported that 'no other segment of the global coffee industry has grown as consistently and as fast as the one for coffees that are certified as sustainable' (p. 3). In fact, coffee is now the most widely traded and consumed ethically certified product (Renard and Peréz-Grovas, 2007).

No doubt, it is the long, exploitative labour history of coffee production that made it an appealing crop for the introduction of ethical sourcing and certification. This history is one of colonial enslavement, indentured servitude on plantations and post-emancipation, impoverished peasant farmers exploited at the hands of middlemen and large transnational corporations (Pendergrast, 1999; Talbot, 2004, 2011; Topik, 2010; Wild, 2004). Because coffee has been traded as a commodity, producers have faced the uncertainty of extreme price fluctuation, and throughout the latter half of the twentieth century, have had neoliberal development schemes imposed on them (Talbot, 2011). This history makes coffee not only an attractive commodity for ethical treatment, but also, a prime case for a culturally grounded analysis of ethical consumption. Because it is the most widely consumed ethically coded product, it is likely to include a more diverse cross-section of consumers than other ethical products on the market, and to include those who apply an ethical lens to other consumer decisions. It stands to reason that a snapshot of consumers of ethical coffee is a reasonable equivalent to a snapshot of ethical consumers in contemporary American society. And, because it is primarily an import product in the United States, and is produced overwhelmingly by people of races other than white, it is an excellent case for considering the raced relations of today's global system of capitalist production and consumption.

Research Settings and Methods

This study was conducted between 2007 and 2009 in Seattle, Washington, Portland, Oregon and in San Francisco and Santa

Barbara, California. All cities are located along the west coast of the United States, and were chosen because they represent the contemporary base of both production and consumption of ethical coffee within the nation, and for their histories as key sites in the development of the specialty coffee industry. Additionally, these locations are ideal sites for research into ethical consumption because they are known for their popular embrace of alternative lifestyles, and are oriented towards socially and environmentally responsible politics and business.

To take the ideological pulse, so to speak, of ethical coffee consumers, I conducted surveys and interviews with participants across these locations. Thirty-two interview participants self-identified in response to advertisements posted at over 250 coffeehouses. In the field I approached patrons of coffeehouses and solicited survey participation, which yielded 144 survey respondents. Participants who completed the two-page survey responded to questions pertaining to their knowledge of ethical coffee sourcing models, and their motivations for patronizing the coffeehouses they do. With interview participants, I held one-on-one conversations ranging from 30 minutes to 1 hour in length. Topics included awareness of ethical coffee, level of commitment to it, reasons for purchasing it, and understanding of how ethical sourcing models affect producers. In addition, we discussed ethical consumption beyond coffee, and their attitudes towards large corporations, small businesses and global capitalism. Interview and survey data were then hand coded and analysed together to identify dominant discursive and ideological patterns.

Overview of Sample Population

Participants in this research are mostly white, middle class, college educated, younger adults, with an average age of thirty-two and half years old. Slightly more are married or partnered than not, and about a third have children. Politically speaking, they skew from centrist to left. About a third are religious, though most of them do not participate regularly in religious events or observances. All are regular consumers of coffee, both at home and in coffeehouses. Most regularly purchase ethical coffee, and select coffeehouses in part based on whether it is served. Notably, nearly a third of interview participants stated that they choose to shop at businesses that serve strictly ethical coffee, thus, eliminating ethics from the decision-making process once they are in the establishment. Many overall exclude or avoid certain locations or businesses due to an absence of ethical options.

In terms of general consumer concerns and awareness, a preference for local products and purchasing directly from producers was expressed by a majority of participants. Some exude an anti-corporate and anti-chain mentality, and prefer to support small, independent businesses. About half prefer to buy organic products due to concerns for the environment, and processes of industrial and large-scale food production. They express a host of concerns related to ecological sustainability, including excessive fuel and energy consumption and the importance of decreasing waste, particularly in terms of plastics, product packaging, shipping and industrial pollution. Thus, many support producing with recycled materials, buying used, and reusing and repurposing goods. In sum, they bring a wide range of ethical concerns to consumption.

Research Findings

Clear trends emerged in interviews and surveys with consumers of ethical coffee. Participants are critical of mainstream American consumerism, and this provides the basic impetus towards ethical consumption. They express an awareness of the privileges they enjoy in comparison to those who produce the goods they consume, and experience feelings of guilt and responsibility because of this. These too serve as motives that coalesce into a dyadic strategy of ethical consumption: do good, and avoid doing harm. Because producers exist in very troubled communities in the American imaginary, participants articulate an interventionist definition of ethical trade that seeks to correct injustices taking place in distant lands. But despite their belief in the power of ethical consumption to effect positive social, economic and environmental change, they experience nagging anxieties about its realities and potential. In what follows, I rely on statements by interview participants to extrapolate these trends. While survey results are included in the description of the sample population provided earlier, they are only included in the following section when specifically stated.

Attitudes towards Consumption

In providing context for why they purchase ethical coffee, many describe problems of mainstream American consumer norms and values. They recognize that American mass consumption patterns produce negative consequences around the world, and consequently feel a responsibility to be a part of a solution, and to the extent that they can avoid reproducing the problem. Nearly half of all interview participants levelled overt critiques at consumerism. Of those, many construed the problem as over-consumption, and bemoaned the pull of consumer desires, like Kate who lamented the fact that 'Things run things' in our society. Similarly, David described himself in juxtaposition to his perception of mainstream consumerism. He said,

> I don't think it's that important to keep up with the Joneses. I think having a nice place to live, a good place to educate my children, access to health care, access to public transportation and good roads, and a safe place to live are the most important things.

What David suggests is there are things that he values above the lifestyle and image that comes with consumerism, and they reflect the basic rights that citizens of the United States are supposed to enjoy. Relatedly, some assert that the American standard of living is higher than is economically sustainable or socially responsible. Karen explained that she had recently had a conversation with her boyfriend about why people were not buying gasoline when prices had spiked, but that they were still living their lives and getting by, and that ultimately this situation was better for the environment. This observation prompted her to ask, 'Would it really be that bad if people couldn't afford gas? Would it really be that bad if McDonald's raised all their prices and people couldn't afford to buy it anymore?' Karen's observation and questions suggest that positive changes would come of Americans adjusting their consumption habits in response to the rising cost of resources.

As a solution to this problem, many describe buying used goods and reducing consumption as ways to help abate the problems they see in the world, like Kristin, who said, 'It's the one thing I feel people can do to curb consumption, and to not be a part of the problem of mass consumption'. Kate explained that it is hard to find goods whose production didn't negatively affect someone, so she consumes very little as a consequence. When discussing how she came to a radical anti-consumerist perspective, Morgan explained that her adolescent rebellion was a rejection of the way of life that surrounded her. She spiritedly communicated to me her teenaged internal monologue: 'Screw capitalism! Screw consumerism!' Sentiments like these are representative of participants' identification of the problematic consequences of consumption of resources, the waste that is generated by consumerism, and the often negative health implications of mass consumer practices. Ultimately, participants critique what they perceive as normal in the American context—the singular importance of goods as they relate to image and lifestyle. They critique the over-consumption of resources, and assert that normative American consumption is unsustainable and irresponsible. Importantly, they position themselves as different from the norm, as a distinctly different kind of consumer, in order to create space for an ethical consumer subjectivity.

Awareness, Guilt and Responsibility

For those I interviewed, with awareness of problems associated with consumerism come feelings of guilt and a sense of responsibility. Many conveyed this when they explained why they purchase ethical products, like Morgan, who said that it is consumers' responsibility 'to demand goods that are good for our conscience'. Lucia echoed this sentiment, saying '... we're the one's buying it. If we don't buy it, they won't make it'. Connected to awareness of the consequences of one's choices is recognition of one's positionality. Some state that it is important to recognize the privileged position that they inhabit as US consumers, particularly in relation to global producers of goods. Eddie explained it is important that people realize they have a stake in producing social injustice. Similarly, Robert said, regarding the disparity between the global north and south, 'To have that kind of inequality, somebody else has to suffer'.

Such statements reveal awareness of the economic and social connections between Americans, and those who produce the coffee that we consume, and that these connections often have harmful consequences for producers and their communities. This level of awareness often leads to feelings of guilt. Thus, some explain that a sense of guilt and desire to make reparations fuels their purchase of ethical coffee. Referencing the historical legacy of 'various forms of imperialism' in coffee producing nations, Carrie asked, 'Don't we owe 'em?' Christopher drove the point home when he exclaimed in exasperation, 'You can't tell suffering people to just wait for the revolution to come, and you know, all of their problems will be solved!'

These participants express recognition of injustice, and a sense of responsibility to address it as consumers. This implies confidence in the power of consumption to be the solution to problems identified, and to salve the guilt they feel. Ethical consumption is a solution that is immediately available to them in their everyday lives, so they experience it as an immediate act of change making. This is a gratifying experience, evidenced by the fact that many state that purchasing ethical coffee feels good. Sadie said, 'It makes me feel good. Like, I'm getting the things that I need and I'm actually helping somebody in the process'. Evelyn said that after a purchase she thinks, 'This bag did somebody good'. Dean said that he 'like[s] being able to make a difference', while Brenda said that now that her son is grown and out of the house that she and her husband 'have more disposable income to do things we feel good about'.

Clearly, participants experience ethical consumption as a feel-good way of fulfilling their needs through consumerism, which they view as otherwise problematic. Ethical products thus afford participants the opportunity to avoid 'bad' consumer choices and practices, and allow them to embody and express a moral consumer subjectivity. Ethical coffee thus responds to and assuages, to a certain extent, the anxieties that participants feel due to their awareness of global inequalities, and their culpability in producing them.

An Ethical Strategy of Consumption

Participants want their choices to produce good, not harm and suffering, and believe that purchasing ethical coffee is a way to achieve this dyadic strategy. Kate put quite simply the power of ethical coffee to achieve this when she said, 'We provide livelihood to farmers by drinking Fair Trade coffee'. Brenda, on the other hand, framed ethical consumption as avoidance: 'People are not suffering to produce the thing we enjoy'. Similarly, Robert explained, 'I wasn't worried too much about exploiting Ethiopian farmers until somebody mentioned, 'Hey, you know there is such a thing as not exploiting them', and then I began to get with the program', while Abby said, 'I just don't like people suffering, or people's lives to go bad because of my personal choices'.

This strategy of avoidance stood out in survey results too. Of the 114 respondents who reported that they intentionally avoid certain coffeehouses, nearly 70 per cent listed an ethical concern first. Whether consumers take a casual or thoughtful approach to purchasing, it is clear that they believe in the promise of ethical sourcing models. In fact, many believe that consumer choice is the only thing that matters to businesses, and thus the only thing capable of changing business practices. Samuel pointed out that Brita, the popular purveyor of water filtration devices, now recycles its filters because of consumer demand. Because they believe in this model, about a third of those who specifically advocated consumer-driven change stated that they are willing to pay more to make an ethical purchase, like Scott, who said, 'For me, it would be worth paying more money so that folks are getting their fair share of the wealth'.

These statements reveal that the foundational logic of ethical consumption is to avoid harmful consequences, and to promote good when making purchases. This strategy of avoidance seems an extension of the tradition of consumer boycotts, but is also reflective of a history of expressing identity through consumption. Participants support the concept of producing social change through consumption, and so implicitly support the notion that positive social change can be produced through the capitalist system. The immediate problems then from the perspective of participants are *un*ethical consumption, and greedy corporations who exploit labourers and the environment, not the capitalist system.

The Coffee Producer in the American Consumer Imaginary

For consumers of ethical coffee, what makes coffee ethical is directly juxtaposed against the poor and difficult conditions they imagine to result from the low wages and exploitative forces and actors, which they know to be true in the typical coffee growing community. This popular image of producing communities, and the suffering experienced within them, fuels the desire to do good and avoid doing harm expressed by participants. For them, coffee can be labelled 'ethical' when it either avoids producing, or responds to, problematic conditions. They envision coffee producers living in impoverished conditions that result from oppressively low wages, exploitation by large corporate buyers, inept and corrupt local and national governments, and political instability throughout their regions. They imagine that producers labour under very poor conditions. Overall, they identify a complex and deeply troubled set of social, economic and political circumstances that plague coffee producing communities.

Many cite bad labour conditions and underpayment as hallmarks of traditional coffee production, like Roderick, who stated,

My assumption is that the conditions tend to be horrendous in less fair places. And the wages would go hand-in-hand. If the conditions are bad, I'm assuming the wages are bad. I think that conditions would horrify me more than wages ... long hours, children working.

Lucia, familiar with the struggles of farm workers in California, explained that she imagines that the experiences of coffee producers is similar to that of field labourers who endure long hours of back-breaking labour under the hot sun, only to receive low pay and abuse due to their immigration status. She emphasized that agricultural labour is very physically demanding, time consuming and typically under-compensated.

How participants imagine conditions of labour at the site of production tends to manifest as in conflict with labour laws within the United States. Yet, they tend to associate these conditions with the parts of the world in which coffee is grown. According to David, 'The worst imaginable place in the United States is the Hilton compared to some of these places'. Some participants explain that these problems are a result of internal conditions in coffee producing nations, such as a lack of labour laws, inept or corrupt governments, and political instability. Using coded language to describe the situation, Drake said 'Coffee comes from a Third World nation, from Central America. I'm sure that the farmers and labourers involved work hard and are probably not compensated well for it'. Lily explained that coffee '[is] grown in really tough parts of the world ... places that are politically complicated'. These imaginaries of coffee growing communities reflect common northern tropes that frame formerly colonized lands as 'Third World' or 'developing', which suggest that these places are unfinished, and deficient when compared with the United States and other Westernized nations.

Within this conceptualization, internal governments and their leaders are often cast as facilitators of bad conditions. Sadie expressed this when she said, '[The] governments don't take care of people, quality of life is low, and governments cater to big US corporations'. Jim explained, 'In Colombia and Guatemala, they have unstable governments, problems with revolutionaries battling counter-revolutionaries, civil war and innocents slaughtered'. While Sadie connects the problems in coffee growing countries to the goals and actions of US corporations, overwhelmingly participants conceptualize such problems as rooted in the communities they describe, like Jim does.

Participants also fault exploitation of farmers by middlemen and large buyers. Scott invoked the struggle of the Immokalee farm workers with Taco Bell when he explained, '[L]arge buyers can bully farm workers because they'll work for less than minimum wage. They work like indentured servants'. Pointing to another problem coffee producers experience as a result of the power of large buyers, Christopher said, 'The mainstream coffee market really serves to isolate and pit farmers against each other'. Thus, despite awareness of their positionality and privilege, they do not view problems in producing communities as embedded in a world-system of capitalist production and consumption, but as a result of select bad actors within those communities.

Notably, this popular imaginary of coffee producers and their communities paints them as victims who presumably do not resist. Thus, the vision of coffee growing communities that emerges out of the ethical consumer imaginary is one populated by disempowered peasant farmers who are exploited by local political elites and buyers, and who suffer the consequences of inept and corrupt governing bodies. These conditions are overwhelmingly understood as particular to these places, and not connected to how we live in the United States.

Ethical Consumption as Benevolent Intervention

Participants rely on several key factors to define ethical trade. First and foremost, they invoke money to define it, using terms like 'living wage' and 'fair wage' to explain what makes ethically sourced coffee distinct from the mainstream. Some discuss this in terms of profit share, and many flag equity and a balance of power as necessary for 'fair' trade. Conditions of labour also figure prominently in how participants define ethical trade, as is clear in the previous description of how participants imagine problems within producing communities. In what follows, I focus on two themes that encapsulate all of these concerns: the environmental and economic sustainability of farms and communities, and producer quality of life.

Participants explain that farm and community sustainability are important markers of ethical sourcing, and are required for ensuring that producers enjoy a minimum quality of life. Participants point to these relations when they state that a 'sustainable livelihood' is a sign of ethical trade. It logically follows then that consumers believe that farm sustainability is directly tied to environmental sustainability. Evelyn expressed this when she said,

> ... what I'm hoping for is that ... the farmer on the picture ... [is] getting good wages, that they're able to grow their coffee in a way that makes sense to the soil, to the area where the coffee is being grown, and that they're getting a fair price for their coffee. And a fair price would mean whatever the margins are that would make sense for them to continue their practices.

Others state that producers are better off when education is made available for children, and when children are not required to work. Many point to availability of food and water, to housing, and to good health and health care as conditions of an ethical situation. Participants expect that with larger income, the ability to meet basic necessities of survival follows. Lily explained that ensuring the availability of food, shelter, clean water and education 'seems only fair'. She stated, 'If we're going to buy something from that part of the world, those people would have the same things [as us]'. And, some connect quality of life directly to wages, like Kristin who said producers should 'Absolutely have the basic necessities, the human necessities of life, shelter, education, food and water. Access to all of those. To have that be guaranteed by the wage'. David explained how increased wages trickle down to bolster a community: 'By increasing the compensation for the employees and improving the working conditions, it will provide them with additional funding which will bring additional services to their communities to make life better for them.'

With these statements participants identify key elements that define ethical coffee sourcing from their perspective: fair price and wages, equitable relations of trade, environmentally sustainable growing practices and the resulting sustainability of the farm. These statements also present a stark contrast to the popular image of 'unethical' coffee production offered by participants: low prices and wages, exploitative relations of trade, concern only for production volume and an impoverished, subsistence level existence. As they understand it, ethical sourcing models respond to the problems that plague growing communities by paying more, adjusting the relations and conditions of production and trade and ultimately, create thriving communities that want for nothing. This model positions consumers as saviours, and offers them the opportunity to inhabit ethical consumer subjectivity.

Anxieties and Contradictions

Those who participated in this research are not full-blown supporters, neither ideologically nor practically, of ethical models of sourcing and production. About a third point out that they have to protect their economic self-interest, and so can't do as much as they might like, given the price premiums of many ethical products. Others explain that buying ethically can sometimes require more time in research and travel to where such goods are available, and so ethical consumption is sometimes more of a hassle than they are willing to tolerate. Regarding this, Natalie said, 'It has to be convenient. Life is so complicated anyway and time is so short during the day, you do what you can in your little area'. When discussing his concerns besides coffee, Roderick explained, 'It's so big that there's really no way for me to know where it's coming from in a timely way'. Describing that he hasn't achieved the ethical consumer status that he would like to, Jake said, 'In an ideal world my relationship to things would be more local, but I haven't gotten to that point yet.'

Some point out that models of ethical sourcing are steps in the right direction, though not solutions for producers around the world. Scott pointed to the contradictions that exist in the purchasing habits of ethical consumers when he said, 'It's great that folks can go and buy Fair Trade coffee, but what does that mean when they're buying a lot of products that there aren't mainstream alternatives for, like socks made in Taiwan?' Because of the limitations they experience and the contradictions they see, some feel a sense of hopeless ambivalence towards social and environmental problems, and recognize that their ability to make change is limited. Reflecting on this, Dean said, 'There's a point where it does become paralyzing'.

No doubt, these sentiments are fuelled by the scepticism of labels and ethical sourcing models that nearly half of participants expressed. Many harbour concern that ethical claims are more marketing ploys or forms of 'washing' than they are indicative of real changes to relations of production and trade. Many also point out that labels have been co-opted by big business and thus have lost meaning and validity. Regarding agricultural products, Michael said, 'Before it meant something certain, but now bigger farms are jumping on board and bending the rules, using fertilizers that shouldn't be used'. Kristin revealed similar concerns: 'It seems like the terms or labels have been watered down. I wonder how true Starbucks' claims are. Now you can find organic Cheerios and major food companies are creating organic stuff. How is it that it's organic?'

Concern for a lack of transparency of sourcing models is another key concern of participants, who admit that they are not certain that they can trust the claims of the businesses they patronize. Lance explained that the direct trade company from which he buys green coffee for home roasting revealed some problems associated with the Fair Trade model in their monthly newsletter. Of this, he said, 'A lot of times the dollars really don't filter down to the actual growers'. Similarly, Brenda admitted that she is sceptical that the model is as good as labels make it out to seem.

With statements like these participants reveal the material and ideological constraints in their lives that shape their ability and desire to pursue ethical consumption. Money and time are limited resources, and they must protect their own economic self-interest and quality of life. Their awareness of corporate bad-actors and mainstream co-optation has raised their suspicions about the sincerity of the claims of those touting ethical business practices and sourcing models. Some of them feel overwhelmed by the many ethical options on the market and the multitude of global social and environmental problems that these options signify. Yet, they consistently purchase ethical coffee, which suggests that despite their scepticism and the contradictions they see in ethical consumption, they believe that consuming for change is what they can do as individuals to make a positive impact on the world.

Conclusion

This research reveals that ethical consumers believe in the power of consumer-driven change. They deploy a dyadic strategy of consumption that targets goods that are marketed as the 'right' choice, and avoid goods that are associated with corporate bad actors. They frame ethical coffee as the 'right' choice because they believe it ensures fair prices to producers, fair wages to labourers, provides for good labour conditions, an acceptable community-wide quality of life and environmental and economic sustainability. Despite the scepticism that some harbour for corporate claims, consumers read ethical coffee as an effective response to the political and economic problems that they perceive to be endemic to 'Third World' and 'developing' nations. Ultimately, they view ethical coffee as a tool of empowerment and change. As consumers with resources and knowledge, they are empowered to change the lives of producers through their consumption choices. They inhabit a moral consumer subjectivity.

Yet despite recognition of problems in coffee growing communities, the situatedness of these within a system of capitalist production and consumption, and the history of this system, goes unrecognized by the vast majority. Disparities in wages due to unjust hierarchies of race and nationality are overlooked, and so it is presumed that because ethical sourcing levels the playing field of the global economy, it gives producers the resources they need to succeed within it. Ethical consumers are unaware that not all producers welcome this kind of benevolent intervention. Many have resisted neoliberal models of development and aid (Neilson and Pritchard, 2007), have objected to the inclusion of transnational corporations and plantations in ethically certified sourcing models (Wilkinson and Mascarenhas, 2007), and have expressed discontent with certification fees and standards imposed from the north (Renard and Peréz-Grovas, 2007; Wilkinson and Mascarenhas, 2007). Often, producer demands for more representation on the boards of certification organizations have gone unheeded (Wilkinson and Mascarenhas, 2007). Further, the notion of ethical consumers reaching in to southern communities to solve their problems vanishes the producer-rooted origin of the Fair Trade system, which was called into being in Mexico as a counter force to the neoliberal globalization of trade (Murray and Raynolds, 2007; Renard and Peréz-Grovas, 2007). The negligible economic in-the-pocket difference between conventional and certified coffee is another reality not understood by consumers.

Given that most have only vague, surface level knowledge of how ethical sourcing models operate, and the realities of their effects in coffee communities, consumer concern ultimately manifests as well-intentioned reactionary purchasing. I see this as evidence of the successful commodification of morality. By disseminating a narrative that features happy producers who thrive due to the choices of consumers, the specialty coffee industry has successfully created a market for morality. Together the discourse and imagery that surrounds the product functions as a sign, in the Saussurian sense, of ethical relations of trade, which signals to the consumer that all is well and they have done the right thing (Saussure [1916] 1983). For these reasons I find it impossible to frame ethical consumption as it exists today as political action or progressive social change.

That said, the genuine concern for the welfare of producers, for global justice, and for planetary sustainability shine through as lights of hope in our contemporary culture. Implicit in ethical consumption is a critique of the dominant relations of global capitalism and the behaviour of large corporations. This is expressed through the construction of 'villains' in consumer discourse on the problems of today's world, and is representative of heightened awareness of the abuses of the system, against which some businesses are framed as 'ethical'. Consumer unease with these conditions is expressed also in the guilt they articulate over not doing more to be ethical actors, shaped by the real material constraints on their own lives—making the 'right' choice often costs more. This is certainly a critical orientation.

The interviews I conducted with consumers, however, revealed that awareness of problems often mushrooms to overwhelming proportions, which generates feelings of hopelessness and ambivalence. For many, awareness is an unfolding process, during which knowledge of corporate abuses builds up, in part due to the marketing of goods as ethical. As awareness grows, so does their understanding of the social-systemic scope of the problem. For some, this produces hopelessness because they feel that no matter what they do, problems will persist. This can result in an ambivalent orientation towards ethical consumption and other politically effective modes of social change.

The act of purchasing an ethically coded good then, such as Fair Trade or 'Farm Direct' coffee, offers a momentary alleviation of the postmodern stress and anxiety that many US consumers feel. When the situation seems hopeless, making the 'right' consumer choice is an available action that resonates with immediacy. The product tells consumers that their act starts a chain reaction of goodness that trickles down to producers in the global south. I suggest then, that the anxieties and critical impulses that tip US consumers towards ethical goods are dampened by the act of ethical consumption. This means that ethical consumption of goods represents an adaptation of consumerism to our contemporary historical moment, not a challenge to it, nor to the norms of global capitalism.

Despite this, I believe that hope lies in the unease, the anxiety, and the discomfort that pushes consumers to harbour suspicions of the relations and conditions of production. But if we are to

make moves towards real social change and global economic justice, we must embrace our anxieties, not assuage them through
the self-gratifying channels of consumption. To the extent that we
opt for the simple fix of ethical consumption we fail to actually
confront the root of the problem that causes these anxieties—the
system of capitalism—and instead we reproduce the very thing
that troubles us. We must confront and marinate in our anxieties,
allow them to trouble us, and then use them as motive to engage
in what Marcuse (1964) called 'negative thinking'—the unthink-
ing of the norms that limit the possibilities for what social and
economic relations can look like. We must meet the challenge of
thinking outside the iron cage of global capitalism. Only then can
we imagine social justice into being.

References

Barrientos, S., Michael, E.C. & Elaine, Jones. 2007. Northern social
    movement and Fair Trade. In L.T. Raynolds, D.L. Murray &
    J. Wilkinson (eds), *Fair Trade: The Challenges of Transforming Globalization*
    (pp. 51–62). New York: Routledge.
Bauman, Z. 2008. *Does Ethics Have a Chance in a World of Consumers?*
    Cambridge: Harvard University Press.
Bolton, D. 2009. Coffee industry shifts under tougher economy. *Specialty
    Coffee Retailer*, 27 July. Available at http://www.specialty-coffee.com/
    ME2/Audiences/dirmod.asp?sid=&nm=&type=MultiPublishing&
    mod=PublishingTitles&mid=8F3A7027421841978F18BE895F87F
    791&AudID=464620AE3F20454894C8CB7CEF72A481&tier=4&i
    d=71C474258D2F46AEAD2BA59307E8002B (accessed on 7 April
    2011).
Cook, I. & Philip, C. 1996. The world on a plate: Culinary culture, displace-
    ment and geographical knowledges. *Journal of Material Culture, 1*(2),
    131–153.
Featherstone, M. 2011. Foreword. In T. Lewis & E. Potter (eds), *Ethical
    Consumption: A Critical Introduction*, pp. 17–28. New York: Routledge.
Goodman, M.K. 2010. The Mirror of consumption: Celebritization,
    developmental consumption and the shifting cultural politics of Fair
    Trade. *Geoforum, 41*(1), 104–116.
Grodnik, A. & Conroy, M.E. 2007. Fair Trade coffee in the United States:
    Why companies join the movement. In L.T. Raynolds, D.L. Murray &

J. Wilkinson (eds), *Fair Trade: The Challenges of Transforming Globalization,* pp. 83–102. New York: Routledge.

Guthman, Julie. 2008. Neoliberalism and the making of food politics in California. *Geoforum, 39*(3), 1171–1183.

Lewis, T. & Potter, E. 2011. Introducing ethical consumption. In T. Lewis & E. Potter (eds), *Ethical Consumption: A Critical Introduction,* pp. 3–24. New York: Routledge.

Littler, Jo. 2009. *Radical Consumption: Shopping for Change in Contemporary Culture.* Maidenhead, Berkshire, UK: Open University Press.

Low, W. & Davenport, E. 2006. Mainstreaming Fair Trade: Adoption, assimilation, appropriation. *Journal of Strategic Marketing, 14*(4), 315–327.

Marcuse, H. 1964. *One-dimensional Man.* Boston: Beacon Press.

Mathur, N. 2010. Shopping malls, credit cards and global brands: Consumer culture and lifestyle of India's new middle class. *South Asia Research, 30*(3), 211–231.

Micheletti, M. 2003. *Political Virtue and Shopping: Individuals, Consumerism, and Collective Action.* New York: Palgrave Macmillan.

Micheletti, M. & Stolle, D. 2008. Fashioning social justice through political consumerism, capitalism, and the internet. *Cultural Studies, 22*(5), 749–769.

Monbiot, G. 2007. Environmental Feedback: A reply to Slive Hamilton. *New Left Review, 45*(May–June). Available at http: www.newleftreview. org/?view=2672 (accessed on 25 September 2011).

Murray, D.L. & Raynolds, L.T. 2007. Globalization and its antinomies: Negotiating a Fair Trade movement. In L.T. Raynolds, D.L. Murray & J. Wilkinson (eds), *Fair Trade: The Challenges of Transforming Globalization,* pp. 3–14. New York: Routledge.

National Coffee Association. 2007. *National Coffee Drinking Trends 2007.* New York: National Coffee Association.

Neilson, J. & Pritchard, B. 2007. Green coffee: The contradictions of global sustainability initiatives from an Indian perspective. *Development Policy Review, 25*(3), 311–331.

Pendergrast, M. 1999. *Uncommon Grounds: The History of Coffee and How It Transformed Our World.* New York: Basic Books.

Pierrot, J. & Giovannucci, D. 2010. *Sustainable Coffee Report: Statistics on the Main Coffee Certifications.* Geneva, SW: International Trade Centre.

Raynolds, L.T. & Long, M.A. 2007. Fair/alternative trade: Historical and empirical dimensions. In L.T. Raynolds, D.L. Murray & J. Wilkinson (eds), *Fair Trade: The Challenges of Transforming Globalization,* pp. 15–32. New York: Routledge.

Renard, M.-C. & Peréz-Grovas, Victor. 2007. Fair Trade coffee in Mexico: At the center of the debates. In L.T. Raynolds, D.L. Murray &

J. Wilkinson (eds), *Fair Trade: The Challenges of Transforming Globalization*, pp. 138–156. New York: Routledge.

Said, E.W. 1978. *Orientalism.* New York: Vintage Books.

Saussure, F. de. 1983. *Course in General Linguistics.* Chicago: Open Court Publishing.

Specialty Coffee Association of America (SCAA). 2010. Sustainable Coffee Certifications: A Comparison Matrix. SCAA.org. Available at http://www.scaa.org/PDF/Sustainable%20Coffee%20Certifications%20Comparison%20Matrix%202010.pdf (accessed on 7 April 2011).

Talbot, J.M. 2004. *Grounds for Agreement: The Political Economy of the Coffee Commodity Chain.* New York: Rowman & Littlefield Publishers, Inc.

——. 2011. The coffee commodity chain in the world-economy: Arrighi's systemic cycles and Braudel's layers of analysis. *Journal of World-Systems Research,* 27(1), 58–88.

Topik, S. 2010. Why do Americans drink coffee? The Boston tea party or Brazilian slavery? Paper presented at University of California, Santa Barbara, March 2010.

Wild, A. 2004. *Coffee: A Dark History.* New York: W.W. Norton and Company.

Wilkinson, J. & Gilberto, M. 2007. Southern social movements and Fair Trade. In L.T. Raynolds, D.L. Murray & J. Wilkinson (eds), *Fair Trade: The Challenges of Transforming Globalization*, pp. 125–137. New York: Routledge.

13

Consumer Culture and Turkish Poor Youth's Identity: Issues of Vulnerability and Exclusion

Melike Aktaş Yamanoğlu

Introduction

Although consumption has always been an important part of the social life, in a consumer society it acquires unprecedented importance for which reason, among others, it has largely been of interest to sociologists. In a general sense, consumer society is understood as one in which a consumption-centred lifestyle is promoted, encouraged and rigorously reinforced. One of the prominent roles of individuals in society is that of a consumer. The performance of 'consumer role' becomes a criterion of assessing success and a principle that regulates the distinction between inclusion in or exclusion from consumer society (Bauman, 2007: 53). While many studies have been performed on the nature of consumption in societies and their transformation into 'consumer societies' (see Baudrillard, 2004; Bauman, 2005, 2007; Cohen, 2003; Jameson, 1983; Miller, 1995; Ritzer and Slater, 2001; Slater, 1997; Trentmann, 2004), there are few that deal with the poor people's encounter with them.

Being poor in a consumer society means, in the words of Bauman (2005: 38) an 'inadequacy, this inability to acquit one-self of the consumer's duties, that turns into bitterness at being left behind, disinherited or degraded, shut off or excluded from the social feast to which others gained entry'. Equating 'normality' with ability to consume, consumer society marginalizes and defines poor as 'deficient', 'invalid' and 'flawed' consumers due to their capability limitations and restrictions (Bauman, 2005, 2007). In a consumer society, there is hardly any need of poor consumers, 'so they are unwanted' (Bauman, 2007: 126). Exclusion from the consumer society may take physical and/or psychological forms. Particularly, poverty-producing mechanisms of the society might be obscured and poverty attached to individual failures thus the empathy to the poor is weakened.

It can be argued that experiencing this process as a poor youth results in compelling exclusion, for the youth have an overall 'privileged' position in consumer society as consumers. As young consumer groups make up a market category with high profitability, they are the object of marketing efforts. The perception of youth as a distinct consumer group accompanied the increase in consumption expenditures and the differentiation of consumption patterns of youth after World War II (Abrams, 1959). The size of the market created by youth reached unprecedented levels, especially in the post-1980 period (Zaim, 2006: 92). Placed on the margins of the consumer market, poor youth are also subject to consumerist pressures, just like their counterparts from higher social strata. Youth is defined in the consumer society as involvement to certain consumption patterns. The adoption of, or the ability to adopt, certain consumption patterns, practices and life styles is the most important criterion differentiating the 'young' from the 'not-young'. It can be argued that being poor and young means experiencing these two phenomena differently. Living as young and as poor in combination is telling because the pressure to consume and join the mainstream is far too high. Their situation is worsened by the fact that they are not adequately equipped to deal with such pressures. Thus, poor youth can be treated as a separate social category differentiated both from youth and poor in general.

With the adoption of outward-looking and free market economy after 1980s, Turkey moved into global consumer culture and especially during the 1990s consumer society is almost settled down entirely with its all constituents. The main driver of this movement in the post-1980s period was Turkey economy's engagement with the global market. Starting from 1980–1983 transformations and completed during 1989–1990, initially commodity market opened to foreign trade and export regimes are liberalized; liberalization of national fiscal market and articulation with foreign finance centres followed this process and Turkish economy transformed into open market economy totally during 1990s (Yeldan, 2005: 25). Neo-liberal policies brought privatization and dissolution of some specific social security practices of welfare state into agenda under the discourse of state's minimization.

The liberalized market economy has led Turkey to open up the world not only economically but also socio-culturally and a shift from scarcity to abundance in goods and services is witnessed (Durakbaşa and Cindoğlu, 2002: 74). By the mid-1980s, with the growth in advertising, mass communication, consumer credit and commercial leisure, urban classes' relationships with consumption dramatically changed both quantitatively and qualitatively (Özyeğin, 2002: 55). However, not all social groups could have enjoyed the opportunity structures offered by the new economic dynamics (Kandiyoti, 2002: 4) and this situation produced widening gaps between them. Economic policies applied post-1980 period gave rise to development of consumer society; however, on the other hand they also contributed to the dissociation of social groups in terms of both income and consumption patterns. The 1990s were the years in which social dissolution and fragmentation became apparent and the neo-liberal politics that was placed into practice produced vast number of excluded consumers (Etöz, 2000: 49). In other words, while consumer society was institutionalized, rich–poor dichotomy has become even more distinct.

The outlook of urban poverty remains different from that observed in other countries for a long time especially until the 2000s. According to Pınarcıoğlu and Işık (2008), the solidarity networks on religious, ethnic and cultural bases that developed among urban poor in Turkey, contributed to the struggle for urban poverty and secured relatively safe place for urban poor during the 1980s and 1990s. The roots of distinctive features of urban poverty in Turkey could be sought in the peculiarities of urban processes. Social actors have taken advantage of informal sector to improve their livelihood conditions (in forms of low rents and informal jobs) and due to the informal sector dynamism, urban poor could overcome the economic hardships. Pınarcıoğlu and Işık (2008) use 'poverty-in-turn' concept to explain the process of 'the web of relations functioned to build up in metropolitan areas (p. 1354). However, those networks have started to disappear faced with the pressure of internal and external factors; thus, 'Turkey now encounters with deepening poverty levels and engendering new forms and dynamics of poverty' (p. 1353).

Urban poor youth in Turkey have no easy access to basic services, such as education, health and housing. They are spatially excluded as well and unable to participate in the labor force because of their low educational qualifications. This chapter focuses on the relationships between urban poor youth and consumer society. It examines (i) the encounter of poor youth residing in squatter areas outside the city centre of Turkey's capital Ankara with consumer society; (ii) how 'youth' and 'poverty' are experienced by the urban poor youth; (iii) how their dreams, desires and aspirations related with the culture of consumption are dealt with; and (iv) the processes of exclusion from consumer society and the counter strategies developed at the grass roots. Considering that exclusion from consumer society results in a more severe experience of class inequalities among the poor and the young poor in particular, the chief question addressed here is: How urban poor youth experience and deal with class inequalities in a consumption-driven society? This chapter is based on in-depth fieldwork carried out in Ankara's Altındağ, Mamak and Sincan districts. The focus, however, was on the Altındağ district because it has the largest squatter population in Ankara. The sample comprised 65 women and men, in a total 58 semi-structured interviews (siblings interviewed together) between 15 and 29 years of age diversified in terms of educational qualifications and nature of employment. Although respondents were not limited by a specific income level since poverty is conceptualized as multi-dimensional phenomenon, it should be noted that the youth whom I interviewed had household incomes that were far below the minimum subsistence level for a family of four. Considering the impact of the place of residence on experience of poverty, people residing in areas known for extreme poverty holding out limited access to resources and deprived of economic, social and cultural capital that could raise their standard of living were included in the study.

The Pressure to Consume

Consumer society makes poor youth aware about the 'normal' and 'legitimate' criteria of consumption principles so that they measure their living conditions and poverty on these bases. The consumption patterns prevalent in consumer society and considered as ordinary are, in fact, regarded as 'rewards', 'passions' or 'dreams' by the poor youth since they are distant from their usual practices. Although they do not have complete knowledge of all the consumption opportunities afforded by consumer society, they treat access to these consumption alternatives as a gateway to living 'a good and comfortable life'. Consumerist pressures coerce them to evaluate their lives, social relations and living conditions based on various criteria. Their deprivation grows exponentially since material constrains prevent them from reaching consumption standards considered as legitimate in consumer society. One informant stated this in following words:

> The dreams we have, things that are not even dreams, things that do not realized ... the reason we are angry and not happy is that we dream the smallest of things, say, for example, I say to my friend let's get two pairs of Adidas trainers, think of it, only 60 liras,[1] dress the same, go buy two sweat suits, two hoodies, have a haircut ... then go sit in a café, we would go now, but we say

we will go later ... (Kemal, 19, M, elementary school graduate, unemployed)

The persistent claims of consumerism transmit the messages that only way for self-realization is to engage with objects of consumption, social status can only be enhanced by the ownership of various consumer goods and social identity could be acquired by the use and display of certain consumer commodities. The association of all sorts of needs with a consumption opportunity aggravates the living conditions of the poor, who do not have access to them. The effect of the consumerist pressures on young people is that they come to believe that life worth living is one in which they are able to participate in various entertainment and consumption patterns, failing which it is wasted.

Processes that preclude the young people from being youthful (family pressure, having to work at a young age, household chores, financial problems, etc.) create even harsher and stricter conditions under the consumerist pressures of the consumer society. Poor youth who do not have access to consumption opportunities and who are not able to 'live like the young' classify themselves among the 'not young'. 'Fast maturation' is experienced as a burden by the poor youth, which 'differentiates' them from their peers and 'not being able to be young' is a source of pain. For instance, Kemal (19, M) and Yelda (15, F) describe the reasons they do not 'feel young' as follows, emphasizing different reasons:

I look at my peers and I am surprised, I talk as if I am older than all, like I am 50 or something. I have seen it all, everything. But nothing satisfied me. I wish I had learnt little by little, like my peers did, say this much (makes a hand gesture) in a year. I wanna be like my peers. I wanna make jokes, laugh, do stuff ... For example, sometimes people older than me come and say 'What's up, uncle Kemal?', and I feel really irritated by that. (Kemal, 19, M, elementary school graduate, unemployed)

I am 16 but I am always depressed, same thing every day. I don't remember a day when I laughed or didn't cry ... I can never go out or go to places, my family reacts very harsh, if I were to be late just a little, then 'where have you been, why are you so late?', excuse my language, 'have you been prostituting yourself?', then, you know, beatings and all that ... I am young but I think old ... I don't want anything in this life, I just wanna smile a bit, that's what I want ...

Question: What would make you smile?

I don't know, I never smiled in my life ... What kind of a life would make me happy? ... mmm. I, personally ... I am not even allowed to come here (meaning the municipal youth centre where the interview was held), I just sneak out. Being allowed to come here would make me happy for example. I am under pressure. And I get beaten for the smallest thing ... why won't they let us see our mistakes by ourselves? (Yelda, 15, F, eighth grader, part-time hairdresser)

Korkut (20, M), an auto mechanic, states he was not able to live his childhood and youth, stating they were not able to 'go out' or 'sit in cafés'. 'Going out', 'discovering new places', 'wandering' and 'spending time in cafés' are considered by many to be the most important entertainment activities of the youth. Being poor is considered to be the single biggest obstacle in front of living one's youth. For example, Hakkı (24, M) born and raised in Altındağ and working in the same place, says that the youth in Altındağ will never have the life style that is desired by all young people and that is mundane for rich youth:

Every young person wants to have a good life, like, you know, have a car, a car that is only his or hers. They wanna see different places, go to different places, you know, wanna have a luxury life, maybe because they emulate luxury lives ... Youth in Altındağ will never have that chance, maybe only once in their lives. (Hakkı, 24, M, security guard at a municipal building)

Fashion and youth magazines, advertisements, television serials and celebrity shows are the most important tools through which urban poor youth learn about various consumption alternatives, different life styles and consumption patterns. For example, Ruken (20, F) says she and others in similar economic and social situation cannot afford expensive magazines, but they share them with friends when they get hold of one. Free youth magazines and newspaper supplements, in particular, are sources for learning about the latest fashion trends and other consumer goods:

> We learn things of fashion from the internet, from celebrity sites etc. Magazines, Trendy, Salsa, Kral.... We check what the fashion is this week, ins and outs of the week.... When we get together, this is what we talk about the most, and computers and mobile phones ... did you see that new phone, etc ... (Ruken, 20, F, high school graduate, office worker)

While urban poor youth develop an understanding of the images of consumer society, they simultaneously internalize their poor conditions. Since the lifestyles transmitted through advertisements, television serials and celebrity shows have no place in the lives of poor youth, some of them develop a negative attitude towards these media. 'Celebrity shows are all about the lives of rich people, things that do not concern me at all', says Onur (16, M), adding that he finds these shows 'ridiculous' because they have nothing to do with his life, and that he 'watch[es] but it makes no sense'. Selçuk (18, M) describes poor youth who are impressed by rich people in these shows as 'wannabes'.

The impact of the information gained from media on the lives of poor youth is mitigated by the idea that it is all fiction and by developing a negative attitude towards these consumption patterns and the people who enjoy them. Youth who confront the images of consumer society in their daily lives, on the other hand, have more dramatic experiences. Experiences gained in shopping malls are particularly important. Shopping malls are places where all sorts of consumption alternatives and objects are on display, and they allow urban poor youth to confront consumer society as a solid reality. As most of the interviewees mentioned that they had never been to a shopping mall, they 'saw them on TV and [were] curious about them' (Melda, 17, F), 'pass through all the time' and 'wondered what all these cars were doing there' (Gonca, 16, F), but they did not want to or did not have the 'opportunity' to go to a shopping mall because 'wouldn't know what to do there' (Mehmet, 21, M), 'shopping malls are not for them', these are 'places for rich people' (Selçuk, 18, M), and they 'don't feel comfortable' (Engin, 20, M) in these places. The few poor youth who go to shopping malls treat these places as a kind of museum, places where they go to learn about the lives of rich people and to 'gain some experience' (Sertaç, 18, M; Aysel, 25, F). Youth who are knowledgeable about the consumption alternatives on offer in these places have a stronger curiosity and interest in the objects of consumer society.

Poor youth, confronting the images of consumer society in various places, develop an interest and curiosity to these consumer commodities and aspiration to have them, their limitations to access them lead to internalization of poverty. Not having access to consumption opportunities of the consumer society aggravates the feelings of dissatisfaction that these young people have with their lives and adds new dimensions to their poverty and they try to deal with the dilemmas by clinging to moral values and by developing a 'virtue made of necessity' (Bourdieu, 1984).

Narratives of Exclusion from Consumer Society

In a consumer society, the ability to consume means the ability to make choices from among the alternatives offered in the market. Bauman (2007) argues that the identification, in consumer societies, of freedom with freedom of choice leads poor leave out from this field freedom. Making consumption choices freely means not having limitations on the part of the consumers nevertheless the insufficient economic resources that poor consumers have restrict their ability to 'make choices' or their 'license to make choices' (Bauman, 2005). Thus, poverty is defined in consumer society as the inability to make consumption choices. This process is central to poor youth's experiences of exclusion from the field of consumption. For example, Umut (15, M) and Oğuz (15, M) say that they cannot afford to buy their favourite clothes, but can only look at them in the showcases of stores:

We go to Sıhhiye or Ulus[2] for a walk. Sometimes to Kızılay[3] as well. When we go there, we walk in front of the stores, sit down and talk. People go there for shopping, we go only when we have money ... I like doing my own shopping. I don't let my parents do the shopping for me, because they buy old stuff.
Question: What style of dress do you like?
I think hoodies and hats make you look better.... You can't take your eyes off of them, the shoes especially. We say let's buy those shoes but we just look at them in the stores, especially at Kiler,[4] and we look at the shoes. We look at clothes in the Russian bazaar.... We see them on TV, in the ads etc. And we see them on guys walking around Kızılay, and it looks so good. We say that looks good on them, would it look good on us too? (Oğuz, 15, M, eight grader)

I am interested in clothes but it's not like I have a lot clothes or anything. I buy what fits my body, sometimes they are too small, and I give them to my younger brother. I would like to buy more if I had more money. I like wearing young stuff, sneakers and all.... It gets attention, people look at you. Everybody wants to dress nice. I want that too. (Umut, 15, M, eight grader)

As consumer culture shortens the lifecycle of goods under the continuous pressure of change, poor consumers have to use what they buy for a long time, keep them in good condition, and maximize their gratification from them. Knowing about the alternatives in consumer society and not being able to access them creates a psychological pressure on poor youth.

[Brands] I like them, of course, and they are the fashion, when I see everybody wearing them and I don't, it makes you feel ... Well, I get sad when I can't buy something when it first comes out ... (Olcay, 17, F, high school student)

Ideal consumers in a consumer society are those who can 'add colour' to their lives by frequent shopping and who never have the time to get bored. The life of poor youth, on the other hand, is a 'boring' and 'monotonic' one because of a lack of involvement in social activities and urban life, besides lack of new experiences.

I don't know, we don't go for a walk, for example.... Some people drink but we fear. Staying out of trouble and out of fights, that's our job…. This life is for them (the rich people) to enjoy, that's just the way it is. We have always been like this, and I don't know if it will ever change … (Selim, 23, M, elementary school graduate, automobile head repair technician)

I am just 19 and about to turn 20. Should I be bored? I mean can you be bored at this age? I feel so tired I barely get out of the bed. I lie down here, look around, and think, what would I do if I were to get up? Then I keep sleeping, till noon. I have nothing else to do … (Kemal, 19, M, elementary school graduate, unemployed)

The 'monotony' of the lives of these young people is related with one of the most critical aspects of consumer society 'commodification of time' in other words 'to avoid work and replace it with leisure or other forms of work' (Urry, 1995: 130). As Veblen (2005) argues, the privilege to have 'leisure time' and to use this time for consumption is a practice of the upper classes. For example, Selim (23, M) describes the results of his constant work as follows, in comparison with rich people:

Because we live in this environment, we don't know about other people's environments. How can we? You know, some people are very rich, they send their kids to schools, and don't leave Sakarya at night. We can't go on vacation in the summer, but they can … I envy them a little bit. I mean, I think [to myself] it would be nice if I we too had some money, went on vacation this summer, for example. But I didn't, I couldn't … (Selim, 23, M, elementary school graduate, automobile head repair technician)

Korkut (20, M), who has been working in car repair shop since he was a kid, says he never has free time because he has to work:

It's not like I can take a walk every once in a while. And we have to be here [the industrial site] all the time during weekdays. We only have Sunday. We get out at seven or eight in the evenings, after the sun sets, and it takes one hour to one hour and a half to get home. After we have dinner, I go out for five minutes, to see friends, have a chat, and come back. This is the only time I go out…. Others go out to cafés and restaurants on weekdays, with their girl friends, I've never done anything like that in my life, I never had that.... You get bored here, you get bored from working. For example, some friends used to go out and invite us too. OK, let's do that, but how? We can't get a day off, it's so busy out here. They go out, you work here, and you get bored, knowing that they are out and you are working ... (Korkut, 20, M, elementary school graduate, automobile head repair technician)

Mustafa (23, M) compares his own situation with that of other youth he meets in shopping malls and says he cannot understand how they find the free time:

I just don't get it, how do they find the free time to go out. This free time, I mean, they should be seeing life as only bumming around.... What do we do? We try to get home as early as we can, that's what we do.... You get home, take a bath, shave, etc, and it takes time. We go home at eight at the earliest, and our houses are far away from here.... Some days I work till eleven, till twelve. I remember working till four in the morning once. (Mustafa, 23, M, elementary school graduate, auto mechanic technician)

The pressure to express feelings by means of consumer goods and in the form of consumption patterns is another example of how urban poor youth feel excluded. Particularly in the romantic relationships poor youth who cannot make 'proper' use of consumer goods, this situation is a source of 'embarrassment' and interpreted as a 'shame'. This is especially the case for males who have difficulty keeping up with the consumption demands of their female friends. In this sense, poverty acts as a barrier to romantic relations between men and women.

It all comes down to money, it always does.... For example, you are going out with a girl, and you don't have any money. The girl says 'could you buy me a coke, please?' What do you do? It is not even about shame, you can't even say you can't buy it. What do you do? You try to do other things. This is how things are among the have-nots, the rich don't have that. Rich girls do not ask, there is no such thing as 'could you buy me a coke,'. He buys it before she asks, there is no need to ask ... (Kemal, 19, M, elementary school graduate, unemployed)

If I had a girlfriend, if we were to go out, I would be both stressed and worried, thinking what if she wants to go to a fancy place? All I have is 20 liras at most, and what would that be worth if she wanted to go to a luxury place? (Yavuz, 17, M, high school student)

Many of them prefer to meet their loved ones in parks and sit on public benches in order that opportunity to spend is closed. Romantic relations do not translate into actual dating, but are maintained through phone messages and Internet chats. Sertaç (18, M) describes romantic friendships between girls and boys in his neighbourhood as follows:

Now some have cell phones but have no pre-paid talktime. In such a case, they ring the phone and hang up. Then the girl rings back, and hangs up. Or they exchange messages. No dates, no going out, nothing. Where would they go if they had a date? To Kurtuluş Park at most, where they would sit in the cold, and then go back home…. When you look at them (youth in shopping malls), everybody wants to be like that. Everyone around here wants to be like them, I mean, go out with their girlfriends, but they can't. They probably could if they had the money, because they would have learnt about life. They would know how to hang in places and then just do it. (Sertaç, 18, M, vocational school graduate, repairman)

Upper-end neighbourhoods with luxury houses, shopping malls, cultural centres, restaurants, luxury brand stores, gymnasiums and beauty salons are places from 'another planet' for the urban poor youth. These places, constructed as if belonging to another world, are places visited like museums by the urban poor youth, and are not only the objects of curiosity but also a source of discomfort. Believing that they are not wanted in these places because of their looks, clothes, speech and manners, people there are disturbed by their presence and treated like thieves and subjected to disrespectful behaviour. In this sense, poverty is experienced as a stigma and hurt to self-esteem.

When I go to luxury places, I feel a little shy, I keep thinking, are these people looking at me?, Should I do this? Would I draw attention if I did that? … (Yavuz, 17, M, high school student)

We go there for a walk, but we just pass by. We never even think about hanging in these places ... I don't feel comfortable. I mean, people in there are different ... their manners, behaviours ... when we go there they stare at us ... they give way, for example, when we walk on the sidewalks ... They understand we are not from there ... (Yıldırım, 19, M, vocational school graduate, plumber)

[Rich neighbourhoods] When we walk there, they [see us] as beasts not as humans, I see it in their eyes, they give way, men look away, girls look differently, plus they make room so you can walk. (Selçuk, 18, M, high school student)

When I go to a theater, the guy gives me this look, as if to say go away, we have no movies to show you ... (A teenager from Kale)

I don't like going to those places at all, I get irritated. You go there, and do nothing but walk around without a purpose.... The rich man's wealth tires the poor's jaw. Did you see this, did you see that, look at this, look at that, it's just weird. (Halil, 19, M, high school graduate, unemployed)

Exclusionist processes experienced by poor youngsters are also related with the suspicions and prejudices concerning them. In both media reports and academic studies, poor youth are the subjects of stories involving 'crime', 'violence' and 'drug abuse', which results in a perception that they are potential 'problems' and 'trouble-makers' (Chin, 2001: 3; Griffin, 1997: 17–20). This affects their relations with people from different social strata, and even discourages them from going to certain districts of the city and places of consumption such as shopping malls, entertainment centres, movie theatres.

Zeynep (19, F) expresses her anguish towards the attitudes of salespeople in a well-known store selling foreign brands as follows:

Employees over there act as if they own the place.... They are showy, they examine you, and when they see a rich person, they run to attend, pushing you around.... They know if you are rich from your bag or shoes, and they know if you are not their customer, saying 'this is here just to have a look'.... After I saw that, I never went back to this place again, I don't think I can buy anything from there anyways ... (Zeynep, 19, F, high school graduate, shop assistant)

Despite a lack of particular treatment or negative attitudes towards them in most cases, youngsters who internalize the suspicions around them have an intense feeling of exclusion, because they take some things personally, define themselves in opposition to members of higher classes and think their poverty is apparent 'no matter how well they try to cover it'. They gave vivid examples from the accounts of well-off people about 'not approving', 'mocking' and 'ridiculing' them. Although it is not easy to estimate the exact situation, it is clear that urban poor youth experience their poverty as feelings of 'shame', 'deficiency' and 'lack of confidence'.[5] Thus, all looks, words and attitudes directed at them are interpreted within this axis, resulting in the internalization of their poverty and reinforcement of stereotypes about rich people. For youth excluded from various consumption opportunities, social inequalities turn into class bitterness and anger. For example, Zehra (19, F) says her classmates 'crushed' her and her low-income friends. The examples she gives make it clear that Zehra felt excluded when her classmates talked about brands, places they visited, movies and music. According to Zehra, these behaviours were aimed at 'humiliating' her and other students with low income. In her words,

Our teachers used to say 'be friends, you are all in the same class, talk to one another', and when we tried to talk, they would do different things. They would change the subject to brands, and say let's go to this place, let's go to that place.... For example, they liked going to Kızılay and sitting in cafés, or going to the movies, going to other place, taking a walk in Tunalı[6].... There were those small radios, we used to listen to them, then they started bringing in mp3 players and listening to them right in front of us. They would show these and say see, this plays video as well, etc., that was another way for them to crush us. (Zehra, 19, F, high school graduate, unemployed)

Umut (15, M) felt that when the 'rich' kids talked about their vacations, it was a sign of contempt for him (or for the poor people in general),

> Rich people like hanging with rich people. They insult the poor.... We have some of them at our school, they boast about 'having gone to Antalya, swimming in the sea' etc., they look down upon us. For example, when something happens in class, they rat on you for the smallest thing.... They think they are bullies, threatening to call hash heads, saying we could get you killed. We are not afraid of them, we are trying to do what is right. When you are afraid, they take advantage of it ... (Umut, 15, M, eight grader)

The most striking result of social inequalities for the poor is a lack of self-respect. The narratives of poor youth cited earlier, describing poverty using concepts indicating 'shame', 'deficiency' and 'lack of confidence', are, in fact, reflection of the emotional-symbolic violence exerted upon them, not of material poverty. In this sense, processes of exclusion created by poverty also threaten the dignity, self-respect and self-confidence of these youth.

Şenol (20, M) explains the direct connection he forms between poverty and lack of self-confidence as follows:

> If you have money in your pocket, then you have confidence, if not, then you don't have confidence. Just think about it, a person who has 100 bucks would of course have self-confidence, go out to places, and what not. People who do not have that kind of money cannot go out to places, they don't feel confident. They look at these people, look at these rich lives, and think, Why don't I have that? (Şenol, 20, M, high school graduate, unemployed)

Engin (20, M) takes security measures in shopping malls personally, and perceives them as the reflection of a 'suspicion' towards himself. This perception can be considered to be a reflection of the 'lack of confidence' arising from living in a consumer society. Similarly, Leman (21, F) believes people think things in their heads about her, exemplifying the 'lack of confidence' surrounding poverty.

I don't like going to shopping malls, I went once, I didn't like it, because they search you every minute, make walk you through the detector, I have a phone in my pocket, I wear a belt, and it keeps beeping. I don't like those places. It's like…. And it needs to be simple, you should walk in, then walk out. (Engin, 20, M, high school graduate, auto mechanic apprentice)

I feel the thoughts of people around me, when they think things in their heads … I am wondering what are they thinking about me? (Leman, 21, F, elementary school graduate, unemployed)

For youth who reside in cities, who are very 'close' to and at the same time very 'far away' from consumption opportunities, exclusionist practices result in contradictory feelings. Some youth observe the consumption opportunities of their peers and see them as 'lucky', others accept this situation as fate and make peace with it, and yet others develop feelings of 'anger' and 'resentment'.

Urban Poor Youth's Response to Exclusion from Consumer Society

Urban poor youth develop practical strategies to deal with the practice of exclusion from consumer society, to deal with the sentiments arouse from these processes and to be included in consumer society and consumer living. The exchange of various consumption goods among friends, use of borrowed or rented products, use of counterfeit brands and having special days for consumption are examples of such strategies. Poor youngsters also try to gain cheaper access to consumer goods by taking an advantage from second-hand stores, bargain shops, street hawkers, bazaars, places that sell stolen goods or clearance sale stores that facilitate their inclusion to world of consumers.

Strategies of the poor youth, as Hill (2002) argues, can be classified into emotional and behavioural strategies. On the one hand, youngsters look for tangible shortcuts that will make it easier for them to participate in consumer society, and on the other, they keep their memories of relatively easier lives in the past alive or comfort themselves by dreams of future opportunities awaiting them.

In addition to practical strategies developed by the poor youth themselves, their families also develop various strategies for the children. Urban poor families sometimes overspend their budgets, as Kochuyt (2004: 145) argues, to create 'an artificial affluence' for their kids (2004: 145). Families sometimes make cuts from spending on basic needs in order to enable satisfaction desired by youngsters as a measure against their experiences of exclusion. Youth interviewed highlighted such 'reversing practices' (Kochuyt, 2004: 145) or strategies developed by families by giving examples from their friends. Consider the following statements of two informants:

A friend of ours used to dress really well, she always looked good and wore brands, then we found out her family was really poor. (Ruken, 20, F, high school graduate, office worker)

My dad does not limit us. He always says, do it, don't feel left behind, I will work and take care of you, I will borrow if I have to, he says, if you want it, then buy and don't envy others ... (Zehra, 19, F, high school graduate, unemployed)

In addition, working youth gave examples of such strategies when they talked about how they spent some of their money for their siblings' needs:

When I have the means, I buy stuff (for my sister). I buy stuff now, too. I give her all the money she needs as she leaves for school in the mornings. I was the one who bought her a mobile phone. (She is young, only 13, but) she asked and I bought.... My dad does not buy anything, of course, but I can't stand that so I buy stuff. I buy it because some of my wishes when I was a kid were not realized. (Yıldırım, 19, M, vocational high school graduate, plumber)

Besides practical strategies, there are also lesser planned ways of resisting the pressure of consumption in society. Whereas the practical strategies of the urban poor youth aim to facilitate participation in consumer society, deal with the pressure and humiliation caused by exclusion and help youth preserve their self-respect; strategies of resistance target consumption patterns that are considered to be 'legitimate' and redefine them. These strategies include reactions to the practice of making social inequalities visible in the field of consumption. The struggle against social distance created by consumption can be interpreted as a strategy of resistance and empowerment among the urban poor youth against class distinctions. Some of the resistance strategies, on the other hand, consist of practices that clearly target images of consumer society, or those who have the means to consume, and contain an anger directed at consumer society itself. In his study of the media representation of youth living in disadvantaged regions of France, Champagne (1999: 59) interprets violent acts by unemployed youth towards images of consumer society and objects of consumption as an attempt to destroy and vandalize symbols of exclusion. Their decision to target shopping malls and to steal, vandalize or burn cars, according to Champagne, is a reflection of the fact that these objects of consumption represent numerous investments (not only economic, but also psychological, social and time investment, etc.) and the indispensible instrument of transportation and leisure. To these youth, cars represent participating in the labour market and symbolize success. The informants also highlighted that not having access to particular consumer goods was a source of tension that sometimes resulted in violent behaviour and could push poor youth to illegal activities such as robbery and extortion:

> Now, they are the haves and you are a have-not, and this is hard to digest.... This is what lies at the source of stealing, you know. Now, this guy looks around, sees some have stuff, others don't, some live like this, others live like that. What do I do? I go steal, I extort, I bribe, I try to earn easy money. (Halil, 19, M, high school graduate, unemployed)

> I am not like this when I am outside, I am more angry. Where does this anger come from? Because there is envy. I say, look at this guy, he bought a car, he is 17 and driving a Mercedes. Why? Why can't I drive one? ... The reason behind stealing is the desire

to live better, wealth and poverty.... Greed takes you to death, takes you to jail, takes you to different environments ... I could do that if I wanted to, I could do the best, the coolest, the greatest ... (Kemal, 19, elementary school graduate, unemployed)

Some youth do not have the financial means, they see such and such have these shoes, they ask their parents, and when it is not bought, they steal or try to get them via other means, I know because I have witnessed it many times.... Sweat suits were stolen, shoes were stolen at our school. It was clear who did it, those who couldn't buy ... (Zeynep, 19, F, high school graduate, shop assistant)

Some poor young people's wrath towards luxury cars or houses, spite and grudge feelings to peers rolling freely with their girlfriends or boyfriends in popular places drive from same longing and the negative attitudes directed to them can be interpreted as practices of resistance in which the resentments towards consumer society becomes most apparent. For example, Halil (19, M) expresses his anger towards people arriving in the Kale neighbourhood in Ankara in luxury cars for touring around and entertainment purposes in following words:

They come here, for example ... I look at them, and they are driving million-dollar cars. It really makes you resentful, you know.... When I see expensive luxury cars around here, I just want to steal them, or scratch the sides with a key ... (Halil, 19, M, high school graduate, unemployed)

Practices of resistance against consumer society are reflected not only in violent behaviours and resentment attitudes, but also in the development of creative individualistic consumption practices. Individual or household consumer goods created or adapted to keep up with fashion by young women using their handiwork skills; fashion patterns and dress styles created by youth themselves; body adornment techniques used to differentiate oneself from others and to express uniqueness and individuality can be interpreted as examples of this type of resistance practice. Ezgi (20, F) says she styles her own clothes using her handiwork skills:

If it meets my needs, if it makes me happy, I don't hesitate, I buy, I make it work ... I buy a dress, with beads and sequins and all, and it is ten million liras. I say, I won't give 10 lira for this. I buy a two-lira dress, take the dress home, work on it, and it becomes so beautiful, it is even better than the 10-lira dress. The product of my own labour. Most of my dresses have beads and sequins. Some even call me a fashionista. It's all my own doing ... I don't buy any shawls or scarves, I make them myself, I sew. Everyone thinks they are ready-made. (Ezgi, 20, F, vocational high school graduate, baby-sitter at a municipal nursery)

Consumption as Symbolic Capital

Consumption practices are not simply reflections of habits that are randomly formed in the daily lives of the agents. Consumption practices as symbolic expressions of class positions are not only stable expressions of these positions, at the same time they act as sources that these positions are developed or preserved (Bourdieu, 1984: 170). They play an instrumental role in the display and creation, struggle and reproduction of class inequalities. The two generative principles of habitus, 'the capacity to produce classifiable practices works and the capacity to differentiate and appreciate these practices and products (tastes)', lead agents to differentiate themselves from other classes and to classify themselves through this classification. In this context, consumption practices function as signs generating class distinctions. Boundaries of class distinctions are challenged through consumption practices; consumption becomes, in the struggle over class distinctions, leverage and target of agents.

For urban poor youth, consumption habits and the use of consumer goods in particular are the most important means through which class hierarchies are made evident. Urban poor youth, who differentiates the rich from themselves with their consumption habits and the use of various goods of consumption, define their consumption practices in opposition to them, and thus make judgements of distinction.

In this context, consumption goods emphasized and underlined by poor youth are mostly material goods of consumption, such as garment styles. The reason for this is the importance attached to clothing by young people and their limited knowledge of wealth and wealthy people. For young people who rarely venture outside their places of residence and work and who have limited opportunity of contacting or meeting rich people in their daily routine, wealth is defined from a very narrow perspective. According to poor youth, recognizing rich people is easy, 'one does not need a guide when the village is in sight':

> From their clothes and looks ... rich people have this nature. You don't need a guide when the village is in sight, it is clear, you know it when you see it, they are very different ... (Ertan, 19, M, elementary school graduate, car repairman)

> The clothes they are wearing and all, it is already clear, one does not need a guide when the village is in sight. (Olcay, 17, F, high school student)

> When I see a rich person, I recognize it from their clothes. If he were poor, he would dress just like me. (Yavuz, 17, M, high school student)

> You can recognize people more or less, their manners, walk, speech, I don't know, clothes give it away. (Haldun, 26, M, waiter in cafeteria)

Similarly, they think rich people can recognize them from their clothes:

> I can't wear the type of shoes a rich person wears, that's how they can recognize me. My shoes and their shoes are different. Their shoes are brand shoes, cleaner, more beautiful. My shoes are not like that. (Zehra, 19, F, high school graduate, unemployed)

Poor youth say they can recognize other poor youth from their clothes. For example, Onur (16, M) says he can recognize youth from his neighbourhood at first sight as follows:

I recognize youth from around here at first sight. This is probably because I am from around here, was born and raised here....
From their clothes, behaviour, everything gives them away. For
example, they would wear pointed shoes, jeans, a white sweater
or something, then an overcoat, and then they would act like they
are ready to pick up a fight any moment ... (Onur, 16, M, high
school student)

Consumption patterns of rich people are defined, in contrast
to those of poor youth, as 'varied', 'luxury', 'comfortable', 'self-
confident', 'fancy', 'branded', 'different' and 'attention grabbing'.
Consumption patterns of poor youth, on the other hand, are
defined as 'ordinary'.

For example, sometimes you wear the same t-shirt every day, say
if you don't have any other, then you have to wear it every day, or
if you have two, you wear them in turns. Rich people don't wear
the same clothes twice. They have so much diversity. They are
not contented with one, and want two to three more.... Most of
them say, I wore this one today, I shouldn't wear it the other day.
(Ruken, 20, F, high school graduate, office worker)

They dress differently, compared to us, you know, a little weird.
Instead of wearing a proper sweater, they tear this part, do something on the other side, they gotta have lots of money ... (Halime,
15, F, high school student)

People around here wear jeans and a t-shirt, their pants and coats
are different, more varied, more beautiful, their hair and make-up
is more fancy.... People here wear ordinary sneakers, they only
wear Converse. (Semra, 16, F, elementary school graduate,
unemployed)

The narratives of poor youth who criticize the lifestyles and
consumption patterns of the rich conform to the images reproduced in products of popular culture that describe the rich as
'useless' and 'snob'. These negative images, which form the basis
of poor youth's perception of rich people, also allow them to
feel empowered against the rich. Poor youth describe themselves as possessing moral values not possessed by the rich, thus

differentiating themselves as a class and striving to turn class distinctions to their own advantage. As a result, it becomes easier for them to develop 'obliged satisfaction' towards their life conditions. In this context, criticisms directed at the source of wealth and the consumption habits of the rich serve to reproduce class distinctions. Poor youth, unlike the consuming rich, 'value modesty', 'can be happy with little things', and are 'rich in their hearts', which forms part of their symbolic capital.

> I am not an immature person. I wouldn't fly high even if I had everything, I am modest. If I were to fly high, that would be a lowly thing for me. I mean, I can be modest even when I climb the ladder.... This is my purpose in life: I think of myself as a kite. How do kites stay upright? Is it because they flow with the wind? No. It's because they stand firm against the wind. I always have this in my mind, and I raise the bar so high that they cannot even see me. (Ezgi, 20, F, vocational high school graduate, baby-sitter at a municipal nursery)

> We are people who can be happy with the smallest of things, we get something out of the smallest things. Rich people cannot do that. A rich person cannot come and talk to me. The atmosphere we have among friends, rich people don't have that. They don't have the atmosphere we create on the street with our small bottle of rakı, cheese and grapes. (Örsan, 20, M, elementary school graduate, unemployed)

Poor youth disavow the excessive consumption practices of the rich on several counts of which prominent one is their dissonance with moral values. The poor derive sense of empowerment by critiquing, what they describe as, 'wasteful', 'extravagant' and 'conspicuous' consumption practices of the rich and celebrating their own anti-consumerist attitude. The basis of the anti-consumerist attitudes in the form of disapproving and condemnation rich's consumption expenditures mostly grounded on religion and traditions.

An informant stated candidly,

> We are stronger than the rich. They are strong in money, we are strong in heart. They cannot enter our places. We gain the seat of

honour in their places with our heart.... I like sharing my bread with the poor, but I don't like giving a single cigarette to the rich, I won't. I wouldn't give a single cigarette if I had a thousand. I don't enter into that dialogue. (Kemal, 19, M, elementary school graduate, unemployed)

(Referring rich person) He has money, he is spoiled. We have money too, but we think before we spend, rich people spend without thinking, they waste the money. When we spend money, we think twice. Should I buy it, should I not buy it ... (Yıldırım, 19, M, vocational school graduate, plumber)

Ideas on the source of wealth, as Erdoğan (2007: 89) argues, lie at the centre of whether social hierarchies are perceived as legitimate. A common emphasis in the narratives of poor youth is that most rich people make money in ways that are not approved morally or canonically legitimate—in other words, *halal*.[7] However, they are quick to add that 'men are not all alike' and that 'some rich people make *halal* money' too. They categorize the rich into two: the 'working' rich who earn their money with the sweat of their brow and others. According to them, rich people who 'humiliate', 'crush' and 'belittle' the poor are 'upstarts' whose 'sources of wealth are shady'. Those, however, who earn money honestly, by working hard, acquiring education and gaining professional expertise do not participate in 'luxury' and 'show-off' consumption culture like other rich people do, 'because they know how hard it is to earn money'. In this context, the relative weight of the cultural capital contained in wealth becomes the criterion for accepting wealth and thereby social hierarchies, as 'legitimate'.

Urban poor youth's practice of differentiating themselves by consumption patterns applies not only to judgements about the rich, but also takes place where there are concrete confrontations with groups who have different tastes. Men, in particular, develop harsh attitudes towards other men they meet in places like Kızılay and differentiate in terms of clothing preferences. Poor youth display cynical, even hostile, attitudes towards these groups who clearly have different cultural capitals.

This is a result of the fact that urban poor youth develop very harsh distinctions concerning gender roles. Thus, urban poor youth differentiate themselves from youth from other strata in this sense as well, and engage in a struggle over tastes in the classification system.

> I don't like three things in men when I take a walk in Kızılay: long hair, earrings, and this attitude, snobbery I mean … you are a man at the end of the day, and you are supposed to cut your hair short. And what's up with the earrings? I get really irritated when I see those, I don't like them at all…. When I see these people on the street, I stare at them directly in the eye, and if they stare back, I jostle shoulders … (Yavuz, 17, M, high school student)

> Types with long hair, wearing earrings, they make no sense to me. Why would any guy wear an earring, have long hair? I don't approve of it at all…. It feels weird. Why? Because it makes no sense to dress like girls. Does it make any sense? No. Why can't they be just normal, like me? (Yıldırım, 19, M, vocational school graduate, plumber)

For urban poor youth, symbolic meanings of consumption goods lie at the centre of the display of social inequalities. The symbolic aspect of consumption is about the social relations formed, developed, preserved and limited by consumer goods. The constraints that urban poor youth have in access to various opportunities of consumption result in feelings of exclusion from certain social relations. As the poor youngsters mention the rich people 'recognize them from their clothes at first sight', 'crush' them because of their different lifestyles, 'exclude' and 'dislike' them, they underline this symbolic aspect of consumption. In this context, various consumption practices become important in drawing the boundaries of social relations. By staying away from rich neighbourhoods and minimizing encounters with the rich, urban poor youth actively participate in the drawing of boundaries, and simultaneously contribute to the reproduction of the boundaries between social classes. Yıldırım (19, M) describes the boundaries between them and the rich as follows:

The Tunalı neighbourhood is not for us, really. People there are weird, I mean, they have a different style. I don't feel free over there, I just can't. I feel trapped…. Rich people don't hang with us, and we don't hang with them. People with money despise us a little, the lower classes. And it irritates me, that's why I don't like them. They don't approve of us, and the environment gets toxic when they display that attitude. It's not like they make it clear, their disapproval, but I get it…. For example, they didn't want to sit with us at school, we used to have tea, three or four friends, and he would stay away, preferring to stay alone. And we used to say to each other: What use do we have for the spoiled child? But he was our mate, we used to sit in the same class, listen to the same lessons. Why would he exclude us? (Yıldırım, 19, M, vocational school graduate, plumber)

I don't have any friends with money. We don't make friends with them. They are high-hat, they go wherever whenever they like, we are not like that. That's why we don't fit. Having money is important; I wouldn't like to have that kind of friend…. For example, they stare at people, at people's clothes, as if they pity them…. When they look at me that way, it makes me mad, and I stare back at them … (Oğuz, 15, M, eight grader)

Yet, boundaries of social relations established through consumption are not rigid. There is a continuing struggle over the marking, establishment and reconversion of these boundaries. Ironically, urban poor youth make active use of consumption patterns that exclude them from consumer society in the process of organizing social relations established via consumption.

The 'symbolic capital' aspect of consumption acquires meaning in this context. According to Bourdieu, symbolic capital is the form of the three basic forms of capital (economic, cultural and social) take when it is grasped through categories of perception (Bourdieu and Wacquant, 1992: 119). In this sense, consumption acts as sign of economic, cultural and social capital in the perceptions of urban poor youth. Urban poor youth, who are lacking in all three basic forms of capital, experience the process by which these forms of capital are turned into symbolic capital by means of consumption as 'symbolic violence'.

When I go to Kızılay, when I come here, I get depressed, that's why I don't go to Kızılay. I look at these girls, all clean, tidy, wearing nice clothes, they maybe spend hours in front of the mirror before they go out, then I see those fag-like types wearing earrings and other rings on their bodies, and I get depressed … I notice this, I notice that, look at this, look at that, it just feels so weird. (Halil, 19, M, high school graduate, unemployed)

Knowledge of brands of consumption goods, their appreciation, and the feeling of shame associated with not knowing enough about brands are examples of the symbolic capital aspect of consumption.

When I say to my friends, look, I bought this Colin's thing, they make fun of me, they laugh at me. They don't believe it, I show the tag, and they say it's a fake. They don't believe it because I live in this neighbourhood, no one believes it…. They say it's not original, you can't afford to buy the original, maybe they don't wanna believe. (Sertaç, 18, M, vocational school graduate, repairman)

I have a friend talking brands all the time. The other day, we went to look at shoes, her father gave her some money, we went in the store, and she keeps asking about brands. Shop owner said, look girl, this is all we got, stop asking about the brands. The guy felt like…. He must have felt a little ignorant too. This is very prevalent among friends, for example, talk of brands. They keep talking about brands, and some do not know about them. Then they feel, well, insufficient. Also, if their parents are not that well-off, they can't wear brands, they wear whatever they can afford, and they feel deficient, they feel shame. (Olcay, 17, K, high school student)

The symbolic capital aspect of consumption also becomes apparent as urban poor youth make active use of consumption to conceal their own poverty (in both economic and cultural forms of capital) and to cover the social distance between them and other classes. Thus, the distinctions formed between classes via consumption are believed to disappear, if only in sight. In addition, they make use of consumption to get rid of the suspicions towards them and to be able to gain access at various places of consumption. Thus, using consumption, they try to re-arrange social relations in a more egalitarian form. Urban poor youth's consumption practices that act as resources to close the gap between positions in social space and to elevate their current positions not only make it easier for them to participate in a consumption society, they are also expressions of the struggle and resistance against distances formed through consumption. Youth interviewed made observations of this case by giving examples from their friends. These observations demonstrated that such initiatives are not approved of and seen as illegitimate efforts. As Bourdieu (1984: 381) mentions, these narratives 'contain a warning against the ambition to distinguish oneself by identifying with other groups, that is, they are a reminder of the need for class solidarity'.

> I had this friend who lived in the neighbourhood next to us, her father was not that well off, they had a small shop, but she used to wear branded shoes and all her clothes were branded clothes, and she liked to act as if they were rich, so that she could get into that world. One day, a teacher asked, Why are you like this, do you have too much money? The kid said they had a shop, a big shop, blah blah, still trying to impress others. People don't know about her, maybe she is trying to crush them this way. (Zehra, 19, high school graduate, unemployed)

> Where I live is a squatter region, but I also have tons of friends living in Çankaya. People in squatters wear dresses even Çankaya residents can't afford. The poor pressure their families to buy them stuff. By wearing expensive clothes, they try to create the impression that they are rich. (Selçuk, 18, M, high school student)

Urban poor youth try to modify perceptions by making use of various consumption goods and patterns. These practices are all about the use of consumption as a symbolic medium in 'impression management'. Yet, what matters here is that these consumption patterns are not prevalent in all aspects of the lives of urban poor youth. In other words, impression management strategies are used by urban poor youth only in places where they would confront people from other classes and in relations formed with them, for the 'symbolic profit' that is expected to accrue. As was mentioned before, consumption practices considered to be routine in the daily lives of other social strata gain a special meaning in the lives of urban poor youth.

While urban poor youth appear to have consumption patterns or own consumer goods that are similar to those of people from the upper classes, such consumption practices among the urban poor youth are not (cannot be) transformed into consumption habits. The limited capital accumulation prevents poor youth from extending these consumption activities to other areas of their lives.

Impression management strategies involving 'disguise' are not approved of by fellow urban poor youth. The effort to erase class distinctions this way is interpreted as a denial of one's own self, and people who engage in these activities are described as 'wannabes'. Ercüment (17, M) talks about a girl in the neighbourhood who tries to look different and thus humiliate her friends, and expresses his anger at and reaction to this behaviour as follows:

> The girl has such attitudes, thinks she is different, she keeps saying to another girls 'look at you, look at your type, how do they let you in, I wouldn't let you in', etc.... And I said to her 'what are you talking about, where do you think you come from, you don't like her but do you think you are really different?' (The other girl) is new to the school, a poor person, and she is trying to make fun of her.... Finally she stopped. She used to have this attitude all the time, forgetting where she comes from. She was such a show-off. She is an ordinary person but she is trying not to look it, she is trying to look different. (Ercüment, 17, M, elementary school graduate, unemployed)

The idea that certain places have certain behaviour and consumption codes represents another dimension of the symbolic capital aspect of consumption.

> In our neighbourhood, I go out at nights with sweat suits and shorts as well, it doesn't matter. They are all friends and acquaintances anyway, they don't care. When I go to Kızılay, for example, things change, it's a bit more like dress style becomes more important. We talk among friends, I ask, we are going to Kızılay, what should I wear? And my friend says 'wear jeans and a sweater,

look a little snobby', etc. (Mehmet, 21, M, high school graduate, potman)

No matter how we are, we care a lot about our dresses. We buy stuff, we try to make things match. It depends, sometimes you wear a skirt, sometimes you wear jeans.... But, for example, I buy a dress, and it is just sitting at home, What am I gonna do with it? We don't go to any places anyways, and yet we dress as if we're attending a wedding ceremony all the time. (Melda, 17, F, elementary school graduate, unemployed)

As they talk about their relations with police officers, Kemal (19, M) and Örsan (20, M) make it clear that symbolic meanings associated with consumption goods change with the spatial context:

To us, they say show me your ID, you son of a blah blah, and when they see someone wearing suits, they are like 'could you please let me see your ID, sir?'.... You are sir if you are wearing a tie, and son of a what not if you are like us. (Örsan, 20, M, elementary school graduate, unemployed)

But wearing a suit is not possible around here.... We always want to wear suits, we always did. But they don't get it. I wore one once, and the police stopped me right away, and asked 'Are you carrying a gun?' ... Here (Yenidoğan) you are treated as if you are the mafia if you wear suits ... (Kemal, 19, M, elementary school graduate, unemployed)

A significant section of the youth whom I interviewed described themselves as people 'who knew what to do and where' and 'who can adapt to different environments'. These statements signify that urban poor youth adopt behaviour codes such as politeness and courtesy, which can be considered forms of symbolic capital, as part of their impression management strategy in their confrontations with people from other social groups. The lack of this symbolic capital in the neighbourhoods where they live is interpreted as an important indicator separating them from the upper classes. For instance, Sertaç (18, M) talks about behaviour codes in shopping malls and his friends' behaviour in these places:

Sometimes I regret taking them there. They think those places are the same as here (referring to Doğantepe/Altındağ). It's not like they irritate me or anything, I am one of them too. But I do everything in its proper place, you are not supposed to do those things over there. Say, you don't speak slang over there, but they sometimes do, they act out of place, that's not for me.... Every place has a rule. You can do them here. Here, people have a different perspective; people over there have another perspective. Let me put it this way, people around here were born and raised in squats, mostly people of modest means. Their manners are a bit odd ... (Sertaç, 18, M, vocational school graduate, repairman)

I can go all places. The only thing that differentiates me from people around here is that I know really well what to do in which place. I keep prayer beads in my hand when I am around here, but I know how to talk smooth when I go to a nice place. There is a place for everything ... (Halil, 19, M, high school graduate, unemployed)

In places where they confront people who have the symbolic capital that they do not, urban poor youth try to cover the social distance between them and people from other social classes by adopting behaviour codes that befit those places. In this sense, various behaviour codes are considered as tools that both differentiate urban poor youth from the upper classes in their life worlds and facilitate more balanced communication with them.

Of the youth interviewed, those who were close to the residential areas of the upper classes were able to make use of their work experiences as symbolic capital. In other words, experiences they gained in these spaces, to which they did not think they belonged, functioned as symbolic capital that could be used in other regions of the city. Hakkı (24, M) who works as a security guard at a luxury estate in Ankara described his experiences as follows:

On the one hand, I am glad I have been to those places and seen these people at a young age. On the other hand, we lived in a squatter house in Altındağ, I did my internship while we were living in squats.... I was nineteen, I wish I.... Of course I wanted to own one of those cars, drive one, etc.... Youth of my age have cars of their own over there, and they can go out with their cars anytime they like, they can go all places. Youth over there are different of course, but I never envied them. I mean I never envied a luxury life. Would it be bad if I had more? No, of course it would be good; everyone likes to live a comfortable life. (Hakkı, 24, M, security guard at a municipal building)

Haldun (26, M) says his work as a waiter made it possible for him to go to places he could not have otherwise thought of. He admitted

Because I worked as a waiter (in the richer neighbourhoods of Ankara), I don't feel strange over there. If I hadn't been to those places, I would be curious too. I used to be curious about the bars. For example, my nephew cannot afford to go to these places, he is curious about cafés. One day I took him to a café, and said here you go, this is what a café looks like ... (Haldun, 26, M, waiter in cafeteria)

On the other hand, poor youth also stated that, attempts directed to close or minimize the social distance by imitating upper classes' consumption patterns and behavioural codes often fail. They are confused with the fact that, these efforts can be easily spotted 'no matter what they do'.

Conclusion

At the centre of urban poor youth's experience of living in a consumer society lie processes of exclusion from consumer society and symbolic struggles against these processes. In consumer societies, which add new implications to the meaning of poverty and youth, poverty is experienced as the most important barrier of being young. Poverty is beyond a lack of material resources and is experienced as a threat to one's 'dignity', 'self-respect' and 'self-confidence'.

Bourdieu's approach in *Distinction* (Bourdieu, 1984) arguing the social groups with low cultural and economic capital accumulation organize their taste and consumption choices through their 'necessities' has important implications; however, only 'taste of necessity' is not adequate to unveil consumption practices of poor youth. Under the pressure of consumer society, urban poor youth still reference necessities in their consumption nevertheless this situation does not point that they only consider 'functionality' of the consumer goods. These young people utilize consumer goods and consumption patterns as a form of symbolic capital to reduce the social distances and develop various relationships. However, the consumption practices based on the efforts to hide the class differences and to sustain more equal relationships lead to reproduction of social hierarchies as a result.

Consumer world is a field of struggle and competition where agents from different social strata meet. Agents compete with each other to monopolize the dominant form of capital in the field, to have an advantage to decide the legitimate and to challenge social order. Occupants of dominant positions in the field tend to pursue 'strategies of conservation', while those in subordinate locations try to deploy 'strategies of subversion' (Wacquant, 2006). These 'strategies of subversion' are shaped, on the one hand, by urban poor youth's descriptions of themselves as 'possessing moral values' not possessed by the rich and the negation of the consumption practices of the rich, and on the other hand, the effort to close social distances symbolized by consumption patterns making use of consumption. Urban poor youth who experience poverty in the consumer society as 'a form of symbolic violence' characterized by 'shame', 'deficiency', 'stigma' and 'humiliation' make use of consumption to resolve the tensions created by processes of exclusion and to reframe inequalities 'if only in appearance'.

As they differentiate themselves from other social strata through their consumption patterns, urban poor youth simultaneously contribute to the reproduction of classification systems. Yet poor youngsters contribute to the reproduction of social hierarchies and class distinctions as they accept the validity and the value of the consumption patterns of upper classes and treat these as major points of reference in their self-evaluations.

Notes

1. One Turkish Lira is nearly 0.53 USD.
2. Sıhhiye and Ulus are old markets of Ankara. Prices are cheaper and especially low income consumers usually make their shopping in these districts. Ulus is the old city centre of Ankara and lost its popularity particularly among young people.
3. Kızılay is the city centre of Ankara. Entertainment, culture and shopping central especially for middle class consumers and students.
4. Kiler is a supermarket chain in Turkey with the slogan of 'economic shopping'. Its stores are mostly concentrated in low-income areas.
5. Taking social relations into consideration and avoiding treating poverty only as an economic situation defined by disadvantages, insecurities and lack of material resources would contribute to understanding the multi-dimensional nature of poverty. The 'relational and symbolic aspects of poverty' associate poverty with concepts such as 'lack of voice; disrespect, humiliation, assault on dignity and self-esteem; shame and stigma; powerlessness; denial of rights and diminishes citizenship' and hence highlight its 'non-material aspects' (Leister, 2004: 7). Various studies focusing on the narratives of poverty emphasize the expression of poverty as a source of shame; deficiency and lack of confidence (see Charlesworth, 2000; Chin, 2001; De Castro, 2006; Hill, 2001).
6. Tunalı or Tunalı Hilmi Street is the new city centre of Ankara where more luxury consumer life is concentrated. It is very popular and lively shopping and entertainment district with global brand stores, expensive butiques, restaurant and cafe chains, etc.
7. *Halal* is a common word used by Turks to express something that is moral and traditionally legitimate.

References

Abrams, M. 1959. *The Teenage Consumer*. London: London Press Exchange.

Baudrillard, J. 2004. *Tüketim Toplumu*. [The Consumer Society]. İstanbul: Ayrıntı.

Bauman, Z. 2005. *Work, Consumerism and the New Poor* (2nd ed). Maidenhead, Berkshire: Open University Press.

———. 2007. *Consuming Life*. Cambridge: Polity Press.

Bourdieu, P. 1984. *Distinction: A Social Critique of the Judgement of Taste*. London: Routledge.

Bourdieu, P. & Wacquant, L.J.D. 1992. *An Invitation to Reflexive Sociology.* Chicago: University of Chicago Press.

Champagne, P. 1999. The view from media. In P. Bourdieu et al. (eds), *Weight of the World: Social Suffering in Contemporary Society*, pp. 46–59. California: Stanford University Press.

Charlesworth, S. 2000. Bourdieu, social suffering and working-class life. In B. Fowler (ed.), *Reading Bourdieu on Society and Culture*, pp. 49–65. Oxford: Blackwell Publishers.

Chin, E. 2001. *Purchasing Power: Black kids and American Consumer Culture.* Minneapolis: University of Minnesota Press.

Cohen, L. 2003. *A Consumer's Republic: The Politics of Mass Consumption in Postwar America.* New York: Alfred A. Knopf.

De Castro, L.R. 2006. What is new in the south? Consumer culture and the vicissitudes of poor youth's identity construction in urban Brazil. *Young, 14*(3), 179–201.

Durakbaşa, A. & Dilek, C. 2002. Encounters at the Counter: Gender and shopping experience. In D. Kandiyoti & A. Saktanber (eds), *Fragments of Culture: The Everyday of Modern Turkey*, pp. 73–89. New Jersey: Rutgers University Press.

Erdoğan, N. 2007. Garibanların Dünyası: Türkiye'de Yoksulların Kültürel Temsilleri Üzerine İlk Notlar. In N. Erdoğan (ed.), *Yoksulluk Halleri: Türkiye'de Kent Yoksulluğunun Toplumsal Görünümleri*, pp. 29–49. İstanbul: İletişim.

Etöz, Z. 2000. Varoş: Bir İstila Bir Tehdit! *Birikim, 132*(Nisan), 49–53.

Griffin, C. 1997. Representations of the youth. In J. Roche & S. Tucker (eds), *Youth in Society: Contemporary Theory, Policy and Practice*, pp. 18–25. London: SAGE.

Hill, R.P. 2001. Surviving in a material world: Evidence from ethnographic consumer research on people in poverty. *Journal of Contemporary Ethnograghy, 30*(4), 364–391.

———. 2002. Consumer culture and the culture of poverty: Implications for marketing theory and practice. *Marketing Theory, 2*(3), 273–293.

Jameson, F. 1983. Postmodernism and consumer society. In H. Foster (ed.), *The Anti-Aesthetic: Essays on Postmodern Culture*, pp. 111–126. Seattle: Bay Press.

Kandiyoti, D. 2002. Introduction: Reading the Fragments. In D. Kandiyoti & A. Saktanber (eds), *Fragments of Culture: The Everyday of Modern Turkey*, pp. 1–24. New Jersey: Rutgers University Press.

Kochuyt, T. 2004. Giving away one's poverty. On the consumption of scare resources within the family. *The Sociological Review, 52*(2), 139–161.

Leister, R. 2004. *Poverty.* Cambridge: Polity Press.

Miller, D. (ed.) 1995. *Acknowledging Consumption: A Review of New Studies.* London: Routledge.

Özyeğin, G. 2002. The doorkeeper, the maid and the tenant: Troubling encounters in the Turkish urban landscape. In D. Kandiyoti & A. Saktanber (eds), *Fragments of Culture: The Everyday of Modern Turkey*, pp. 43–72. New Jersey: Rutgers University Press.

Pınarcıoğlu, M. & Oğuz, Işık. 2008. Not only helpless but also hopeless: Changing dynamics of urban poverty in Turkey, the case of Sultanbeyli, İstanbul. *European Planning Studies, 16*(10), 1353–1370.

Ritzer, G. & Don, S. 2001. Editorial. *Journal of Consumer Culture, 1*(1), 5–8.

Slater, D. 1997. *Consumer Culture and Modernity.* Cambridge: Polity Press.

Trentmann, F. 2004. Beyond consumerism: New historical perspectives on consumption. *Journal of Contemporary History, 39*(3), 373–401.

Urry, J. 1995. *Consuming Places.* London: Routledge.

Veblen, T. 2005. *Aylak Sınıfının Teorisi.* [The theory of leisure class]. İstanbul: Babil.

Wacquant, L.J.D. 2006. Pierre Bourdieu. Retrieved from http://www.umsl.edu/~keelr/3210/resources/PIERREBOURDIEU-KEYTHINK-REV2006.pdf, accessed on 23 December 2011.

Yeldan, E. 2005. *Küreselleşme Sürecinde Türkiye Ekonomisi: Bölüşüm, Birikim ve Büyüme.* 11. Baskı. İstanbul: İletişim.

Zaim, A. 2006. 80 Sonrası Orta Sonıf Gençliğinin Kendini Farklılaştırma Stratejileri. *Birikim, 208*(Ağustos), 89–96.

About the Editor and Contributors

Editor

Nita Mathur is Professor of Sociology at the Indira Gandhi National Open University, New Delhi, India. She is the author of *Cultural Rhythms in Emotions, Narratives and Dance*, 2002 and editor of *Santhal Worldview*, 2001. Her research interests range from arts and lifestyles to emotions across cultures and indigenous vision. Currently she is working in the area of consumer culture, modernity and fashion in India.

Contributors

Nicki Lisa Cole is a Visiting Scholar in Sociology at Pomona College in Claremont, California. Her research focuses on the connections between consumerism and inequality in the context of global capitalism. She is currently studying and writing about the brand power and supply chain of Apple, Inc. She is published in the journal *Race, Class & Gender*, in the volume Censored 2014: Fearless Speech in Fateful Times, and is a contributor to Contexts, Sociological Images, and Pacific Standard. She is the Founder and Head Writer of 21 Century Nomad, a public sociology blog.

Steve Derné is Professor of Sociology at SUNY, Geneseo. He has received fellowships from the Fulbright programme (1986–1987, 2012), the Rockefeller Foundation (2002), the National

Endowment for the Humanities (1997, 2005), and the American Institute of Indian Studies (1991). In five research stints over more than 25 years, he has conducted 31 months of fieldwork in India. His previous books explore family life and emotion in India (*Culture in Action*, 1995), filmgoing in India (*Movies, Masculinity and Modernity*, 2000), and cultural, economic and family changes since India's economic liberalization (*Globalization on the Ground*, 2008). In 2007 and 2011, he (along with Meenu Sharma and Narendra Sethi) conducted over 200 interviews about well-being with a diversity of Indians in Dehradun.

Mike Featherstone is founding editor of the journal *Theory, Culture & Society* and the *Theory, Culture & Society* Book Series. He is the Editor-in-Chief of the journal *Body & Society*. Author of *Consumer Culture and Postmodernism* (2nd edition, 2007) and *Undoing Culture: Globalization, Postmodernism and Identity* (1995). He is also the co-author of *Surviving Middle Age* (1982). He is the editor of over a dozen of books and author of numerous journal articles and book chapters on social and cultural theory; consumer and global culture; ageing and the body. His books and articles have been translated into 16 languages. He has also spent time as a visiting professor in Barcelona, Geneva, Kyoto, Recife, São Paulo, Singapore, Tokyo and Vancouver.

Olga Gurova (Ph.D., Cultural Studies) holds the position of the Academy of Finland Research Fellow at the Department of Social Research, the University of Helsinki, Finland. Previously she served as a Docent in Sociology at the National Research University—Higher School of Economics in St. Petersburg (Russia) and was a research fellow at the Helsinki Collegium for Advanced Studies, the University of Michigan at Ann Arbor, USA; University of Illinois at Urbana-Champaign, USA; and at the Central European University, Budapest, Hungary. She is the author of *The Soviet Underwear: Between Ideology and Everyday Life* (2008). Her current research interests include consumption, fashion, socialist and post-socialist cultures of consumption.

Douglas Kellner is George Kneller Chair in the Philosophy of Education at University of California, Los Angeles (UCLA) and is the author of many books on social theory, politics, history and culture, including works on cultural studies such as Media Culture and Media Spectacle. His *Guys and Guns Amok: Domestic Terrorism* and *School Shootings from the Oklahoma City Bombings to the Virginia Tech Massacre* won the 2008 AESA award as the best book on education. His book *Cinema Wars: Hollywood Film and Politics in the Bush/Cheney Era* got published in 2010 and another book *Media Spectacle and Insurrection, 2011: From the Arab Uprisings to Occupy Everywhere* got published in 2012.

William Mazzarella is Professor of Anthropology at the University of Chicago. He is the author of *Shovelling Smoke: Advertising and Globalization in Contemporary India* and *Censorium: Cinema and the Open Edge of Mass Publicity.*

Shelly Pandey is presently working as Senior Fellow at Women's Studies and Development Studies, University of Delhi, India. Her doctoral research is from Indian Institute of Technology (IIT) Delhi on Women Working in Call Centre in India. She is recipient of M.N. Srinivas Memorial Prize 2012 for her paper 'Private space in public transport: locating gender in Delhi Metro' published in *Economic and Political Weekly*. Her research interests include gender, space, globalization and work.

Robert Rattle is an independent researcher, consultant, author and scholar with interests in sustainable consumption, social determinants of health, health impact assessment, aboriginal well-being, Internet and communication technologies and globalization. He also teaches at the natural resources and social studies departments at Sault College. Through his research and policy, programme and project activities, his primary focus is on the social and cultural contexts of sustainable consumption, lifestyles and provisioning. He is the author of *Computing Our Way to Paradise? The Role of Internet and Communication Technologies in Sustainable Consumption and Globalization* along with numerous book chapters, journal articles and other publications.

Marketa Rulikova is currently a visiting assistant professor of sociology at Williams College and has also taught at Bennington College, Keene State College, Charles University, and New York University in Prague. She received her Ph.D. from the Institute of Philosophy and Sociology at the Polish Academy of Sciences. She was awarded a scholarship from the Soros Foundation (1996–2001) and received a fellowship from the International Sociological Association (2001). Her research focuses on global migration, social stratification and cultural transformation in post-socialist Europe. She is currently working on a book about undocumented Eastern European immigrants in the United States, based on a longitudinal ethnographic field study in Chicago.

Roberta Sassatelli is an Associate Professor of Cultural Sociology at the University of Milan, Italy. She is editor of the Journal *Studi Culturali* and has published widely on the culture of consumption, cultural theory and the sociology of the body, gender, and sexuality. She is currently researching on how the crisis has impacted the Italian middle classes and their consumption attitudes and practices as well as quality networks in the food sector in Northern Italy. She is completing a monograph on Embodiment, Culture and Gender. Among others, she is the author of *Fitness Culture, Gyms and the Commercialization of Discipline and Fun*, 2010, and *Consumer Culture: History, Theory and Politics*, 2007.

Narendra Sethi is Editor of the *Shah Times* in Dehradun, India. Being a long-time journalist, he has previously been with cable and print news organizations, including *TV 100* and the *Dainik Jagaran* in Dehradun.

Meenu Sharma is a lecturer at Divya Drishti Institute of Advanced Studies in Dehradun, India. She has submitted her thesis in education for a doctoral degree to the H.N.B. Garhwal University, Srinagar, Uttarakhand.

Sanjay Srivastava is Professor of Sociology at the Institute of Economic Growth, New Delhi, India. His research interests include masculinities, consumerism and urban studies. His key publications include *Constructing Postcolonial India: National Character and the Doon School,* 1998, *Asia: Cultural Politics in the Global Age,* 2001, co-author, *Sexual Sites, Seminal Attitudes: Sexualities, Masculinities and Culture in South Asia,* 2004, contributing editor, *Passionate Modernity: Sexuality, Class and Consumption in India,* 2007, *The Sexualities Reader,* 2012, contributing editor and *Entangled Urbanism: Slum, Gated Community and Shopping Mall in Delhi and Gurgaon.*

Melike Aktaş Yamanoğlu is an Assistant Professor at the Faculty of Communication, Ankara University, Ankara, Turkey. She received her MA in Marketing degree from University of Nottingham in 2002 and Ph.D. from Ankara University Institute of Social Sciences in 2008. Her research interests include consumption relationships in modern societies, class distinctions of consumption practices, inequality and social exclusion, media consumption and public relations.

Index

se/046/f